THE

HORS D'OEUVRE

BOOK

CORALIE CASTLE

ILLUSTRATIONS BY KAREN LYNCH

101 PRODUCTIONS

The recipe for Sikotaka Tighanita (Greek Fried Liver Bits) on page 91
is from *Greek Cooking for the Gods* by Eva Zane (101 Productions,
1970). Reprinted by permission of the publisher.

Printed and bound in the U.S.A.
Published by 101 Productions and distributed by Ortho Information
Services, Box 5047, San Ramon, CA 94583

 2 3 4 5 6 7 8 9
89 90 91 92 93 94

Library of Congress Catalog Card Number 88-71974
ISBN 0-89721-170-7

THE
HORS D'OEUVRE
BOOK

INTRODUCTION

Hors d'oeuvres present the home cook with a fascinating, challenging way of entertaining, of pleasing the eye and palate with thoughtfully prepared food. They afford the chance to experiment, to try new recipes, and to use the artistic skills we all possess but may have perhaps ignored. Best of all, they provide a most appreciated opportunity: the chance to be with friends and family and together enjoy the fine art of delicious, beautiful food.

For many people, the word "hors d'oeuvre" brings to mind visions of elegant, elaborate morsels presented at formal parties in fancy homes or clubs. Yet the setting does not have to be formal and the foods need not be intricate. Serving hors d'oeuvres is just as appropriate at a picnic or in a mountain cabin as at a black-tie affair.

Offer a few appetizers before a lovely, small sit-down luncheon or evening meal, or serve several as a prelude to a large formal dinner. Plan menus in which hors d'oeuvres comprise the entire meal, or bring out one or two items when friends drop in unexpectedly.

When you are serving both hors d'oeuvres and dinner to guests, select the dishes for each carefully. A light dinner may be preceded by richer, heavier foods, such as phyllo triangles, a creamy brie torta, or an elaborate terrine. A richer meal calls for delicate starters—filled raw mushrooms or Belgian endive leaves, gravlax on rye rounds, or a simple hot or cold canapé. If your guests are going on to dinner elsewhere, serve a fish or vegetable terrine, a cream cheese mold, or perhaps an assortment of dips and spreads. For ideas on serving an "hors d'oeuvre meal,"see the Buffets chapter. Whatever the occasion, garnish your dishes with care. An attractive presentation is important to the overall success of all gatherings.

If you are a novice cook, *The Hors d'Oeuvre Book* will help you become a confident, competent giver of parties, large or small. It will allow you to present imaginative dishes in a relaxed atmosphere without having to rely on costly caterers. If you are an accomplished cook, you will find many new ideas and challenging recipes as well as simplified methods within these pages. Most importantly, whether experienced or not, you will be proud of the results of your culinary efforts.

Dishes suitable for all kinds of hors d'oeuvre parties are found in these pages. I have, however, limited the recipes to preparations that can be picked up with fingers, cocktail picks, small, two-pronged forks, or chopsticks, or to those that are spread or placed on or scooped up with bread or crackers. Many of the dishes can be made ahead and kept on hand in the refrigerator or freezer, and many of them use foods already in your pantry.

Careful planning—developing a menu, shopping ahead, organizing your kitchen time—will make all your cooking easier. And the feeling of accomplishment you derive from being able to say "I prepared everything myself" will far outweigh the time spent in the kitchen.

A self-confident chef is never offended if some dishes are not universally popular. People have definite likes and dislikes that have nothing to do with how well something is prepared. One person will adore the caviar-topped mushroom, while another will pass it by. Taramosalata will garner raves from a few guests and be avoided by others.

Nor does a secure chef become flustered if a dish doesn't look absolutely perfect. A "goof" can be artistically camouflaged: an irregularly shaped galantine can be masked with aspic, or any imperfections in a mold can be hidden with garnitures. No one will notice dolmades that have begun to unravel, or a phyllo triangle that has sprung a leak in baking. In every case, the flavor is what counts.

For many of the recipes, I have included information on how far in advance they can be made and/or how long they can be stored. Three symbols desig-nate this information:

● means that a dish may be *completely readied* six or more hours in advance of serving.

■ means that a dish may be frozen the time specified in the recipe.

○ means that a dish *must* be made six or more hours in advance of serving.

Even if a recipe does not have a symbol, some aspects of prepa-ration can be done in advance. For example, skewered marinated meats can be refrigerated up to two days or frozen for up to three weeks before barbecuing. The fillings for many of the stuffed vegetables can be pre-pared several days in advance, or the ingredients for a chafing dish recipe can be readied the night before the party.

Read the recipes and note the symbols and storage times, and then choose hors d'oeuvres that fit your schedule. The storage times are conservative estimates, but keep in mind that most foods have better flavor if not kept too long.

Recipe yields are given in cup measurements, in numbers, or in individual servings. The latter do not refer to the number of people that can be served, how-ever, but rather to the number of "bites," so plan your menu accordingly. Some recipes include among their ingredients other recipes in the book. These are indicated by initial capitals and the page on which they appear can be found in the index.

The book is organized into two types of chapters. First there are those defined by the method of preparation, that is, canapés; spreads and dips; pâtés, terrines, galantines, and molds; chafing dish; and pastries. Then, there are those defined by the principal ingredients, including cheese, eggs, vegetables, and fish, poultry, and meats. There is also a chapter devoted to basics—sauces, stocks, breads, aspics, garnitures, and kitchen hints. Here you will find any unfamiliar ingredients or cooking terms and methods. Finally, there is a chapter on buffets, which includes eight international menus and all you need to know to host a spectacular "hors d'oeuvre meal."

THE
HORS D'OEUVRE
BOOK

● May be made ahead
■ May be frozen
○ Must be made ahead

CANAPES

Canapés, small open-face sandwiches that can be easily eaten in a bite or two, have been neglected by many cooks for two reasons: they are time-consuming to assemble and they must be made shortly before serving. This is a shame, for canapés make attractive additions to any hors d'oeuvre party.

If you include make-ahead foods on the menu, the last few hours before guests arrive can be devoted to preparing canapés. These petite sandwiches are perfect to make when you have volunteered to contribute to a friend's gathering, as you can lavish your complete attention on their preparation.

To streamline the assembly, have the breads sliced, the spreads and other ingredients prepared, and the garnishes ready. A wide variety of breads may be used: homemade-style white or whole wheat, french, Italian, light or dark rye, pumpernickel, or black. It is important that they be fine-textured, rather dense loaves, and that the canapé topping complement, not mask the flavor of the bread. If there is a good commercial bakery in your community, purchase the bread to save yourself time in the kitchen. Baguettes and rye bread (sometimes baked in baguette form upon request) are usually available. Miniature bagels, halved crosswise, and Fried Bread are also good canapé bases.

Any bread loaves should be sliced 1/4 inch thick. Then, with specially designed metal hors d'oeuvre cutters or cookie cutters, cut the bread slices into the shapes desired—rounds, ovals, half moons, diamonds, spades, hearts, squares. For rectangles, cut evenly by hand. Each cutout should be approximately 1-1/4 to 1-1/2 inches in diameter, or an equivalent surface measure if the shape is other than a round. Save bread crusts and other scraps for making crumbs. If you are using baguettes or buffet rye, simply slice 1/4 inch thick and do not remove the crusts.

The bread base for hot canapés should always be toasted before it is covered with a spread or other topping. Opinion differs on the need to toast the bases for cold canapés. Some cooks find toasted bread is easier to handle and holds up better. Others prefer the softer quality of an untoasted base.

To toast canapé bases, arrange on a baking sheet and place in a preheated broiler just until bread turns golden. Remove from the broiler, transfer to a wire rack or flip over on the baking sheet, and let cool. Always arrange the canapé topping on the *untoasted* side of the bread.

The spread that covers the canapé base may be plain or seasoned butter or mayonnaise or a more complex mixture. In spread recipes calling for cream cheese, always have the cheese at room temperature so that it can be easily softened with cream or mayonnaise. Also, butter or a spread that has been made ahead and refrigerated should be at room temperature before using.

For additional canapé spread suggestions, see Spreads and Dips.

Garnishes must be selected and arranged with care. The well-received canapé is one that is colorful, tasty, and imaginatively decorated. Don't overlook the serving plate or tray. It requires the same thoughtful presentation.

COLD CANAPES

These are delicate creations that must be carefully put together. A light coating of butter on the base keeps the bread from absorbing moisture and becoming soggy. Meats, cheeses, smoked fish, vegetables such as tomatoes and cucumbers, hard-cooked eggs, or other similar ingredients that will be placed on the bread should be *very thinly sliced*. For a "perfectly formed" canapé, cut the bread into shapes after it has been topped with meat or cheese and then decorate.

Cucumber canapés are popular, but they require special attention because cucumbers tend to "weep" once they are sliced. To prevent the slices from giving off moisture that will dampen the bread, place them in a colander, lightly sprinkle with salt, and let drain thirty minutes. Rinse with cold water to wash off salt. With the back of a wooden spoon, press

out as much moisture as possible, then pat each slice dry with paper toweling.

For the cold canapé suggestions that follow, any type of suggested bread cut into any shape (see chapter introduction) is appropriate, unless otherwise specified. The ingredients are mentioned in the order they are to be spread or layered. Some suggestions call for "piping" an ingredient onto the bread. Refer to the Basics chapter for directions on piping techniques.

As the canapés are made, place them on refrigerator trays or serving plates and cover tightly with plastic wrap. Refrigerate or keep in a cool place until ready to serve. Try to keep the holding time to a minimum.

- Unsalted butter, rolled caper-filled anchovy with a little of its oil, tiny parsley leaf.
- Unsalted butter, Mustard Mayonnaise, cooked shrimp halved lengthwise, sprinkling of paprika, tiny watercress leaf.

- Unsalted butter, prepared mustard, slice of Gruyère cheese, rows of thinly sliced radish.
- Horseradish Butter, tiny roll of thinly sliced rare roast beef, chopped green onion.
- Butter, slice of tomato, sprinkling of sieved hard-cooked egg, anchovy curl in center.
- Unsalted butter, spread of equal parts crumbled Gorgonzola cheese, cream cheese, and well-drained crushed pineapple, seedless grape halves (cut lengthwise).
- Almond Butter, slice of cooked chicken or turkey, tiny watercress leaf.
- Avocado Butter, cooked shrimp or flaked cooked crab meat, tiny lemon peel.
- Shrimp Butter, flaked cooked crab meat, border of piped Shrimp Butter, drained caper and parsley leaf in center.
- Horseradish Butter, Esrom or other creamy semisoft cheese, slice of cherry tomato, overlapping row of tiny cooked shrimp, sprinkling of finely minced fresh parsley.
- Butter, swirls of cream cheese softened with a little Basic Mayonnaise and flavored with anchovy paste, tiny parsley leaf.
- Bread diamond, Smoked Salmon Butter, lightly blanched asparagus tip placed on diagonal, tiny pimiento or Roasted Pepper strip.

- Bread rectangle, unsalted butter, 2 narrow strips Gruyère cheese, row of tiny cooked shrimp between cheese strips, dots of Basic Mayonnaise, tiny watercress or parsley leaf.
- Bread rectangle, unsalted butter, deviled ham, cross bars of cheese strips, tiny green bell pepper strips.
- Bread rectangle, butter, slice of hard-cooked egg in center, slice of cherry tomato on each end topped with an anchovy curl, sprinkling of minced fresh chives.
- Bread round, butter, slice of tiny cooked beet, slice of cucumber or sweet onion, finely minced hard-cooked egg white.
- Rye bread, butter, Steak Tartare, border of tiny cooked shrimp, dab of raw egg yolk with drained caper in center.
- Dark rye bread, butter, sour cream mixed with prepared horseradish and Worcestershire sauce, slice of corned beef, blanched shredded cabbage tossed with vinegar, caraway seeds, and salt and pepper to taste.
- Dark rye or pumpernickel, Mock Liver Pâté, slice of sweet onion, dabs of sour cream and caviar, tiny lemon peel.
- Rye bread, butter, Mustard Mayonnaise, finely shredded lettuce, tiny roll of thinly sliced smoked ham.

- Rye bread, butter, Steak Tartare, border of finely minced onion, well of lumpfish caviar, tiny grating of horseradish, drained caper, sieved hard-cooked egg.
- Rye bread round, Mustard Butter, round slice of smoked ham, slice of heart of palm, tiny pimiento or Roasted Pepper strip.
- Rye bread, Mustard Butter, slice of cooked tongue, sliced pimiento-stuffed olive, parsley leaf in center, sieved hard-cooked egg border.
- Rye rectangle, butter, thin slice of smoked ham spread with Chicken Liver Pâté, rolled into a cylinder, and placed on diagonal, tiny piece of pickle on each side.
- Pumpernickel round, Anchovy Butter, well-drained marinated artichoke bottom (trim to small sizes and use trimmings in tossed salad) with a piping of cream cheese softened with sour cream, tiny watercress leaf.
- Rye bread, Smoked Salmon Butter mixed with anchovy paste, fresh lemon juice, crumbled dried dill, and black pepper to taste, drained caper in center.
- Fried Bread, Anchovy Butter mixed with sieved hard-cooked egg yolk and a few drops olive oil, sprinkling of sieved hard-cooked egg white, light dusting of paprika.

- Toast, equal parts butter and finely shredded Cheddar or Monterey Jack cheese, slices of gherkin, pimiento or Roasted Pepper strips.
- Fried Bread or Melba Toast round, slice of hard-cooked egg, border of Watercress Butter, watercress leaf in center.
- Fried Bread or Melba Toast round, slice of onion, slice of salted and drained cucumber, dab of lumpfish caviar, squeeze of fresh lemon juice, minced fresh chives, border of sieved hard-cooked egg.
- Butter, equal parts cream cheese and Basic Mayonnaise, sliver of Pumate, dab of cream cheese, chopped fresh chives or tiny piece of smoked salmon.
- Tomato Butter, slice of cooked lobster or Steamed Monkfish, ripe olive half, light coating of Fish Aspic, border of hard-cooked egg mixed with Basic Mayonnaise.
- Bread round, unsalted butter, piping of cream cheese softened with Crème Fraîche, daisy design of slivered blanched almonds with center of sieved hard-cooked egg yolk.
- Bread round, butter, red onion round to fit bread, sprinkling of ground cumin and chili powder, dab of Basic Mayonnaise, fresh coriander leaf.
- Bread round, Watercress Butter, slice of mushroom rubbed with

fresh lemon juice, tiny piece of pimiento or Roasted Pepper on either side of mushroom stem, light sprinkling of paprika.
• Butter, salted and drained cucumber slice, sprinkling of white pepper and paprika, tiny watercress leaf.
• Rye bread, cream cheese softened with heavy cream, thin slice of smoked salmon, sprinkling of minced fresh dill.
• Butter, Mock Liver Pâté, thin slice of tomato, thin slice of onion, drained caper in center.
• Dark rye, Mock Liver Pâté, crumbled crisply cooked bacon, minced fresh chives or green onion tops.
• French bread, Lemon Butter seasoned with Tabasco sauce, slice of smoked ham, sprinkling of black pepper.
• Toast, unsalted butter, chèvre and/or cream cheese, Pumate strips, tiny fresh basil leaf.
• Rye bread, butter, cream cheese softened with Basic Mayonnaise, overlapping slices of radish or carrot, tiny watercress leaf.
• Brown bread, cream cheese softened with heavy cream or Crème Fraîche, dab of pepper jelly.
• Pumpernickel, Hazelnut Butter, slice of smoked turkey, ripe olive slivers, tiny parsley leaf.

• Egg Yolk Butter, cooked shrimp half (cut lengthwise), dab of red caviar, tiny sprig of dill.
• Pumpernickel rectangle, Chutney Butter, slice of smoked turkey, seedless grape half (cut lengthwise) placed on each end, tiny fresh coriander leaf in center.
• Whole-grain bread, unsalted butter, Salmon Mayonnaise, slice of smoked salmon, slice of onion, sprinkling of black pepper.
• Rye or pumpernickel, Avocado Butter, crumbled crisply cooked bacon, tiny fresh coriander leaf.
• Miniature bagel half, unsalted butter, crumbled blue cheese softened with a little light cream, sprinkling of chopped pecans, tiny parsley leaf.
• Whole-wheat bread, unsalted butter, crumbled blue cheese softened with a little light cream, thin slice of apple rubbed with fresh lemon juice.
• Rye bread, butter, slice of cooked pork roast, ribbon of drained and chopped chutney, tiny fresh coriander leaf.
• Rye bread, Mustard Butter, slice of raw beef steak such as New York cut, drained capers, freshly ground black pepper, tiny parsley leaf.

HOT CANAPES

As with cold canapés, any type of bread or bread shape described in the chapter introduction can be used for preparing hot canapés. In general, though, the toppings for hot canapés are delicately flavored, making mild-flavored rye, whole-wheat, and white breads the best choices. Be sure to toast the bread on one side before topping, then spread or layer the untoasted side.

The yields for these recipes are based on using bread cutouts, which will each take about one teaspoon of "spread." If you are using the slightly larger baguette or buffet slices, plan on fewer individual servings.

Adjust your broiler rack so that it is approximately five inches from the heat. Preheat the broiler fully so that the canapés cook quickly and evenly.

Most hot canapés can be prepared a day ahead, covered with plastic wrap, and refrigerated, or sheet frozen for up to one month and then defrosted in the refrigerator before broiling. Recipes that fall into these categories have been indicated by symbols.

These satisfying appetizers taste best straight out of the broiler, so schedule their appearance with this in mind.

CRAB AND CLAM CANAPES ● ■

Makes Six to Seven Dozen
8 ounces cream cheese, softened
One 7-1/2-ounce can minced clams, drained (save liquid for fish stock)
3/4 cup flaked cooked crab meat (approximately 3 ounces)
2 teaspoons grated onion
2 tablespoons minced fresh chives
1 teaspoon Worcestershire sauce
1/2 teaspoon garlic powder
1/2 teaspoon freshly ground white pepper
Dash Tabasco sauce
Paprika
6 to 7 dozen prepared bread cutouts of choice

Combine cream cheese, clams, crab, onion, chives, Worcestershire sauce, garlic powder, pepper, and Tabasco sauce. Spread mixture on untoasted side of bread, sprinkle with paprika, and broil until bubbly.

RIPE OLIVE CANAPES WITH CHEDDAR ● ■

Makes Approximately Four Dozen
One 4-1/2-ounce can chopped ripe olives
1/4 cup finely minced green onion and tops
1/4 teaspoon finely minced garlic
3/4 cup finely shredded sharp Cheddar cheese
Commercial mayonnaise to make spreading consistency
Curry powder to taste
Paprika
4 dozen prepared light-rye bread cutouts

Combine olives, onion, garlic, cheese, mayonnaise, and curry powder. Spread mixture on untoasted side of bread, sprinkle with paprika, and broil until bubbly.

GREEN OLIVE CANAPES WITH PECANS ● ■

Makes Approximately Four Dozen
4 ounces cream cheese, softened
2 teaspoons commercial mayonnaise
1/4 cup finely chopped pimiento-stuffed olives
1/4 cup finely chopped pecans
1/2 teaspoon Worcestershire sauce
6 drops Tabasco sauce, or to taste
Paprika
4 dozen prepared light- or dark-rye bread cutouts

Combine cream cheese, mayonnaise, olives, pecans, Worcestershire sauce, and Tabasco sauce. Spread mixture on untoasted side of bread, sprinkle with paprika, and broil until bubbly.

MUSHROOM CANAPES ●■

Makes Six to Seven Dozen
8 ounces cream cheese, softened
1/2 pound mushrooms, *very finely* minced
1 tablespoon grated onion
1/2 teaspoon grated or pressed garlic
3 tablespoons finely minced fresh chives or green onion tops
1/2 tablespoon fresh lemon juice
1/2 teaspoon Worcestershire sauce
1/2 teaspoon salt
1/4 teaspoon freshly ground white pepper
2 or 3 drops Tabasco sauce
Paprika
6 to 7 dozen prepared bread cutouts of choice

Combine cream cheese, mushrooms, onion, garlic, chives, lemon juice, Worcestershire sauce, salt, pepper, and Tabasco sauce. Cover and chill several hours.
Spread mixture on untoasted sides of bread, sprinkle lightly with paprika, and broil until bubbly.

GORGONZOLA CANAPES ●■

Makes Approximately Four Dozen
6 ounces Gorgonzola or other blue cheese, crumbled
1/4 pound butter, softened
1/2 teaspoon celery salt
1/3 cup finely chopped pecans
Paprika
4 dozen prepared light-rye bread cutouts

Combine cheese, butter, celery salt, and pecans. Spread mixture on untoasted side of bread, sprinkle with paprika, and broil until bubbly.

ARTICHOKE-PARMESAN CANAPES

Makes Approximately Five Dozen
One 8-1/2- ounce can (drained weight) water-pack artichoke hearts, drained
1 cup commercial mayonnaise
1 tablespoon grated onion and juices
2/3 cup freshly grated Parmesan cheese
5 dozen prepared bread cutouts of choice

In a blender or food processor, finely mince the artichoke hearts. Add mayonnaise, onion, and 1/3 cup of the cheese. Whirl until well mixed.

Spread mixture on untoasted sides of bread, sprinkle lightly with remaining cheese, and broil until bubbly.

SHRIMP CANAPES WITH WATER CHESTNUT

Makes Two Dozen
2 tablespoons butter, at room temperature
1/4 cup finely minced cooked shrimp
2 teaspoons minced fresh chives
1 teaspoon soy sauce
2 tablespoons finely minced water chestnuts
Freshly ground white pepper to taste
Sour cream or Crème Fraîche, as needed
2 dozen prepared sourdough bread cutouts
Paprika
2 dozen tiny cooked shrimp
2 dozen tiny parsley leaves

Combine butter, shrimp, chives, soy sauce, water chestnuts, and pepper. Add sour cream to make firm spreading consistency and spread mixture on untoasted side of bread rounds. Sprinkle with paprika and broil until bubbly. Top each hot canapé with a shrimp and a tiny parsley leaf.

TOMATO-CHEESE ROUNDS

These canapés are demanding of the cook's time, but are worth the effort. Plan to serve them when you have no other last-minute items on your menu.

Makes Approximately Four Dozen
1/2 cup grated sharp Cheddar
    cheese
1/3 cup mayonnaise
1/4 cup very finely minced green
    onion and tops
3 tablespoons very finely minced
    green bell pepper
1/8 teaspoon garlic powder
1/8 teaspoon salt
1/8 teaspoon cayenne pepper
Mayonnaise for spreading
Cherry tomatoes, thinly sliced
Bacon
Paprika
4 dozen prepared bread rounds
    of choice

Combine cheese, mayonnaise, onion, green pepper, and seasonings. Spread untoasted side of bread rounds with a little mayonnaise, top with a tomato slice, mound about 1 teaspoon of the cheese mixture on the tomato slice, and top with a tiny piece of bacon. Sprinkle with paprika and broil until bubbly.

    Let canapés cool slightly before serving, as the tomato retains heat.

HOT CANAPE SUGGESTIONS

Here are some quick-to-assemble hot hors d'oeuvres. For basic guidelines, see the general introduction to hot canapés. Unless otherwise specified, any type of bread cut into any shape may be used for these suggestions. Ingredients that are to be sliced, such as cheeses, meats, onion, tomato, and so on, must be sliced *very thinly*. Spread or layer ingredients in order given, then broil until bubbly.
- Butter, slice of red onion, grated or finely shredded cheese, sprinkling of paprika.
- Butter, slice of water chestnut, slice of Cheddar or Monterey Jack cheese, sprinkling of paprika; after broiling, sprinkle with minced parsley.
- Butter, finely shredded Cheddar cheese combined with minced cooked ham, chopped ripe olives, and minced drained chutney, sprinkling of freshly grated Parmesan cheese.
- Pumpernickel, butter, slice of Münster, Cheddar, or Monterey Jack cheese, slice of onion, light sprinkling of ground cumin or chili powder.
- French bread, mixture of equal amounts commercial mayonnaise and freshly grated Parmesan or Romano cheese and dry sherry or Marsala to taste.

- Sourdough french bread rounds, mayonnaise thinned with a little Garlic Olive Oil, generous sprinkling of freshly grated Romano or Parmesan cheese, light sprinkling of paprika.
- Sourdough french-bread fingers, Roasted Garlic Purée, sprinkling of paprika.
- Tiny English muffin halves, seasoned ground lean raw beef, few pieces of Pumate, slice of mozzarella cheese.
- Dark rye bread, butter, slice of cooked chicken or turkey, slice of Monterey Jack cheese; after broiling garnish with a tiny piece of spiced peach or crabapple.
- Whole-wheat bread or crackers, slice of mozzarella cheese, sprinkling of minced fresh basil, slice of ripe tomato, sprinkling of freshly grated Parmesan cheese.
- Butter, slice of sharp Cheddar cheese, dab of mango or other chutney.
- Mustard Butter, slice of smoked ham, grated Gruyère cheese, sprinkling of paprika. ■
- French bread, Duxelle, sprinkling of paprika. ■

SPREADS & DIPS

Some hors d'oeuvres are suitable for almost any occasion: as the prelude to an elegant dinner party, the food for an afternoon of bridge, or the mainstay of a large buffet. Spreads and dips fall into this category. Several factors contribute to their popularity: they are generally quick and easy to prepare, can be made in advance, keep well, and add a festive touch to any gathering.

The density of a mixture determines whether it is a spread or a dip. A spread must be firm enough to be applied with a small knife or other similar utensil, but not so stiff that it will not flow easily. A dip, in contrast, should be thin enough to be "scoopable" with a vegetable dipper or a tortilla chip, but not runny. Spreads may be thinned to dip consistency by the addition of mayonnaise, sour cream, or whatever liquid is called for in the recipe.

In general, the ingredients for spreads and dips are most easily mixed in a food processor. It saves your "beating arm," creates a smooth, even mixture, and allows you to make a larger batch than is possible in a blender.

EGGPLANT-TOMATO SPREAD O

Makes Approximately Three Cups
One 1-1/2-pound eggplant
1/3 cup olive oil
4 large garlic cloves, minced
1 large onion, minced
1/2 green bell pepper, minced
2 large ripe tomatoes, peeled
   and chopped
1 tablespoon fresh lemon juice
1 teaspoon salt
1/2 teaspoon granulated sugar
1/8 teaspoon cayenne pepper
Roasted Pepper, drained and cut
   into thin strips
Minced fresh parsley
French bread or dark rye

Bake eggplant in a preheated 400° F oven 30 minutes, or until soft to the touch. Alternatively, halve eggplant lengthwise, place cut side up on rack over boiling water, and steam 12 minutes, or until tender. When cool enough to handle, peel eggplant and chop into 1- or 1-1/2-inch cubes; set aside.

In a large nonstick skillet, heat oil over medium heat and add garlic, onion, and green bell pepper. Cover skillet and cook 5 minutes. Add reserved eggplant, tomatoes, lemon juice, salt, sugar, and cayenne pepper and stir well. Cook, uncovered, over medium-low heat, stirring often, until mixture thickens to spreading consistency. Taste and adjust seasonings. Cool, cover, and refrigerate at least 6 hours or overnight to blend flavors.

To serve, stir mixture well and transfer to a shallow serving bowl. Decorate with pepper strips and sprinkle liberally with minced parsley. Serve with french bread.

LAYERED TACO SPREAD

This wonderful, eye-catching layered spread is always a big hit, especially when served with freshly made tortilla chips. It may be assembled a few hours in advance and refrigerated, in which case let it warm to room temperature before serving.

Approximately Thirty Servings
1-1/3 cups refried beans (preferably homemade)
1-1/2 cups Tomatillo Sauce
2/3 cup sour cream
1 large ripe avocado, peeled, pitted, and mashed with 2 to 3 teaspoons fresh lemon juice
2 medium-size ripe tomatoes, diced and drained
1/2 to 2/3 cup finely chopped ripe olives
6 green onions, white and 2 inches of green tops, finely minced
2 cups very finely shredded iceberg lettuce
3/4 cup finely shredded Monterey Jack cheese
Tortilla Chips

Combine beans with 1 cup of the tomatillo sauce, mix well, and spread in the center of a large round platter, making a round approximately 10 inches in diameter. Spread sour cream evenly over the bean mixture and then layer with remaining sauce, avocado mixture, tomatoes, olives, green onions, and lettuce. Sprinkle with cheese and serve with tortilla chips.

BABA GHANNOUJ
(Eggplant and Sesame Spread) ●

For the fullest flavor, prepare this Middle East classic the day before serving. Break up lahvosh rounds or crisp pita bread in a hot oven and separate into serving pieces. Serve bread in a basket alongside the spread.

Makes Approximately Two Cups
One 1-pound eggplant
3 tablespoons tahini (sesame-seed paste), at room temperature
2 tablespoons water
3 tablespoons fresh lemon juice, or to taste
2 large garlic cloves, finely minced
2 tablespoons minced green onion and tops
1/2 teaspoon salt
1/2 teaspoon freshly ground black pepper

PRESENTATION
Olive oil
Lightly toasted sesame seeds
Coriander sprigs
Lahvosh or pita bread

Prick eggplant in several places with a cake tester or thin metal skewer. Place on broiler rack and broil 4 inches from heat 20 minutes, turning until all sides are evenly charred. Remove eggplant from the broiler, and when cool enough to handle, peel and chop coarsely. With a potato masher, mash chopped eggplant until it forms a purée. Set the purée aside.

In a large mixing bowl, stir the tahini with a wooden spoon to soften, then gradually work in the water and lemon juice to form a smooth, well-blended mixture. Stir in the garlic, green onion, reserved eggplant, salt, and pepper. Mix well, taste, and adjust seasonings. Cover and refrigerate at least 4 hours or overnight to allow flavors to blend.

To serve, mound eggplant mixture in a shallow bowl and let come to room temperature. Just before serving, drizzle with olive oil, sprinkle with sesame seeds, and garnish with coriander. Serve with lahvosh or pita bread.

CAPONATA
(Italian Eggplant Spread) ○

Use a dense Italian loaf to make fried bread to accompany this Sicilian eggplant dip. High-quality vinegar is a must, and as with Baba Ghannouj, overnight chilling and subsequent warming to room temperature improves the flavor.

Makes Approximately Two Cups
One 1-pound eggplant
1 teaspoon salt
4 tablespoons olive oil, or as needed
1/2 cup chopped onion
1/2 cup chopped celery
1 bay leaf, broken
2 tablespoons tomato paste, diluted in 1 tablespoon warm water
1/3 cup high-quality red wine vinegar
1/2 tablespoon granulated sugar
2 to 3 teaspoons drained capers
1/3 cup pitted green olives, sliced crosswise
1/2 teaspoon salt
1/2 teaspoon freshly ground black pepper
Pumate strips
Fried Bread

Chop unpeeled eggplant into 1/2-inch pieces and sprinkle with salt. Place in a colander and let drain 45 minutes. Pat eggplant dry with paper toweling.

In a large skillet, sauté the eggplant in 2 tablespoons of the oil until lightly browned, adding additional oil if pan becomes too dry. Remove eggplant with a slotted spoon and set aside.

Add remaining 2 tablespoons oil to skillet and sauté the onion and celery until lightly browned. Add reserved eggplant, bay leaf, diluted tomato paste, vinegar, sugar, capers, olives, salt, and pepper. Cook gently 15 minutes, stirring occasionally. Taste and adjust seasonings. Remove skillet from the heat and transfer eggplant mixture to a storage container. Let cool, cover, and refrigerate overnight.

To serve, mound mixture in a shallow bowl and let come to room temperature. Decorate with pumate strips and accompany with fried bread.

SKORDALIA
(Greek Garlic-Potato Spread) ●

A smooth and creamy mixture that will win the praise of garlic lovers. Surround the serving bowl with thin slices of crusty sourdough baguette.

Approximately Twenty Servings
1 small thick-skinned potato, scrubbed and quartered
4 to 5 large garlic cloves
1/4 teaspoon salt
1/3 cup olive oil
2 tablespoons fresh lemon or lime juice
Parsley leaves

Place potato in a saucepan and add water to cover barely. Cover saucepan, bring water to a boil, lower heat slightly, and cook until potato is tender. Drain (reserve liquid for breads or soup stocks) and return saucepan with potato to burner to rid the potato of any remaining moisture. Force potato through a ricer and keep warm.

In a blender or food processor, finely mince the garlic with the salt. Add 1 cup of the riced potato and mix with on and off pulses; be careful not to overmix or the potato will become gummy. With motor running, add oil alternately with lemon juice. Transfer mixture to a bowl and stir well. Taste and adjust seasonings with salt, then cool, cover, and refrigerate.

The potato mixture will keep for up to 2 days. To serve, stir well and transfer to a serving bowl. Let come to room temperature and garnish with parsley leaves. Serve with baguette slices.

HOT ARTICHOKE SPREAD WITH PARMESAN ●

If there is a chance this delicious spread may cool before it is all eaten, keep it warm on a hot tray.

Approximately Thirty Servings
One 8-1/2-ounce can (drained weight) water-pack artichoke hearts
One 4-ounce can chopped mild green chili peppers or chopped ripe olives
1 cup freshly grated Parmesan cheese
1 cup commercial mayonnaise
1/4 cup finely minced green onion and tops
1/2 teaspoon garlic powder
1/2 teaspoon freshly ground white pepper
Salt to taste
Paprika
Unsalted crackers or sliced baguette or buffet rye

Preheat oven to 350° F. Drain artichoke hearts and chop coarsely. Combine with chilies, all but 2 tablespoons of the cheese, mayonnaise, green onion, garlic powder, white pepper, and salt. Spoon mixture into a well-buttered 3-cup shallow baking dish (attractive enough to serve from). Sprinkle evenly with remaining cheese and with paprika.

Bake in the preheated oven 30 minutes, or until the mixture is bubbly and the top is lightly browned. Serve with crackers.

If making ahead, cover unbaked spread with plastic wrap and refrigerate for up to 1 day. Bring to room temperature before baking.

CREAM CHEESE SPREADS

Cream cheese spreads are versatile concoctions. They are an excellent way to use up small amounts of foods in your refrigerator, plus they can be the perfect answer for what to serve last-minute guests.

Here are six recipes for cream cheese spreads, followed by thirteen quick-and-easy cream cheese blends. Serve all of these spreads in attractive high-sided bowls or crocks, accompanied with breads or crackers (see Ways with Breads). Provide small broad-bladed knives for spreading.

Alternatively, fill Belgian endive leaves, cooked artichoke bottoms, hollowed-out cherry tomatoes or cooked beets, or celery ribs with cream cheese spreads and dust the tops with paprika.

AVOCADO CREAM CHEESE SPREAD ●

This simple spread is especially good served with smoked salmon and buffet rye bread.

Makes Approximately One Cup
1 medium to large ripe avocado
2 teaspoons fresh lemon juice
3 ounces cream cheese, at room temperature
1 tablespoon heavy cream or Crème Fraîche, or as needed
1/4 teaspoon salt
1/8 teaspoon freshly ground white pepper
Tiny lemon peel slivers

Peel and pit avocado and place pulp on a plate or cutting board. With a fork, mash avocado with lemon juice; set aside.

In a mixing bowl, combine cream cheese and cream and beat with a wooden spoon until well blended, soft, and smooth. Beat in avocado mixture, adding additional cream as needed to make spreading consistency. Season with salt and pepper. Taste and adjust with lemon juice and seasonings. Pack spread into a small bowl or crock and garnish with lemon peel.

If not using spread immediately, cover with plastic wrap and refrigerate for up to 1 day. Let come to room temperature before serving.

MUSHROOM CREAM CHEESE SPREAD ●

Makes Approximately Three-fourths Cup
4 ounces cream cheese, at room temperature
3 tablespoons Crème Fraîche, or as needed
1/2 cup finely minced raw mushrooms
1 teaspoon fresh lemon juice
1 teaspoon grated onion and juices
1/4 teaspoon garlic powder
1/8 teaspoon ground oregano
1/4 teaspoon salt
1/8 teaspoon freshly ground white pepper
Tiny watercress leaves

In a mixing bowl, combine cream cheese and crème fraîche and beat with a wooden spoon until well blended, soft, and smooth. Stir in mushrooms, lemon juice, onion and juices, and seasonings. Mix in additional crème fraîche as needed to make spreading consistency. Taste and adjust with lemon juice and seasonings. Pack spread into a small bowl or crock and garnish with watercress leaves.

If not using spread immediately, cover with plastic wrap and refrigerate for up to 2 days. Let come to room temperature before serving.

PECAN CREAM CHEESE SPREAD ●

Makes Approximately One Cup
4 ounces cream cheese, at room temperature
1/2 cup sour cream
1 tablespoon very finely minced onion
1 tablespoon finely minced celery
2 teaspoons minced fresh chives
1/4 cup finely chopped lightly toasted pecans
Salt and freshly ground white pepper to taste
Crisply cooked bacon, crumbled

In a mixing bowl, combine cream cheese and sour cream and beat with a wooden spoon until well blended, soft, and smooth. Stir in onion, celery, chives, pecans, and salt and pepper. Pack spread into a small bowl or crock and sprinkle liberally with crumbled bacon. Offer a small bowl of additional bacon on the side.

If not serving spread immediately, cover with plastic wrap and refrigerate for up to 3 days. Let come to room temperature before serving.

CHESTNUT CREAM CHEESE SPREAD ○

Approximately One and One-third Cups
4 ounces cream cheese, at room temperature
2 to 3 teaspoons sour cream
1 cup Chestnut Purée
2 tablespoons grated raw chestnut
1/4 teaspoon salt
1/4 teaspoon freshly ground white pepper
Dash cayenne pepper (optional)
Paprika
Minced fresh parsley
Melba Toast and/or plain crackers

In a mixing bowl, combine the cream cheese and sour cream and mix with a fork until smooth and softened. Gradually stir in chestnut purée, raw chestnut, salt, and white and cayenne peppers. Taste and adjust seasonings.

Pack chestnut mixture into a crock or bowl and dust with paprika. Cover and refrigerate at least 6 hours to mellow the flavors, or for up to 2 days.

To serve, bring spread to room temperature. Sprinkle with minced parsley and serve with melba toast and/or crackers.

OLIVE CREAM CHEESE SPREAD ●

*Makes Approximately
Two-thirds Cup*
3 ounces cream cheese, at room
temperature
2 tablespoons mayonnaise, or
as needed
1/4 cup finely chopped ripe
olives
2 tablespoons finely minced
green bell pepper
2 tablespoons finely chopped
well-drained pimiento or
Roasted Pepper
1 teaspoon grated onion
Salt and freshly ground white
pepper to taste
Green bell pepper slivers

In a mixing bowl, combine cream
cheese and mayonnaise and beat
with a wooden spoon until well-
blended, soft, and smooth. Stir
in olives, bell pepper, pimiento,
onion, and salt, and white
pepper. Mix in additional mayonnaise as needed to make spreading consistency. Taste and adjust
seasonings. Pack spread into a
small bowl or crock and garnish
with bell pepper slivers.
    If not using spread immedi-
ately, cover with plastic wrap
and refrigerate for up to 3 days.
Let come to room temperature
before serving.

SHRIMP CREAM CHEESE SPREAD ●

*Makes Approximately
Three-fourths Cup*
4 ounces cream cheese, at room
temperature
2 tablespoons sour cream, or
as needed
1 tablespoon fresh lemon juice
1 teaspoon grated onion
2 teaspoons minced garlic chives
1/4 pound shrimp, cooked,
shelled, and finely minced
Salt and freshly ground white
pepper to taste
Lightly toasted slivered blanched
almonds

In a mixing bowl, combine cream
cheese and sour cream and beat
with a wooden spoon until well
blended, soft, and smooth. Stir
in lemon juice, onion, and chives.
Mix in additional sour cream as
needed to make spreading consistency. With a fork, stir in
shrimp and salt and pepper.
Taste and adjust seasonings. Pack
spread into a small bowl or
crock and sprinkle with almonds.
    If not using spread immedi-
ately, cover with plastic wrap
and refrigerate for up to 2 days.
Let come to room temperature
before serving.

QUICK-AND-EASY CREAM CHEESE SPREADS ●

All of these spreads may be
prepared up to three days in
advance, unless otherwise noted.
Cover tightly and refrigerate
until about one hour before
serving, then allow to come to
room temperature.
    For easy mixing, have the
cheese and butter at room temperature, and use *freshly ground*
black or white pepper for fullest
flavor.
● 3 ounces cream cheese, 3
tablespoons unsalted butter,
mayonnaise to make spreading
consistency, 3/4 cup finely minced
watercress leaves, and Beau Monde
seasoning, salt, and white pepper
to taste.
● Equal amounts cream cheese
and minced cucumber (peel, slice,
sprinkle with salt; let stand 30
minutes, drain, and dry with
paper toweling before mincing),
mayonnaise to make spreading
consistency, and grated onion,
salt, and white pepper to taste.
● Cream cheese, mayonnaise to
make spreading consistency, well-
drained finely minced pimiento
or Roasted Pepper, and salt and
white pepper to taste.
● 3 ounces cream cheese; mayonnaise to make spreading consistency; 2/3 cup coarsely ground
or very finely minced cooked
ham or beef; 2 hard-cooked

eggs, sieved; 1/3 cup grated sharp Cheddar cheese; and salt and white pepper to taste.

• Equal parts cream cheese and chèvre, ground thyme or finely minced fresh thyme to taste, and light cream to make spreading consistency. Top with finely shredded daikon or other white radish.

• Cream cheese, softened with white Dubonnet, and anchovy paste, minced fresh chives, and Worcestershire sauce to taste. Garnish with ripe olive halves or slivers.

• 4 ounces cream cheese, 1/2 cup finely chopped and drained ripe tomato, 2 tablespoons minced fresh parsley, 1/2 teaspoon pressed garlic, and salt and white pepper to taste.

• 3 ounces cream cheese, softened with a little light cream; one 2-1/4-ounce can deviled ham; and grated onion, prepared horseradish, salt, and black pepper to taste. Garnish with tiny sliver of gherkin.

• 3 ounces cream cheese, 1/4 cup sour cream, and onion powder, garlic powder, Worcestershire sauce, and anchovy paste to taste.

• 4 ounces cream cheese, mayonnaise to make spreading consistency, 1 cup firmly packed minced watercress leaves, 1/2 teaspoon *each* salt and paprika, and 1/4 teaspoon curry powder,

or to taste. Or omit curry powder and season with prepared horseradish to taste; thin with light cream instead of mayonnaise. Refrigerate for no more than 2 days.

• 4 ounces cream cheese, mayonnaise to make spreading consistency, 1/2 cup finely minced celery, and cayenne pepper to taste.

• 4 ounces cream cheese; 2 hard-cooked eggs, sieved; 2 tablespoons *each* finely minced green or red bell pepper and green onion and tops; 1 tablespoon minced gherkin; and salt and white pepper to taste. Garnish with crumbled crisply cooked bacon.

• 4 ounces cream cheese, at room temperature; 1/4 cup small curd low-fat cottage cheese; 2 garlic cloves, finely minced; 3 tablespoons finely minced fresh parsley; 1 tablespoon minced fresh chives; and ground thyme, salt, and white pepper to taste.

SPREAD SUGGESTIONS ●

Like the preceding cream cheese spreads, these spreads go together quickly and easily and will keep up to three days in the refrigerator, unless otherwise specified. Serve the spreads lightly chilled, except for those made with butter, which should be served at room temperature. Accompany with breads and/or crackers (see Ways with Breads).

Remember to use *freshly ground* white or black pepper and to have cheeses and butter at room temperature for ease of mixing.

• 1/2 cup finely diced Brie or Camembert cheese, equal parts sour cream and mayonnaise to make spreading consistency, 1/2 cup finely diced tart apple, and 2 tablespoons finely chopped walnuts or pecans.

• 1/2 cup small-curd low-fat cottage cheese, 2 tablespoons *each* crumbled blue cheese and chopped radishes, and 1 tablespoon minced fresh parsley and/or chives; top with thinly sliced radishes. Refrigerate no more than 2 days.

- One 4-3/8-ounce can sardines, drained and mashed, 2 tablespoons minced fresh parsley, 2 teaspoons minced shallots, 1 tablespoon fresh lemon juice, and salt and white pepper to taste. Garnish with a tiny parsley leaf.
- Ground cooked chicken, finely minced water chestnuts, mayonnaise to make spreading consistency, and salt and white pepper to taste.
- 1/2 cup *each* finely minced cooked ham and chicken, 2 tablespoons *each* finely chopped Brazil nuts or pecans and fresh chives, 1 tablespoon finely minced gherkin, mayonnaise to make spreading consistency, and salt and black pepper to taste.
- Ground cooked ham, minced dill pickle, mayonnaise to make spreading consistency, and ground allspice and black pepper to taste.
- 1/2 cup *each* minced cooked tongue and chicken or turkey, 4 tablespoons butter, and Dijon-style mustard, salt, and black pepper to taste.
- 1/2 cup Basic Mayonnaise; 2 hard-cooked eggs, sieved; 1/2 cup *each* minced radishes, watercress, and cucumber (peel cucumber, slice, sprinkle with salt, and let stand 30 minutes; drain and dry with paper toweling before mincing); 1/4 cup minced green onion and tops; 1 tablespoon minced fresh dill; and salt and

white pepper to taste. Refrigerate no more than 1 day.
- 1/2 cup Basic Mayonnaise; 1 cup minced cooked shrimp or crab meat; 1 tablespoon minced shallots or 2 tablespoons minced green onion and tops; 1 to 2 teaspoons drained capers, minced; and white pepper to taste. Refrigerate no more than 1 day.
- 1/2 cup shredded Steamed Pollack or Monkfish; 1 hard-cooked egg, sieved; 2 tablespoons minced cucumber (peel, slice, sprinkle with salt, and let stand 30 minutes; drain and dry with paper toweling before mincing); mayonnaise to make spreading consistency; and salt and pepper to taste. Refrigerate no more than 1 day.
- 4 hard-cooked eggs, finely chopped; 2 slices bacon, cooked and crumbled; mayonnaise to make spreading consistency; and Worcestershire sauce, salt, and white pepper to taste. Refrigerate no more than 1 day.
- 4 ounces liver sausage (liverwurst); sour cream to make spreading consistency; 2 green onions and tops, finely minced; 1 tablespoon minced fresh parsley; 2 teaspoons minced fresh chives; and prepared horseradish and Tabasco sauce to taste.

DIPS AND DIPPERS

A spectacular presentation is important to the success of a dip, whether it be the single offering at a small gathering or part of a large buffet. Select the container with color and material in mind. For example, a crystal bowl would beautifully set off the lovely salmon color of the Lima Beans with Roasted Pepper dip at an elegant affair, while a black lacquer vessel would complement the soft green of Guacamole for a more casual evening. Whatever container you settle on, it should be shallow for easy dipping. It is important, too, to take the time to garnish a dip attractively (see Garnitures).

Vegetable "bowls" make stunning dip containers. Hollow out eggplant halves, red cabbages, or bell peppers and use as serving vessels. In the fall months, a dumpling squash or small pumpkin filled with a vibrantly colored dip would add a bright touch to the buffet table.

Dippers, the edible scoops with which guests serve themselves, can be any number of items. Garden-fresh vegetables are popular choices, as they are healthful and low in calories. These dippers, called here by the French term "crudité," include both raw and lightly blanched vegetables. Those that are to be served raw should be cut at the last minute to preserve vitamins. If your schedule doesn't permit this, prepare the vegetables several hours ahead and refrigerate in sealed plastic bags.

In my opinion, certain vegetable dippers taste best when blanched briefly, no more than twenty seconds. These include asparagus tips, green beans (unless very young), and broccoli florets. Plunge them into ice water immediately to cool, then drain, pat dry with paper toweling, arrange in a nonmetallic container, cover, and refrigerate until ready to serve.

Suggested crudités, and directions for cutting them, follow. Keep color and texture in mind when deciding on which crudité best complements a particular dip. Emulate the Japanese way with vegetables: trim them to a graceful, easy-to-manage size.

- asparagus tips
- tender young green beans
- cauliflower or broccoli, broken into florets
- cherry tomatoes
- mushrooms, halved if large and rubbed with fresh lemon juice
- jicama, carrots, turnips, beets, cucumbers, kohlrabi, celery, fennel, zucchini, or green or red bell peppers, sliced or cut into fingers
- Belgian endive leaves
- sugar snap peas

Other items also make good dippers: chunks of cooked lobster, monkfish, or pollack; cooked shrimp, scallops, or squid; miniature breadsticks; flour or corn Tortilla Chips; potato chips; thin, firm crackers; french bread fingers; pita bread; lahvosh.

Dips may be stored in tightly covered nonmetallic containers in the refrigerator until serving time. Keeping times are indicated in the recipes.

BEAN DIPS

You'll never again buy commercial bean dips once you've made your own. The recipes that follow are nutritious, tasty creations that feature some unusual combinations and a wide variety of legumes.

Do not resort to using canned beans to prepare these delicious dips. Cook the beans yourself so that you can add seasonings to the pot such as garlic, onion, and parsley. When done, the beans should be soft, but not dry. Drain them and reserve the cooking liquid; it may be combined with the dip ingredients to achieve the proper consistency. Each recipe gives you the quantity of dried beans you will need to cook in order to end up with the required cooked measure.

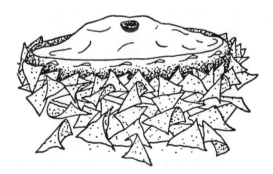

PINTO BEANS
WITH OREGANO ○

Makes Approximately Two Cups
2 tablespoons minced onion
1 large garlic clove, minced
2 cups cooked pinto beans
  (1 cup dried)
1/2 teaspoon crumbled dried
  oregano
2 teaspoons olive oil
1/2 teaspoon salt
1/4 teaspoon freshly ground
  black pepper
2 tablespoons cooking liquid or
  water, or as needed
Quartered cherry tomatoes
Parsley leaves
Tortilla Chips and/or crudités

In a blender or food processor,
purée onion, garlic, beans, oregano, oil, salt, and pepper. Add
cooking liquid and purée to
make dipping consistency. Taste
and adjust seasonings. Cover and
refrigerate overnight, or for up
to 3 days.

   To serve, bring bean dip to
room temperature, stir well, and
mound in a shallow serving bowl.
Decorate with tomatoes and parsley and serve with tortilla chips
and/or crudités.

WHITE BEANS
WITH ALMONDS ○

Design a spoke pattern of green
beans or asparagus tips on a
round serving plate and place
the bowl of bean dip in the
center.

Makes Approximately
One and One-half Cups
1 large garlic clove, minced
2 tablespoons minced red onion
1/4 cup parsley leaves
1-1/2 cups cooked white beans
  (1 cup plus 2 tablespoons dried)
2 tablespoons olive oil
1 tablespoon fresh lemon juice
1/4 cup light cream
1/2 teaspoon salt
1/4 teaspoon freshly ground
  white pepper
Bean cooking liquid or water
  as needed
1/2 cup sliced almonds, lightly
  toasted and finely chopped
Tiny strips of drained Pumate
Green beans or asparagus

In a blender or food processor,
whirl garlic, onion, and parsley
until very finely minced. Add
beans, oil, lemon juice, cream,
salt, and pepper. Purée, adding
cooking liquid as needed to
make dipping consistency. Taste
and adjust seasonings. Add
almonds and whirl just to mix.
Transfer to a storage container,

cover, and refrigerate at least
overnight or for up to 2 days.

   To serve, bring mixture to
room temperature, stir well, and
mound in a shallow serving bowl.
Decorate with pumate strips and
serve with green-bean dippers.

HUMMUS
(Garbanzo Bean Spread) ●

Makes Approximately
Two and Two-thirds Cups
2 or 3 large garlic cloves, minced
2 tablespoons minced fresh
  parsley
3/4 teaspoon salt
1 teaspoon ground cumin
1/2 teaspoon freshly ground
  black pepper
1/8 teaspoon cayenne pepper
2 cups cooked garbanzo beans
  (1 cup dried)
Bean cooking liquid or water
  as needed
2/3 cup tahini (sesame-seed paste)
1/3 cup fresh lemon juice, or
  to taste

PRESENTATION
1 to 2 tablespoons olive oil
Paprika
Minced fresh parsley
Slivered Mediterranean-style
  olives
Pita bread, warmed and torn
  into pieces

In a mortar with a pestle, mash garlic, 2 tablespoons parsley, salt, cumin, black pepper, and cayenne pepper; set aside.

Reserve 10 garbanzo beans. In a blender or food processor, purée remaining garbanzo beans, adding a little cooking liquid as needed to form a thick, smooth mixture. Blend in garlic mixture, tahini, and lemon juice, adding cooking liquid to make dipping consistency. Taste and adjust seasonings. Then, with a spatula, form mixture on a serving plate in a circle or an oval about 3/4-inch high. If not serving immediately, cover with plastic wrap and refrigerate for up to 2 days.

To serve, bring dip to room temperature. Make a shallow indentation in the center of the circle of bean dip and pour olive oil into the hollow. Sprinkle entire surface with paprika and decorate with minced parsley, slivered olives, and reserved whole garbanzo beans. Serve with pita bread.

REFRIED BEANS WITH CHILI PEPPER ●

For the best result, use homemade refried beans to create this pleasantly fiery dip. Arrange a basket of crisp tortilla chips alongside the serving bowl.

Makes Approximately
One and One-half Cups
1 cup refried beans (1/2 cup dried)
1/2 cup sour cream
1/4 cup finely minced onion
1 large garlic clove, very
    finely minced
1 to 3 tablespoons Tomatillo
    Sauce
1/2 teaspoon crushed dried red
    chili pepper, or to taste
Salt and freshly ground black
    pepper to taste
Bean cooking liquid or water
    as needed
Green bell pepper rings
Tortilla Chips

In a mixing bowl, combine refried beans, sour cream, onion, garlic, tomatillo sauce, crushed red pepper, salt, and black pepper. Beat until smooth, adding liquid as needed to make dipping consistency. Taste and adjust seasonings. If not serving immediately, cover and refrigerate for up to 3 days.

To serve, bring mixture to room temperature, stir well, and mound in a shallow serving bowl. Decorate with bell pepper rings and serve with tortilla chips.

BLACK-EYED PEAS WITH PUMATE O

Makes Approximately One Cup
1 small garlic clove, minced
2 teaspoons minced red onion
2 teaspoons Pumate Purée
1 cup cooked black-eyed peas
    (1/2 cup dried)
2 teaspoons olive oil
1/4 teaspoon salt
1/4 teaspoon freshly ground
    black pepper
1/4 teaspoon chili powder
Cooking liquid or water
    as needed
3 tablespoons finely chopped
    ripe olives
Ripe olive slivers
Crudités

In a blender or food processor, whirl garlic, onion, pumate purée, beans, oil, salt, pepper, and chili powder. Purée, adding cooking liquid as needed to make dipping consistency. Add minced olives and whirl just to mix. Taste and adjust seasonings. Cover and refrigerate overnight, or for up to 3 days.

To serve, let bean dip come to room temperature, stir well, and mound in a shallow serving bowl. Decorate with olive slivers and serve with crudités.

HOT BLACK-EYED PEAS WITH CHEDDAR

Makes Approximately
One and One-half Cups
1 large garlic clove, minced
3 tablespoons chopped onion
1 cup cooked black-eyed peas
  (1/2 cup dried)
1 fresh jalapeño pepper, seeded
  and chopped
1 tablespoon butter
1/4 teaspoon chili powder
1/4 teaspoon salt
1/8 teaspoon freshly ground
  black pepper
3/4 cup shredded sharp Cheddar
  cheese
1/4 cup diced canned mild green
  chili peppers
1/2 tablespoon pea cooking liquid
  or water, or as needed
Coriander sprigs
Crudités and/or bread rounds

In a blender or food processor, whirl the garlic and onion. Add peas, jalapeño pepper, butter, and seasonings. Purée until smooth. Transfer mixture to a fireproof earthenware pan or heavy saucepan and place over medium heat. Add cheese and cook, stirring almost constantly, until cheese is melted. Stir in canned chilies and cooking liquid, adding more liquid if needed to make dipping consistency. Taste and adjust seasonings.

Place pan over a spirit stove. Garnish with coriander and serve with crudités and/or bread rounds.

LIMA BEANS WITH ROASTED PEPPER ○

Lima beans are given an elegant treatment in this easy-to-prepare dip. Its gorgeous salmon color and pronounced roasted-pepper flavor make it an irresistible addition to any hors d'oeuvre table.

Makes Approximately Two Cups
2 cups cooked lima beans
  (3/4 cup dried)
2 tablespoons minced lightly
  drained Roasted Pepper
1/2 teaspoon oil from Roasted
  Pepper
1 teaspoon salt
1/4 teaspoon freshly ground
  white pepper
2 teaspoons fresh lemon juice
3 tablespoons cooking liquid or
  water, or as needed
Additional Roasted Pepper,
  drained and cut into slivers
Lahvosh bread or miniature
  breadsticks

In a blender or food processor, purée beans, 2 tablespoons roasted pepper, oil, salt, white pepper, and lemon juice. Add cooking liquid and purée to make dipping consistency. Taste and adjust

seasonings. Cover and refrigerate overnight, or for up to 2 days.

To serve, bring bean mixture to room temperature, stir well, and mound in a shallow serving bowl. Decorate with roasted pepper slivers. Serve with lahvosh.

CREME FRAICHE WITH ROASTED PEPPER ●

Makes Approximately
Three-fourths Cup
1/2 cup Crème Fraîche
1/4 cup minced well-drained
  Roasted Pepper
1 tablespoon finely minced ripe
  olive
1 tablespoon minced fresh
  parsley
1 teaspoon fresh lemon juice,
  or to taste
1 teaspoon anchovy paste, or
  to taste
Salt and freshly ground black
  pepper to taste
Crudités

In a mixing bowl, combine crème fraîche, roasted pepper, olive, parsley, lemon juice, anchovy paste, salt, and black pepper. Taste and adjust seasonings.

Transfer dip to a shallow serving bowl, cover, and refrigerate until well chilled, or for up to 2 days. Serve with crudités.

LEMONY SPINACH-SORREL DIP ●

*Makes Approximately
One and One-half Cups*
1 large garlic clove, chopped
1 egg
1 tablespoon fresh lemon juice
1/4 cup firmly packed parsley
    or watercress leaves
1/4 cup minced green onion tops
1/4 cup firmly packed finely
    shredded spinach leaves
1/4 cup firmly packed finely
    shredded sorrel leaves
1/2 teaspoon Worcestershire
    sauce
1/2 teaspoon salt, or to taste
1/4 teaspoon freshly ground
    white pepper, or to taste
1 cup olive or safflower oil
1/2 cup Crème Fraîche or
    sour cream
Paprika
Crudités

In a blender or food processor, finely mince the garlic. Add egg, lemon juice, parsley, green onion tops, spinach, sorrel, Worcestershire sauce, salt, and pepper. Blend to mince herbs and vegetables finely and to mix well.

With motor running, pour in oil in a slow, steady stream. Whirl in crème fraîche, taste, and adjust seasonings.

Transfer dip to a shallow serving bowl, cover, and refrigerate until well chilled, or for up to 2 days. Just before serving, stir well and sprinkle lightly with paprika. Accompany with crudités.

VARIATION Add 1 tablespoon Dijon-style mustard and/or 1 tablespoon drained capers with the egg.

PEANUT DIP WITH CHILI ●

*Makes Approximately
One and One-half Cups*
1 medium onion, minced
2 large garlic cloves, minced
1 or 2 small fresh hot chili
    peppers, seeded and minced
1/2 teaspoon finely minced
    ginger root
2 tablespoons peanut oil
1 cup coconut milk
1 cup chunky peanut butter
1-1/2 tablespoons white rice
    vinegar
1 teaspoon soy sauce
1 teaspoon brown sugar
Fresh coriander leaves
Unsalted crackers, miniature
    breadsticks, and/or crudités

In a large covered nonstick skillet, sauté onion, garlic, chili pepper, and ginger root in oil until softened. Stir in coconut milk, peanut butter, vinegar, soy sauce, and brown sugar. Cook, stirring almost constantly, until mixture is well blended and smooth. Remove from the heat and let cool.

Mound dip in a shallow serving bowl and garnish with coriander leaves. Serve with crackers, breadsticks, and/or crudités.

This dip may be made 1 day in advance of serving. Any leftover dip will keep up to 3 days. Cover and store in the refrigerator. Bring to room temperature and stir well before garnishing and serving.

GUACAMOLE

One of the most popular of all dips, guacamole can be prepared in a blender or food processor so that it is very smooth, or it can be mixed with a fork to form a coarse mixture, as is done in this recipe.

Some cooks believe the avocado pits help retard the discoloration of the guacamole, but I have found they make little difference. Lemon juice is what keeps the avocado fresh-looking, but it will not do so for more than four or five hours, so make this one of the "last-minute" items on your menu.

Don't throw out any dip that is left over, as the discoloration will not affect the taste. Thin the dip with a little sour cream or vinaigrette and use it the next evening to dress salad greens. Two days, however, is the maximum it will hold.

Makes Approximately Two Cups
2 large ripe avocados, peeled
    and pitted
2 tablespoons fresh lemon or
    lime juice
2 teaspoons grated onion
1/2 teaspoon grated garlic
3/4 teaspoon salt
1/4 teaspoon freshly ground
    white pepper
1/8 teaspoon ground cumin

1/8 teaspoon chili powder
1 medium-size ripe tomato,
    cut into tiny dice and drained
3 or 4 tiny parsley leaves
Tortilla Chips, cooked lobster,
    monkfish, or pollack chunks,
    and/or crudités

With a fork, mash avocados and lemon juice until lemon juice is incorporated and avocado is mashed to desired consistency. Stir in onion, garlic, salt, pepper, cumin, and chili powder. Taste and adjust seasonings.

Transfer to a serving dish, cover tightly with plastic wrap, and refrigerate several hours until well chilled. Just before serving, make a border of the diced tomato around the rim of the avocado dip and tuck the parsley leaves into the center. Serve with tortilla chips, seafood chunks, and/or crudités.

VARIATIONS
• Mix the tomato dice directly into the dip before adding the seasonings. At the same time, add 1/3 cup minced well-drained canned mild green chili peppers. Omit the parsley leaves and garnish with finely minced fresh coriander.
• Season the dip with Tabasco sauce and/or prepared horseradish to taste. Just before serving, sprinkle with paprika.

YOGHURT DIPS

Serve an array of crudités with any one of these four low-cholesterol yoghurt dips, all of which taste best when eaten slightly chilled. They may be made one day in advance of serving and any left-over dip will keep for up to three days, unless otherwise specified. To store, cover tightly and refrigerate. Stir well before garnishing and serving.

AVOCADO YOGHURT DIP

Makes Approximately Three Cups
2 to 3 shallots, cut up
1 small sweet red or white onion,
    cut up
1/2 small green bell pepper,
    cut up
2 tablespoons chopped green
    onion tops
2 large ripe avocados, peeled,
    pitted, and cut up
1-1/2 tablespoons fresh lemon
    juice, or to taste
1/2 cup plain yoghurt, sour
    cream, or Crème Fraîche
1/4 cup Basic Mayonnaise
1 teaspoon crumbled dried dill
    or tarragon, or to taste
1/4 teaspoon salt
1/4 teaspoon freshly ground
    white pepper
Coriander sprigs
Tortilla Chips

In a blender or food processor, finely mince shallots, onion, bell pepper, and green onion tops. Add avocados and lemon juice and whirl until smooth. Add yoghurt, mayonnaise, dill, salt, and white pepper. Whirl until smooth, then taste and adjust seasonings.

Transfer dip to a shallow serving bowl, cover, and refrigerate several hours to chill thoroughly. Just before serving, garnish with coriander sprigs. Serve with tortilla chips.

This dip should be kept no longer than 1 day.

SPINACH YOGHURT DIP ●

Makes Approximately Two and One-half Cups
2 large garlic cloves, chopped
2 green onions and tops, chopped
1 cup firmly packed *well-drained* chopped cooked spinach (one 10-ounce package frozen chopped spinach)
2 cups plain yoghurt
1/2 tablespoon fresh lemon juice, or to taste
1/2 teaspoon salt
1/4 teaspoon freshly ground white pepper
1/4 teaspoon paprika
1/8 teaspoon cayenne pepper
Additional paprika
Crudités

In a blender or food processor, finely mince garlic and green onion. Add spinach and whirl to chop finely. Add yoghurt, lemon juice, salt, white pepper, paprika, and cayenne pepper; blend to mix well. Taste and adjust seasonings.

Transfer dip to a shallow serving bowl, cover, and refrigerate at least 1 hour. Just before serving, sprinkle lightly with paprika. Serve with crudités.

VARIATIONS
● Omit paprika and season with 1/2 teaspoon curry powder, or to taste. Just before serving, sprinkle with very finely minced fresh coriander.
● Just before serving, stir in 2/3 cup very finely minced cooked shrimp or crab meat. (Yield will increase to approximately 2 cups). Keep no longer than 2 days.
● Add one 8-1/2-ounce can (drained weight) water-pack artichoke hearts, well drained, and 1 teaspoon minced fresh dill with the spinach. (Yield will be increased to approximately 2 cups.)

MINTED YOGHURT DIP ●

Makes Approximately One Cup
1 cup plain yoghurt
2 tablespoons fresh lemon juice
2 tablespoons finely minced fresh mint

1 teaspoon finely minced garlic
1/4 teaspoon salt
1/4 teaspoon freshly ground white pepper
Fresh mint leaves
Crudités

In a mixing bowl, combine yoghurt, lemon juice, minced mint, garlic, salt, and pepper. Taste and adjust seasonings.

Transfer dip to a shallow serving dish, cover, and refrigerate 1 hour. Just before serving, garnish with mint leaves and surround with crudités.

CURRIED YOGHURT DIP ●

Makes Approximately One Cup
3/4 cup plain yoghurt
1/4 cup sour cream
2 teaspoons curry powder, or to taste
2 teaspoons fresh lemon juice
1/4 teaspoon salt
1/4 teaspoon freshly ground white pepper
Parsley or watercress leaves
Crudités

In a mixing bowl, combine yoghurt, sour cream, curry powder, lemon juice, salt, and pepper. Taste and adjust seasonings.

Transfer dip to a shallow serving dish, cover, and refrigerate at least 1 hour. Just before serving, garnish with parsley leaves and serve with crudités.

ZUCCHINI CREAM CHEESE DIP ●

Makes Approximately Two and One-half Cups

2 cups diced zucchini (10 to 12 ounces)
2 tablespoons minced onion
1 teaspoon minced garlic
2 parsley sprigs, chopped
1/2 tablespoon minced fresh basil
1/2 teaspoon salt
1/2 teaspoon paprika
1/4 teaspoon freshly ground black pepper
8 ounces cream cheese, cut into cubes and at room temperature
1/2 teaspoon Worcestershire sauce
1 teaspoon fresh lemon juice
1/2 teaspoon crumbled dried mixed Italian herbs
Crème Fraîche or sour cream
Additional paprika
Minced fresh parsley
Crudités

In a large nonstick skillet, combine zucchini, onion, garlic, parsley sprigs, basil, salt, paprika, and pepper. Cover and cook over medium heat 15 minutes, or until vegetables are very soft. Cool and purée in a blender or food processor. (At this point, the mixture may be frozen for up to 2 months. Bring to room temperature before proceeding with recipe.)

In a mixing bowl, combine cream cheese, Worcestershire sauce, lemon juice, and Italian herbs and beat with a wooden spoon until cheese is softened and smooth. Gradually work in the zucchini mixture until well blended, adding crème fraîche as needed to make dipping consistency. Taste and adjust seasonings.

Transfer zucchini mixture to a shallow serving bowl and sprinkle with paprika and minced parsley. Place bowl on a plate and surround with crudités.

This dip may be made 1 day in advance of serving. Cover and store in the refrigerator. Any left-over dip can be refrigerated for up to 3 days. Bring to room temperature and stir before garnishing and serving.

ARTICHOKE CREAM CHEESE DIP ●

The secret of this simple dip is how the artichokes are prepared. Cook whole artichokes in rich stock with lots of garlic, onion, oregano, and fresh lemon juice and reserve the bottoms to use in this recipe. Do not purchase canned or jarred artichoke bottoms, for the proper flavor will be lacking.

Makes Approximately One Cup

3 ounces cream cheese, at room temperature
1 tablespoon heavy cream or Crème Fraîche, or as needed
2/3 cup very finely minced or lightly mashed cooked artichoke bottoms
2 teaspoons fresh lemon juice
1/4 teaspoon Worcestershire sauce
1/4 teaspoon freshly ground white pepper
1/8 teaspoon salt
Dash cayenne pepper
Paprika
Watercress leaves
Miniature breadsticks and crudités

In a mixing bowl, combine cream cheese and cream and beat with a wooden spoon until softened and smooth. Stir in artichokes, lemon juice, Worcestershire sauce, white pepper, salt, and cayenne pepper. Add additional cream as needed to make dipping consistency. Taste and adjust seasonings.

Transfer artichoke mixture to a shallow serving bowl, sprinkle with paprika, and garnish with watercress leaves. Stand breadsticks upright in a mug or other high-sided container and arrange the crudités in a basket. Place the breadsticks and crudités alongside the dip.

This dip may be made 1 day in advance of serving. Cover and

store in the refrigerator. Any left-over dip may be refrigerated for up to 3 days. Bring to room temperature and stir before garnishing and serving.

OLD-FASHIONED CLAM DIP ●

This cream cheese–based dip is an old standby, favored particularly by young people, who prefer potato chips for dipping.

Makes Approximately
Two and One-half Cups
8 ounces cream cheese, at
    room temperature
1/2 cup sour cream
2 tablespoons mayonnaise
1 tablespoon finely grated onion
    and juices
2 tablespoons chopped drained
    pimiento (optional)
2 tablespoons minced fresh dill
3 dashes Tabasco sauce (optional)
One 7-ounce can minced clams,
    drained (save juices for fish
    stock or to make cream sauce
    for fish)
Paprika
Potato chips or crudités

In a large mixing bowl, beat cheese with a wooden spoon until smooth. Add sour cream, mayonnaise, onion, pimiento, dill, and Tabasco sauce and mix until well blended. Stir in clams and transfer to a shallow serving bowl. Sprinkle with paprika and serve with potato chips or crudités.

This dip may be made 1 day in advance of serving. Cover and store in the refrigerator. Any left-over dip can be refrigerated for up to 3 days. Bring to room temperature and stir well before garnishing and serving.

TAHINI DIP ●

Tahini, or sesame-seed paste, made from ground raw sesame seeds with no salt added can be purchased in jars in natural- and health-food stores and some supermarkets. It is very thick and needs to be stirred well before using, to mix in the oil that has separated from the paste. Storing upside down, then turning right side up for several hours before using will help distribute the oil. Once opened, store in the refrigerator for up to three months.

Makes Approximately Two Cups
4 or 5 large garlic cloves, minced
1 teaspoon salt
1 cup tahini, at room temperature
1 cup fresh lemon juice
Cold water, if needed
2 tablespoons minced fresh
    coriander
1/2 teaspoon salt
1/4 teaspoon freshly ground
    white pepper
1/8 teaspoon cayenne pepper
Green bell pepper strips
Halved cherry tomatoes
Cauliflower florets

In a mortar and pestle, mash garlic with salt. In a separate bowl, stir tahini with a wooden spoon to soften. Gradually add lemon juice to form a workable mixture. Combine with garlic-salt mixture, then beat in water 1 tablespoon at a time to make dipping consistency. Mix in coriander, salt, white pepper, and cayenne pepper. Taste and adjust seasonings.

To serve, let dip come to room temperature, stir well, and mound in a shallow serving bowl. Garnish with green pepper strips and cherry tomatoes. Serve with cauliflower florets.

This dip may be made 2 days in advance of serving. Any left-over dip will keep up to 3 days. Cover and store in the refrigerator.

VARIATION Peel and pit 2 medium-size ripe avocados and mash with a fork. Stir mashed avocado into tahini dip, combining thoroughly. Store tightly covered in the refrigerator no more than 2 days.

TAPENADE WITH EGGS AND CAULIFLOWER ●

Tapenade, the garlicky anchovy dip from Provençal, is a versatile creation. This version is accompanied with hard-cooked egg halves and cauliflower florets, but other raw vegetables would be equally good (see Dips and Dippers for suggestions).

This full-bodied dip can also be a filling for stuffed mushrooms, artichoke bottoms, or cherry tomatoes, or can be combined with sieved hard-cooked egg yolks as a filling for stuffed eggs.

Makes Approximately Twenty-four Egg Servings; Approximately Forty-eight Cauliflower Servings
One 7-1/2-ounce can oil-packed tuna fish
6 anchovy fillets
3 tablespoons drained capers
3 large garlic cloves, minced
20 medium-size pitted ripe olives
6 tablespoons fresh lime or lemon juice
1/2 teaspoon freshly ground black pepper
4 to 6 tablespoons olive oil
2 to 3 tablespoons brandy

PRESENTATION
12 small hard-cooked eggs, halved
3 to 4 cups cauliflower florets
12 pitted ripe olives, halved
Parsley and watercress sprigs

In a blender or food processor, purée tuna and its oil, anchovies and their oil, capers, garlic, olives, lime juice, and pepper. With motor running, pour in olive oil in a slow, steady stream until sauce is the consistency of mayonnaise. Mix in brandy, then taste and adjust seasonings. Transfer to a storage container, cover, and refrigerate several hours or until well chilled.

To serve, spoon a dollop of the chilled dip on each egg half and garnish each with an olive half. Spoon remaining tapenade into a shallow bowl and place in the center of a large round platter. Arrange eggs around bowl alternately with cauliflower florets and tuck parsley and watercress sprigs in around eggs and florets. Guests help themselves to eggs and dip the florets into the tapenade.

This dip may be made 1 day in advance of serving. Any leftover dip will keep up to 3 days. Cover and store in the refrigerator.

BAGNA CAUDA
(Italian Anchovy-Garlic Dip)

Serve this Piedmontese specialty in the earthenware or other heavy saucepan in which it has been made. Place the vessel over a spirit stove to keep the dip warm. The pronounced garlic and anchovy flavors call for crusty sourdough bread fingers and crudités.

Makes Approximately One Cup
3/4 cup butter
1/4 cup olive oil
4 large garlic cloves, finely minced
10 anchovy fillets packed in oil, rinsed in cold water, patted dry, and finely minced
1 tablespoon fresh lemon juice, or to taste (optional)
Freshly ground black pepper to taste
Sourdough french-bread fingers
Crudités

In a fireproof earthenware pan or heavy saucepan, heat butter with oil until butter is melted. Add garlic and cook slowly until garlic is very soft. Do not allow garlic to brown. Remove pan from heat and with a wooden spoon, stir in anchovies. Return saucepan to low heat and, stirring constantly, cook mixture until anchovies become a paste. Stir in lemon juice and pepper.

Place saucepan over a spirit stove and serve at once with french-bread fingers and crudités.

TARAMOSALATA
(Greek Caviar Dip) ●

Makes Approximately Two Cups
5 slices white bread, crusts
    removed
One 8-ounce jar tarama (salted,
    preserved cod, carp, or mullet
    roe)
2 tablespoons minced onion
1 to 1-1/2 cups olive oil
1/3 to 1/2 cup fresh lemon juice
Freshly ground black pepper

PRESENTATION
Minced fresh parsley
Chopped hard-cooked eggs
Slivered Mediterranean-style olives
Pita bread, warmed and torn
    into pieces
Carrot and celery sticks

Soak bread in water to cover until soft, squeeze dry, and set aside. In a mixing bowl, stir tarama with a wooden spoon to soften. Gradually stir in onion and a little of the oil to make a smooth paste. Alternately beat in lemon juice, reserved bread, and remaining olive oil until mixture is smooth. Season with pepper to taste, cover, and refrigerate at least 1 hour.

To serve, mound mixture in a shallow serving bowl and sprinkle with parsley. Decorate with chopped eggs and slivered olives. Serve with pita bread and carrot and celery sticks.

This dip may be made 1 day in advance of serving. Any leftover dip will keep for up to 3 days. Cover and store in the refrigerator.

BLACK PEPPERCORN–ANCHOVY DIP ●

This rich mayonnaiselike dip is for those who like peppery foods. Carrot and/or zucchini sticks or asparagus tips are the ideal dippers.

Makes Approximately
One and One-half Cups
15 to 20 black peppercorns
1 large garlic clove
2-1/2 tablespoons prepared
    mustard
One 2-ounce can anchovy fillets
    packed in oil
1 egg
1 cup safflower oil
Parsley leaves
Crudités

In a blender or food processor, whirl peppercorns, garlic, mustard, and anchovies and their oil until smooth. Add egg and blend 1 minute. With motor running, slowly pour in safflower oil in a steady stream.

Transfer mixture to a shallow serving bowl, cover, and refrigerate until chilled. Just before serving, garnish with parsley leaves. Serve with crudités.

This dip may be made 1 day in advance of serving. Any leftover dip will keep for up to 3 days. Cover and store in the refrigerator.

EGGS

Eggs are a must on any large hors d'oeuvres menu. They are an economical buy that can be transformed into a variety of tasty, attractive dishes to satisfy both good-sized appetites and sophisticated palates.

The unique texture of stuffed eggs—the firmness of the whites contrasting dramatically with the smooth yolk-based fillings—is a good counterpoint to other dishes, and some twenty-five recipes for these longtime favorites appear here. There are also frittatas, dense with vegetables and cheese, that provide substantial mouthfuls, and a Spanish-style omelet that successfully combines the commonplace potato with delicate seafood.

For a colorful, edible garnish, prepare Red Eggs or Tea Eggs and use as a decorative addition to a meat platter. See the Pastries chapter for a delectable array of egg-rich quiches.

STUFFED EGGS

The following stuffing recipes will fill 14 small eggs. If small eggs are not readily available where you shop, you can special order them through the dairy manager of your market or the local farmers' market. Eggs are best for hard cooking when they are about 2 weeks old; fresher eggs are difficult to peel and their yolks tend to discolor when cooked.

Eggs may be hard-cooked 1 day ahead and refrigerated unpeeled until ready to fill. Once filled, they should be refrigerated and served within 3 or 4 hours. Leftovers can be eaten on the following day, but should be kept no longer.

To cook, pierce a hole in the center of the blunt end of each unshelled egg with a sewing needle. Put the eggs in a saucepan with cold water to cover and bring slowly to a boil. Simmer gently 2 minutes, remove from the heat, cover, and let stand 15 to 18 minutes. Plunge into cold water, chill, and peel.

Halve the peeled eggs lengthwise or crosswise. Cut off a thin slice of the white on the bottom of each egg half so that the whites, when filled, will stand straight. Carefully remove the yolks. Place the whites on a plate or platter lined with paper toweling; cover with plastic wrap and refrigerate.

With a spoon, push yolks through a 1/4-inch-mesh sieve into a bowl. With a fork, combine the yolks with one of the following suggested fillings, adjust seasonings, and mound mixture in egg-white halves.

Some of the fillings call for butter or cream cheese, which must be quite soft for easy mixing with the yolks. Bring these ingredients to room temperature and then mash them with a fork until smooth. Unless otherwise specified, when pepper is listed, white or black may be used, according to your preference. The pepper should always be freshly ground, however.

Smooth fillings may be piped into the whites (see Basics for piping instructions), resulting in a more professional look. If the filling is too coarse to go through the pastry tube, reserve the yolks of 5 of the eggs, mix them with mayonnaise to make the correct consistency for use with a pastry tube, and then finish the mounding of the yolk mixture with an attractive piping.

After filling the eggs, decorate them as suggested in the recipes. Place them in a nonmetallic pan, cover with plastic wrap, and refrigerate until serving time.

There are specially designed plates with indentations for serving stuffed eggs. Use one of these, or arrange the eggs on a shallow platter and garnish the platter with complementary herbs or greens (see Simple Garnishes).

MUSTARD FILLING Mix sieved yolks with 2 tablespoons butter, 1/2 teaspoon *each* dry mustard and salt, 1/4 teaspoon white pepper, and Herb Mayonnaise to moisten. Sprinkle with paprika and top with a tiny cooked shrimp and a parsley leaf.

CURRY FILLING Mix sieved yolks with 1 to 2 teaspoons curry powder, 1 teaspoon soy sauce, 1 to 2 teaspoons fresh lemon juice, Shallot Mayonnaise to moisten, and white pepper to taste. Top with a tiny piece of chutney.

CHILI SAUCE FILLING Mix sieved egg yolks with 1/4 cup Chili Sauce; 1 tablespoon minced fresh parsley; 3 tablespoons finely minced green onion and tops; 2 tablespoons finely minced celery; salt, pepper, and Dijon-style mustard to taste; and Lemon/Lime Mayonnaise to moisten. Top with a tiny celery leaf.

MUSHROOM FILLING Mix sieved egg yolks with 3/4 cup finely minced mushrooms; fresh lemon juice, ground oregano, white pepper, and salt to taste; and Tarragon Mayonnaise to moisten. Top with a tiny watercress leaf.

OLIVE FILLING Mix sieved egg yolks with 1/2 cup minced ripe olives, salt, pepper, and dry mustard to taste, and Basic Mayonnaise to moisten. Sprinkle with paprika.

YOGHURT FILLING Mix sieved egg yolks with 1/4 cup plain yoghurt; 2 tablespoons finely minced pimiento-stuffed olives; 1 tablespoon *each* minced fresh parsley, fresh chives, and celery; and salt, pepper, and Dijon-style mustard to taste. Top with a tiny sliver of green bell pepper.

GREEN ONION FILLING Mix sieved egg yolks with 1/3 cup finely minced green onion and tops; 3 tablespoons minced drained sweet pickle relish; Dijon-style mustard, salt, and cayenne pepper to taste; and mayonnaise to moisten. Top with a tiny sliver of ripe olive.

SORREL FILLING In a covered nonstick skillet, cook 1 cup finely minced sorrel and 3 tablespoons finely minced shallots in 4 tablespoons butter until shallots are soft. Cool, mix with sieved egg yolks, and season to taste with salt, pepper, fresh lemon juice, and anchovy paste (optional) to taste. Top with a tiny walnut meat.

PIMIENTO FILLING Mix sieved egg yolks with 2 tablespoons butter, 1/4 cup finely chopped drained pimiento or Roasted Pepper, salt and white pepper to taste, and mayonnaise to moisten. Top with a tiny watercress leaf.

CHICKEN FILLING Mix sieved egg yolks with 1/2 cup ground cooked chicken or turkey; crumbled dried basil, ground cumin, ground turmeric, chili powder, or curry powder to taste; and mayonnaise to moisten. Top with a tiny slice of cherry tomato.

HAM FILLING Mix sieved egg yolks with 1/2 cup mayonnaise, 1/2 cup ground cooked ham, 1/2 tablespoon Dijon-style mustard, 2 teaspoons grated onion, and Worcestershire sauce, salt, and black pepper to taste. Garnish with a tiny coriander leaf.

PARMESAN CHEESE FILLING Mix sieved egg yolks with 2 tablespoons cream cheese, 1/4 cup freshly grated Parmesan cheese, 1 teaspoon minced fresh dill, salt and white pepper to taste, and mayonnaise to moisten. Top with 2 or 3 drained capers or a dab of red or black caviar.

GRUYERE CHEESE FILLING Mix sieved egg yolks with 1/2 cup grated Gruyère cheese, 5 tablespoons softened butter, and salt, pepper, and Tabasco sauce to taste. Decorate with tiny strips of Gruyère cheese.

FETA CHEESE FILLING With a fork, mash 1/2 cup crumbled feta cheese with 2 tablespoons olive oil. Stir in sieved egg yolks, 3 tablespoons *each* finely minced fresh parsley and chives, salt and white pepper to taste, and plain yoghurt to moisten. Top with a tiny dill feather.

CREAM CHEESE FILLING Mix sieved egg yolks with 4 ounces cream cheese, 2 tablespoons minced fresh chives or green onion tops, and sour cream to moisten; fold in 2 to 3 tablespoons red caviar. Garnish with a tiny dab of caviar and a tiny lemon peel.

CAVIAR FILLING Mix sieved egg yolks with 1/2 cup lumpfish caviar; dry mustard, Worcestershire sauce, and white pepper to taste; and mayonnaise to moisten. Top with a tiny sliver of lemon peel.

SMOKED SALMON FILLING Mix sieved egg yolks with 1/3 cup Shallot Mayonnaise, 1/3 cup finely minced smoked salmon, 1 tablespoon finely minced pimiento or drained Roasted Pepper, 2 teaspoons minced fresh dill, and prepared horseradish, salt, and white pepper to taste.

TUNA FISH FILLING Mix sieved egg yolks with 1/2 cup mayonnaise; one 7-ounce can waterpack tuna fish, drained and flaked; 1/3 cup finely minced celery; and Dijon-style mustard, salt, and white pepper to taste. Top with a tiny celery leaf.

OYSTER FILLING In a blender or food processor, combine and purée 2/3 cup smoked oysters, 2 tablespoons chopped green onion, and 2 tablespoons butter. Stir in sieved egg yolks, 2 tablespoons minced fresh parsley, Basic Mayonnaise to moisten, and salt, pepper, garlic powder, and curry powder to taste. Sprinkle with paprika and decorate with a ripe olive half.

DUXELLE FILLING Mix sieved egg yolks with 2/3 cup Duxelle and sour cream if needed to moisten. Top with a dab of sour cream and a tiny parsley leaf. Sprinkle with paprika.

CAPER AND ANCHOVY FILLING Mix sieved egg yolks with 1/2 cup mayonnaise, 1 teaspoon pressed garlic, or to taste, 2 teaspoons chopped drained capers, 2 teaspoons fresh lemon juice, and salt and white pepper to taste. Garnish with a rolled anchovy fillet and a tiny parsley leaf.

BEARNAISE SAUCE FILLING Mix sieved yolks with 1/2 cup Béarnaise Sauce. Top with a tiny parsley or watercress leaf.

PESTO FILLING Mix sieved egg yolks with 2/3 cup Pesto and mayonnaise to moisten. Top with a tiny basil leaf.

SOUR CREAM FILLING Mix sieved yolks with 2/3 cup sour cream and salt and white pepper to taste. Decorate with a tiny lemon slice and a dab of lumpfish caviar.

PUMATE FILLING Mix sieved egg yolks with 1/3 cup *each* mayonnaise, sour cream, and finely minced drained Pumate, and salt and white pepper to taste. Garnish with a dab of sour cream and a tiny piece of Pumate.

CHICKEN LIVER PATE FILLING Mix sieved yolks with 1/2 cup of the mushroom variation of Chicken Liver Pâté. Decorate with a thin slice of ripe olive.

TAPENADE OR TARAMOSALATA FILLING Mix sieved egg yolks with 2/3 cup Tapenade or Taramosalata. Top with a tiny watercress leaf or a sliver of ripe olive.

CHESTNUT PUREE FILLING Mix sieved egg yolks with 2/3 cup Chestnut Purée, salt and white pepper to taste, and sour cream to moisten. Top with a sprinkling of grated raw chestnut, dust with paprika, and garnish with a tiny parsley leaf.

RED EGGS ○

As mentioned in the introduction to this chapter, these beet-tinted eggs and the tea-flavored eggs that follow make excellent garnishes for meat platters. Halve crosswise and nestle in the greenery that decorates the meats, or slice and arrange in overlapping semicircles or flower patterns at the edge of the platter. They may also be halved or quartered lengthwise and placed on the crudité plate that you assemble to accompany dips.

To hard-cook the eggs, see the preceding directions for Stuffed Eggs.

Sixteen Servings
1 cup beet juice*
1 cup cider vinegar
1 large garlic clove, lightly mashed
1 small onion, sliced
1 small bay leaf
2 tablespoons granulated sugar
3/4 teaspoon salt
1/4 teaspoon ground cloves
1/4 teaspoon ground allspice
1/4 teaspoon freshly grated nutmeg
8 hard-cooked eggs, shelled

In a large saucepan, combine beet juice, vinegar, garlic, onion, bay leaf, sugar, salt, and spices. Bring to a boil, lower heat, and simmer 10 minutes. Remove from heat and cool briefly. Place eggs in a glass bowl or 2 quart jars and pour in beet liquid.

Cool to room temperature, cover container(s), and refrigerate eggs at least 1 day before serving. The longer the eggs stay in the pickling mixture, the spicier they will be. The eggs should be kept no longer than 1 week.

*Water in which 3 or 4 beets have been cooked.

TEA EGGS ○

Sixteen Servings
1 cup strong brewed tea
3/4 cup cider vinegar
1 tablespoon granulated sugar
1/2 teaspoon salt
3 slices ginger root (1-1/2 inches in diameter)
8 hard-cooked eggs, shelled

In a saucepan, combine tea, vinegar, sugar, salt, and ginger root. Bring to a rapid boil, remove from heat, and cool briefly. Place eggs in a glass bowl or in 2 quart jars and pour in tea liquid.

Cool, cover container(s), and refrigerate eggs at least 2 days before serving. The eggs should be kept no longer than 1 week.

CHOPPED EGG WITH CHESTNUT PUREE ●

Approximately Two Cups
1/2 cup Chestnut Purée
1/4 cup Crème Fraîche or
   sour cream, or as needed
2 tablespoons grated raw
   chestnut
2 tablespoons minced fresh
   parsley
1/4 teaspoon salt
1/4 teaspoon freshly ground
   white pepper
1/8 teaspoon ground thyme
6 hard-cooked eggs, finely
   chopped
Paprika
Tiny geranium leaves
Rye or whole-wheat Melba Toast

In a mixing bowl, combine chestnut purée and crème fraîche and stir with a fork until smooth. Stir in raw chestnut, parsley, salt, pepper, thyme, and eggs. Taste and adjust seasonings and add additional crème fraîche if needed to make spreading consistency. Cover and refrigerate at least 2 hours, or for up to 1 day.

   To serve, mound egg mixture in the center of a shallow bowl, sprinkle with paprika, and surround with geranium leaves. Place a basket of melba toast nearby.

CAVIAR SURPRISE ●

Present this impressive creation with a basket of unsalted crackers and small knives for spreading. Any that is left over may be used as a stuffing for cherry tomatoes.

Approximately Twenty-five Servings
2 tablespoons butter, at room
   temperature
2 green onions and tops,
   finely minced
2 tablespoons finely minced
   fresh parsley
1 tablespoon Dijon-style mustard
2 tablespoons Garlic Mayonnaise
1/2 teaspoon fresh lemon juice,
   or to taste
1/4 teaspoon Worcestershire
   sauce, or to taste
4 drops Tabasco sauce, or to taste
2 hard-cooked eggs, finely
   chopped
1/2 cup sour cream
One 2-ounce jar lumpfish caviar
Unsalted crackers or Melba Toast
   rounds

Place butter in a mixing bowl and cream with a wooden spoon until smooth. Stir in onions, parsley, mustard, mayonnaise, lemon juice, and Worcestershire and Tabasco sauces. With a fork, stir in eggs just until mixed. Taste and adjust seasonings. Pack mixture into a small round-bottomed bowl, cover with plastic wrap, and refrigerate at least 2 hours or for up to 1 day.

   To serve, carefully ease egg mixture out of bowl with a thin-bladed spatula knife, inverting it onto a round serving plate. With a spatula, smooth into an even mound shape. Spread sour cream over the mound and then mask with caviar, covering the mound completely. Cover and refrigerate at least 1 hour, or up to 6 hours. Serve with crackers or toast rounds.

FRITTATAS

These colorful Italian-style omelets are perfect fare for a large gathering. They can be cooked a few hours ahead of serving, and then left out at room temperature until the guests arrive.

   Brush Lecithin Oil on the baking dish and coat with bread crumbs before adding the egg mixture. These two steps will ensure easy removal of the bite-size squares.

SPINACH-HAM FRITTATA

Approximately Forty Servings
3 tablespoons fine dry bread
   crumbs
4 eggs
1/2 cup finely minced green
   onion and tops
1/2 tablespoon minced fresh
   oregano
3/4 teaspoon salt
1/2 teaspoon freshly ground
   white pepper
1/4 teaspoon freshly grated
   nutmeg
1 cup low-fat ricotta cheese
1-1/4 cups freshly grated Romano
   or Parmesan cheese
1/2 cup coarsely ground or
   finely minced cooked ham
1-1/2 cups cooked white or
   brown rice
2 cups *well-drained* finely chopped
   cooked spinach (two 10-ounce
   packages frozen spinach)
Lemon curls

Oil a 1-1/2-quart (10 by 6 by 2
inches) shallow baking dish with
Lecithin Oil. Sprinkle dish with
bread crumbs, tilting to coat
bottom and sides evenly. Preheat
oven to 325° F.

Break eggs into a large mixing
bowl and beat lightly with a
fork. Stir in onion, oregano,
salt, pepper, nutmeg, ricotta
cheese, Romano cheese, ham,
rice, and spinach. Pour spinach
mixture into prepared dish.

Place frittata in the preheated
oven and bake for 30 minutes,
or until eggs are set and mixture
is firm. A cake tester inserted in
center should come out clean.
Remove frittata to a wire rack
and cool at least 10 minutes.

To serve, cut frittata into
small squares and lift squares
out with a spatula. Arrange the
squares on a serving plate. Garnish
the plate with lemon curls and
serve the frittata at room temperature with cocktail picks.

CHILI-OLIVE FRITTATA

Approximately Forty Servings
3 tablespoons fine dry bread
   crumbs
4 eggs
1 teaspoon dry mustard
1 teaspoon crumbled dried
   oregano
1/2 teaspoon salt
1/4 teaspoon freshly ground
   black pepper
Dash cayenne pepper
One 4-1/2-ounce can chopped
   ripe olives
1/2 cup minced drained canned
   mild green chili peppers
2 tablespoons minced fresh
   parsley

PRESENTATION
Ivy or other green leaf
4 or 5 fresh small red or green
   chili peppers
6 or 7 ripe olives

Oil a 1-1/2-quart (10 by 6 by 2
inches) baking dish with Lecithin
Oil. Sprinkle dish with bread
crumbs, tilting to coat bottom
and sides evenly. Preheat oven
to 325° F.

Break eggs into a large mixing
bowl and beat lightly with a
fork. Stir in mustard, oregano,
salt, black pepper, cayenne pepper,
olives, minced chilies, and parsley.
Pour olive mixture into prepared
baking dish.

Place frittata in the preheated
oven and bake 35 minutes, or
until eggs are set and mixture is
firm. A cake tester inserted in
center should come out clean.
Remove frittata to wire rack and
let cool at least 10 minutes.

To serve, place the ivy leaf in
the center of a serving plate.
Arrange whole chili peppers on
leaf in a spoke pattern and tuck
olives around them. Cut frittata
into small squares and lift out of
dish with a spatula. Arrange
squares on the garnished serving
plate. Serve at room temperature
with cocktail picks.

ZUCCHINI FRITTATA WITH MIXED HERBS

Approximately Fifty Servings
3 tablespoons fine dry bread
    crumbs
14 ounces zucchini, sliced
    1/4 inch thick
One 8-1/2-ounce can (drained
    weight) water-pack artichoke
    hearts, drained and finely
    chopped
2 large garlic cloves, finely
    minced
1 cup minced green onion
    and tops
1 teaspoon minced fresh
    rosemary
1 teaspoon minced fresh thyme
1 teaspoon minced fresh sage
2 tablespoons olive oil
4 eggs
1/2 cup minced fresh parsley
1 cup well-drained finely chopped
    cooked swiss chard
1 cup freshly grated Romano
    or Parmesan cheese
1 teaspoon salt
1/2 teaspoon freshly ground
    black pepper
Parsley sprigs

Oil a 1-1/2-quart (10 by 6 by 2
inches) baking dish with Lecithin
Oil. Sprinkle dish with bread
crumbs, tilting to coat bottom
and sides evenly. Preheat oven
to 350° F.

In a large nonstick skillet,
combine zucchini, artichoke
hearts, garlic, green onion, rosemary, thyme, sage, and olive oil.
Cover and cook 5 to 8 minutes,
stirring occasionally to coat evenly
with oil and to cook lightly the
vegetables. Remove skillet from
heat and let vegetable mixture
cool slightly.

Break eggs into a large mixing
bowl and beat lightly with a
fork. Stir in parsley, swiss chard,
cheese, salt, and pepper. Add
the zucchini mixture and mix
well. Pour vegetable mixture
into prepared baking dish.

Place frittata in preheated oven
and bake 30 minutes, or until
eggs are set and mixture is firm.
A cake tester inserted in center
should come out clean. Remove
frittata to wire rack and let cool
at least 10 minutes.

To serve, cut frittata into
small squares and lift out of dish
with a spatula. Arrange squares
on a serving plate. Garnish the
plate with parsley sprigs and
serve the frittata at room temperature with cocktail picks.

TORTILLA DE PATATA
(Spanish Potato Omelet)

Approximately Twenty-four Servings
1 large baking potato
    (approximately 10 ounces)
1/2 large onion, very thinly sliced
2 tablespoons olive oil,
    or as needed
2 large garlic cloves,
    very finely minced
2 eggs
1/2 cup finely flaked steamed
    pollack (see Basics) or other
    firm white fish
1/4 cup minced fresh parsley
1/4 teaspoon salt
1/4 teaspoon freshly ground
    black pepper
Parsley sprigs

Scrub potato well and slice as
thinly as possible. Layer the
potato slices alternately with the
onion slices in a large nonstick
skillet. Drizzle with 2 tablespoons
olive oil, sprinkle with garlic,
and cover skillet. Cook over low
heat 20 minutes, or until potato
and onion are soft. Lift and turn
the layers occasionally and do

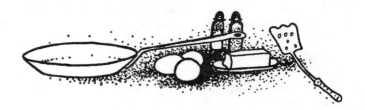

not allow to brown. (It does not matter if the potatoes break up.)

Transfer potato mixture to a colander set over a bowl and let drain 20 minutes. Put the oil that has drained into the bowl into a 7-inch skillet and add additional oil as needed to make 1 tablespoon. Set skillet aside.

In the same bowl, beat eggs lightly with a fork and add pollack, minced parsley, salt, and pepper. Stir to mix well. Add the potato mixture and stir to coat the slices of potato and onion with the egg mixture as thoroughly as possible.

Heat the reserved oil over medium heat and pour the egg mixture into the skillet. Cover and cook over medium-low heat 10 minutes, or until bottom is golden brown. Slide omelet out onto a plate. Invert the skillet on the plate and turn the skillet right side up, holding the plate in place. Remove the plate, return the skillet to the heat, and brown the omelet on the second side.

To serve, slide omelet onto a serving plate and garnish plate with parsley sprigs. Let cool at least 5 minutes before serving. Guests cut their own wedges or squares.

SMOKED SALMON AND BROCCOLI CUSTARD

Almost like a quiche without the crust, this custard is as delicious as the colorful ingredients that bespeckle it. It is very delicate, but firm enough to cut into small squares that can be speared with cocktail picks.

The egg mixture may be made one day in advance and refrigerated. Bring to room temperature before proceeding.

Approximately Sixty Servings
1-1/4 cups minced onion
2 tablespoons butter
6 eggs
1 cup heavy cream
5 ounces smoked salmon, finely shredded (approximately 3/4 cups)
3/4 cup very finely chopped lightly blanched broccoli
1-1/2 tablespoons minced fresh dill
1/2 teaspoon freshly ground white pepper, or to taste
Salt
Carrot Ribbons or Twists
Dill feathers

In a covered nonstick skillet, cook onion in butter over medium heat 5 minutes, or until soft. Remove cover and let cook, without browning, until almost all moisture has evaporated. Remove from heat and let cool.

Preheat oven to 300° F. Butter a shallow straight-sided baking dish approximately 7-1/2 by 10 inches. Set dish in a roasting pan and have a kettle of boiling water ready on the stove.

In a mixing bowl, lightly beat eggs with a fork and then beat in cream. Stir in reserved onion and the salmon, broccoli, dill, and pepper. Sauté a small amount of the egg mixture until set, taste, and adjust seasonings, adding salt if needed.

Pour egg mixture into prepared dish, place dish in center of roasting pan, and pour boiling water into roasting pan to come halfway up sides of dish. Place custard in the preheated oven and bake 30 minutes, or until a cake tester inserted in center comes out clean and the eggs are set. Remove from water bath and let cool on a wire rack at least 10 minutes.

To serve, garnish a serving plate with carrot ribbons and dill. Cut custard into small squares and carefully lift out of dish with a small metal spatula. Arrange squares on the garnished serving plate and set a container of cocktail picks nearby. Serve warm or at room temperature.

The custard can be made 3 to 4 hours before serving. Let cool, cover with plastic wrap, and set in a cool place. Bring to room temperature before serving.

CREPES ●■

Tiny crêpes can become wrappers for all sorts of fillings: lightly blanched vegetables, elegant lumpfish caviar, or delicate Duxelle. The crêpes must be tightly wrapped so they do not come apart when speared with a cocktail pick.

Use an eight-inch skillet with straight sides for cooking the crêpes and cut four three-inch rounds from each crêpe. The scraps should not be thrown away. If you don't eat them all while you're working with the crêpes, shred them and add to broth, or heat them in butter and serve with fried eggs, or sprinkle them with curry powder or ground ginger and fry quickly in hot oil and butter and serve as an appetizer. They are also good warmed in butter and sprinkled with a little confectioner's sugar, then served with jam.

Makes Four Dozen
1-1/3 cups milk, or as needed
4 eggs
1 cup unbleached flour
1/2 teaspoon salt
1 tablespoon safflower oil or
   melted butter
1 tablespoon finely minced fresh
   parsley or chives (optional)
Butter for cooking crêpes

Place milk, eggs, flour, salt, and oil in a blender or food processor and whirl until well blended. Scrape down sides of container several times to incorporate all the flour. Add optional parsley and whirl just to mix. Cover and refrigerate for at least 2 hours, or for up to 3 days.

Heat an 8-inch skillet over medium heat. To test for proper temperature, flick a few drops of water on the surface of the pan. If the drops dance about on the surface, the pan is ready. Butter the pan lightly. When the butter bubbles, lower heat slightly, stir batter, and pour 2 to 2-1/2 tablespoons of batter into the pan. Do not use more batter than this, or the crêpes will be too thick. (To judge how much you are using, measure 2-1/2 tablespoons water into a 1/4-cup measuring cup and note how high it reaches in the cup. Pour out the water and fill to that line with batter. Continue to use the cup as a measure.)

Quickly tilt the pan from side to side to coat the bottom as thinly, evenly, and completely with the batter as possible. Cook the crêpe until golden, then transfer it to a plate, using a flexible spatula and your fingers. If you are not planning to reheat the crêpe once it is filled, flip the crêpe over and cook the second side briefly before stacking. Repeat with remaining batter, adding more butter to the pan occasionally (after every 3 or 4 crêpes) and stirring 1 or 2 teaspoons milk into the batter when it thickens. Stir the batter well each time before you pour it into the cup.

While each crêpe is cooking, cut the previously cooked crêpe into four 3-inch rounds, and stack the rounds on a small plate.

The crêpes may be filled immediately, or they may be wrapped and refrigerated for up to 2 days, or frozen for up to 2 months. Defrost in the refrigerator and bring to room temperature before proceeding.

FILLINGS FOR CREPES

• Place a lightly blanched 3-1/2-inch-long asparagus tip, miniature carrot or carrot stick, or whole young green bean across the center of the crêpe, allowing the tip to extend approximately 3/4 inch beyond the edge of the crêpe. Put a tiny dab of cream cheese about one-third of the way up from the bottom of the asparagus tip. Bring one side of the crêpe up over the asparagus, overlapping it slightly and holding it in place by pressing it onto the cream cheese. The bottom of the crêpe should be tight against the asparagus and the top of the crêpe should remain flared. Place a dab of cream cheese on the crêpe covering the asparagus and bring the other side of the crêpe up and over the first, pressing firmly to hold the crêpe in place and again allowing the top of the crêpe to flare. The crêpe-wrapped asparagus will have the appearance of a just-opened calla lily. Place on a round serving plate, arranging in a spoke pattern. Set a small bowl of Crème Fraîche or Curry Mayonnaise at the center of the spokes and ring the bowl with parsley or watercress sprigs. Tuck a few sprigs in between the crêpes. Guests pick up a roll with their fingers and dip it into the sauce. Alternatively, spread crêpe with room temperature Boursin or similar cheese before topping with vegetable. Serve without sauce.

• Place 1/2 teaspoon lumpfish caviar about 1/2 inch from edge of a crêpe. Top caviar with 1/4 teaspoon Crème Fraîche. Roll crêpe, making one turn to cover the filling. Fold in sides and continue to roll to form a tight cylinder. Arrange seam side down on a serving plate and garnish the plate with small Lemon Twists and parsley leaves.

• Place about 3/4 teaspoon Duxelle, Tomato and Ham Filling, or Crab Filling (at room temperature) on a crêpe and roll as above. In a large skillet, melt enough butter to cover the bottom of the skillet with a thin film. Place the rolls in the skillet seam side down, cover skillet, and place over medium-low heat 5 minutes, or until just heated through. Carefully transfer the filled crêpes to a chafing or equivalent dish and keep warm. Guests spear the crêpes with cocktail picks.

CHEESE

Cheese is experiencing a "boom market." Specialty shops now offer a myriad of choices that include both domestic and imported products. There is a galaxy of blues, dozens of double- and triple-creams, and seemingly endless varieties of chèvre.

This bounty can leave the shopper feeling bewildered, however. The only answer to sorting out the complex world of international cheeses is to find a reputable merchant who will steer you to the best buys, in terms of both quality and price. A less-than-superb cheese will produce a mediocre dish, so you must shop wisely. With purchases in hand, you can begin preparing some of the very special dishes found here.

Tantalizing creations such as tortas, various fried cheeses, and savory cheese-based cakes and pies make a dramatic showing in this chapter, along with such long-admired standards as potted cheeses and cheese balls. Additional recipes in which cheese plays a starring role can be found in Pastries and in Spreads and Dips.

CLAM AND VEAL CREAM CHEESE BALLS ●

Makes Approximately Four Dozen
6 ounces cream cheese, at
    room temperature
One 7-1/2-ounce can minced
    clams, drained (save liquid for
    fish stock)
1-1/2 cups ground cooked veal
1 teaspoon fresh lemon juice
1/2 teaspoon paprika
1/4 teaspoon freshly ground
    white pepper
1/4 teaspoon garlic powder
1/2 teaspoon anchovy paste, or
    to taste
Finely minced fresh parsley
Parsley sprigs
Tiny pretzel sticks (optional)

In a mixing bowl, soften the cheese with a wooden spoon and gradually work in clams, veal, lemon juice, paprika, pepper, garlic powder, and anchovy paste. Mix until well blended, then taste and adjust seasonings. Cover and refrigerate 1 to 2 hours until stiff enough to handle.

Form clam mixture into balls about 3/4 inch in diameter and gently roll each ball in minced parsley to cover completely. Place balls in a single layer in a shallow dish. Cover with plastic wrap and refrigerate at least 1 hour or for up to 2 days.

To serve, arrange balls attractively on a serving plate and garnish with parsley sprigs. Serve with tiny pretzel sticks or cocktail picks.

GORGONZOLA AND CREAM CHEESE BALLS ●

Makes Approximately Three Dozen
6 ounces cream cheese, at room
    temperature
1/2 cup crumbled Gorgonzola
    or other blue cheese
    (2 ounces)
2 tablespoons finely minced
    celery
2 tablespoons finely minced
    fresh parsley
1 tablespoon finely minced onion
2 teaspoons minced fresh chives
Salt, freshly ground white pepper,
    and cayenne pepper to taste
Coarsely ground or very finely
    chopped walnuts
Watercress sprigs
Tiny pretzel sticks (optional)

In a mixing bowl, soften the
cream cheese with a wooden
spoon and gradually work in
Gorgonzola. Stir in celery, parsley,
onion, chives, and seasonings.
Mix until well blended, then
taste and adjust seasonings. Cover
and refrigerate 1 to 2 hours until
stiff enough to handle.

Form cheese mixture into
small balls about 3/4 inch in
diameter and gently roll each
ball in walnuts to cover completely. Place balls in a single
layer in a shallow dish. Cover
with plastic wrap and refrigerate
for at least 1 hour or for up to
2 days.

To serve, arrange balls attractively on a serving plate and
garnish with watercress sprigs.
Serve with tiny pretzel sticks or
cocktail picks.

VEGETABLE CREAM CHEESE PIE ●

A variety of vegetables gives this
rich creation a colorful appearance. For the garnish, cut raw
carrots, zucchini, and/or celery
into small finger shapes and
stand them upright in the cheese
mixture in a decorative pattern.
Guests may eat the vegetable
fingers in between bites of the
cheese pie spread on bread cutouts.

Approximately Twenty-five Servings
8 ounces cream cheese, at room
    temperature
2 to 3 tablespoons Crème Fraîche
2 teaspoons fresh lemon juice
1/2 teaspoon Worcestershire
    sauce
2 tablespoons finely minced
    carrot
2 tablespoons finely minced
    radish
2 tablespoons finely minced
    green or red bell pepper
2 tablespoons finely minced
    green onion and tops
2 tablespoons finely minced
    pimiento-stuffed olives
1/4 teaspoon freshly ground
    white pepper
Minced fresh parsley
Small-cut raw vegetables
Whole-grain bread cutouts or
    slices

In a mixing bowl, combine cream
cheese and crème fraîche, soften
with a wooden spoon or fork,
and then beat until smooth. Stir
in lemon juice, Worcestershire
sauce, carrot, radish, bell pepper,
onion, olives, and white pepper.

Transfer cheese mixture to a
shallow bowl, smoothing with a
rubber spatula or the back of a
wooden spoon. Cover and refrigerate 2 hours, or for up to 2 days.

To serve, let pie come to
room temperature and sprinkle
generously with parsley. Decorate
with small-cut raw vegetables.
Place bowl on a serving plate,
and surround bowl with bread
cutouts.

CREAM CHEESE CAVIAR PIE

For many years this "pie" has garnered raves from my guests. It is simple to make, extraordinarily delicious (even for those who claim to dislike caviar), and lovely to look at, especially when presented in a shallow crystal bowl.

The cheese base can be readied the day before, and the eggs and onions chopped and refrigerated for easy assembly the next morning. Once the pie is made, cover it tightly with plastic wrap and refrigerate. Bring to room temperature before serving.

Melba toast rounds or unsalted crackers such as water wafers or Cracotte brand are excellent accompaniments.

Approximately Forty Servings
8 ounces cream cheese, at room temperature
2 tablespoons mayonnaise
1 tablespoon grated onion
1 teaspoon Worcestershire sauce (optional)
2 teaspoons fresh lemon juice
3 or 4 drops Tabasco sauce, or to taste (optional)
3 tablespoons finely minced fresh parsley
One 3-3/4-ounce jar lumpfish caviar
1/2 to 2/3 cup minced green onion and tops

2 hard-cooked eggs, yolks and whites sieved separately
Paprika
Freshly grated lemon peel
Unsalted crackers or Melba Toast rounds

In a mixing bowl, combine cream cheese and mayonnaise, soften together with a fork or wooden spoon, and then beat until smooth. Stir in grated onion, Worcestershire sauce, lemon juice, Tabasco sauce, and parsley until well blended.

Transfer the cheese mixture to a shallow crystal bowl about 10 or 11 inches in diameter and 2 or 3 inches deep. With a rubber spatula or the back of a wooden spoon, spread the mixture evenly in the bowl, bringing it up to within about 1 inch of rim. When finished, the cheese mix should form an even lining, or shell.

Spread caviar evenly over surface of cheese shell, sprinkle with onion, and decorate with egg. The cream cheese shell should be completely covered with the caviar, onion, and egg. Sprinkle with paprika and strew lemon peel over. Serve with melba toast or crackers.

EDAM CHEESE WITH OLIVES ●

Approximately Twenty Servings
One 7-ounce Edam cheese, at room temperature
2 tablespoons butter, at room temperature
2 teaspoons grated onion
1 teaspoon dry mustard
1/4 teaspoon garlic powder
1/4 teaspoon freshly ground white pepper
1/4 teaspoon Worcestershire sauce
1 tablespoon brandy
1/3 cup finely chopped pimiento-stuffed olives
2 tablespoons minced fresh chives
1/4 to 1/3 cup minced fresh parsley
Unsalted crackers and/or Melba Toast

Slice the cheese into small pieces and place in a blender or food processor. Add butter, onion, mustard, garlic powder, pepper, Worcestershire sauce, and brandy. Whirl until very smooth. Add olives and chives and whirl briefly just to mix. Taste and adjust seasonings. Pack cheese mixture into a round-bottomed bowl, cover, and refrigerate at least 2 hours, or for up to 2 days.

To serve, gently ease the cheese mixture out of the bowl with a thin-bladed spatula knife, inverting it onto a serving plate. Let come to room temperature and sprinkle evenly with parsley to cover completely. Surround with crackers and/or melba toast.

HERBED CHEVRE O

Twenty to Twenty-five Servings
2 large garlic cloves, minced
5 green onions and tops, chopped
1/4 cup firmly packed Italian parsley leaves
8 ounces Montrachet or similar chèvre, at room temperature
4 tablespoons unsalted butter, at room temperature
2 teaspoons fresh lemon juice, or to taste
1 teaspoon Worcestershire sauce or to taste (optional)
Heavy cream
Salt, freshly ground white pepper, and cayenne pepper to taste
Italian parsley leaves
Whole-grain crackers or bread cutouts

In a blender or food processor, whirl garlic, green onion, and parsley leaves until finely minced. Add chèvre, butter, lemon juice, and Worcestershire sauce and whirl until mixture is smooth. A teaspoonful at a time, add heavy cream until mixture forms a

spreading consistency. Season with salt, white pepper, and cayenne pepper. Pack cheese mixture into a round-bottomed bowl, cover with plastic wrap, and refrigerate at least 2 days.

To serve, gently ease cheese mixture out of the bowl with a thin-bladed spatula knife, inverting it onto a serving plate. Smooth the surface and decorate with parsley leaves. Let come to room temperature and serve with crackers or bread.

LIPTAUER CHEESE O

Popular in Europe, this highly seasoned spread is traditionally made from sheep's milk cheese, giving it an especially fresh, tangy flavor. Cream cheese is a good substitute, though less full-bodied. Paprika or caraway seeds are generally considered a must.

Forty to Fifty Servings
6 tablespoons unsalted butter, at room temperature
1 pound cream cheese, at room temperature
6 ounces sharp Cheddar cheese, finely shredded
2 teaspoons Dijon-style mustard, or to taste
3 tablespoons very finely minced sweet red or white onion
2 garlic cloves, pressed or very finely minced (optional)

1 teaspoon anchovy paste, or to taste (optional)
2 teaspoons caraway seeds, or 1 teaspoon paprika

PRESENTATION
Parsley sprigs
Chopped anchovy fillets, drained capers, and/or minced green onion and tops, radishes, well-drained cucumber, and gherkins
Black bread

In a large mixing bowl, beat butter with a wooden spoon until soft, then gradually beat in cream cheese. When well mixed, gradually stir in Cheddar cheese, mustard, onion, garlic, anchovy paste, and caraway seeds. Beat until well blended and smooth. Pack mixture into a round-bottomed bowl, cover with plastic wrap, and refrigerate for at least 3 days.

To serve, gently ease the cheese mixture out of the bowl with a thin-bladed spatula knife, inverting it onto a large serving plate. Smooth the surface and place a small parsley sprig in the center. Surround the cheese with an assortment of garnishes and a few parsley sprigs. Let come to room temperature and serve with black bread.

This cheese will keep in the refrigerator for up to 1 week.

TORTAS

A new star has appeared on the hors d'oeuvre table. It is called a torta and consists of cheese layered with other ingredients, such as nutmeats, pumate, herbs, and so on. The torta is formed in one of two ways: it is shaped in a mold and then removed to a plate for serving, or a whole cheese, such as a Brie or Camembert, is cut in half and layered with the other ingredients directly on the plate.

Provide knives for guests to cut portions of the torta and french bread or buffet rye slices, unsalted crackers, melba toast, grape clusters, and apple or pear wedges as accompaniments.

The proper preparation of the mold for the *molded* torta is very important. Oil the pan or other container into which you will pack the torta with Lecithin Oil and then line it with two strips of cheesecloth in a cross pattern. Let the cheesecloth strips overhang the edge of the pan by about one inch. When the torta is ready to unmold, use the cheesecloth ends to help ease it out of the mold.

All of the tortas that follow may be assembled a day in advance. Suggestions for garnishing are given with each recipe, but feel free to add your own imaginative touches.

TRICOLOR TORTA ●

Twenty to Twenty-five Servings
3 ounces drained Pumate
    (1/2 cup firmly packed)
4 ounces Kalamata (Greek)
    olives, pitted
10 ounces Montrachet or similar
    chèvre
Watercress sprigs
Cherry tomatoes

Prepare a 2-cup mold or straight-sided pan as directed in introduction to tortas. In a blender or food processor, purée the pumate to form a paste. Set aside. Make a paste of the olives in the same manner. In a mixing bowl, mash the cheese with a wooden spoon.

Press the pumate paste into the bottom of the prepared container, being careful not to get any on the sides. Press half the cheese on top, then cover with a layer of the olive paste, and finally a layer of the remaining cheese. Cover with plastic wrap and refrigerate at least 3 hours.

To serve, ease the torta out of the pan with the help of the cheesecloth, inverting it onto a serving plate. Carefully remove and discard cheesecloth. Let torta come to room temperature and garnish with watercress and tomatoes.

ENGLISH TORTA ●

Thirty to Forty Servings
6 tablespoons butter, at room
    temperature
1 pound white Cheddar cheese,
    grated
2 tablespoons port
2 cups coarsely ground walnuts
8 ounces Stilton cheese, crumbled
Parsley sprigs

Prepare a 9-inch round cake pan as directed in introduction to tortas. Place 4 tablespoons of the butter in a mixing bowl, and beat with a wooden spoon until softened. With a fork, alternately work in the white Cheddar cheese and port. Press half of this cheese mixture into the prepared pan. Sprinkle half of the walnuts over the cheese layer and press in firmly.

Combine the remaining 2 tablespoons butter and the Stilton in the same manner as the Cheddar. Press the Stilton mixture evenly on top of the walnut layer. Sprinkle with remaining walnuts, press in firmly, and layer the remaining Cheddar mixture on top, again pressing down firmly. Cover with plastic wrap and refrigerate at least 3 hours.

To serve, ease the torta out of the pan with the help of the cheesecloth, inverting it onto a serving plate. Carefully remove and discard cheesecloth. Let torta come to room temperature and garnish with parsley.

CREAM CHEESE–PESTO TORTA ●

Forty to Fifty Servings
1 pound unsalted butter, at room temperature
1 pound cream cheese, at room temperature
2/3 cup Pesto
Basil leaves

Prepare a 3-cup mold as directed in introduction to tortas. In a mixing bowl, cream the butter with a fork or wooden spoon until soft. Gradually stir in cream cheese until well blended and smooth.

Place a basil leaf on the bottom of the prepared mold and pack in half the cheese mixture. Top with pesto, pressing down firmly, and cover with remaining cheese mixture, again pressing down firmly. Cover with plastic wrap and refrigerate at least 3 hours.

To serve, ease the torta out of the pan with the help of the cheesecloth, inverting it onto a serving plate. Let torta come to room temperature and garnish with additional basil leaves.

PESTO-BRIE TORTA ●

Twenty to Thirty Servings
4 ounces cream cheese, at room temperature
1 cup Pesto, at room temperature
One 8-ounce wheel Brie or Camembert cheese, chilled
Basil leaves or parsley sprigs

In a mixing bowl, beat the cream cheese with a fork or wooden spoon until soft and smooth. Gradually stir in pesto until well blended.

With a sharp knife, split the cheese wheel in half horizontally. Place one half cut side up on a large round serving plate. Spread with cream cheese mixture, pressing down firmly. Top with second half, cut side down. Cover tightly with plastic wrap and refrigerate at least 3 hours.

To serve, let torta come to room temperature and garnish with basil leaves.

WALNUT-BRIE TORTA ●

Twenty to Thirty Servings
3 ounces cream cheese, at room temperature
2 tablespoons light cream
1-1/2 cups coarsely chopped walnuts
One 8-ounce wheel Brie or Camembert cheese, chilled
Grape clusters

In a mixing bowl, beat the cream cheese and cream with a fork or wooden spoon until smooth. Gradually stir in walnuts until well blended.

With a sharp knife split cheese wheel in half horizontally. Place one half cut side up on a large round serving plate. Spread with walnut mixture, pressing down firmly. Top with second half, cut side down. Cover tightly with plastic wrap and refrigerate at least 3 hours.

To serve, let torta come to room temperature and garnish with grape clusters.

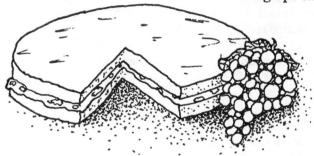

HERB-BRIE TORTA ●

Twenty to Thirty Servings
3 ounces cream cheese, at room
  temperature
3 tablespoons unsalted butter,
  at room temperature
3/4 cup crumbled blue cheese
  (3 ounces)
3/4 cup finely shredded sharp
  Cheddar cheese (3 ounces)
1 large garlic clove, pressed or
  very finely minced
3 tablespoons finely minced
  green onion and tops
2 tablespoons minced fresh
  parsley
1 tablespoon minced fresh basil
  or oregano
1 teaspoon minced fresh thyme
1/2 teaspoon minced fresh
  rosemary
One 8-ounce wheel Brie or
  Camembert cheese, chilled
Rosemary, oregano, or parsley
  sprigs

In a mixing bowl, beat the
cream cheese with a fork or
wooden spoon until softened.
Stir in butter until mixture is
smooth, and then stir in blue
and Cheddar cheeses, garlic, onion,
and herbs. Beat until mixture is
well blended.

With a sharp knife, split cheese
wheel in half horizontally. Place
one half cut side up on a large
round serving plate. Spread with
cheese mixture, pressing down
firmly. Top with second half, cut
side down, cover tightly with
plastic wrap, and refrigerate at
least 3 hours.

To serve, let torta come to
room temperature and garnish
with rosemary sprigs.

NUT-FILLED BRIE TORTA ●

Twenty to Thirty Servings
1-1/4 cups coarsely chopped
  unsalted pistachios or pine nuts
3 tablespoons unsalted butter
One 8-ounce wheel Brie or
  Camembert cheese, chilled
Mint sprigs

In a small skillet, lightly brown
pistachios in butter; let cool.

With a sharp knife, split cheese
wheel in half horizontally. Place
one half cut side up on a large
round serving plate. Spread walnuts and butter evenly over
cheese, pressing down firmly,
and top with second half, cut
side down. Cover tightly with
plastic wrap and refrigerate at
least 3 hours.

To serve, let come to room
temperature and garnish with
mint sprigs.

PECAN-BRIE TORTA ●

Twenty to Thirty Servings
4 tablespoons unsalted butter,
  softened
3/4 cup lightly toasted, finely
  chopped pecans
1 teaspoon Worcestershire sauce,
  or to taste
1 tablespoon fresh lemon juice,
  or to taste
Cayenne pepper to taste
One 8-ounce wheel Brie or
  Camembert cheese, chilled

PRESENTATION
Pecan halves
Small ivy leaf
Ripe olive half (slice crosswise)

In a mixing bowl, combine butter,
pecans, Worcestershire sauce,
lemon juice, and cayenne pepper
and mix thoroughly with a fork
or wooden spoon. Taste and
adjust seasonings.

With a sharp knife, split cheese
wheel in half horizontally. Place
one half cut side up on a large
round serving plate. Spread with
pecan mixture, pressing down
firmly. Top with second half, cut
side down, cover tightly with
plastic wrap, and refrigerate at
least 3 hours.

To serve, let torta come to
room temperature and garnish
with halved pecans arranged in a
daisy pattern on a small ivy leaf
with olive half in center.

AVOCADO-SALMON TORTA ●

Twenty to Thirty Servings
8 ounces unsalted butter, at
    room temperature
8 ounces cream cheese, at room
    temperature
1/2 cup Guacamole
1 cup very finely minced smoked
    salmon
Coriander sprigs

Prepare a 2-cup mold as directed
in introduction to tortas. In a
mixing bowl, cream the butter
with a fork or wooden spoon
until soft and then gradually stir
in the cream cheese. Stir 1/2 cup
of the cheese mixture into the
guacamole, mixing until smooth.
Press half of the remaining cream
cheese mixture into the prepared
mold. Arrange the salmon over
the cheese layer, pressing down
firmly. Spread with guacamole
mixture and top with remaining
cream cheese mixture. Cover
with plastic wrap and refrigerate
at least 3 hours.

To serve, ease the torta out of
the pan with the help of the
cheesecloth, inverting it onto a
serving plate. Carefully remove
and discard cheesecloth. Let torta
come to room temperature and
garnish with coriander sprigs.

OLIVE-CHEESE TORTA ●

Select Explorateur, Brillat-Savarin,
or St.-André triple-cream cheese
for this sinfully rich, irresistible
torta.

Thirty to Forty Servings
12 ounces triple-cream cheese,
    at room temperature
8 ounces Gruyère cheese, grated
1/2 cup drained Roasted Pepper,
    minced
8 ounces cream cheese, at room
    temperature
4 ounces Kalamata (Greek)
    olives, pitted and finely minced
1 cup minced green onion and
    tops
Green Onion Brushes

Prepare a 9-inch round cake pan
as directed in the introduction
to tortas. In a mixing bowl,
mash triple-cream cheese with a
fork. Gradually work in Gruyère
until well combined and then
stir in roasted pepper. Press half
this mixture into the prepared
pan.

In another mixing bowl, mash
cream cheese with a fork until
soft and then gradually blend in
olives and minced green onion.
Spread the cream cheese mixture
on top of triple-cream mixture,
pressing down firmly. Top with
remaining triple-cream mixture,
cover tightly with plastic wrap,
and refrigerate at least 3 hours.

To serve, ease the torta out of
the pan with the help of the
cheesecloth, inverting it onto a
serving plate. Carefully remove
and discard cheesecloth. Let torta
come to room temperature and
garnish with green onion brushes.

POTTED CHEESES

These flavorful cheese mixtures should be prepared at least two days in advance of serving to permit flavors to mellow. Pack into crocks, cover, and refrigerate up to one week. Bring to room temperature before serving with melba toast rounds, unsalted crackers, miniature breadsticks, or lahvosh.

Potted cheeses will keep in the freezer for up to one month. Defrost in the refrigerator.

POTTED DILLED CHEVRE ○■

*Makes Approximately
One and One-half Cups*
4 ounces Montrachet or similar chèvre, crumbled (1 cup)
3/4 cup sour cream
1 teaspoon fresh lemon juice, or to taste
1/4 teaspoon crumbled dried dill, or to taste
2 tablespoons finely minced fresh parsley

In a mixing bowl, mash cheese with a fork and then stir in sour cream, lemon juice, dill, and parsley until well blended. Pack into a crock, cover with plastic wrap, and refrigerate.

POTTED BRIE WITH COGNAC AND ALMONDS ○■

Makes Approximately Two-thirds Cup
4 ounces Brie or Camembert cheese, cut up and at room temperature
6 tablespoons unsalted butter, at room temperature
1/2 cup chopped sliced almonds, lightly toasted
4 teaspoons Cognac, or to taste
1/8 teaspoon ground thyme, or to taste
1/8 teaspoon freshly ground white pepper, or to taste

In a mixing bowl, cream together the cheese and butter with a fork or wooden spoon until smooth. Stir in almonds, Cognac, and seasonings and mix until well blended. Pack into a crock, cover with plastic wrap, and refrigerate.

POTTED BRIE AND CREAM CHEESE WITH WALNUTS ○■

Makes Approximately Two-thirds Cup
4 ounces Brie or Camembert cheese, cut up and at room temperature
2 ounces cream cheese, at room temperature
2 teaspoons unsalted butter, at room temperature
6 tablespoons chopped walnuts, lightly toasted
2 teaspoons fresh lemon juice
2 teaspoons minced fresh chives

In a mixing bowl, cream together the Brie, cream cheese, and butter with a fork or wooden spoon until smooth. Stir in walnuts, lemon juice, and chives, blending thoroughly. Pack into a crock, cover with plastic wrap, and refrigerate.

POTTED BLUE CHEESES ○■

Here are four potted blue cheese mixtures that go together quickly and easily. Use Stilton, Roquefort, Gorgonzola, or any high-quality domestic blue-veined cheese. Each recipe makes approximately one cup.

CHEESE I

1/2 cup crumbled blue cheese
(2 ounces)
1/2 cup plain yoghurt
1 teaspoon fresh lemon juice
3 tablespoons lightly toasted
chopped pecans
Freshly ground white pepper
to taste
Worcestershire sauce to taste
(optional)

In a mixing bowl, mash blue
cheese with a fork. Stir in yoghurt,
lemon juice, pecans, pepper, and
Worcestershire sauce, blending
thoroughly. Pack into a crock,
cover with plastic wrap, and
refrigerate.

CHEESE II

1 small garlic clove, chopped
3 tablespoons chopped parsley
leaves
3 tablespoons chopped green
onion tops
3/4 cup crumbled blue cheese
(3 ounces)
1/3 cup Crème Fraîche

In a blender or food processor,
finely mince garlic, parsley, and
green onion tops. Add blue cheese
and crème fraîche and whirl just
until mixed. Pack into a crock,
cover with plastic wrap, and
refrigerate.

CHEESE III

4 ounces cream cheese, at room
temperature
1/2 cup crumbled blue cheese
(2 ounces)
1 tablespoon unsalted butter,
at room temperature
1/2 tablespoon fresh lemon juice
1/4 teaspoon Worcestershire
sauce, or to taste

In a mixing bowl, beat cream
cheese with a fork or wooden
spoon until softened. Stir in
blue cheese, butter, lemon juice,
and Worcestershire sauce, blending thoroughly. Pack into a crock,
cover with plastic wrap, and
refrigerate.

CHEESE IV

2 ounces cream cheese, at room
temperature
3/4 cup crumbled blue cheese
(3 ounces)
1 tablespoon very finely minced
green onion and tops
1/2 tablespoon fresh lemon juice
1 teaspoon anchovy paste,
or to taste

In a mixing bowl, beat cream
cheese with a fork or wooden
spoon until softened. Stir in
blue cheese, onion, lemon juice,
and anchovy paste, blending thoroughly. Pack into a crock, cover
with plastic wrap, and refrigerate.

HEATED CHEESE DISHES

Cooked-cheese dishes are now in
vogue, whether baked, fried, or
broiled. Soft cheeses, such as a
mozzarella, Camembert, Brie,
certain chèvres, and Monterey
Jack, and firm ones like Cheddar
all take well to heating, and the
resulting lovely texture and spectacular appearance ensure an
enthusiastic response at any
gathering.

Baked chèvre that has been
soaked in olive oil and dusted
with bread crumbs is a mainstay
of the new California cuisine.
Cheddar, Monterey Jack, or mozzarella is delicious handled in
the same way. Italians and Greeks
have long been frying breaded
cheese cubes. An even simpler
skillet treatment is whole Brie
or Camembert wheels lightly
browned in unsalted butter.

For a more elegant presentation, encase a Brie round in puff
pastry or buttered phyllo sheets,
bake until the wrapper is crisp
and golden, and serve straight
from the oven.

The greatest room for error
when preparing hot cheese dishes
is overcooking them. Heat just
until the cheese is soft and
slightly runny; if left beyond this

point, the cheese is apt to toughen. Serve these dishes immediately, as the cheese will harden as it cools.

The heated cheeses should be served with sliced baguettes. Set a shallow dish of warm Roasted Garlic alongside. You will also find here the traditional Swiss fireside preparation called raclette and the classic French fondue.

SAGANAKI
(Greek Fried Cheese)

The Greeks flame this spectacular fried cheese dish after dousing it with the national brandy, Metaxa. This critical step takes some practice. Use Kasseri or Kefalotyri cheese, which can be found in Greek delicatessens and many cheese specialty stores.

The Yugoslavs prepare a similar dish, called *pohovani kackavalj,* which they serve with lemon wedges or tartar sauce. It is easier to prepare than Greek-style fried cheese, because there is no tradition of flaming with brandy.

Saganaki requires deft, quick work, as it must be piping hot when served. If you don't have a skillet large enough to cook all of the cheese cubes at once, fry them in two batches.

Approximately Twenty-five Servings
1/2 pound Kasseri cheese
1 egg
1-1/2 tablespoons milk
1/2 cup unbleached flour, or as needed
Olive oil, or combination of olive oil and butter
1 to 2 tablespoons Metaxa or brandy
1 lemon, halved
Lemon slices
Greek bread or baguette slices

Cut the cheese into 3/4-inch squares and refrigerate the squares until well chilled. In a mixing bowl, beat the egg with the milk. Mound the flour on a plate or piece of waxed paper. Heat about 1 inch of oil in a large skillet or electric frypan to 375° F, or until a small piece of bread sizzles when added. In a small saucepan, heat the Metaxa and keep hot. Put a heatproof serving platter in the oven and turn the oven to 325° F.

To fry the cheese, dip each cube into the egg mixture and then coat lightly with the flour. Arrange coated cheese cubes in the oil about 1-1/2 inches apart and brown on one side. Turn the cubes over and fry just until the second side starts to brown. Quickly transfer the cubes to a heated platter, pour Metaxa over them, and light with a match.

Let burn 30 seconds, then squeeze the lemon halves over to extinguish the flames.

Garnish the platter with lemon slices and serve immediately with bread slices to eat with the cheese cubes and to dip into the juices.

FRIED BRIE WITH HERBS AND PECANS

Approximately Twenty Servings
1 egg, beaten
1/4 teaspoon ground basil, thyme, or oregano
One 8-ounce wheel Brie or Camembert cheese, chilled
1/2 to 2/3 cup lightly toasted finely chopped pecans, almonds, or walnuts
1-1/2 tablespoons butter
1-1/2 tablespoons olive oil
6 garlic cloves, halved
Finely minced green onion tops
Sliced pears and apples
Sourdough baguette slices, toasted

In a shallow dish, beat together egg and thyme. Dip cheese wheel in egg mixture, then into chopped nuts to coat evenly. Cover loosely and refrigerate at least 1 hour or up to 3 hours.

In a small skillet, slowly heat butter and oil with the garlic 15 minutes. Remove and discard garlic. Heat butter and oil mixture to 375° F, or until a piece of bread sizzles when added. Fry the coated cheese 1 or 2 minutes to brown lightly, then turn and lightly brown second side.

Transfer cheese to a round serving plate and sprinkle onion tops over. Arrange pear and apple slices around the wheel and serve baguette slices in a basket on the side.

FRIED MONTEREY JACK WITH GARLIC AND CHILIES

Approximately Thirty Servings
1 pound Monterey Jack or
   mozzarella cheese
1/2 cup unbleached flour,
   or as needed
1/4 teaspoon freshly ground
   white pepper
2 cups fine dry bread crumbs,
   preferably sourdough
2 eggs
3 tablespoons milk
Olive oil
8 garlic cloves, lightly crushed
2 small dried hot red chili
   peppers

Cut cheese into 1-inch cubes and chill. Combine flour and white pepper and mound on a plate or a piece of waxed paper. Mound bread crumbs on a separate plate or piece of waxed paper. In a mixing bowl, beat eggs and milk. Coat cheese cubes lightly with flour mixture, then dip in egg mixture. Gently roll cubes in bread crumbs, forming a coating that entirely encloses the cheese. Chill coated cheese cubes at least 1 hour or for up to 3 hours.

Pour oil to a depth of 1 inch in a large skillet or electric frypan. Add the garlic cloves and chili peppers and cook over low heat 15 minutes. Remove and discard garlic and peppers. Heat oil to 375° F, or until a piece of bread sizzles when added. Arrange prepared cheese cubes at least 1-1/2 inches apart in oil and fry until golden, turning once. Drain on paper toweling and keep warm in a moderate oven until all cubes are fried.

Serve fried cheese immediately with cocktail picks.

BAKED BRIE WITH ALMONDS

Approximately Twenty Servings
4 tablespoons butter
2 large garlic cloves, lightly
   crushed
1/2 cup sliced almonds
One 8-ounce wheel Brie cheese
Melba Toast rounds

Preheat the oven to 400° F. In a small skillet, melt the butter over medium-low heat, add the garlic, and cook slowly for 10 minutes. Remove and discard the garlic. Raise the heat slightly, add the almonds, and brown the almonds and the butter until a light hazelnut color.

Place the Brie in the center of a shallow ovenproof serving dish. Pour the butter and almonds over to cover the cheese evenly. Bake in the preheated oven 5 minutes, or until cheese just starts to soften. Remove from the oven and serve at once with melba toast.

RACLETTE

A small fall or winter gathering is the perfect occasion for a party featuring raclette, literally "scraper," a pale yellow, mild-flavored cheese from the Swiss canton of Valais. Traditionally, the cheese is placed in a pan and melted on the hearth of a glowing fireplace, but an oven can also be used. If raclette is not available in your area, Fontina, Swiss, Swiss Bagnes, Gruyère, Samsoe, or Monterey Jack may be substituted. Plan on about four ounces of cheese for each guest.

Trim the rind from the block or wedge of cheese and place the cheese in a heavy, shallow skillet or pan. Set the pan on the hearth near the fire so the cheese melts gradually. Provide each guest with a plate, a large spoon, and a fork. Nearby, set out a peppermill and containers of french bread slices, unsalted butter, tiny gherkins cut into fan shapes, freshly boiled or steamed tiny new potatoes, and pickled onions (see Pickled Vegetables).

As the cheese melts, guests scrape a spoonful from the liquid area, spread it on top of a potato, and then grind pepper over the top. Other accompaniments are eaten as desired.

If you are using an oven for melting the cheese, preheat it to 375° F. Place the cheese in the oven and heat for five to ten minutes until the surface is runny. Alternatively, briefly place the cheese under a preheated broiler. Remove the cheese from the stove, let guests help themselves, and then return the unmelted portion to the oven or broiler. Repeat melting procedure as often as is necessary.

CHEESE FONDUE

In French the word *fondant* means melting, juicy, luscious, a most apt trio of adjectives to describe cheese fondue. This very special dish can be simply described as pieces of bread skewered on long forks and dipped in a pot of melted cheese seasoned and thinned to the right consistency with white wine and kirsch or brandy.

A traditional fondue pot or a pot with a lower pan for hot water, like a double boiler, controls the temperature for cheese fondues that tend to curdle if allowed to become too hot.

The best bread to serve is one with a chewy crust, such as a sourdough. The bread should be cubed, leaving the crust on one face of each piece. Wine and brandy should be of good quality. If the consistency in the pot is just right, the coated morsel will trail strings of cheese as it is removed. A quick twirl and a flourish are required to overcome the reluctance of the cheese to leave the pot.

1 large garlic clove
6 ounces Emmenthaler cheese,
   grated
6 ounces Gruyère cheese, grated
1 tablespoon potato flour or
   cornstarch
1/4 teaspoon salt
1/4 teaspoon freshly ground
   white pepper
1 cup good-quality light dry
   white wine
2 teaspoons Dijon-style mustard
   (optional)
2 tablespoons kirsch or Cognac
Sourdough bread cubes

Halve the garlic and rub over
the bottom and sides of a fondue
pot, heavy earthenware casserole,
or chafing dish. In a large mixing
bowl, toss together the cheeses,
potato flour, and seasonings.

Pour the wine into the pot
and heat until bubbles start rising
to the surface. Do not boil.
With a fork or wooden spoon,
stir in a handful of cheese mixture
at a time, stirring until cheese is
melted before adding another
handful. Add mustard and kirsch,
taste, and adjust seasonings with
salt and pepper. Once ingredients
are blended and heated, do not
cook further; adjust heat to
keep the fondue just at serving
temperature.

Serve fondue at once with
bread cubes arranged in a basket
alongside.

CHEVRE CHEESECAKE

Serve this extremely rich cheesecake for a large party. Select a
soft, medium-flavored chèvre
such as Montrachet or Bucheron.

Approximately Thirty Servings
1 tablespoon butter
1/4 cup fine fresh bread crumbs
3 tablespoons finely chopped
   pecans
1 pound, 2 ounces cream cheese,
   cut up and at room
   temperature
6 ounces chèvre, cut up and
   at room temperature
3 eggs
1/2 teaspoon grated or pressed
   garlic
1/2 teaspoon fresh lemon juice
1/4 teaspoon freshly grated
   lemon peel
1/4 teaspoon salt
1/8 teaspoon freshly ground
   white pepper
6 tablespoons heavy cream
Lemon Flowers
Baguette slices, Melba Toast
   rounds, and/or buffet-rye
   slices

Preheat oven to 325° F. Butter a
springform pan 8 inches in diameter and 2 inches deep. Toss
bread crumbs and nuts together
and toast lightly in the oven
while it is preheating. Sprinkle
crumb mixture over the bottom

of the springform pan and tilt to
coat sides and bottom evenly.
Refrigerate the prepared pan.

Have ready a kettle of boiling
water and a baking pan large
enough to hold the springform
pan.

In a blender or food processor,
whirl the cheeses until softened.
Add eggs, garlic, lemon juice,
lemon peel, salt, pepper, and
cream. Scraping down sides of
container frequently, whirl until
mixture is well blended and very
smooth. (If your processor or
blender is too small to mix all of
the ingredients at once, prepare
the cheese mixture in 2 batches.)

Carefully pour the cheese
mixture into the prepared springform pan and set it in the
baking pan. Pour boiling water
into baking pan to come two-
thirds up the sides of the springform. Place cheesecake in the
preheated oven and bake 1 hour
and 15 minutes. Turn off oven
heat and let cheesecake cool
1 hour with oven door open
slightly. Remove cheesecake to
wire rack and cool completely.

To serve, remove the cake
from the pan by pushing the pan
bottom up through the rim.
Run a flexible spatula under the
cake and carefully transfer it to
a round serving plate. Garnish
with lemon flowers and serve
with baguettes, melba toast
rounds, and/or buffet rye.

CHEESE CRISPS

Nachos are tortilla chips arranged on a baking sheet and covered with grated Monterey Jack or Cheddar cheese, then baked in a hot oven until the cheese is melted. A Tucson, Arizona variation called a cheese crisp can best be described as a tortilla "pizza." A whole crisped tortilla is covered with shredded cheese and then placed in a hot oven until the cheese melts and is bubbly. In more elaborate versions, sliced ripe olives, chorizo, mushrooms, tomato, bell pepper, minced onion, and/or jalapeño pepper are layered over the tortilla and then topped with the shredded cheese.

Deep fry tortillas in 375° F corn oil just until golden and crisp. Drain on crumpled paper toweling and let cool. Top the cooled tortilla with cheese, or with other ingredients, and then cheese. Bake in a preheated 400° F oven 5 minutes, or until cheese is melted and bubbly.

To serve, immediately place cheese crisp on a round plate. Guests break off their own servings.

Deep-fried tortillas without topping may be stored in an airtight container for up to 2 days, or frozen for up to 2 months.

CHEESE TRAYS

An assortment of cheeses is a popular addition to any buffet table: guests enjoy the opportunity to sample a variety and the host or hostess needs to spend little more time than it takes to shop for the selections.

When making your choices at the cheese store, several factors must be considered. There should be a variety of colors, shapes, and textures on the tray, as well as a range of flavors: a snow-white, tangy chèvre balanced against a mild, pale orange Gouda, a four-inch round of Camembert alongside a square Pont l'Evêque, or a creamy triple-cream as a counterpoint to a semifirm Pyrénées de Brebis. Be flexible when you shop. If what you want is not available, be ready with alternatives or listen to the suggestions of the clerk. Most stores offer customers a taste of the cheeses to help them decide what they want.

For fullest flavor, the cheeses must be at room temperature when they are served. Some warm more quickly than others. This will mean removing a very ripe Brie or similar cheese from the refrigerator forty-five minutes before guests arrive and a firm cheese, such as a Cheddar, up to two hours ahead of time.

When serving cheeses, set them on surfaces that will not take away from their own attractiveness. A simple wooden board or plate, a slab of marble, a heavy lucite tray, or a ceramic platter would be appropriate. Fresh grape, fig, or ivy leaves placed beneath unripened cheeses add to the presentation. Lemon or other citrus leaves or small bouquets of fresh herbs are good decorative touches. Separate the stronger-tasting cheeses from the milder ones, and put out knives for each if possible. This way flavors will not be passed from one cheese to another.

The best accompaniments are breads, crackers, and fruit. A baguette is good for serving with the softer cheeses, such as Camembert, Coulommiers, or the creamy blues. Firmer cheeses like Gruyère or the Cheddars go best with coarser breads. Crackers should have a "neutral" flavor; water crackers or Cracotte brand are suitable (see Ways with Breads).

Set out crocks of unsalted butter for those who like to coat their bread or crackers before topping them with a strong-flavored cheese such as Roquefort. Apples, pears, grapes, and plums complement most cheeses; in summer, berries go wonderfully with fresh chèvres or other mild cheeses.

Allow two to three pounds of cheese for a party for twelve. The cheese trays that follow can be scaled up or down according to your needs. The third and fourth trays are particularly suitable for dessert.

TRAY I

- Caprin (French; leaf-wrapped triangular-shaped chèvre with subtly sour flavor) or Montrachet (French; cylindrical chèvre with pleasantly sour flavor, sometimes coated with ash)

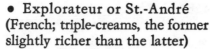

- Explorateur or St.-André (French; triple-creams, the former slightly richer than the latter)
- Bleu d'Auvergne or Roquefort (French; blue-veined)
- Fontina (Italian; buttery, nutty flavor with a natural sweetness)
- Pont l'Evêque (French; firm and yellow, pungent monastery type)

TRAY II

- Gouda or Edam (Dutch; soft, smooth, mild, the former with a bright red paraffin coating) or Jarlsberg (Norwegian; mild, slightly sweet, yellow, with holes)
- English Farmhouse Cheddar (English; yellow, dense, hard textured, the term "farmhouse" indicates produced on one of about two dozen farms in England)
- Monterey Jack (U.S.; buttery, mellow, pale yellow)
- Cantal (French; smooth, close textured, nutty flavored, with a dusty rind) or Comté (French; firm, smooth, golden, with round holes)
- Maytag (U.S.; blue-veined)

TRAY III

- Camembert or Brie (French; edible rind, soft, creamy, with a pale yellow interior)
- Bavarian Blue or Blue Castello (German and Danish respectively; blue-veined double-creams)
- California chèvre (U.S.; variety of shapes; solid consistency, well-developed flavor)
- Brillat-Savarin or Boursault (French; triple-creams)
- Oka or Port Salut (Canadian and French, respectively; velvety textured monastery types)

TRAY IV

- Zola (Italian; sometimes called Torta Gaudenzio as well as other names, alternating layers of blue-veined Gorgonzola and creamy Mascarpone)
- Caprini (Italian; cylindrical, creamy, mild-flavored chèvre) or Bucheron (French; cylindrical, drier, with mild, distinct goat flavor)
- Coulommiers or Brie (French; soft, creamy, pale yellow)
- Boursin or Fontainebleau (French; triple-creams, the former mixed with herbs and the latter with whipped cream)
- Bel Paese (Italian; very creamy, mild flavored with pleasant aftertaste)

SUGGESTIONS FOR CHEESE

- Soften cream cheese with cream or mayonnaise and mound in the center of a large round platter. Sprinkle with paprika and arrange an assortment of smoked oysters, clams, and/or octopus around. Tuck sprigs of parsley in and around the seafood and surround with an assortment of crackers.
- Evenly cut Monterey Jack or sharp Cheddar cheese into 1/2-inch cubes. Lightly roll each cube in cayenne pepper, ground oregano, or chili powder. Arrange cubes on a lightly buttered baking sheet, placing them at least 3 inches apart. Place in a preheated 300° F oven, and bake 10 minutes, or until cubes have melted and edges have become lightly browned and lacy. Immediately remove to a rack and serve piping hot.

- Brush a baking sheet with melted butter. Arrange round won ton or gyoza skins on sheet and brush each with melted butter. Evenly sprinkle each round with finely shredded Parmesan cheese and top with a dusting of ground thyme. Place in a preheated 350° F oven and bake 5 minutes, or until cheese has melted and is bubbly. Immediately remove to a rack and let cool slightly before serving, or serve at room temperature.
- Marinate 1- to 2-ounce chèvres in olive oil to cover with mixed crumbled dried herbs, pressed garlic, crumbled dried red chili peppers, and lightly crushed white peppercorns. Cover and let stand at room temperature 24 hours, carefully turning cheeses several times so the flavorings are distributed evenly. Serve with sliced baguettes or crackers.
- On a wooden platter arrange dark bread, slices of chèvre, walnut halves, green onion lengths, and radishes. Garnish with fresh coriander sprigs.
- Skewer a small cube of white Cheddar and a piece of canned hot green chili pepper. Serve with Tortilla Chips.

- Mash cream cheese, at room temperature, with Crème Fraîche, sour cream, or mayonnaise to make spreading consistency. Spread a 1/2-inch layer in a shallow crystal bowl. Cover with very thin slices of smoked salmon, sprinkle with minced fresh dill and freshly grated lemon peel, and carefully spread softened cream cheese over, making a layer approximately 1/2 inch thick. Repeat with salmon and softened cream cheese. Sprinkle top with paprika. Serve with Melba Toast rounds, buffet rye slices, and/or baguette slices. If not serving at once, cover with plastic wrap and refrigerate for up to 2 days. Bring to room temperature before serving.
- In a crystal serving bowl, combine cubed feta cheese, cherry tomatoes, artichoke hearts, and minced parsley. Toss in fresh lemon juice, olive oil, and freshly ground black pepper to taste. Cover and refrigerate, tossing occasionally, at least 2 hours, or for up to 6 hours. Serve at room temperature with cocktail picks.

VEGETABLES

Vegetable dishes offer an alternative to the richer, more caloric hors d'oeuvres that customarily adorn a buffet table. They are attractive, colorful additions with a wide variety of textures and tastes.

A whole range of stuffed vegetables, hot and cold, appear here. A platter of mushrooms filled with a smoked salmon mixture or a tray of cherry tomatoes mounded with sauerkraut will beautifully round out almost any buffet menu. Tiny new potatoes crowned with lumpfish caviar and sour cream, and hot artichoke bottoms with a creamy chestnut purée are just two more of the dozens of ideas included. A complementary garnish is important to the presentation of all stuffed vegetables; devote careful thought to creating an eye-appealing plate.

There are also recipes for tiny spinach and Parmesan balls straight from the oven, rolled grape leaves with a choice of three fillings, two mushroom

"caviars," pickled and marinated vegetables, marinated olives, and flavored roasted nuts.

Crisp crudités, raw cut vegetables used for scooping up mouthfuls of tasty dips, are described in Spreads and Dips. Pumate, roasted peppers, and roasted garlic, all basic vegetable preparations that are used in a number of dishes, can be found in Basics.

COLD STUFFED MUSHROOMS

Trim discolored ends off mushroom stems and clean mushrooms with a mushroom brush, or wipe gently with a lightly dampened paper towel (do not wash, as the mushrooms will become soggy). Carefully snap off stems close to the caps and reserve for stocks or sauces. Rub the caps inside and out with fresh lemon juice.

If you don't like the raw taste of mushrooms, they may be blanched or steamed before stuffing. Blanch the caps (do not rub with lemon juice) in water to which fresh lemon juice has been added (1 tablespoon lemon juice to 2 cups water) for 1 to 2 minutes; or rub with fresh lemon juice, set on a rack over boiling water, and steam for 1 to 2 minutes. In either case, pat dry with paper toweling before filling.

Each of the following fillings makes approximately 1 cup, enough for 24 medium-size mushrooms about 1-1/2 inches in diameter (1-1/2 pounds), or approximately 2 teaspoons for each mushroom. Have cheeses and butter at room temperature before beginning to mix the fillings, and always freshly grind the white or black pepper.

The mushrooms may be filled several hours ahead of serving. Arrange on a serving plate, cover with plastic wrap, and set in a cool place. If the mushrooms are to be served chilled, refrigerate them until the guests arrive.

There are a number of other recipes in this book that would

make suitable stuffings for cold mushrooms. For example, use Almond-Chicken Balls, Eggplant-Tomato Spread, Taramosalata, Tahini Dip, Salmon Mayonnaise Sauce, or one of the Potted Cheeses.

• Mash 3 ounces cream cheese with 1 cup crumbled blue cheese (4 ounces) and 2 tablespoons softened butter. Season to taste with grated onion, Worcestershire sauce, salt, and white pepper to taste. Fill mushroom caps and top with minced green or red bell pepper. Chill.
• Combine 1-1/4 cups crumbled blue cheese (5 ounces), 2 tablespoons sour cream, and 1 teaspoon minced fresh chives. Add brandy to taste. Fill mushroom caps and sprinkle with paprika. Chill.
• Combine 1 cup crumbled blue cheese (4 ounces), 3 tablespoons unsalted butter, 3 tablespoons lightly toasted finely chopped walnuts, 2 tablespoons finely minced fresh parsley, 2 teaspoons finely minced fresh chives, and dry vermouth and white pepper to taste. Fill mushroom caps and sprinkle lightly with paprika. Chill.
• Soften 6 ounces cream cheese with 2 tablespoons light cream.

Stir in 1/4 pound finely minced smoked salmon until well blended. Add freshly grated lemon peel, minced fresh dill, and white pepper to taste. Fill mushroom caps and sprinkle with additional minced dill or with paprika. Chill.
• Mash 6 ounces cream cheese with enough sour cream to make a creamy, spreadable mixture. Season to taste with fresh lemon juice and white pepper. Fill mushroom caps just to the rim, then top the filling with red caviar and a tiny lemon peel. Chill.
• Sauté 2 cups Seasoned Bread Crumbs in 3 to 4 tablespoons butter. Stir in 1 tablespoon *each* minced fresh parsley and chives. Fill mushroom caps and sprinkle with freshly grated Parmesan cheese. Serve at room temperature.
• Season 1 cup ricotta cheese to taste with salt, curry powder, grated onion, and minced fresh chives. Fill mushroom caps and sprinkle with paprika. Chill.
• Fill mushroom caps with lumpfish caviar, sprinkle lightly with fresh lemon juice, and garnish with sieved hard-cooked egg yolk and a tiny parsley leaf. Chill.
• Fill mushroom caps with Chicken Liver Pâté, then top with crumbled crisply cooked bacon or lightly toasted chopped pistachio nuts. Serve at room temperature.

FILLED CHERRY TOMATOES

Cut a tiny slice from the top of tomato, scoop out pulp with a small spoon, and turn tomato upside down on a rack to drain. The stem end should be flat enough so that the tomatoes will stand upright. Each tomato will take 1 to 1-1/2 teaspoons of filling; allow 1 to 1-1/2 cups of filling for 40 to 50 tomatoes.

Fill the tomatoes the day of the party, cover with plastic wrap, and refrigerate. Arrange on a serving plate and decorate the plate with appropriate garnishes (see Garnitures). Many of the recipes in the Spreads and Dips chapter, such as Taramosalata or Tapenade, would also

make delicious fillings, or fill with Caviar Surprise or one of the Potted Cheeses.

Have the cheeses and butter at room temperature for easy mixing. The white and black peppers should always be freshly ground.

• 5 hard-cooked eggs, sieved and then mixed with 4 tablespoons softened butter, 2 to 3 teaspoons anchovy paste, 2 teaspoons *each* minced fresh parsley and chives, garlic powder and white pepper to taste, and Crème Fraîche to make a creamy consistency. Briefly invert filled tomatoes on finely minced parsley so that the tops are completely coated with the parsley.

• 1 cup low-fat small-curd cottage cheese, 1 tablespoon *each* finely minced fresh chives and parsley, 2 tablespoons finely grated raw carrot, and salt and white pepper to taste. Top with a dab of lumpfish caviar.

• 4 ounces cream cheese; 3 tablespoons butter; 2 tablespoons fresh lemon juice; 2 teaspoons minced fresh dill; 1 tablespoon minced fresh parsley; 1 hard-cooked egg, finely chopped; 1 cup flaked cooked salmon; and brandy to taste. Top with a tiny sliver of lemon peel.

• 4 ounces cream cheese softened with 2 tablespoons light cream, 1/2 cup crumbled blue cheese (2 ounces), and grated onion, minced fresh chives, and white pepper to taste. Top with a tiny sliver of ripe olive.

• 6 ounces cream cheese softened with 2 tablespoons sour cream or Crème Fraîche; 1/4 cup *each* finely minced celery, carrot, and green onion and tops; 1 tablespoon finely minced fresh parsley; 1 teaspoon finely minced fresh dill; and garlic powder and white pepper to taste. Top with a tiny celery leaf.

• 6 ounces cream cheese softened with 2 tablespoons light cream, 2/3 cup minced cooked shrimp, 3 tablespoons minced watercress leaves, and Worcestershire sauce, Tabasco sauce, and white pepper to taste. Top with a tiny watercress leaf.

• 8 ounces cream cheese softened with 3 tablespoons sour cream or Crème Fraîche, 2 tablespoons minced fresh basil, and fresh lemon juice, salt, and white pepper to taste. Top with a tiny basil leaf.

• 1 cup crumbled chèvre (4 ounces) softened with 2 tablespoons heavy cream, 1 teaspoon *each* minced fresh parsley, basil, and oregano, and fresh lemon juice and white pepper to taste. Top with a tiny piece of Pumate.

• 1-1/2 to 2 cups rinsed and well-drained sauerkraut. Generously fill the tomatoes so the filling is nicely mounded.

• 3/4 cup finely minced cooked shrimp; 1/2 tablespoon finely minced celery; 3 tablespoons finely minced ripe olives; 1/4 teaspoon ground oregano; salt, white pepper, and Tabasco sauce to taste, and mayonnaise to make a creamy consistency. Top with a tiny coriander leaf.

• Jellied consommé or aspic (see To Prepare Aspic Jelly). Top with a dab of sour cream or Crème Fraîche.

• Smoked oysters and a tiny parsley leaf.

• Hard-cooked egg yolks, mashed and seasoned to taste with anchovy paste, minced drained capers and ripe olives, prepared mustard, and mayonnaise to make a creamy mixture. Top with a tiny sliver of ripe olive.

NEW POTATOES
FILLED WITH CAVIAR

Select new potatoes no larger than 1-1/2 inches in diameter. Scrub them well but do not peel. Steam 10 minutes, or until just barely tender, over water to which a spoonful of pickling spices has been added (see Steaming). Cool potatoes slightly.

Cut potatoes in half crosswise. Cut a tiny slice off rounded (uncut) part of each half so that the half will stand upright. With a small spoon, hollow out the center of each half, leaving a 1/4-inch-thick shell.

Fill each potato boat with lumpfish or red caviar, top with a dab of sour cream, and garnish with a tiny parsley or dill leaf. Alternatively, broil unfilled potato boats until heated through and light golden in color. Quickly fill and serve.

A faster way to prepare this elegant hors d'oeuvre and achieve much the same result is to slice the steamed potatoes crosswise into 1/4-inch-thick slices, spread each slice with caviar, and top with a dollop of sour cream and a tiny dill feather.

The potato boats can also be stuffed with the fillings for Cold Stuffed Mushrooms or those for Other Cold Filled Vegetables.

OTHER
COLD FILLED VEGETABLES

Filled artichoke bottoms, beets, bell peppers, celery ribs, Belgian endive leaves, snow peas, and zucchini also make attractive hors d'oeuvres. Directions on how to ready each of these vegetables for filling and suggested fillings follow. No proportions are given for some of the mixtures, as they are only ideas on which to build.

Have cheeses and butter at room temperature for easy mixing, and always freshly grind the white or black pepper. Arrange the filled vegetables on an imaginatively garnished platter and serve chilled.

ARTICHOKE BOTTOMS Use cooked artichoke bottoms about 1-1/2 inches in diameter (or trim larger bottoms by cutting to size with a cookie cutter), or drained marinated artichoke bottoms (reserve marinade for salad dressings and sautéing), trimmed if necessary. Dry artichoke bottoms with paper toweling, then sprinkle lightly with fresh lemon juice, salt, white pepper, and paprika. Each bottom will hold 2 to 3 teaspoons of filling.
• Cream cheese softened with Crème Fraîche or light cream to make a spreading consistency and paprika for color. Top with

lumpfish caviar and a tiny lemon peel and parsley leaf.
• Chicken Liver Pâté or Mock Liver Pâté. Garnish with a tiny watercress leaf.
• Crumbled feta cheese or chèvre mashed with sour cream to make a spreading consistency and combined with minced fresh chives and parsley. Garnish with a sprinkling of paprika and a tiny parsley leaf.
• Finely minced Gravlax or smoked salmon moistened with Crème Fraîche and seasoned with white pepper, dry mustard, and ground coriander to taste. Garnish with a dab of Crème Fraîche and a drained caper.

BEETS Cut a small slice off tops of tiny cooked beets about 1-1/2 inches in diameter. Hollow them out to form a 1/4-inch-thick shell. Each beet will hold approximately 2 teaspoons filling.
• Chopped hard-cooked egg combined with mashed sardines or anchovies and minced drained capers and gherkins. Top with a drained caper and a tiny parsley leaf.
• Sieved hard-cooked eggs combined with finely chopped watercress, minced celery, Curry Mayonnaise, and Tabasco sauce to taste. Top with a tiny watercress leaf.

• Crème Fraîche mixed with anchovy paste to taste. Sprinkle with finely minced fresh chives.

BELGIAN ENDIVE Separate leaves of Belgian endive and wash well. Drain, wrap in a terry towel, and refrigerate. Just before serving, pipe (see Basics) or spread the fillings for cherry tomatoes, beets, or celery onto the leaves. Chill no more than 30 minutes. Serve immediately.

CELERY RIBS Separate inner ribs from the celery and cut them into 3-inch lengths. Place the pieces in a bowl of ice water to crisp, drain, and pat dry with paper toweling. Allow approximately 1 tablespoon filling for each piece of celery. Use a small butter knife or spatula or a piping apparatus (see Basics) to apply filling.
• Chopped hard-cooked eggs combined with minced celery and fresh parsley, mashed sardines or anchovies, salt and white pepper to taste, mayonnaise to bind. Garnish with a tiny parsley leaf.
• Cream cheese softened with heavy cream and combined with minced ripe olives, chopped unsalted cashews, Worcestershire sauce, and onion powder to taste. Garnish with a tiny sliver of ripe olive.

• Two parts cream cheese and one part unsalted butter combined with minced anchovies and fresh lemon juice to taste. Garnish with a tiny strip of lemon peel.
• Equal parts cream cheese and crumbled blue cheese combined with Pumate Purée or tomato paste, minced fresh parsley and chives, white pepper, and Tabasco sauce to taste. Garnish with a tiny piece of Pumate.
• Cream cheese combined with prepared horseradish, crumbled crisply cooked bacon, minced fresh parsley, and black pepper to taste. Garnish with crumbled crisp bacon.
• Mock Liver Pâté. Garnish with 2 or 3 ripe olive slices (slice crosswise).
• Tapenade or Taramosalata. Garnish with a coriander or parsley leaf.

BELL PEPPERS Cut bell peppers in quarters lengthwise. Cut quarters crosswise into 2 or 3 pieces to form "boats." Fill with any of the fillings for cherry tomatoes, artichoke bottoms, or celery.

SNOW PEAS Filling snow peas is a time-consuming job that really needs two people, one to hold the pea pod, the other to pipe the filling. Only plan to serve these delicious and lovely-to-

look-at morsels when you are having a small gathering or when you're sure to have lots of help.

Trim and remove strings from snow peas and blanch the peas for 15 seconds. Drain, plunge into ice water, drain, and pat dry with paper toweling. With the tip of a sharp, thin-bladed knife, carefully slit the rounded side of the pea, opening the pod to within 1/4 inch of each end. Pipe the filling (see Basics) into the pod. Use any of the cream cheese-based fillings for cherry tomatoes, artichoke bottoms, or celery, or fill with one of the Potted Cheeses.

Arrange the filled pea pods on a serving plate in a spoke pattern and intersperse with rows of tiny cooked shrimp and parsley sprigs. Provide cocktail picks for the shrimp; guests pick up the pea pods with their fingers.

ZUCCHINI Cut raw zucchini (about 1-1/2 inches in diameter) into 1-inch-thick slices and hollow out centers to make a shell approximately 1/4 inch thick. Alternatively, cut zucchini in half lengthwise and then cut into 2-inch pieces and hollow out. Fill with any of the fillings for cherry tomatoes, artichoke bottoms, or celery ribs.

MUSHROOM AND SHALLOT CAVIAR ●

Vary this delicate spread by adding one-half cup finely chopped pine nuts, pecans, almonds, or walnuts. Serve with melba toast rounds, unsalted crackers, or slices of dense black bread.

Makes Approximately
One and One-half Cups
2/3 cup finely minced shallots
5 tablespoons butter
12 ounces fresh mushrooms, very finely minced
1/2 teaspoon ground oregano
1/2 teaspoon salt
1/4 teaspoon freshly ground white pepper
Dash cayenne pepper
3 large garlic cloves, finely minced
1-1/2 tablespoons fresh lemon juice
3 tablespoons sour cream
Melba Toast rounds, unsalted crackers and/or slices of dense black bread

In a large covered nonstick skillet, cook shallots in butter over medium-low heat 3 minutes. Uncover, raise heat to high, and add mushrooms. Sprinkle mush-rooms with oregano, salt, and pepper and, stirring frequently, cook 5 minutes. Add garlic and lemon juice, stir well, and cook 2 minutes, or until moisture has evaporated.

Remove skillet from heat and let mushroom mixture cool. Add sour cream and blend well. Taste and adjust seasonings. Pack "caviar" into a crock or serving bowl, cover with plastic wrap, and refrigerate for at least 1 hour, or for up to 2 days.

To serve, place crock on a serving plate and surround with melba toast, unsalted crackers, and/or black bread.

CURRIED MUSHROOM CAVIAR ●

Makes Approximately One Cup
2-1/2 tablespoons rendered chicken fat and/or butter
3 tablespoons minced shallots
2 tablespoons minced green onion
3/4 teaspoon curry powder
6 ounces mushrooms, thinly sliced
1/2 teaspoon crumbled dried basil
1/4 teaspoon freshly ground white pepper
1/3 cup lightly toasted coarsely ground almonds
3 tablespoons Crème Fraîche
Radish Roses
Parsley sprigs

In a large nonstick skillet, heat chicken fat over medium heat. Add shallots and green onion and sprinkle with curry powder. Cook and stir 2 minutes, then toss in mushrooms, basil, and pepper. Cover skillet and cook until mushrooms are tender. Uncover and let almost all of the moisture cook away.

Cool mushroom mixture briefly, then whirl in a blender or food processor *just* until puréed; do not allow the mixture to become a paste. Transfer purée to a mixing bowl and, with a fork, stir in almonds and crème fraîche. Taste and adjust seasonings. Cover and refrigerate for at least 2 hours, or for up to 2 days.

To serve, mound mixture on a serving plate. Garnish with radish roses tucked into parsley sprigs.

PICKLED AND MARINATED VEGETABLES

A number of vegetables, alone or in combination, lend themselves to pickling or marinating. The critical step in these preparations is the cooking of the vegetables. The vegetables must remain crisp, which is made difficult by the fact that they continue to cook as they cool.

Suitable vegetables for pickling or marinating include the following, beginning with the longest-cooking ones. Approximate cooking times are given; keep in mind that the age of the vegetable and how it is cut will make the timing vary.

Artichoke hearts, small whole: 15 minutes

Beets, tiny young whole or sliced (best cooked and served alone): 12 to 15 minutes

Carrots, tiny young whole, sliced, or cut into sticks: 10 to 12 minutes

Turnips, tiny young whole or cut into sticks: 10 minutes

Celery, cut into sticks: 7 to 10 minutes

Celery hearts: 7 to 10 minutes

Fennel hearts: 7 minutes

Brussels sprouts, small whole: 6 to 7 minutes

Pearl onions, whole: 6 minutes

Broccoli or cauliflower florets: 5 minutes

Eggplant fingers: 4 minutes

Green onions, whole with 1 inch of green top: 3 minutes

Bell peppers, cut into eighths: 3 minutes

Green beans, young whole: 3 minutes

Button mushrooms, whole: 2 minutes

Zucchini or other summer squash, sliced or cut into sticks: 1 to 2 minutes

Asparagus spears: 1 to 2 minutes

PICKLED VEGETABLES ○

Approximately Fifty Servings

PICKLING LIQUID
1 cup distilled white vinegar
1 cup water
1/3 cup olive oil
2 teaspoons granulated or brown sugar
2 teaspoons salt
1 to 2 teaspoons pickling spices
8 whole cloves
1 medium-size onion, finely minced
5 large garlic cloves, finely minced

4 cups readied vegetables (1 vegetable or a combination)
1 cup slivered drained Roasted Peppers
Minced fresh parsley and chives

Combine all ingredients for pickling liquid in a saucepan, cover, and bring to a boil. Lower heat slightly and boil 15 minutes, stirring once to dissolve sugar.

Raise heat and add the longest-cooking vegetable. In order of how much cooking time each needs, add additional vegetables, cover, bring back to a rapid boil, lower heat slightly, and boil until *barely* tender. Remove from heat, uncover, and let cool.

Pour vegetables and liquid into a nonmetallic container, cover, and refrigerate overnight, or for up to 3 days. With a slotted spoon, transfer vegetables to a shallow crystal serving dish and stir in roasted peppers with a fork. Sprinkle with parsley and chives. Serve with cocktail picks.

MARINATED VEGETABLES ○

Zucchini and yellow squash sticks, tiny onions, button mushrooms, and cherry tomatoes (uncooked) make a delicious, colorful marinated vegetable combination. If the stock you are using is very gelatinous, thin with water and add chicken stock base to strengthen the flavor.

Approximately Twenty-five Servings

MARINADE
1 cup chicken stock
1/2 cup dry white wine
3 tablespoons fresh lemon juice
1 small onion, sliced
2 large garlic cloves, minced
1 small celery rib and leaves, finely chopped
4 Italian parsley sprigs
3 thyme sprigs
1 oregano sprig
6 white or black peppercorns, lightly crushed
1/4 teaspoon salt

2 cups readied vegetables (1 vegetable or a combination)
1/4 cup olive oil
Minced fresh parsley and chives

Combine all marinade ingredients in a saucepan, cover, and bring to a boil. Lower heat and simmer 20 minutes. Strain and return liquid to saucepan.

Bring strained marinade to a boil and add the longest-cooking vegetable. In order of how much cooking time each needs, add additional vegetables, cover, bring back to a rapid boil, lower heat slightly, and boil until *barely* tender. Remove from heat, uncover, add olive oil, and let cool.

Pour vegetables and liquid into a nonmetallic container, cover, and refrigerate overnight, or for up to 2 days. With a slotted spoon, transfer vegetables to a shallow crystal serving dish. Sprinkle with parsley and chives. Serve with cocktail picks.

DILLED VEGETABLES ○

The flavor of young whole green beans, miniature carrots, pearl onions, brussels sprouts, and cauliflower is enhanced by preserving in dill and garlic. The procedure is simple: the vegetables are packed into sterilized jars with dill seeds and garlic cloves and a hot vinegar solution is poured into the jar to cover them completely. Once sealed, the vegetables should stand at least one week before opening to allow flavors to blend.

For 6 or 7 half-pints, combine in a saucepan 2-1/2 cups cider or distilled white vinegar, 2-1/2 cups water, 1/4 cup salt, and 1 bay leaf. Bring to a boil, stir to dissolve salt, and boil 6 minutes.

Lower heat and keep mixture hot.

Treat each vegetable separately. Stand trimmed whole young green beans or blanched miniature carrots in hot sterilized jars, or pack the jars with blanched pearl onions, brussels sprouts, or small cauliflower florets. Add to each jar 1 large garlic clove, halved; 1/4 to 1/2 teaspoon crushed dried red pepper; and 1/4 to 1/2 teaspoon *each* dill seeds and mustard seeds. Pour in hot vinegar solution to within 1/4 inch of jar rim, making sure the vegetables are covered. Cover jar with sterilized lid and screw lid on tightly.

Place jars on a low rack in a large kettle. Add boiling water to cover jars by 1/2 inch, cover kettle, bring water back to a boil, and boil 5 minutes. Remove jars to work surface and let cool. Do not move the jars for 24 hours. If the lids do not appear slightly indented, a sign that they are properly sealed (you will hear a loud "pop" at the moment of sealing), store the jars in the refrigerator for up to 1 month. Properly sealed jars may be stored in a cool, dark place for up to 4 months, after which time, refrigerate.

Serve the dilled vegetables in a shallow dish garnished with Lemon Twists.

MARINATED OLIVES ○

A touch of garlic, lemon, and oregano will enhance the flavor of Kalamata, ripe, or green olives.

For 1 pound olives, combine 1/2 cup olive oil; 2 tablespoons fresh lemon juice; 1-1/2 table-spoons balsamic vinegar; 1 table-spoon minced fresh oregano; 4 large garlic cloves, chopped; 1/4 teaspoon salt; and 6 black pepper-corns, lightly crushed.

If the olives are purchased in liquid, drain them and then place in a nonmetallic container. (Rinse Kalamata or other Mediterranean-style olives in 6 or 7 cold water baths.) Pour the olive oil mixture over olives, cover container, and refrigerate for at least 1 day, preferably 3 days, or for up to 1 week.

To serve, remove olives from marinade and place in a crystal serving bowl. Alternatively, toss olives with cubed feta cheese and cherry tomatoes. Provide cocktail picks for spearing.

ROASTED SEASONED NUTS ●

A bowl of specially flavored nuts is always popular at any gathering. Pecans, walnuts, almonds (blanched or unblanched), or cashews can be prepared in either of the following ways.

● Melt 3 tablespoons unsalted butter with 2 tablespoons soy sauce and 1/8 teaspoon ground ginger. Toss 1 pound (3-1/2 to 4 cups) nuts with butter mixture and spread nuts on a baking sheet with sides. Stirring occasion-ally, toast in a 250° F oven for 35 to 45 minutes, or until just starting to turn golden. Remove from oven, transfer to paper toweling, and cool completely. Store in an airtight container up to 2 weeks, or freeze for up to 6 months.
● Generously butter a large baking sheet with sides. In a large mixing bowl, beat 1 egg white until light and frothy. Stir in 2 teaspoons coarse sea salt and 1/2 teaspoon garlic powder, 1/4 teaspoon ground cumin or chili powder, or dash cayenne pepper. Add nuts to bowl and toss to mix well with egg white and seasoning. Spread nuts on the buttered baking sheet and place in a 300° F oven. Stirring occasionally, toast 30 minutes, or until golden brown. Cool and store as directed above.

POTATO BALLS

With a melon ball scoop, make balls from pared raw thick-skinned potatoes, dropping the balls into acidulated water as they are formed. Drain the balls and place in a saucepan with salted water to cover. Place a lid on the pan, bring to a boil, reduce heat slightly, and cook balls just until tender, about 10 minutes. Drain balls and let cool.

Toss cooled balls with chopped sweet red onion and Sour Cream Mayonnaise seasoned to taste with curry powder. Alternatively, toss balls with minced celery and shallots and sour cream seasoned to taste with prepared horseradish, red wine vinegar, salt, and freshly ground white pepper.

Cover the coated potato balls with plastic wrap and chill at least 1 hour, or for up to 3 hours. Sprinkle with minced fresh parsley and/or chives and serve with cocktail picks.

VEGETABLE AND FRUIT IDEAS

• Wrap lightly blanched asparagus spears in prosciutto, thinly sliced smoked salmon or Gravlax, or thinly sliced salami. Secure with a toothpick and arrange in a spoke pattern on a serving tray. Garnish tray with small parsley sprigs and halved ripe olives, Pumate strips, or cherry tomatoes.

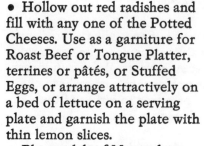

• Hollow out red radishes and fill with any one of the Potted Cheeses. Use as a garniture for Roast Beef or Tongue Platter, terrines or pâtés, or Stuffed Eggs, or arrange attractively on a bed of lettuce on a serving plate and garnish the plate with thin lemon slices.
• Place a dab of Mustard or Curry Mayonnaise on the end of a small leaf of Belgian endive or cooked artichoke, top with a cooked shrimp or a bit of crab meat, and garnish with a tiny parsley leaf. Arrange in spoke fashion on a large round serving platter.
• Slice jicama or young kohlrabi thinly and drizzle with fresh lemon juice. Sprinkle slices with seasoned salt or herb salt or seasoning and refrigerate 1 to 2 hours. Serve as a refreshing non-caloric hors d'oeuvre.

• Wrap lemon-coated avocado balls or melon, papaya, or mango balls in prosciutto and secure with cocktail picks.
• Sprinkle fresh figs with black pepper, wrap in prosciutto, and secure with cocktail picks.
• Dip apple cubes in fresh lemon juice. Thread on bamboo skewer or cocktail pick with a cube of Brie or Camembert cheese.
• Soak pitted prunes in rum for several hours, drain, and stuff with cream cheese softened with sour cream or Crème Fraîche.
• Sandwich large pecan halves together with cream cheese mixed with anchovy paste.

HOT VEGETABLES

BAKED
STUFFED MUSHROOMS

Twenty-four Servings
Purchase 24 uniform medium-large mushrooms (approximately 1-1/2 pounds). Trim discolored ends from mushroom stems and clean mushrooms with a mushroom brush or wipe with a lightly dampened paper towel (do not wash, or mushrooms will become soggy). Brush the caps with melted butter and set aside. Finely mince the stems.

In a skillet, melt 3 tablespoons butter and sauté minced stems with 2 tablespoons finely minced onion and 1 large garlic clove, finely minced. Combine this mixture with one of the following filling suggestions, mound mixture into caps, and sprinkle with paprika.

Arrange filled caps, touching, in a shallow baking dish. Bake in a preheated 400° F oven 10 to 15 minutes until mushrooms are tender and tops are lightly browned. Transfer to a warmed serving plate and serve at once.

WALNUT FILLING Combine sautéed mushroom stem mixture with 1 cup fine dry bread crumbs, 1/3 cup freshly grated Parmesan cheese, 1/4 cup lightly toasted finely chopped walnuts, Worcestershire sauce, salt, and freshly ground black pepper to taste, and chicken stock if needed to moisten. Bake as directed and garnish each mushroom with a tiny parsley leaf.

ALMOND FILLING Combine sautéed mushroom stem mixture with 1/4 cup lightly toasted finely chopped blanched almonds, 1/4 cup *each* Herb Mayonnaise and fine dry bread crumbs, and 1/4 cup finely grated Monterey Jack or sharp Cheddar cheese. Fill caps and sprinkle with finely chopped slivered blanched almonds and paprika. Bake as directed.

SPINACH OR SWISS CHARD FILLING Combine sautéed mushroom stem mixture with 1/2 cup *well-drained* and very finely chopped cooked spinach or swiss chard; 2 ounces feta cheese, crumbled (1/2 cup); 1/2 cup fine dry bread crumbs; and Worcestershire sauce, crumbled dried dill, salt, and freshly ground white pepper to taste. Fill caps and sprinkle with finely shredded Gruyère cheese. Bake as directed.

PESTO FILLING Combine sautéed mushroom stem mixture with 3/4 cup Pesto and 1/4 cup fine fresh bread crumbs. Fill caps and sprinkle with freshly grated Parmesan cheese. Bake as directed.

HAM FILLING Combine sautéed stem mixture with 1 cup ground cooked ham, 1/3 cup sour cream, 2 tablespoons *each* minced fresh parsley and chives, and salt and freshly ground white pepper to taste. Fill caps and sprinkle with finely shredded Monterey Jack cheese. Bake as directed.

CRAB OR SHRIMP FILLING Prepare 1 recipe Crab or Shrimp Filling and combine with sautéed stem mixture. Fill caps and sprinkle with freshly grated Parmesan cheese. Bake as directed.

BLUE CHEESE FILLING Do not sauté the mushroom stems as above; chop them finely and combine with 1/4 cup crumbled blue cheese (1 ounce); 2 tablespoons unsalted butter, at room temperature; 1 cup fine fresh bread crumbs; 3 tablespoons minced fresh parsley; 2 teaspoons fresh lemon juice; and freshly ground white pepper to taste. Fill caps and sprinkle with paprika. Bake as directed.

DOLMADES
(Greek Stuffed Grape Leaves) ●■

The following filling recipes are for one 12-ounce jar of grape leaves preserved in brine, approximately 50. Any unfilled leaves can be used as a bed under the rolls when cooking them, or on the serving platter as a bed and/or garnish. The same method can be used to fill swiss chard leaves and large spinach, nasturtium, or fresh grape leaves. Blanch these leaves just until wilted, pat dry with paper toweling, and place vein side up on a work surface. Fill and roll as with brined grape leaves.

Remove the brined grape leaves from the jar, unfold, and rinse in cold, then hot water. Drain, pat dry with paper toweling, and spread 6 or 8 leaves at a time, shiny side down, on the work surface. Remove the tough stem at the base of each leaf and then cut out any tough stem that extends up into the leaf. Place 2 to 3 teaspoons filling on stem end of leaf and fold over one turn to encase the filling. Fold in sides of leaf lengthwise, then continue to roll toward the tip. (If leaves are very large, or if smaller dolmades are preferred, cut leaves in half). At this point, dolmades may be covered and refrigerated 1 day, or they may be sheet frozen for up to 1 month. Defrost in one layer before cooking.

To cook the dolmades, pour olive oil into a large kettle or electric frypan to a depth of 1/8 inch. Arrange dolmades close together in kettle seam side down. Tuck small parsley sprigs between them and carefully pour in a mixture of 1-2/3 cups rich beef stock (or one 10-1/2-ounce can consommé diluted with 1/2 cup water) and 1/4 cup fresh lemon juice. Place a heavy plate on top of dolmades to weight them down. Cover kettle, bring stock to a gentle boil, lower heat, and cook, adding more stock if needed, 15 minutes for large dolmades, or 10 to 12 minutes for small.

To serve the dolmades hot, immediately transfer them to a chafing or equivalent dish. Be careful when moving them, or they will begin to unwrap. The simplest presentation is to pour the hot cooking liquid over them. Alternatively, combine the liquid with 1/2 cup sour cream or tomato purée, or thicken the liquid with 2 beaten egg yolks (beat yolks, whisk in a little hot sauce, then whisk into remaining sauce). Reheat but do not boil and then spoon the sauce over the dolmades.

To serve at room temperature, arrange dolmades on a serving platter (on the bed of grape leaves, if desired) and garnish with clusters of fresh grapes. Place a bowl of Yoghurt Sauce next to the platter and provide cocktail picks.

Cooled cooked dolmades may be transferred to a shallow freezer container with their cooking liquid, covered, and frozen up to 1 month. Defrost in the refrigerator before reheating in a microwave oven or in a covered nonstick skillet on top of the stove.

The filling recipes that follow will yield enough to fill approximately 30 large or 50 small dolmades.

LAMB FILLING

1/4 cup minced onion
2 large garlic cloves, finely minced
2 tablespoons minced fresh parsley
2 tablespoons minced fresh mint
1 teaspoon minced fresh oregano
1/2 teaspoon minced fresh thyme
1/2 teaspoon salt
1/2 teaspoon freshly ground black pepper
1 cup finely chopped ripe tomato, well drained
2 tablespoons tomato paste
1/4 cup chopped pine nuts (optional)
1 pound lean ground lamb

In a mixing bowl, combine onion, garlic, parsley, mint, oregano, thyme, salt, pepper, tomato, tomato paste, and pine nuts and stir to mix well. Add lamb and mix with hands until smooth. Pinch off a small amount of mixture and sauté until cooked through. Taste and adjust seasonings.

RICE FILLING

1/4 cup dried currants
2 tablespoons dry white wine
1 cup minced onion
1/2 teaspoon salt
1/4 teaspoon freshly ground
    black pepper
1/4 cup olive oil
1 cup raw long-grain white rice
1-1/2 cups water
2 tablespoons fresh lemon juice
1/4 cup minced fresh parsley
3 tablespoons lightly toasted
    pine nuts
1 tablespoon minced fresh mint
1/2 tablespoon minced fresh
    oregano
1/4 teaspoon ground allspice
1/4 teaspoon ground cinnamon

Soak currants in wine 1 hour; drain, reserving wine, and set aside.

In a covered nonstick skillet, cook onion, salt, and pepper in oil over medium heat 5 minutes, or until onion is soft. Add rice, water, lemon juice, and reserved wine. Cover, bring to a gentle boil, and cook 10 minutes to cook the rice partially. Uncover skillet and let all remaining moisture cook away. Toss in reserved currants, parsley, pine nuts, mint, oregano, allspice, and cinnamon. Taste and adjust seasonings.

PORK AND BEEF FILLING

3/4 cup minced onion
1/2 cup minced fresh parsley
1-1/2 tablespoons fresh lemon
    juice
1 teaspoon minced fresh basil
3/4 teaspoon salt
3/4 teaspoon minced fresh
    marjoram
1/4 teaspoon freshly ground
    black pepper
1 pound ground lean beef
1/2 pound ground lean pork

In a mixing bowl, combine onion, parsley, lemon juice, basil, salt, marjoram, and pepper and stir to mix well. Add beef and pork and mix with hands until smooth. Pinch off a small portion and sauté until cooked through. Taste and adjust seasonings.

BAKED FILLED ARTICHOKE BOTTOMS

Ready artichoke bottoms as directed in Other Cold Filled Vegetables. You will need 1 to 1-1/2 cups filling for 24 artichoke bottoms, or about 2 to 3 teaspoons filling for each. Mound one of the following mixtures in the bottoms, dust tops lightly with paprika, and bake in a preheated 350° F oven 10 to 15 minutes, or until heated through. Garnish with sieved hard-cooked egg and arrange on a warmed serving plate. Serve at once.

• Combine *well-drained* finely chopped cooked spinach with enough Cream Sauce to make a smooth mixture. Season to taste with grated onion and garlic, salt, freshly ground white pepper, and freshly grated nutmeg. Fill artichoke bottoms with spinach mixture. Bake and garnish as directed.
• Fill artichoke bottoms with Duxelle. Bake as directed and garnish each artichoke bottom with a thin slice of raw mushroom in place of the hard-cooked egg.
• Fill artichoke bottoms with Chestnut Purée. Bake and garnish as directed.

MUSHROOMS FILLED WITH SNAILS

These rich, elegant mouthfuls are lovely served on a white ceramic platter. The fried bread rounds should be the same diameter as the mushroom caps.

Twenty-four Servings
1/4 pound unsalted butter, at room temperature
4 large garlic cloves, finely minced
2 teaspoons very finely minced parsley
2 teaspoons fresh lemon juice
1/2 teaspoon Worcestershire sauce
6 to 8 drops Tabasco sauce
24 medium-size mushrooms
Two 7-1/2-ounce cans snails, drained
2 tablespoons fine dry bread crumbs
Paprika
24 Fried Bread rounds
Lemon Twists

In a mixing bowl, combine butter, garlic, parsley, lemon juice, and Worcestershire and Tabasco sauces and mix with a fork to blend thoroughly. Ready the mushrooms as for Baked Stuffed Mushrooms, but reserve the stems for another use. Tuck a snail into each of the mushroom caps and top each snail with 1/2 teaspoon of the butter mixture. Arrange filled mushroom caps in a shallow baking dish and sprinkle with bread crumbs and paprika. Bake as directed in Baked Stuffed Mushrooms.

To serve, arrange bread rounds on a serving platter and top each round with a mushroom cap. Drizzle any butter in the baking dish over the mushroom caps and garnish with lemon twists. Serve at once.

POTATO SKINS

These crisp morsels are perfect for an informal gathering. Peel thick-skinned (baking) potatoes, removing enough of the potato with the peel to form a strip 1/8 inch thick. Deep-fry the peels until crisp in 375° F peanut oil, drain on crumpled paper toweling, and sprinkle lightly with salt and freshly ground black pepper. Serve at once.

Alternatively, bake potatoes as usual, halve lengthwise and scoop out the pulp, leaving a shell about 1/4 inch thick. Cut each half into 4 to 6 pieces. Brush pieces with melted butter and soy sauce; spread with equal parts Crème Fraîche and freshly grated Parmesan cheese; or sprinkle with shredded Monterey Jack or sharp Cheddar cheese.

Place skins on a baking sheet in a single layer, and bake in a preheated 450° F oven 10 minutes, or until crisp. Serve at once.

ZWIEBELKUCHEN
(Onion Pie)

The inspiration for this onion pie comes from Alsace-Lorraine, where the flavor is enhanced by baking on a wooden plaque in a huge brick oven. It may be eaten at room temperature, or wrapped loosely in aluminum foil and reheated, though it is best freshly baked and cooled only slightly.

*Approximately
Twenty-four Servings*
1 recipe Pizza dough
2 pounds onions, minced (approximately 5 cups)
4 ounces lean bacon, minced
1 tablespoon butter
1/2 teaspoon salt
1/4 teaspoon freshly ground white pepper
2 tablespoons unbleached flour
3 eggs, lightly beaten
1-1/3 cups sour cream
1 cup creamed small-curd cottage cheese
1 to 2 teaspoons caraway seeds
Bits of butter or of additional bacon

Prepare the pizza dough and set it aside to rise.

In a large covered nonstick skillet, cook onion and bacon in butter over medium heat 5 minutes, or until onion is soft. Remove cover and sprinkle with salt, pepper, and flour. Cook and stir 3 minutes and remove from the heat. Cool and stir in eggs, sour cream, cottage cheese, and caraway seeds, blending until smooth. Taste and adjust seasonings. Set aside.

Butter a 10-inch straight-sided pie tin. After pizza dough has risen and rested, roll and pat out into a round approximately 1/4 inch thick. Carefully transfer round to prepared pie tin and trim edges even with rim of tin. Cover with a tea towel and let rise in a warm place 20 minutes, or until half again as high.

Preheat oven to 375° F. Pour onion mixture into pie shell and dot with butter or bits of bacon. Bake in the preheated oven 50 minutes, or until top is golden and a cake tester inserted in center comes out clean.

To serve, cut into wedges and arrange on a serving plate.

SPINACH BALLS ●■

Make these balls ahead and freeze for up to two months. They are a satisfying and filling addition to any buffet and need no dipping sauce. Garnish the serving platter with lemon curls for color contrast.

Approximately Fifty Servings
1 large onion, chopped
4 or 5 large garlic cloves, minced
3/4 cup unsalted butter, cut up and at room temperature
4 eggs
2 cups fine dry bread crumbs
1 cup freshly grated Parmesan cheese
1 teaspoon salt
1/2 teaspoon freshly ground black pepper
1/2 teaspoon freshly grated nutmeg
1/2 teaspoon crumbled dried oregano
1/4 teaspoon crumbled dried basil
2 tablespoons fresh lemon juice
2 cups *well-drained,* finely chopped firmly packed cooked spinach (two 10-ounce packages frozen chopped spinach, cooked and all moisture pressed out)
1-1/2 cups crushed lightly toasted sesame seeds (optional)
Lemon curls

In a blender or food processor, finely mince the onion and garlic. Add butter and process until well mixed. With motor running, add eggs one at a time and process just until mixed. Transfer mixture to a large mixing bowl.

Toss together bread crumbs, Parmesan cheese, seasonings, and herbs. With a fork, stir crumb mixture into butter mixture and blend lightly just until well mixed. Stir in lemon juice and spinach to incorporate evenly, cover bowl, and refrigerate at least 1 hour.

Form spinach mixture into balls about 1-1/2 inches in diameter (no larger) and roll in sesame seeds to coat lightly. Arrange balls, not touching, on baking sheet. At this point, spinach balls may be covered and refrigerated for up to 1 day, or they may be sheet frozen for up to 2 months. If defrosting before baking, defrost in single layer in refrigerator.

To bake, preheat oven to 350° F. Bake room-temperature spinach balls 10 to 15 minutes and frozen balls 20 minutes, or until heated through. Serve at once with cocktail picks.

FISH, POULTRY, & MEAT

This chapter contains easy-to-prepare seafood, poultry, and meat dishes that can play central roles in a buffet—boiled shrimp presented on a bed of ice, steak tartare with an elaborate array of accompaniments, chicken wings fashioned into fanciful shapes, sea-fresh oysters on the half shell, roasted and boiled meats served with a variety of sauces, and so on. You will also find more complex preparations, such as baked clams, rillettes made of duck and of pork, and stuffed squid rings.

You will not, however, find a shellfish mousse, chicken liver pâté, or sautéed liver, for example, for those dishes are in chapters where the preparation or serving method rather than the ingredient defines what is included. The mousse would be with the other molds, the pâté with the pâtés, and the liver in Chafing Dish.

Thus, this is something of a catchall chapter, but a very important one. Many of the recipes represent the most substantial part of your menu, the focus that determines what other dishes will be served.

A section on barbecuing, with more than a score of imaginative marinades, falls at the end of the chapter.

FISH AND SHELLFISH

SHRIMP ON ICE ●

Serve this special treat with one or more of the sauces suggested. Reserve a supply of shrimp for latecomers or they will surely miss out.

Approximately Thirty Servings
2 pounds medium-large shrimp
2 quarts water
3/4 cup fresh lemon juice
3 tablespoons salt
2 bay leaves, broken

PRESENTATION
Romaine lettuce leaves
Parsley or watercress leaves
Avocado Dip
Chili Sauce
Mayonnaise Variations

Remove shells from shrimp. With a sharp knife, cut a slit 1/8 inch deep along the curved back of the shrimp. Discard the black- or coral-colored vein and rinse the shrimp in cold water.

In a large saucepan, combine water, lemon juice, salt, and bay leaves. Over high heat bring to a rolling boil and add shrimp all at once. Stir with a fork and let water come back to a hard boil. Boil 2 minutes and then check for doneness by cutting a shrimp in half; the shrimp should look opaque and taste *barely* cooked through. Pour shrimp into a strainer and immediately plunge into ice water to prevent further cooking.

To serve, line a crystal serving bowl with lettuce leaves. Drain shrimp, pat dry with paper toweling, and mound in the serving bowl. Tuck parsley or watercress leaves around the shrimp and nestle the bowl in a larger bowl filled with crushed ice. Serve with one or more of the sauces.

Shrimp may be cooked 2 days in advance of serving. Place the shrimp in a nonmetallic container, cover with salted water (1 table-spoon salt for each quart water), cover container, and refrigerate. Drain and add fresh salted water each day.

STUFFED SHRIMP WITH TWO FILLINGS

Other filling mixtures, such as Avocado, Mushroom, or Pecan Cream Cheese Spread, or any one of the Potted Cheeses, may be substituted for either of the fillings that follow.

Thirty-six Servings
36 large shrimp
Blue Cheese Filling or Feta
   Cheese Filling (following)
Very finely minced fresh parsley,
   dill, or watercress
Cherry tomatoes
Parsley or watercress sprigs

Clean and cook the shrimp as directed in Shrimp on Ice, pre-ceding. After plunging them in ice water, drain the shrimp and then deepen the slit along the curved back of each shrimp, being careful not to cut the shrimp in half. (Should you make that mistake, pretend the shrimp halves are the bread for a sand-wich.)

Prepare one of the fillings and fill the slit of each shrimp with about 2 teaspoons filling, mounding the filling attractively. Roll the filled curve in minced fresh parsley, dill, or watercress. Place the shrimp in a single layer in a shallow nonmetallic container, cover with plastic wrap, and refrigerate 1 hour.

To serve, skewer each shrimp on a small wooden skewer with a small cherry tomato. Arrange skewers on a serving plate and garnish the plate with cherry tomatoes nestled in a bed of parsley or watercress.

BLUE CHEESE FILLING ●

3 ounces cream cheese, at
   room temperature
1/4 cup crumbled blue cheese
   (1 ounce)
1/2 teaspoon dry mustard
1 tablespoon minced fresh
   parlsey
1 green onion and top,
   finely minced
One 4-ounce can chopped
   ripe olives
Freshly ground white pepper
   to taste
Tabasco sauce to taste (optional)

In a mixing bowl, mash the cream cheese with a fork to soften and then blend in blue cheese. When well mixed, add mustard, parsley, onion, olives, pepper, and Tabasco sauce. Cover and chill at least 30 minutes, or for up to 2 days.

Bring to room temperature and stir well before filling shrimp as directed.

FETA CHEESE FILLING ●

3 ounces cream cheese, at room
   temperature
3/4 cup crumbled feta cheese
   (3 ounces)
2 teaspoons minced fresh parsley
2 teaspoons minced fresh dill
2 teaspoons fresh lemon juice
1/8 teaspoon salt
1/4 teaspoon freshly ground
   white pepper
Dash cayenne pepper

In a mixing bowl, mash the cream cheese with a fork to soften and blend in feta cheese. When well mixed, add parsley, dill, lemon juice, salt, and peppers. Taste and adjust seasonings. Cover and chill at least 30 minutes, or for up to 2 days.

Bring to room temperature and stir well before filling shrimp as directed.

SHRIMP IN THE SHELL, SPANISH STYLE

In Spain, shrimp are often cooked and served in the shell. If you prefer not to have your guests shell their own shrimp, shell and devein them before cooking. The texture will be slightly different, but the flavor will be quite similar.

Quick cooking is essential in either case, so have all ingredients ready before proceeding with this recipe and be especially careful not to overcook, and thus toughen, the shrimp.

Approximately Thirty-six Servings
1 pound medium-large shrimp in the shell
1/3 cup Fish Stock
1/16 teaspoon ground saffron, or saffron threads pulverized in a mortar and pestle
1/2 teaspoon arrowroot
3 tablespoons olive oil
1/3 cup minced onion
4 large garlic cloves, finely minced
1/4 teaspoon salt
1/4 teaspoon freshly ground black pepper
1/2 cup dry white wine
1/2 cup minced fresh parsley
2 lemons, cut into wedges

With small scissors, cut a slit along the rounded back portion of the shell of the shrimp. With the tip of a small knife, remove the vein along the slit, being careful not to pull the shell away from the shrimp. Rinse the shrimp well under running cold water, especially at the slit, place in a colander to drain, and pat dry with paper toweling. Set aside.

In a small saucepan, combine fish stock, saffron, and arrowroot. Heat over medium heat, stirring to dissolve saffron and arrowroot, until thickened. Lower heat to very low and keep warm.

Heat the oil in a large skillet over medium heat. Add onion and garlic and sauté 1 minute. Raise heat to high and add shrimp. Quickly sprinkle shrimp with salt and pepper and cook, tossing and turning the shrimp so they are coated with oil and turn pink on both sides. This should take about 1 minute. Add wine and boil, stirring almost constantly, 2 minutes, or until wine has almost evaporated. Add fish stock mixture and cook 1 minute.

Remove shrimp from heat and toss in parsley. Mound shrimp in a serving bowl and garnish with lemon wedges. Serve immediately with plenty of napkins and a receptacle for the shells.

POTTED SHRIMP ●

For variety, spread this delicate mixture on cucumber slices and garnish with an anchovy curl. The cucumbers will have to be salted, drained, and patted dry with paper toweling before topping. Arrange the topped slices on a garnished platter that has been covered with paper toweling and then an attractive doily.

Makes One Cup
1 pound medium-size shrimp, shelled and deveined
1 bay leaf, broken
6 tablespoons unsalted butter, at room temperature
2 tablespoons fresh lemon juice
1/2 teaspoon Beau Monde seasoning or curry powder
1/4 teaspoon freshly ground white pepper
Salt to taste
1 tablespoon finely minced fresh chives
Melba Toast rounds or baguette or buffet rye slices

Cook shrimp as for Shrimp on Ice, adding the bay leaf to the cooking water. Mince the drained shrimp very finely and set aside.

In a mixing bowl, combine butter, lemon juice, seasonings, and chives and stir with a fork until smooth and creamy. Stir in minced shrimp. Taste and adjust seasonings.

Pack shrimp mixture into a 1-cup crock, cover with plastic wrap, and refrigerate at least 2 hours, or for up to 3 days. Bring to room temperature before serving with melba toast.

SEVICHE ○

Just-caught fish is the secret to this refreshing appetizer in which lime or lemon juice "cooks" the seafood. For a zestier seviche, omit Tabasco sauce and add crumbled dried hot chili peppers or finely minced hot fresh chili peppers to taste.

Small oyster or clam shells are ideal "plates" and tiny forks can be used to "spear" and eat the portions. Serve with crusty french bread.

Approximately Forty Servings
1-1/2 pounds very fresh fish, such as tuna or sea bass
1 cup fresh lime or lemon juice
2 tablespoons finely minced green or red bell pepper
3 tablespoons finely minced onion
1/4 cup olive or safflower oil
1/2 teaspoon salt
1/4 teaspoon freshly ground black pepper
3 drops Tabasco sauce
1/4 cup minced fresh coriander
1/2 cup peeled, seeded, and Coriander sprigs

Place fish in a nonmetallic container, pour lime juice over, cover, and refrigerate 3 hours, tossing occasionally. With a fork, stir in bell pepper, onion, oil, salt, black pepper, Tabasco sauce, and minced coriander. Cover and refrigerate several hours until well chilled.

Adjust seasonings with salt, black pepper, and Tabasco sauce. Transfer seviche to an attractive crystal serving bowl and garnish with coriander sprigs.

SCALLOP SEVICHE ○

Sea scallops or bay scallops may be used for this version of seviche. Sea scallops should be sliced, bay scallops left whole.

Approximately Forty Servings
1-1/2 pounds scallops
1 cup lime or lemon juice
1/4 cup olive or safflower oil
1 large sweet red or white onion, very finely minced
1/2 to 1 teaspoon very finely minced garlic
1/4 cup finely minced green onion tops
1/4 cup finely chopped drained Roasted Peppers or pimiento
3 tablespoons minced fresh parsley

1/2 teaspoon granulated sugar
1 teaspoon crumbled dried red pepper
1/4 teaspoon salt
1/4 teaspoon freshly ground white pepper

PRESENTATION
Avocado balls rubbed with fresh lemon juice
Halved cherry tomatoes
Parsley leaves

Rinse scallops under cold running water, drain, and pat dry with paper toweling. Cut sea scallops into 3 or 4 slices. Place scallops in a nonmetallic container, pour lime juice and oil over, cover, and refrigerate at least 6 hours or overnight.

In a mixing bowl, combine onion, garlic, green onion tops, roasted peppers, parsley, sugar, dried pepper, salt, and white pepper. With a fork, toss with scallops and the lime juice and oil. Cover and refrigerate at least 3 hours. Taste and adjust seasonings with dried peppers, salt, and white pepper.

To serve, transfer seviche to a shallow crystal serving bowl. Arrange a ring of avocado balls and cherry tomatoes around the outside edge of the seviche and make a circle of parsley leaves in the center.

OYSTERS

Raw oysters on the half shell are always a treat. If you live in an area where oysters are harvested, the oyster company staff usually includes someone who can be hired to shuck them at your party.

If you are entertaining outdoors, there is nothing better than fresh oysters barbecued over charcoal. Guests can cook their own oysters, removing them to a plate after ten minutes (or when they have started to open). The shells can be easily pried apart and a small fork will pop the succulent meat out of the shells. Chili Sauce laced with Tabasco sauce and a squeeze of lemon is the perfect complement.

Barbecuing in this manner can be rather messy, though. You may prefer to open the osyters prior to your guests' arrival and top them with a mixture of minced fresh parsley, minced garlic, and freshly grated lemon peel. Grill the oysters over the charcoal when your guests are assembled. The oyster meats should be heated through and bubbly.

Baked oysters are also popular buffet fare, but their preparation is a bit more complex than that of raw or barbecued oysters. The toppings, however, can be prepared several hours ahead of party time, a boon to the busy host or hostess. A recipe for baked oysters with a choice of toppings follows.

TO SHUCK OYSTERS

You will need a stiff-bristled brush and an oyster knife, a special short broad-bladed tool with a horizontal "guard." Scrub the oyster shells well under running cold water with the brush. Working over a sieve set in a mixing bowl to catch the oyster liquor, cup the rounded side of the oyster in the palm of your hand, with the hinged end facing you (you may want to protect your hand with a heavy cloth). Position the hand holding the oyster over a bowl to catch any oyster liquor that may spill from the shell. Slip the oyster knife between the shells an inch or so from the hinge and twist the knife to pry the shells apart. Break off and discard the upper, or flat, shell. Slide the knife under the oyster to sever the muscle. Jar, cover, and refrigerate the oyster liquor. Place the oysters in a nonmetallic container, cover, and refrigerate.

BAKED OYSTERS ON THE HALF SHELL

Here are two toppings for baked oysters, the first one a version of the famous oysters Rockefeller and the second one a lovely sorrel and watercress blend. Regardless of which topping you decide to make, the oysters are arranged in rock salt and baked in the same way.

For two dozen oysters, you will need four eight-inch pie tins. Fill them with rock salt to make a layer about one-half inch thick. Fifteen minutes before you plan to bake the oysters, position the oven rack in the center of the oven. Place the tins on the rack and turn oven heat to 425° F. When the oven is heated and the oysters are readied, nestle them in the bed of rock salt and bake them eight minutes, or until they begin to curl at the edges and the topping is bubbly. Transfer the baking tins to a warming tray and serve immediately. Place two-pronged cocktail forks and a receptacle for the shells nearby.

Twenty-four Servings
2 dozen shucked oysters
  (preceding)
Rock salt
Oyster liquor, reserved from
  shucking the oysters

TOPPING I
(OYSTERS ROCKEFELLER)
1-1/2 pounds spinach, washed,
  drained, and patted dry with
  paper toweling
6 tablespoons butter
3 green onions, minced
1 shallot, minced
1 small celery rib, minced
1/3 cup minced Italian parsley
2 large garlic cloves, minced
1/4 teaspoon fennel seeds,
  crushed in a mortar and pestle
2 teaspoons fresh lemon juice
1/2 tablespoon anchovy paste
3 drops Tabasco sauce
1/4 teaspoon salt
1/4 teaspoon freshly ground
  white pepper
1/2 cup fine dry bread crumbs
1/4 cup reserved oyster liquor
1/4 cup freshly grated Parmesan
  cheese

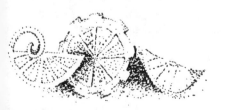

TOPPING II
1 recipe Cream Sauce
Oyster liquor
1/2 cup finely minced
  watercress leaves
1/4 cup finely minced sorrel
1/2 cup very finely minced
  cooked shrimp
1/4 cup minced fresh chives
1 teaspoon finely minced fresh
  tarragon or basil
1/4 teaspoon salt
1/4 teaspoon freshly ground
  white pepper
1/2 cup finely shredded
  Gruyère cheese
1/2 cup fine dry bread crumbs,
  tossed with 2 tablespoons
  melted butter
Paprika

To prepare topping I, chop
spinach finely and set aside. Melt
4 tablespoons of the butter in a
large nonstick skillet over medium
heat. Add green onions, shallot,
celery, parsley, and garlic. Cover
and cook 5 minutes. Add spinach
and fennel seeds and toss to coat
with butter. Cover skillet and
cook 3 minutes, or until spinach
is wilted.

Remove skillet from heat and
let cool briefly. Transfer spinach
mixture to a blender or food
processor, add lemon juice and
anchovy paste, and purée just
until ingredients are very finely
minced. Transfer mixture to a
mixing bowl and stir in Tabasco
sauce, salt, pepper, 1/4 cup of
the bread crumbs, and 2 tablespoons of the oyster liquor.
Taste and adjust seasonings.

Moisten each oyster in its
shell with remaining 2 tablespoons
oyster liquor. Spoon spinach
mixture over each oyster, dividing it equally among the oysters.
Melt remaining 2 tablespoons
butter and toss in remaining 1/4
cup bread crumbs and Parmesan
cheese. Sprinkle the bread crumb
mixture evenly over the topped
oysters and bake as directed in
introduction.

To prepare topping II, make
cream sauce, using any oyster
liquor in place of the stock
called for in the recipe. Stir in
watercress and sorrel and cook 2
minutes. Add shrimp, chives,
tarragon, salt, and pepper and
mix well. Taste and adjust seasonings.

Spoon cream sauce over each
oyster, dividing it equally among
the oysters. Sprinkle each oyster
with Gruyère cheese and then
with buttered bread crumbs.
Bake as directed in the introduction.

SQUID RINGS

Try steaming squid as described here, rather than boiling or sautéing them. I find that steamed squid are always perfectly tender. These rings can be marinated and served Italian style or tossed with a full-bodied green sauce as described in the following recipes, or they can be arranged on a garnished platter and served with Chili Sauce, Tomatillo Sauce, or Pesto on the side.

Being careful not to break the body's filmy skin (it turns a lovely purple when the squid are steamed), rinse each squid under running cold water. Pull the head with tentacles attached gently from the body, then pull the transparent piece of cartilege from the body. Insert your index finger into the body to pull out any entrails. Rinse the body again and place in a colander to drain. Lay the head on a cutting board and make a V-shaped slit between the eyes to cut the tentacles from the head. If a small round piece of cartilege is lodged in the base of the tentacles, pop it out by squeezing gently. Rinse the tentacles and add to the colander.

Pat the body and tentacles dry with paper toweling and cut the body into crosswise slices about 3/4 inch thick; leave the tentacles intact. Place the squid rings and tentacles in a single layer on a steamer rack placed over boiling water. Cover pot and steam 2 minutes. Check 1 ring; the squid should be just barely tender to the bite. Overcooking will toughen them, so immediately remove the squid from the steamer to stop the cooking.

Toss squid with olive oil to coat lightly, then sprinkle with a little fresh lemon juice. Let squid cool completely, cover, and refrigerate up to 4 hours. Bring to room temperature before serving.

MARINATED CALIMARI

No Italian buffet would be complete without calimari, or squid, steamed to perfection and marinated in a spicy olive oil and vinegar mixture, which must be made at least a day ahead. Provide cocktail picks for those who want just the calimari, and a slotted spoon for those who prefer their tidbit on a slice of crusty bread.

Approximately Fifty Servings
1-1/2 pounds squid

MARINADE
1/4 cup olive oil
2 tablespoons red wine vinegar
1 tablespoon fresh lemon juice
1 tablespoon freshly grated
   Parmesan cheese
1 tablespoon grated or finely
   minced onion
1 large garlic clove, finely minced
1/2 teaspoon salt
1 teaspoon minced fresh basil
1 teaspoon minced fresh oregano
1/2 teaspoon crumbled dried
   hot red chili pepper
1/4 teaspoon freshly ground
   black pepper
1 large ripe tomato, finely diced
   and well drained

PRESENTATION
Spinach leaves
Freshly grated lemon peel
Italian bread slices
Mediterranean-style olives

To make the marinade, combine oil, vinegar, lemon juice, cheese, onion, garlic, salt, basil, oregano, chili pepper, and black pepper in a jar. Shake well, taste, and adjust seasonings. Cover and refrigerate at least 1 day, or for up to 5 days.

Squid that are about 5 to 6 inches long are the best to use for this dish. There will be about 12 squid of this size in 1-1/2 pounds.

Clean and steam the squid as directed in Squid Rings, preceding, then transfer the squid to a non-metallic container.

Bring the marinade to room temperature and shake well. Add the tomato and toss to mix. Pour marinade over the squid and toss with a fork to coat each piece. Cover and refrigerate at least 3 hours, but no more than 5 hours.

To serve, line a shallow crystal serving dish with spinach leaves, allowing the leaves to stick slightly up beyond the rim of the bowl. Lift squid from marinade with a slotted spoon and mound it on the bed of spinach. Sprinkle with freshly grated lemon peel. Place a basket of Italian bread and a bowl of Mediterranean-style olives alongside.

STUFFED SQUID ROUNDS

These delicious morsels will become an instant topic of conversation, whether or not your guests relish squid. Mound the steamed tentacles in the center of a round serving plate and surround them with the stuffed squid. Tuck lemon twists and tiny parsley sprigs in and around the squid.

When you purchase the squid, be sure the bodies are six to seven inches long. There will be six or seven in each pound.

Twenty to Thirty Servings
1 pound squid
1/4 cup finely minced onion
2 large garlic cloves, very finely minced
1-1/2 tablespoons olive oil
3/4 teaspoon curry powder
1/4 teaspoon salt
1/4 teaspoon freshly ground black pepper
3/4 cup very finely chopped cooked broccoli
2 teaspoons chicken stock
2/3 cup fine dry bread crumbs
1/4 cup freshly grated Parmesan cheese
2 teaspoons fresh lemon juice
3 tablespoons minced fresh parsley
Lemon Twists
Parsley leaves

Clean squid as directed in Squid Rings and set tentacles aside. Cut fins from bodies (be careful not to cut too deeply so that you pierce the body) and mince; set bodies aside. In a covered nonstick skillet sauté fins, onion, and garlic in olive oil, sprinkling with curry powder, salt, and pepper, until onions are soft. Remove from heat.

In a blender or food processor, combine the broccoli and stock and purée until smooth. Transfer the purée to a mixing bowl and stir in bread crumbs, cheese, lemon juice, minced parsley, and onion mixture. Taste and adjust seasonings.

Pat squid bodies dry with paper toweling and stuff with the broccoli mixture, dividing filling evenly among the bodies and stuffing (pack gently) to within about 1/2 inch from end of opening.

Arrange stuffed squid at least 1 inch apart on a steamer rack over boiling water. Cover steamer, bring water back to a boil, and steam 2 minutes. Add tentacles to the rack and steam an additional 2 minutes. Immediately remove from heat and transfer bodies and tentacles to a wire rack to cool. Place on a plate, cover with plastic wrap, and refrigerate at least 3 hours, but no more than 5 hours.

To serve, arrange tentacles in the center of a large round serving plate. Cut stuffed squid crosswise into slices approximately 1/2 inch thick. Arrange the slices around the tentacles and garnish plate with lemon twists and parsley leaves. Guests may use their fingers or cocktail picks.

SQUID RINGS
IN GREEN SAUCE

Approximately Thirty Servings
1 pound squid
Lemon Twists or Cups
Finely minced fresh parsley

GREEN SAUCE
4 large garlic cloves
1/2 cup fresh parsley leaves
1/2 cup watercress leaves
1/4 cup chopped green onion
   tops
4 large basil leaves, chopped
2 tablespoons fine fresh bread
   crumbs
2 tablespoons freshly grated
   Parmesan cheese
1 hard-cooked egg yolk
2 teaspoons fresh lemon juice
1/4 teaspoon salt
1/4 teaspoon freshly ground
   white pepper
1 cup olive oil
Lemon Twists
Finely minced fresh parsley

To prepare the sauce, whirl the garlic, parsley leaves, watercress, green onion tops, and basil in a blender or food processor until finely minced. Add bread crumbs, cheese, egg yolk, lemon juice, salt, and pepper and blend until well mixed, scraping down sides of blender or processor bowl several times. With motor running, pour in olive oil in a slow, steady stream and whirl until all

oil is incorporated. Taste and adjust seasonings.

Squid that are about 5 to 6 inches long are the best to use for this dish. There will be about 8 squid of this size in a pound. Clean and steam the squid as directed in Squid Rings and transfer to a nonmetallic bowl. Pour green sauce over squid and toss with a fork to coat each piece.

Mound squid in a crystal serving bowl. Let stand in a cool place at least 30 minutes, or for up to 2 hours. Garnish with lemon twists and sprinkle with minced parsley. Serve with cocktail picks for spearing.

If not using the sauce immediately, jar, cover, and refrigerate for up to 2 days. Bring to room temperature before tossing with squid.

PICKLED SQUID ○

Prepare 1 recipe Pickling Liquid (see Pickled Vegetables), adding 2 teaspoons minced fresh oregano. Ready and steam squid as for Squid Rings, using the pickling liquid in place of water (do not steam in an aluminum saucepan). When squid are tender, remove them to a nonmetallic container

and pour the pickling liquid over them. Cool, cover, and refrigerate overnight.

To serve, remove squid rings with a slotted spoon to a shallow serving dish. Toss rings with 3 tablespoons finely minced parsley. Garnish with Lemon Twists.

STUFFED CLAMS OR MUSSELS
WITH TWO FILLINGS

These stuffed clams or mussels can be readied the morning of the party and then baked just before serving. (Save the cooking broth, for it is excellent as is, or can be reserved to use as fish stock or in clam chowder).

Bake stuffed shellfish in an attractive flameproof dish and serve them directly from it. The number of servings will vary, as any clams that do not open must be discarded.

Approximately Twenty-four Servings
2 dozen small clams or mussels
1/2 cup water
1/2 cup dry vermouth or
   white wine
1 small onion, chopped
3 large garlic cloves, chopped
6 parsley sprigs
3 thyme sprigs
4 black peppercorns, lightly
   crushed
Citrus Flowers made with lemons

FILLING I

1/3 cup minced onion
2 large garlic cloves, finely
  minced
1 tablespoon olive oil
1 tablespoon butter
3/4 cup cooked brown rice
1/2 cup finely chopped well-
  drained cooked spinach or
  swiss chard
1/4 cup finely chopped
  lightly toasted pine nuts
3 tablespoons minced fresh
  parsley
1 tablespoon minced fresh chives
1/2 teaspoon minced fresh thyme
1 teaspoon fresh lemon juice
1/4 teaspoon salt
1/4 teaspoon freshly ground
  white pepper
Reserved broth, if needed
1/2 cup freshly grated Parmesan
  cheese
Paprika

FILLING II

1/2 cup fine fresh bread crumbs
1/2 cup crumbled crisply cooked
  bacon
1/4 teaspoon freshly ground
  white pepper
1 to 2 tablespoons clam cooking
  broth, or as needed
Bell Pepper Butter

Soak clams or mussels in salted water (1 tablespoon salt for 1 quart water) for 1 to 2 hours. Scrub well with a wire brush, pulling the "beards" from the mussels. Discard any clams or mussels that are cracked or open. In a large saucepan, combine water, vermouth, onion, garlic, parsley and thyme sprigs, and peppercorns. Add clams, bring to a boil, and cook 6 to 8 minutes, or until clams open. Remove from heat and strain, reserving cooking broth.

Set clams aside, discarding any that have not opened. When cool enough to handle, lift clams from shells, mince finely, and set aside in a mixing bowl. Wash half the shells and set aside to dry; discard remaining shells.

Prepare one of the fillings. To make filling I, combine onion, garlic, oil, and butter in a covered nonstick skillet. Cook over medium heat 5 minutes, or until soft. Remove from heat and stir in minced clams, rice, spinach, pine nuts, minced parsley, chives, thyme, lemon juice, salt, and pepper. Taste and adjust seasonings. If mixture appears dry, stir in a little of the reserved broth.

To make filling II, combine bread crumbs, bacon, and minced clams in a mixing bowl and toss with a fork to mix well. Stir in white pepper and enough broth

to moisten. Taste and adjust seasonings.

Preheat oven to 400° F. Mound the clam mixture in the shells and place the filled shells in a shallow flameproof dish or pan (or dishes if you do not have a large enough one to hold all the clams). For filling I, sprinkle cheese evenly over the top and dust lightly with paprika. For filling II, top each filled shell with 1/2 teaspoon bell pepper butter. Bake stuffed clams in the preheated oven 5 minutes, or until the filling is bubbly.

Arrange the baked clams on a platter, if not serving directly from the cooking vessel. Garnish with citrus flowers. Set dish on a warming tray and place tiny forks and a receptacle for the shells nearby.

If making ahead, cover baking sheet of filled shells tightly with plastic wrap and refrigerate for up to 5 hours. Bring to room temperature before baking, or allow 3 or 4 minutes additional baking time if the clams are chilled.

SMOKED SALMON AND GRAVLAX O

A smoked salmon board is the epitome of luxury. The four common types—Scotch, Norwegian, Atlantic, and Pacific—of this highly prized fish, which is cured by salting and smoking, vary in flavor and texture according to whether the salmon is wild or commercial and how and where it was smoked.

Delicatessens ask a high price for all smoked salmon. If you have fresh salmon available, you may opt to make the unsmoked northern European variation called gravlax, or gravad lax. The salmon is treated with salt, sugar, dill, peppercorns, and sometimes brandy, vodka, or Aquavit. It is extraordinarily good and much less expensive than smoked salmon. The directions for preparing and serving gravlax appear here; smoked salmon should be presented in the same way.

Gravlax can be made with a fresh whole salmon or a pair of fillets. If purchasing the salmon whole, make sure it has been scaled and gutted. To fillet the fish, you will need a very sharp, thin, slightly flexible knife. Place the fish on several thicknesses of newspaper covered with brown paper. Starting at the tail end of the salmon, insert the tip of the knife into the flesh along the back ridge until you feel the backbone against the knife, then make a slit along the backbone to the head. Turn the cutting edge of the knife toward the tail, and keeping knife blade flat against the backbone, cut the fillet from the backbone, lifting it away from the bone as you cut. The fillet should come off in a single piece. Remove the backbone from the second fillet in the same manner, this time lifting the backbone from the bottom fillet as you cut. Cut off head and tail, fins, and any bony areas. Check the fillets carefully for stray bones and pull out any you find with tweezers.

Rinse fillets in cold running water and pat dry with paper toweling. Place one fillet skin side down on a platter slightly larger than the fillet. For a 4-pound salmon, combine 1/4 cup coarse salt (not iodized) and 2 to 4 tablespoons granulated sugar in a mixing bowl and stir well. Sprinkle the mixture over the surface of the fillet and cover completely with a layer of coarsely chopped fresh dill (dried will not do). Sprinkle lightly crushed white peppercorns over and cover with the second fillet, skin side up.

Cover fillets with plastic wrap and then aluminum foil, place a board or a heavy plate on top and weight down with unopened canned goods, a brick wrapped in aluminum foil, or other heavy objects. Refrigerate 48 hours, turning the sandwiched fillets over and basting the cut sides with the accumulated juices 3 or 4 times daily.

Other seasonings, such as minced onion, finely minced drained green peppercorns, and minced fresh thyme, chervil, and/or tarragon, may be strewn between the fillets the last 24 hours.

To serve the gravlax, scrape off the salt mixture, dill, and peppercorns and pat the fillets dry with paper toweling. Place fillets skin side down on an attractive wooden board or a serving platter and surround with lots of lemon wedges and parsley sprigs. Set bowls of unsalted butter, drained capers and/or green peppercorns, finely minced sweet red or white onion, and Mustard-Dill Sauce (following) on the table next to the board.

A smoked salmon platter is served in the same manner, but in place of the mustard sauce offer Avocado Cream Cheese Spread or cream cheese softened with Crème Fraîche and mixed with minced fresh dill.

With a very sharp knife, guests slice off thin (you hope) pieces of salmon, cutting them at a 45-degree angle away from the skin. The salmon can then be placed on a buttered or plain miniature split bagel or rye or pumpernickel bread round. One or more of the accompaniments can be arranged on top, and as a last gesture, guests add a squeeze of lemon juice.

A yield is difficult to determine, for some guests may eat nothing but the gravlax. Each fillet, how-ever, should provide approxi-mately 50 small slices.

To store any uneaten salmon, fold the skin left from the eaten portion over the remaining flesh, wrap in plastic wrap and aluminum foil, and refrigerate for up to 4 days, or freeze for up to 1 month. The texture of the fish after freezing will not be as firm, so you may want to use it only as an ingredient in dips or spreads.

MUSTARD-DILL SAUCE ●

The mustard sauce usually served with gravlax presented as an appetizer or main course is too thin to use as a topping for the salmon canapés fashioned above, so this sauce is a departure from the traditional one.

Makes Approximately
One and One-fourth Cups
1 egg
1 tablespoon fresh lemon juice
1 tablespoon white wine vinegar
1 tablespoon Dijon-style mustard
1-1/2 to 2 teaspoons dry mustard
1 to 2 teaspoons granulated sugar
1/2 teaspoon salt
1/4 teaspoon freshly ground
   white pepper
1 cup safflower oil
1/3 to 1/2 cup minced fresh dill

Place egg, lemon juice, vinegar, mustards, sugar, salt, and pepper in a blender or food processor. Whirl to mix well. With motor running, pour in oil in a slow, steady stream until it is all incorporated and sauce is smooth and glossy. Taste and adjust seasonings. Just before serving, stir in dill.

To store, transfer to a non-metallic container, cover, and refrigerate for up to 1 week.

SMOKED SALMON ROLL-UPS

Cut thin slices of smoked salmon or Gravlax thinly on the bias and spread with cream cheese softened with Crème Fraîche, sprinkle with minced fresh dill and parsley, drizzle a little fresh lemon juice over, and roll like a jelly roll. Arrange the rolls seam side down on a serving platter and garnish each roll with a tiny lemon peel or parsley leaf. Garnish the serving platter with parsley sprigs and lemon wedges and provide slices of pumpernickel or light rye for those who want to make their own canapé.

The thin slices are also delicious when wrapped around lightly blanched asparagus tips.

POACHED WHOLE SALMON ○

During salmon season, plan on making a poached whole salmon the centerpiece of the buffet table, especially if you are lucky enough to know a fisherman who will part with his catch.

It is important not to overcook the salmon; it should be firm and just to the point of flaking. To present the fish intact, easy removal from the poaching water is imperative. If you do not own a fish poacher with a removable rack, you must wrap the fish in cheesecloth so it can be lowered into and removed from the liquid easily. It is difficult, however, to check a wrapped fish for doneness. The method described in this recipe is an unorthodox one that makes checking unnecessary whether or not you have a fish poacher.

If the size of the fish precludes using an ordinary skillet, use a fish poacher or a roasting pan set on two burners. The fish should just fit inside the vessel and the lid of the vessel should be tightly fitting.

Cooling the poached fish in the poaching liquid improves the flavor, helps keep the flesh intact, and allows you to prepare the fish in advance. It should be thoroughly cooled before attempting to remove it from the pan.

Presentation of the poached salmon is important. Choose from the suggestions given or create your own. The salmon may be set out as is, coated with aspic (see To Prepare Aspic Jelly; use the poaching liquid for the liquid), or masked with Avocado Cream Cheese Spread, Crème Fraîche, or sour cream mixed with a little fresh lemon juice and minced fresh dill. In each case, decorate imaginatively and serve with slices of buffet rye, sourdough baguette, and/or black bread.

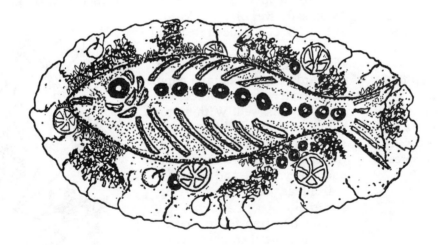

Approximately Sixty Servings
One 5- to 7-pound whole salmon,
   scaled and gutted
White wine
1 celery stalk and leaves, chopped
2 bay leaves
4 parsley sprigs
2 thyme sprigs
1 onion, sliced
1 lemon, sliced
4 allspice berries, lightly crushed
6 black peppercorns, lightly
   crushed
1 teaspoon salt

PRESENTATION
Parsley or watercress sprigs
Flowers such as chrysanthemums,
   daisies, or geraniums
Vegetable Cutouts or other
   garnitures
Lemon Twists and slices
Minced parsley
Hard-cooked eggs, yolks and
   whites sieved separately
Cooked artichoke hearts, halved
Cherry tomatoes, halved if large
Lettuce cups filled with Basic
   Mayonnaise or a variation
Ripe olives sliced crosswise or
   quartered lengthwise
Drained capers and/or green
   peppercorns
Black bread, buffet rye, and/or
   sourdough baguette

Rinse salmon under cold running water, drain well, and pat dry with paper toweling. To measure the amount of poaching liquid needed, place the fish in the cooking vessel and add water to cover. Remove the fish and pour the water into a large measuring cup. Pour off half the water and replace with dry white wine. Pour the water and wine into the cooking vessel and add celery and leaves, bay leaves, parsley, thyme, onion, lemon, allspice berries, peppercorns, and salt. Slowly bring to a boil and boil, uncovered, 5 minutes.

If not using a fish poacher, wrap fish in cheesecloth with folds on top so they can be grasped to remove the fish. Bring the liquid to a rolling boil, lower fish into it, cover, and let water come back to a boil. Lower heat slightly and boil *gently* 5 minutes, then remove the vessel from the heat and cool the fish in the liquid.

Remove the fish from the poaching liquid and place on a board or work surface. Reheat the poaching liquid, drain, jar, cool, and refrigerate for up to 2 days, or freeze for up to 3 weeks.

Unwrap the salmon and slowly peel off the skin and carefully pull the fins from the flesh with your fingers and a knife. Scrape out any fatty dark flesh along the center of the fish and gently turn the salmon over onto a large oval serving platter. Peel off the skin and cover tightly with plastic wrap. Refrigerate at least 3 hours or overnight.

To serve, stuff parsley sprigs in the mouth of the salmon and form a "collar" of small parsley sprigs on the fish just back of the gills. Surround the salmon with parsley sprigs, tucking the stems under the flesh, and decorate it artistically with flowers and/or vegetable cutouts and lemon twists. Sprinkle with minced parsley. Arrange a choice of presentation ingredients around the edge of the platter to accompany the salmon.

If masking the salmon, carefully and evenly cover the entire surface of the fish with one of the suggested mixtures and then decorate as above. Serve with black bread, buffet rye, and/or sourdough baguette.

PICKLED HERRING

Approximately Fifty Servings

4 or 5 Atlantic herring packed
  in brine (about 2 pounds)
2 large onions, chopped
2 lemons, thinly sliced
2 teaspoons black peppercorns
2 tablespoons mustard seeds
2 bay leaves
1/2 cup dill feathers
3 cups distilled white vinegar,
  or as needed

PRESENTATION
Wedges of hard-cooked egg
Cherry tomatoes, halved
Curry Mayonnaise, mixed with
  minced fresh dill to taste
Unsalted butter
Black bread rounds

If the heads are still attached to
the herring, remove and discard
them. Rinse the fish under running
cold water, cleaning the cavities
well. Place in a large nonmetallic
bowl, add cold water to cover,
and refrigerate overnight.

Remove the fish from the
water and place on a work
surface. With a small, sharp
knife, fillet the herring by running
the blade along the length of the
backbone on both sides of each
fish, cutting the flesh away from
body cavity. Trim fins from fillets,
but leave the skin intact. Cut
each fillet crosswise into 1/8-
inch-wide strips.

In a large crock or wide-
mouthed jar, layer one-third of
the herring. Top with one-third
of the onion, and then one-third
of the lemon slices. Repeat layers
twice, ending with lemon. Combine peppercorns, mustard seeds,
bay leaves, and dill in a cheesecloth bag and add to crock. Pour
in enough vinegar to submerge
layers completely. Cover and
refrigerate for 5 days, then remove
cheesecloth bag. The herring
will keep refrigerated for up to 2
months.

To serve, lift herring and
onion from vinegar with a slotted
spoon and arrange on a serving
platter. (Lift out and discard
lemon slices.) Garnish platter
with hard-cooked eggs and cherry
tomatoes. Set bowls of butter
and curry mayonnaise and a
basket of bread alongside; provide small forks and broad-bladed
knives. Guests spread the bread
with butter or mayonnaise and
then top it with the savory
herring and onion mixture.

COOKED SEAFOOD PLATTER

A lovely platter of seafood, artistically arranged, imaginatively garnished, and accompanied by small
bowls of dipping sauces, can be
the highlight of the buffet table.
Purchasing of these perishable
and expensive fish must be done
no more than a day in advance,
and the arranging must be done
only a few hours ahead of serving
time.

The following suggestions give
no yields. It is up to the host or
hostess to decide how much of
each fish to purchase, as the
amounts will depend upon what
other dishes are being offered.

Cooked crab claws and lobster
meat are available at fish markets.
Shrimp, squid, and sea scallops
should be cooked at home. To
prepare the shrimp, see Shrimp
on Ice, and to prepare the squid,
see Squid Rings. To prepare the
scallops, rinse them in running
cold water, drain well, and place
in a single layer on a steamer
rack set over boiling water.

Sprinkle with fresh lemon juice, cover pan, and steam 2 minutes (See Steaming). Immediately remove from the heat and plunge in ice water to prevent further cooking. Drain, pat dry with paper toweling, and place in a nonmetallic container. Pour fresh lemon juice over and sprinkle with minced fresh chives and parsley. Cover and refrigerate overnight, tossing with a fork occasionally to distribute the lemon juice and herbs evenly.

Shortly before serving, line a platter with young kale or young turnip greens or redleaf lettuce leaves. Arrange the crab claws and lobster around the edge of the platter, form a ring of shrimp inside the crab and lobster, and a ring of squid inside the shrimp ring. Mound the scallops in the center. Tuck small bowls of dipping sauces—any of the Basic Mayonnaise variations, Salmon Mayonnaise Sauce, Horseradish Sauce, and/or Chili Sauce—in among the shrimp. Garnish the platter with parsley or watercress sprigs and small wedges of lemon or lime.

Provide two-pronged wooden cocktail forks or large cocktail picks so guests can spear a morsel and dip it in the sauce of their choice.

POULTRY

CHOPPED CHICKEN LIVER ●

Makes Approximately Two Cups
1 pound chicken livers
Marsala to cover
1/2 cup finely minced onion
2 large garlic cloves, finely minced
3 tablespoons rendered chicken fat
1/2 teaspoon salt
1/4 teaspoon ground thyme
1/2 teaspoon freshly ground white pepper
2 teaspoons fresh lemon juice
2 teaspoons Cognac
3 to 4 tablespoons butter, at room temperature
Tiny lemon curl
Sourdough Melba Toast rounds

Trim any fat from chicken livers and discard. Cut each liver into 2 or 3 pieces and place in a nonmetallic container. Add Marsala, cover container, and refrigerate 3 hours, or overnight.

Drain livers and pat dry with paper toweling. In a large covered nonstick skillet, cook onion and garlic in rendered chicken fat over medium heat 3 minutes. Remove lid, raise heat slightly, and add livers to the skillet. Sprinkle with 1/4 teaspoon salt, thyme, and pepper and cook, stirring and turning often, 5 minutes, or until livers are lightly browned but still slightly pink in the center.

With a slotted spoon, remove livers to a chopping board. Reserve onion-garlic mixture and pan juices. Chop liver finely or coarsely, depending on preference, and transfer to a mixing bowl. Add onion-garlic mixture and juices from skillet, lemon juice, Cognac, and remaining 1/4 teaspoon salt; mix well. Gradually work in butter to make a spreadable mixture. Taste and adjust seasonings. Pack into a crock or bowl, garnish with a lemon curl, and serve with melba rounds.

Liver may be covered and refrigerated for up to 3 days. Bring to room temperature and stir well before garnishing and serving.

VARIATION Mix 1 hard-cooked egg, finely chopped, and/or 1 teaspoon dry mustard into the chopped liver after adding the butter.

CHOPPED CHICKEN LIVER AND MUSHROOMS ●

Makes Approximately
Two and One-fourth Cups
1 pound chicken livers
Dry vermouth to cover
1/4 cup finely minced onion
1/4 cup finely minced shallot
2 large garlic cloves, finely
    minced
3 tablespoons bacon drippings
    and/or butter
4 ounces mushrooms, very finely
    minced (do not mince in
    a blender or food processor)
1/4 teaspoon ground oregano
1/2 teaspoon freshly ground
    white pepper
Dash cayenne pepper
1/2 teaspoon salt
1-1/2 tablespoons dry vermouth
3 to 4 tablespoons butter,
    at room temperature
Parsley leaves
Light rye bread slices or
    rye Melba Toast rounds

Trim any fat from livers and discard. Cut each liver into 2 or 3 pieces and place in a nonmetallic container. Cover with dry vermouth, cover container, and refrigerate 3 hours, or overnight.

Drain livers and pat dry with paper toweling. In a large covered nonstick skillet, cook onion, shallot, and garlic in bacon drippings over medium heat 2 min-

utes. Remove lid and add mushrooms. Cook and stir 2 minutes, then push onion-mushroom mixture to edges of skillet, raise heat slightly, and add livers. Sprinkle with oregano, peppers, and 1/4 teaspoon of the salt. Cook, stirring and turning livers often, 5 minutes, or until livers are lightly browned but centers are still slightly pink.

With a slotted spoon, remove livers to a chopping board. Reserve onion-mushroom mixture and pan juices. Chop livers finely or coarsely, depending upon preference, and transfer to a mixing bowl. Add onion-mushroom mixture and juices, vermouth, and remaining 1/4 teaspoon salt. Taste and adjust seasonings. Pack into a crock or bowl, garnish with parsley leaves, and serve with rye bread or toast.

Liver may be covered and refrigerated for up to 3 days. Bring to room temperature and stir well before garnishing and serving.

VARIATION Mix 1 hard-cooked egg, finely chopped, and 3 tablespoons finely minced fresh parsley into the prepared chopped liver and mushroom mixture.

CHICKEN WINGS ●■

At parties, chicken wings disappear with surprising rapidity, so plan on at least two per guest. If the party is long, bring the wings out in several batches, with a rest in between. Freshly garnish each platter with tender kale, young turnip greens, or with parsley or watercress sprigs.

There are numerous marinades that can be used before either baking or barbecuing the wings. They can be readied in advance and sheet frozen, then defrosted and cooked. Once they are on the table your only concern is to refill the serving platter.

Many supermarket poultry departments sell what they call "drumettes," the first joints of chicken wings, all neatly aligned in packages. One pound contains approximately 12 small or 9 large drumettes. It is usually more economical, however, to buy whole chicken wings and disjoint them yourself, reserving the tips and second joints for soup stocks. There are 4 to 6 whole wings in 1 pound.

Once you have removed the tips and second joints, trim the loose, thick skin from the first joint and marinate the wings as directed below. Alternatively, tackle the time-consuming job of making "drumsticks," which look like mushrooms on a stick and are easier to eat. In this case, gather your friends around to help if you are preparing a large number of drumsticks, for the job is a tedious one.

With a sharp knife trim and scrape the meat away from the length of the bone, then pull the pieces of meat around the round end bone to form a knob. Tuck any floppy bits of meat into the mushroom-shaped mass of meat. Arrange the drumsticks in a shallow nonmetallic dish and marinate as directed in the following instructions.

If you plan to barbecue the chicken wings, refer to the poultry and game marinades in the Barbecue Cookery section. Place the wings in a nonmetallic container, pour marinade over (approximately 1/2 cup marinade for 2 pounds wings), and cover. Let stand, turning wings occasionally, 3 hours, or refrigerate overnight. Prepare a fresh batch of marinade, adding 1/4 cup corn oil if marinade recipe contains no oil. Barbecue the wings over hot coals 20 minutes, or until tender, basting frequently with the marinade.

For crumb-coated and baked chicken wings, marinate in Yakitori, Teriyaki, or any of the poultry and game marinades, allowing approximately 1/2 cup marinade for 2 pounds of drumettes or "drumsticks." Arrange the drumettes or drumsticks in a nonmetallic container, pour marinade over, cover, and let stand at room temperature, turning occasionally, 3 hours, or refrigerate overnight.

In a shallow dish, beat 1 egg with 1 tablespoon fresh lemon or lime juice, dry sherry, or sake. Mound Seasoned Bread Crumbs or equal amounts Seasoned Bread Crumbs and freshly grated Parmesan or Romano cheese (you will need approximately 3 cups) on a piece of waxed paper. One at a time, lift a drumette from the marinade and let excess marinade drip off. Dip the drumette in the egg mixture to coat all sides, then roll in bread crumbs to cover completely. Arrange the crumb-coated drumettes in a single layer on a wire rack to dry for at least 30 minutes.

The drumettes may be readied and refrigerated 1 day in advance, or they may be sheet frozen for up to 2 months. Defrost before proceeding.

Preheat oven to 350° F. Place drumettes in a buttered shallow baking pan and carefully drizzle melted butter over each drumette to moisten lightly. Bake in the preheated oven 30 minutes, or until tender. Transfer drumettes to a heated serving platter and garnish as desired. If serving a large number of drumettes, keep them warm on a warming tray. Provide plenty of napkins and a receptacle for the bones.

CHICKEN CHUTNEY BALLS ●

Approximately Two Dozen
1 cup firmly packed diced cooked chicken or turkey
1/3 to 1/2 cup drained chopped chutney, such as mango, plum, or fig
3/4 teaspoon curry powder
3/4 teaspoon salt
1/8 teaspoon freshly ground white pepper
1 teaspoon fresh lemon juice
Finely chopped almonds
Citrus Twists

In a blender or food processor, whirl the chicken just until finely ground into a fluffy consistency. Add chutney, curry powder, salt, pepper, and lemon juice. Blend until well mixed, taste, and adjust seasonings. Transfer to a mixing bowl, cover, and refrigerate 3 hours or until mixture is firm.

Form chicken mixture into small balls about 3/4 inch in diameter and roll each ball in chopped almonds, gently but firmly pressing to coat ball completely. Arrange on a serving plate, cover with plastic wrap, and refrigerate for at least 1 hour, or for up to 1 day. Garnish the plate with citrus twists and serve with cocktail picks.

ALMOND CHICKEN BALLS ●

The ingredients for these tasty spheres may be mixed two or three days in advance of serving. The mixture also makes an excellent filling for cherry tomatoes or other vegetables, or can be mixed with the sieved yolks of hard-cooked eggs to prepare stuffed eggs. If thinned with Crème Fraîche, sour cream, or heavy cream, the mixture becomes a spread or dip.

For variety and eye appeal, arrange the balls on the serving plate with an assortment of stuffed vegetables.

Makes Four Dozen
1-1/4 cups diced cooked chicken or turkey
4 ounces cream cheese, cut into 12 cubes and at room temperature
2/3 cup lightly toasted finely chopped almonds
1 teaspoon fresh lemon juice
1/2 to 1 teaspoon curry powder
1/4 teaspoon salt
1/4 teaspoon freshly ground white pepper
Finely grated dessicated (dried) coconut
Watercress leaves

In a blender or food processor, whirl the chicken just until finely ground into a fluffy consistency. Add cream cheese and whirl to mix well. Add almonds, lemon juice, curry powder, salt, and pepper. Blend until mixture is smooth. Taste and adjust seasonings. Transfer to a mixing bowl, cover, and refrigerate at least 3 hours, or until mixture is firm.

Form chicken mixture into small balls about 3/4 inch in diameter and roll each ball in coconut, gently but firmly pressing to coat ball completely. Arrange on a serving plate, cover with plastic wrap, and refrigerate at least 1 hour or for up to 1 day. Garnish the plate with watercress and serve with cocktail picks.

APRICOT CHICKEN ROLL SPIRALS ○ ■

Make these colorful spirals ahead and have on hand in the freezer for a quick canapé appetizer or for a large buffet. Select a firm-textured rye or dark bread and cut thin slices into rounds slightly larger than the spiral rounds. Spread bread rounds lightly with butter. Place a spiral on a round and garnish with a tiny parsley or watercress leaf.

The rolls may also be made with boned chicken thighs or with very thin slices of turkey breast meat (available in most

markets). The filling may be varied as well. Duxelle, Chicken Liver Pâté, or thin sticks of mozzarella or Monterey Jack cheese wrapped in prosciutto with a sprinkling of minced fresh sage and parsley are just a few of the choices. Allow three to four tablespoons filling or two or three sticks of prosciutto-wrapped cheese for each breast.

Approximately Thirty Servings
2 large chicken breasts, boned, skinned, and halved
1/3 cup fresh lemon or lime juice
6 tablespoons Crème Fraîche
1/4 cup finely chopped dried apricots (cut with kitchen shears)
1/4 to 1/2 teaspoon ground allspice
1/4 teaspoon freshly ground white pepper
1/4 teaspoon salt
2 tablespoons mild honey

Being careful not to tear the meat, gently pound the chicken breasts between waxed paper to flatten to about 1/8 inch. Place chicken in a nonmetallic shallow dish and pour lemon juice over. Let stand, turning several times, 3 to 4 hours.

Remove chicken breasts from container and pat dry with paper toweling. Place the breasts flat on a work surface and spread each with 1-1/2 tablespoons of the crème fraîche. Strew 1 tablespoon of the apricots over each breast and sprinkle with allspice, pepper, and salt. Drizzle honey evenly over filling. Starting at a long edge, roll each breast into a tight cylinder. Place roll on a piece of aluminum foil seam side down and wrap tightly, keeping the cylinder intact. Freeze until solid, or for up to 2 weeks. (The freezing keeps the rolls from coming apart.)

To cook, place frozen rolls directly on a rack over boiling water. Cover pot and steam 40 to 45 minutes (see Steaming). Remove rolls from pot and let cool on a wire rack. Refrigerate at least 2 hours, or for up to 2 days.

To serve, unwrap rolls and cut into 3/8-inch-thick slices. Place on bread rounds and serve as suggested in introduction.

SMOKED TURKEY APPETIZER TRAY

If you have access to a caterer's supply house, you will find smoked turkey at a more moderate price than you would buying it by the quarter pound at a delicatessen. It would be best to plan to serve the turkey at a large gathering and buy the entire smoked turkey breast, then slice it paper thin at home or ask your regular butcher to do it for you on his machine. The breast, approximately 7 pounds, is enough for 100 servings, at almost half the price of already-sliced turkey.

Arrange the turkey slices on a large platter in an overlapping pattern. Tuck the watercress sprigs in and around the slices, and arrange edible garnishes such as pine nuts, crumbled chèvre, chopped Pumate, and/or marinated artichoke hearts in individual red cabbage or lettuce "cups" around the rim of the turkey. Offer bowls of Shallot Mayonnaise and/or your favorite mustard and place a basket of whole-grain and/or soft rye bread alongside so guests can fashion their own sandwiches.

TURKEY SAUSAGES

Turkey link sausages with no preservatives and a spicy flavor are becoming more readily available in delicatessens and supermarkets. They may be stored in the freezer up to 2 weeks, so keep them on hand for a quick appetizer.

Brown the sausages on all sides in a little butter. Cut into quarters and serve with cocktail picks and Chili Sauce as a dip.

DUCK RILLETTES ○ ■

You will be deemed a gourmet chef if you produce this dish for your next party. Because the rillettes are very rich, guests need only help themselves to a small amount of this delicately flavored poultry mixture. Baguette slices are ideal for serving, as their mild flavor will not detract from the very special "topping."

There are two bonuses to making this recipe. The bones and some of the skin become the base for stock that can be used to make future sauces and soups, and the excess rendered duck fat can be used for sautéing and in pâtés.

Approximately Two Cups
One 4- to 4-1/2-pound duckling
Herb salt
Rendered duckling fat
4 cups water
3/4 teaspoon salt

BOUQUET GARNI
12 juniper berries, lightly
    crushed
10 black peppercorns, lightly
    crushed
3 rosemary sprigs
6 thyme sprigs

Rosemary sprigs
Baguette slices

Remove the liver, gizzard, and heart from the duckling's cavity and set aside. Rinse the duckling under running cold water and pat dry with paper toweling. Place the duckling on a cutting board and cut away the skin. Pull off and reserve the large pockets of fat that cling to the skin. Cut the skin into tiny strips to measure 1/2 cup and set aside. Put the remaining skin in a roasting pan. Cut the flesh from the bones and set aside. Add the bones to the roasting pan with the skin, sprinkle with herb salt, and bake in a 350° F oven until nicely browned, about 45 minutes.

While the bones and skin are browning, cut the reserved fat into 1/4-inch cubes or tiny strips and place in a heavy skillet. Render the fat over medium-low heat until the pieces have shrunk to almost nothing.

While the fat is rendering, slice the reserved duckling flesh, heart, and gizzard into 1/16-by-1/2-inch pieces; set aside. Chop the liver finely; set aside.

Strain all but 1/4 cup of the rendered fat into a jar and set aside. Return any bits of fat in the sieve to the skillet and place the skillet over medium-high heat. Add the reserved 1/2 cup skin, duckling meat, gizzard, and heart pieces. Brown the pieces, stirring often with a fork to scrape up all the little bits. Add the liver and brown briefly. The pieces should be evenly golden and crisp. Add 2 cups of the water, again scraping the bottom of the skillet to loosen the pieces. Stir in salt and add bouquet garni. Cover the skillet (if it does not have a tight-fitting lid, transfer the duckling mixture to a saucepan), bring to a boil, lower heat, and cook 4 hours. Stir often and check to make sure the water doesn't boil away. Add water as needed to keep mixture at a simmer.

When the bones and skin have browned, transfer them with tongs from the roasting pan to a kettle. Strain the fat in the pan into a jar and set aside. Scrape any bits on the bottom of the pan into the kettle. To prepare the stock, see Game Stock in Basics. If not preparing the stock immediately, refrigerate for up to 2 days, or freeze for up to 3 months.

When the duckling pieces have cooked 4 hours they should be very tender and have absorbed the flavor of the herbs. Uncover the skillet, discard bouquet garni, and raise heat slightly. Let almost all moisture cook away, leaving only a little fat, then mash the flesh with a potato masher until finely shredded. Taste and adjust seasonings.

Pack the rillettes into two 1-1/2-cup crocks and slowly pour reserved duckling fat (reheat if it has congealed) into the crock, letting it seep down through to the bottom and covering the rillettes completely. Cool, cover crocks with plastic wrap, and refrigerate at least overnight, or for up to 3 days.

To serve, place crock(s) on a serving plate and garnish the plate with rosemary sprigs. Arrange baguette slices around the crock.

Rillettes may be frozen for up to 1 month. Defrost in the refrigerator and bring to room temperature before serving. The fat will keep, covered and refrigerated, for up to 2 weeks, and may be frozen for up to 3 months.

MEATS

SIKOTAKA TIGHANITA
(Greek Fried Liver Bits)

This oregano-scented Greek specialty is adapted from a recipe in the popular *Greek Cooking for the Gods* by Eva Zane.

Approximately Twenty-five Servings
1 pound calves' liver, sliced
   3/4-inch thick
2 large garlic cloves, very finely
   minced
1-1/2 tablespoons very finely
   minced fresh oregano
1/2 teaspoon salt
1/4 teaspoon freshly ground
   black pepper
3 tablespoons olive oil,
   or as needed
3 tablespoons dry white wine
3 tablespoons fresh lemon juice
Finely minced fresh parsley
Baguette slices
Beef or chicken stock, if needed

Cut the liver into 1-inch cubes and toss with garlic, oregano, salt, and pepper. In a large heavy skillet, heat the olive oil over medium-high heat. Add the liver mixture and quickly brown the cubes on all sides, stirring with a fork and adding additional oil if needed to prevent liver cubes from sticking. Add wine and lemon juice and scrape up any browned bits that have adhered to the pan.

Transfer liver cubes to a chafing or equivalent dish. Let stand, covered, 5 minutes, then sprinkle generously with parsley. Serve with cocktail picks and baguette slices.

If the liver cubes begin to dry out in the chafing dish, add a little beef stock to the dish to moisten them.

MIDDLE EAST
BEEF BALLS ●■

The spicy-sweet flavor of these meatballs is pronounced, especially when they are offered just slightly warmer than room temperature. Serve plain or with Yoghurt Sauce prepared without mint.

Approximately Fifty Meatballs
1 egg
2 tablespoons cold water
1 cup fine dry bread crumbs,
   or as needed
1 teaspoon salt
1/2 teaspoon ground cumin
1/2 teaspoon freshly grated
   nutmeg
1/2 teaspoon freshly ground
   black pepper
1/4 teaspoon ground cinnamon
1 cup very finely minced onion
1 pound ground lean beef
Coriander sprigs

In a large mixing bowl, beat egg and water together lightly with a fork or whisk. Stir in 1/2 cup of the bread crumbs, salt, cumin, nutmeg, pepper, cinnamon, and onion. Mix well and with fingers blend in meat. Pinch off a small portion and sauté until cooked through. Taste and adjust seasonings.

Oil a shallow baking pan with Lecithin Oil. Mound remaining bread crumbs on a piece of waxed paper. Form meat mixture into balls about 1 inch in diameter and gently roll in bread crumbs to coat lightly and evenly. At this point meatballs may be sheet frozen for up to 2 months. Defrost before proceeding.

Preheat oven to 375° F. Arrange meatballs, 1 inch apart, on prepared baking sheet. Place in the preheated oven and bake 15 minutes, or until cooked through and barely browned.

To serve, transfer meatballs to a serving platter and let cool slightly. Garnish the platter with coriander sprigs. Provide cocktail picks with which to spear the meatballs.

PORK RILLETTES ●■

Though the procedure for making this French standard is time-consuming, it isn't very difficult, and the rich, delicious result is worth the time spent in the kitchen. Then, too, a small portion spread on fresh bread goes a long way.

Set crocks of rillettes on round serving plates and garnish with coriander or parsley sprigs.

Makes Approximately Three Cups
1-1/2 pounds lean pork butt
1/4 cup rendered pork fat
3/4 pound fresh pork fatback, thinly sliced and cut into small pieces (see General Instructions for Terrines)
3 cups water
1/2 tablespoon salt

BOUQUET GARNI
2 large bay leaves
1/2 onion
6 garlic cloves
6 whole cloves
6 sage leaves
3 thyme sprigs
2 rosemary sprigs
6 Italian parsley sprigs
10 black peppercorns, lightly crushed

Sourdough french bread slices

Shred pork into very tiny pieces and, in small batches, pound in a mortar and pestle until pork is very finely shredded. In a heavy, large-bottom skillet, brown pork well in rendered fat, stirring and scraping bottom of skillet often. Pieces should be golden and crisp.

Add fatback, water, and salt to skillet and stir well to loosen meat from bottom of skillet. Add bouquet garni, cover, bring to gentle boil, lower heat, and simmer slowly 5 hours. Stir occasionally and add more water if meat starts to dry out. Fat will be melted in that time and pork will be very tender and will have absorbed the flavor of the herbs.

Discard bouquet garni and pour meat and fat into a strainer set over a bowl. Pack the meat into two 2-cup crocks and pour enough of the reserved fat over each to cover meat with a 1/4-inch layer of fat. Cool, cover, and refrigerate at least 3 hours. Bring to room temperature and serve with french bread slices.

Rillettes may be made 2 or 3 days in advance or they may be frozen up to 1 month. Defrost in the refrigerator. Jar and chill any juices from the strained meat. When the fat has congealed, discard it and add the juices to soup stock.

BACON ROLL-UPS ●■

These rolls are variations on the hors d'oeuvre called rumaki in which bacon is wrapped around chicken livers and broiled. They can be made 1 day in advance or sheet frozen up to 1 month. Make a variety to keep on hand. Defrost before broiling.

Allow 1/2 piece of thinly sliced bacon for each roll-up. Partially cook bacon in a microwave oven or skillet until limp. Cool, wrap around any of the following suggestions, and secure with a toothpick. Just before serving, broil about 4 inches from source of heat until bacon is crisp, unless otherwise indicated.

● Chicken liver and/or water chestnut, marinated in Teriyaki Marinade, if desired.
● Chicken liver and a small piece of bell pepper or sweet gherkin.
● Pitted prune stuffed with a pecan half.
● Pitted date stuffed with a cube of Monterey Jack cheese.
● Pitted date marinated in brandy or sherry and stuffed with a piece of water chestnut.
● Lightly cooked shrimp sprinkled with ground ginger and black or cayenne pepper.

- Cooked sweetbread piece (see Basics) marinated in fresh lemon juice.
- Pitted ripe olive stuffed with a piece of sharp Cheddar cheese.
- Anchovy- or pecan-stuffed olive marinated in dry vermouth.
- Small raw mushroom cap sprinkled with fresh lemon juice and ground oregano.
- Fresh figs, or pineapple or apple chunks.
- Raw Olympia oyster, drained and patted dry, sprinkled with a little Tabasco sauce.
- Cube of cooked veal and Gruyère cheese.
- Dip raw oysters in melted butter and coat with Seasoned Bread Crumbs with or without freshly grated Parmesan cheese.

STEAK TARTARE

Simplicity is the key to the perfect steak tartare. Use fat- and sinew-free top or bottom round, which has more flavor than sirloin. The meat must be freshly ground, so it is best to grind it yourself in a meat grinder or food processor.

If guests prefer to mask the "pure" taste of raw beef, let them help themselves to the assortment of condiments you have provided. To complement the flavor, serve with rye or pumpernickel bread.

If you prefer a more highly seasoned preparation, add Worcestershire sauce, Dijon-style mustard, anchovy paste, or minced shallots. Be careful, however, not to overmix the meat or it will become mushy and unappealing. It should look fresh and appetizing. Mix the morning of the day you plan to serve it.

For more ideas on serving steak tartare, see below, or see Pastry Balls.

Forty to Fifty Servings
1 unbeaten egg white
1/3 cup grated onion
1 to 2 teaspoons grated garlic
1 teaspoon salt, or to taste
1/4 teaspoon freshly ground
    black pepper
1 pound completely fat-free
    round steak, freshly ground

PRESENTATION
1 thin onion ring
1 raw egg yolk
Minced fresh parsley and chives
Hard-cooked eggs, whites and
    yolks sieved separately
Green onions, whites and tops
    minced separately
Cross-cut slices of pimiento-
    stuffed olives
Sliced ripe olives

Minced gherkins
Cornichons
Chopped toasted walnuts
Drained capers
Drained green peppercorns
Finely chopped anchovy fillets
Lumpfish caviar and finely
    minced onion
Rye or pumpernickel slices

In a large bowl, lightly beat egg white with a fork. Stir in onion, garlic, salt, and pepper. With hands, mix in meat just until well blended; handle as little as possible. Taste and adjust seasonings, cover, and refrigerate 2 hours or up to 6 hours.

To serve, mound meat mixture on a serving platter and form into a mound with a flat top. Press down in center of top to make a hollow, place onion ring around hollow, and place the egg yolk in center of onion ring. Choose 5 or 6 of the presentation suggestions and decorate the meat and the serving platter with them. Place a basket of rye and/or pumpernickel alongside.

STEAK TARTARE BALLS

Steak tartare may also be formed into small balls, no larger than 3/4 inch in diameter. Arrange them attractively on a serving plate, garnish the plate with parsley sprigs, and put a small cocktail pick into each ball.

STEAK TARTARE GRILLED SANDWICHES ■

Popular as steak tartare is, if you are offering a host of other delectable dishes, you may have some left over.

Thinly slice sourdough french bread and spread 1 piece with a generous portion of the meat mixture. Cover with another slice of bread and lightly butter both outer sides of sandwich. Broil until toasted, then turn and toast other side. The meat should still be a little raw inside. These may also be sheet frozen before broiling for up to 2 months. Broil while still frozen and the meat will be almost raw, as it was at the start.

KIBBEH ●

A Middle Eastern *mezze* table will always include *kibbeh* (or *kibbi, kobba,* or *kubba*), a bulghur and ground lamb mixture that is served cooked or raw, the latter the Mideast version of steak tartare. Traditionally, the bulghur is pounded by hand to soften it, then pounded with the lamb to a doughlike consistency. Soaking the fine bulghur before kneading it into the raw ground lamb, however, makes a good facsimile and is far easier on the cook.

Approximately Fifty Servings
1 cup very fine bulghur wheat
1 pound lamb cut from leg of
lamb, trimmed of all fat
1 teaspoon salt
1/4 teaspoon ground allspice
1/8 teaspoon freshly ground
black pepper
1/8 teaspoon cayenne pepper

PRESENTATION
2 tablespoons olive oil
1 cup very finely minced onion
Pita (pocket) bread, warmed and
torn into pieces
Pistachio or pine nuts

Soak bulghur in cold water to cover 15 minutes. Drain through several layers of cheesecloth and squeeze dry.

Using the finest blade of a meat grinder, grind lamb 3 times. Combine bulghur, lamb, salt, allspice, and peppers in a mixing bowl. With fingers, work ingredients together, kneading the mixture until it is smooth. Taste and adjust seasonings. Form the meat mixture into a ball, wrap in waxed paper or plastic wrap, and refrigerate at least 3 hours or overnight.

To serve, form lamb mixture into a large patty about 2 inches thick and place in the center of a good-sized round serving plate. Make a hollow in the center of the patty large enough to hold the oil and pour in the oil.

Arrange the minced onion on the platter around the edges of the patty. Encircle the patty and ring of minced onion with pita bread. Serve bowls of pistachio or pine nuts on the side for guests to help themselves.

ROAST BEEF ROLLS

Slice rare roast beef paper thin and spread with softened Mustard Butter made with Dijon-style mustard. Place a lightly blanched asparagus tip or a watercress sprig across one corner. Roll meat around asparagus to form a cylinder and arrange seam side down on a serving plate. Cover with plastic wrap and refrigerate at least 1 hour, or up to 3 hours. Garnish the plate with watercress sprigs.

Alternatively, bring any of the Potted Cheeses or Blue Cheeses to room temperature and spread on the thin roast beef slices. Roll into a cylinder and place seam side down on a serving plate. Cover with plastic wrap and refrigerate at least 30 minutes, or up to 1 hour. Garnish the plate with parsley sprigs.

RAW BEEF ROLLS

Slice fat-free raw top sirloin or tenderloin very thinly on the bias. Place slices between sheets of waxed paper and pound lightly to make them paper thin. Spread each slice with room-temperature Mustard Butter and sprinkle with very finely minced green onion and tops. Roll into a cylinder and arrange seam side down on a serving plate. Cover with plastic wrap and refrigerate at least 2 hours, or for up to 6 hours. Garnish the platter with parsley sprigs.

HAM ROLLS

Slice baked ham paper thin. Spread with a mixture of equal amounts cream cheese and chèvre, at room temperature. Sprinkle liberally with minced fresh chives and parsley and roll into a cylinder. At this point the rolls may be refrigerated for up to 3 hours before proceeding. Place seam side down on a finger of black or rye bread spread lightly with unsalted butter. (The bread finger should be slightly larger than the ham roll.)

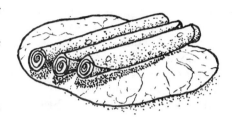

RAW BEEF PLATTER

An aspic coating made with Consommé or Madeira Aspic Jelly would make this presentation a truly stunning one.

Slice fat-free raw top sirloin or tenderloin very thinly on the bias. Place in a nonmetallic dish and moisten with Oregano Marinade in the proportion of 1/2 cup marinade to each pound of meat. Cover dish and refrigerate at least 2 hours, or for up to 4 hours.

To serve, pat each beef slice dry with paper toweling and arrange in an overlapping pattern on a serving platter. Garnish platter attractively with pickled onions (see Pickled Vegetables), cornichons, and capers. Serve with a selection of prepared mustards and sliced pumpernickel.

ROASTED OR BOILED MEAT PLATTERS

Attractively garnished platters of thinly sliced roasted or boiled meats or poultry not only serve as hearty fare for the hungry guest, but also allow the host or hostess to relax once the initial preparations have been made.

Offer a variety of breads, such as miniature Parker House rolls, small croissants, or crusty fresh baguettes, with these platters. Cut bread slices slightly larger than those usually served with spreads and pâtés. Guests spread breads or rolls with prepared horseradish or Horseradish Sauce, mustard, seasoned butter, or other sauce, and then make their own "sandwiches."

Following are a number of platter ideas with approximate yields and garnishing suggestions. Use your imagination and elaborate on what is presented here.

Tongue should be boiled one day in advance and beef should be roasted in plenty of time for it to be chilled to facilitate slicing. Ham and corned beef may be served on the same day they are baked, but the corned beef must be marinated thirty-six hours in advance.

ROAST BEEF PLATTER

Present a lovely platter of top round, sirloin, or filet mignon, roasted until done to your taste and then cooled, chilled, and sliced paper thin. Arrange the slices in an overlapping pattern on a large platter and surround them with a generous garnish of broken chicory or mustard greens. Grind black pepper over and tuck Cold Stuffed Mushrooms around the meat. Place bowls of Horseradish Sauce and an assortment of mustards alongside. Serve with Parker House rolls or black bread.

A 12-pound piece of meat will yield approximately 100 slices.

HAM A L'ORANGE

Score the top surface of a 10- to 12-pound bone-in ham to form diamond shapes and bake in a preheated 350° F oven for 15 minutes. Remove from oven and pack a 1/4-inch layer of brown sugar on top of ham. Place a whole clove in the center of each diamond and top ham with orange slices. Return to the oven for 10 minutes.

Melt 4 tablespoons butter and add one 6-ounce can concentrated frozen orange juice, thawed and undiluted, and 1 cup ginger ale. Mix well and baste ham with this mixture. Return the ham to the preheated oven and bake 2 to 3 hours, basting with orange juice mixture every 15 to 20 minutes (consult your butcher or the directions on the ham for exact time; the manner in which the ham has been cured will determine its cooking time).

Remove the ham from oven and transfer to a serving platter. Let stand 15 minutes before carving. Ham may be brought to the table for guests to cut their own slices, or may be sliced and the slices arranged on a platter. Whichever way you decide to serve the ham, garnish with appropriate garnitures such as poached pear halves, sliced pineapple, dried figs or prunes, and/or curly endive or parsley sprigs. Serve with an assortment of rye and black breads and/or tiny halved cornmeal muffins.

A 10- to 12-pound ham will yield approximately 100 slices.

CORNED BEEF PLATTER O

Plan ahead if serving this meat platter, for the corned beef must be marinated several days before baking. Purchase a 3-1/2-pound center-cut corned beef brisket.

Place the brisket in a nonmetallic container and cover with cold water. Strew 2 tablespoons pickling spices over the brisket and top with 2 lemons, sliced. Cover container with plastic wrap and refrigerate the meat for 36 hours, turning it over several times during this period.

Drain the meat and discard water, spices, and lemon slices Pat the brisket dry with paper toweling and place fat side up on a rack in a shallow baking pan. Spread a generous amount of Dijon-style mustard over the meat (or combine 2 parts French's mustard and 1 part prepared horseradish and spread on the meat). Bake the brisket in a preheated 350° F oven 1-1/2 to 2 hours, or until fork tender.

Remove corned beef from the oven and let stand at least 20 minutes before slicing. Thinly slice the meat and arrange slices overlapping on a serving platter. Garnish the rim of the platter with parsley sprigs and tuck Lemon Twists in and around the meat slices. Serve with bowls of assorted mustards, Horseradish Sauce, and cornichons. Place a basket of whole-grain, rye, and black bread slices alongside.

A 3-1/2-pound corned beef will yield approximately 50 paper-thin slices.

TONGUE PLATTER

Fresh beef tongue, usually 3-1/2 to 4 pounds, and smoked tongue, weighing 4 to 5 pounds, are equally good. Plan ahead for serving either one, for they both should be cooled in their cooking liquid and then refrigerated overnight before serving.

Smoked tongue must be covered with water and refrigerated 24 hours before cooking. Add several lemon slices, 2 or 3 crushed juniper berries, and a bay leaf to the soaking water. Just before you are ready to cook the tongue, drain off and discard the water.

Place fresh or smoked tongue in a dutch oven or heavy saucepan just large enough to hold it. Pour chicken or pork stock over meat to cover barely. Add 2 or 3 leeks, chopped; 1 parsley root, chopped (optional); 1 onion studded with 2 or 3 whole cloves; 2 celery ribs and leaves, chopped; 3 parsley sprigs; 4 thyme sprigs; 10 black peppercorns and 6 juniper berries, lightly crushed; and 1 lemon, sliced. Cover dutch oven, bring stock to a gentle boil, lower heat, and simmer 3 hours, or until meat is tender.

Remove the tongue from the broth and let stand just until cool enough to handle. Peel off skin and cut out any visible fat and gristle. Taste the broth and adjust seasonings with salt, then return tongue to pan. Let tongue and broth cool completely, then cover and refrigerate overnight. Remove tongue from broth and pat dry with paper toweling. Reheat broth, strain, jar, cool, cover, and refrigerate to use as stock or for a soup.

To serve, thinly slice the tongue and arrange slices overlapping on a serving platter. Garnish the rim of the platter with young kale leaves and tuck tiny steamed or boiled new potatoes (unpeeled) and tiny raw cauliflower florets in the bed of kale.

A 4- to 5-pound tongue will yield approximately 50 slices.

BRATWURST CUPS

Slice bratwurst 1/8-inch thick and sauté slices in butter over medium heat until browned. The slice will curl up to form a cup, which then can be quickly filled with Chili Sauce, chutney, or mustard.

The only way for guests to eat these hors d'oeuvres is to pick them up with their fingers! Offer napkins to make transport easier.

BEEF MARROW ROUNDS

Ask your butcher to cut beef marrow bones into 2-inch lengths. Rinse the bones, place in a saucepan, cover with cold water, and bring to a boil. Boil 1 minute, then drain, rinse bones and saucepan, and return bones to saucepan. Add rich beef stock to cover, 1 or 2 bay leaves, and several black peppercorns, lightly crushed. Cover saucepan, bring stock to a boil, lower heat, and simmer 10 to 15 minutes, or until marrow just starts to pull away from the sides of the bone.

Drain bones, reserving stock for another use, and let bones cool briefly. With a small spoon, scoop marrow from bones onto a plate or cutting board. Mash lightly with a fork and spread on freshly made toast rounds. Arrange marrow-topped toast on a platter, garnish platter with watercress sprigs, and serve immediately.

Alternatively, spread on toast, arrange on a baking sheet, and cover with plastic wrap. Marrow rounds will stay fresh several hours. When ready to serve, uncover and heat until bubbly in a preheated 400° F oven. Transfer to a serving platter and garnish with watercress sprigs.

BARBECUE COOKERY

Cooking skewered morsels on a charcoal grill well removed from the hors d'oeuvre table has two advantages: it helps to disperse the crowd that inevitably forms around the main buffet table and it lightens the pressure on the kitchen. An assistant chef should take charge; he or she may find the job easy if eager guests enter into the fun of barbecuing their own servings.

Purchase 6- to 7-inch bamboo skewers and soak them in water several hours. Cut the foods to be skewered into bite-size pieces (3/4-inch squares, or thin strips about 2 inches long) and thread 2 or 3 squares or weave 1 strip on each skewer. Arrange the skewers on a serving platter and decorate the platter with an appropriate garnish.

Place the platter alongside the grill so the chef or guests have easy access, and provide a fresh platter for those kebabs that are ready but have not yet been snatched from the grill. Have a stack of paper napkins handy, as well as a receptacle for the used skewers.

Shellfish, firm fish, meats (and their innards), and poultry and game (including livers and hearts) are delicious barbecued if properly marinated, frequently basted, and not overcooked. Five inches, at least, is required between glowing coals and skewered foods, and the skewers must be constantly turned. Arrange skewers around the periphery of the grill for easy manipulation and retrieval.

Herbs impart special flavors to barbecued meats. Skewer the leaves between the chunks of meat for kebabs—sage with pork, rosemary with lamb, thyme with beef, bay leaf and lemon slices with fish. Use complementary herb sprigs as the basting brush, and baste frequently.

It is not difficult to judge the doneness of small chunks of meat on a skewer, for usually they are cooked when nicely browned. In the case of shellfish and fish, the morsels should be just opaque. Overcooking any food will dry it out and toughen it. Watch the foods carefully, and remove them from the grill while they are still juicy.

When barbecuing a whole flank or skirt steak to be thinly sliced and served with rolls or croissants, barbecue it over a very hot fire and allow only a few minutes cooking on each side; judge by slicing off a small bit to see how rare it is. A butterflied leg of lamb will take considerably longer over a medium-hot fire.

Vegetables and/or fruits may be skewered with meats or seafood. Good combinations include sea scallops and button mushrooms, shrimp and cherry tomatoes, lamb and blanched wedges of green or red bell pepper, beef and blanched pearl onions, ham and blanched wedges of green bell pepper and cubes of fresh pineapple, turkey and small pitted black olives, and chicken and orange sections. You can also barbecue Bacon Roll-ups (see Meats), Stuffed Mushrooms with Blue Cheese Filling (see Vegetables), or water chestnuts wrapped in very thin slices of beef.

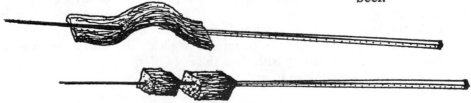

The marinades that follow are sufficient for 1 pound of meat, fish, or poultry, which will yield approximately 50 half-inch pieces or 30 3/4-inch pieces. For fullest flavor, always freshly grind the pepper called for in the recipe. The marinating may be done in a plastic bag or a *nonmetallic* container, at room temperature for short periods, under refrigeration if held overnight. Make sure all the pieces of meat are evenly coated with the marinade.

Do not reuse any marinade in which food has been marinating for more than 2 or 3 hours, for juices from the meat may have "contaminated" it with bacteria. Marinade that is used for a shorter time can be strained and refrigerated for no more than 2 days. Before using, bring to a boil and simmer for 5 minutes. Cool and use on the same type of meat it was used on previously.

Unless otherwise specified, baste grilling meat frequently with marinade, strained if desired. If the marinade contains no oil, add 2 to 4 tablespoons safflower, peanut, or olive oil when basting.

MARINATING TIMES

Fish and shellfish: 30 to 40 minutes.
Ham: 1 to 2 hours.
Cut-up poultry and game birds: 1 to 3 hours.
Meats and game meats (and their innards): 2 to 4 hours.
Large pieces of meat such as flank or skirt steak and butterflied leg of lamb: 4 to 6 hours, or overnight.

MARINADES FOR SEAFOOD

LEMON-GARLIC MARINADE Combine 1/4 cup *each* olive oil and fresh lemon juice; 1 or 2 garlic cloves, finely minced or pressed; 1/4 teaspoon *each* salt and white pepper; and 1 sprig *each* thyme and rosemary, or 2 sprigs *each* parsley and oregano or tarragon.

WHITE WINE MARINADE Combine 1/4 cup *each* olive oil and dry white wine; 1 or 2 shallots, finely minced; 1 teaspoon Worcestershire sauce; 2 tablespoons minced fresh parsley; 1 teaspoon minced fresh thyme; and 1/4 teaspoon white pepper. After using, strain the marinade and heat with 2 tablespoons butter until butter is melted. Use for basting. This is especially good with shrimp.

MARINADES FOR LAMB, BEEF, AND THEIR INNARDS

DILL MARINADE Combine 1/3 cup olive oil, 2 tablespoons fresh lemon juice, 1/2 teaspoon salt, 1/4 teaspoon black pepper, 2 garlic cloves, halved, and 3 to 4 tablespoons minced fresh dill.

MINT MARINADE Combine 1/4 cup *each* olive oil and fresh lemon juice, 1/2 teaspoon salt, 1/4 teaspoon black pepper, 2 large garlic cloves, finely minced, and 1/3 cup minced fresh mint.

OREGANO MARINADE Combine 1/4 cup *each* olive oil and fresh lemon juice, 1/2 teaspoon salt, 1 tablespoon minced fresh oregano, and 1/4 teaspoon black pepper.

RED WINE VINEGAR MARINADE Combine 1/3 cup olive oil, 2 tablespoons red wine vinegar, 4 slices onion, 1 garlic clove, sliced, 1/2 teaspoon salt, 1/4 teaspoon *each* black pepper and paprika, 2 thyme sprigs, and 8 mint sprigs.

TOMATO MARINADE Combine 1 cup chopped peeled ripe tomatoes; 1/4 cup grated onion; 1 bay leaf, crumbled; 1/4 teaspoon *each* black pepper, crumbled dried oregano, and granulated sugar; 3 tablespoons minced fresh parsley; and 1/4 teaspoon ground cinnamon (optional). Baste with olive oil.

YOGHURT MARINADE Combine 1/2 cup plain yoghurt; 3 tablespoons minced onion; 1/2 teaspoon salt; 1/4 teaspoon *each* crumbled dried hot red chili pepper, ground cumin, and confectioner's sugar; and 1/8 teaspoon *each* ground cardamom, black pepper, ground cinnamon, and powdered cloves. This marinade is also good with chicken.

MARINADE FOR GAME

RED WINE MARINADE Combine 1/2 cup red wine; 1 tablespoon fresh lemon juice or wine vinegar; 2 tablespoons minced onion; 1 tablespoon minced carrot; 1 bay leaf, crumbled; 2 parsley sprigs; 2 thyme sprigs; 2 whole cloves; and 4 peppercorns, lightly crushed.

MARINADES FOR POULTRY AND GAME BIRDS

CHILI-LEMON MARINADE Combine 1/3 cup fresh lemon juice, 3 tablespoons safflower or olive oil, 1/2 teaspoon salt, and 1/2 to 1 teaspoon chili powder.

CORIANDER MARINADE Combine 1/2 cup olive oil, 1 teaspoon salt, 1/4 teaspoon black pepper, 1/2 teaspoon Worcestershire sauce, 1 teaspoon minced garlic, and 1/3 cup finely chopped fresh coriander.

MARINADES FOR PORK

BOURBON MARINADE Combine 1/3 cup bourbon; 2 tablespoons honey; 2 tablespoons minced onion; and 2 garlic cloves, minced. Strain and add 1/4 cup peanut oil for basting.

CHILI PEPPER MARINADE Combine 1/4 cup *each* soy sauce, peanut oil, and chopped green onion and tops; 2 large garlic cloves, minced; 2 slices ginger root, minced; 1 teaspoon granulated sugar; 1 to 2 teaspoons crumbled dried red chili pepper; 2 teaspoons lightly toasted sesame seeds; and 1/4 teaspoon black pepper.

OLIVE OIL MARINADE Combine 1/2 cup olive oil; 1/4 cup minced onion; 2 large garlic cloves, finely minced; 2 tablespoons minced fresh parsley; 1 teaspoon minced fresh thyme; 1 teaspoon ground cumin; 1/2 teaspoon *each* paprika and chili powder; 1 bay leaf, crumbled; 1/2 teaspoon salt; and 1/4 teaspoon black pepper, or to taste. Strain before basting.

MARINADES FOR HAM

MADEIRA OR SHERRY MARINADE Combine 1/3 cup Madeira or dry sherry, 3 tablespoons safflower oil, 1/2 teaspoon dry mustard, and 1/4 teaspoon *each* ground allspice, ground cloves, and black pepper. After using, heat with 2 tablespoons butter until butter is melted. Use for basting.

MUSTARD-PINEAPPLE MARINADE In a saucepan, combine 1/4 cup brown sugar, 2 tablespoons cider vinegar, 2 to 3 teaspoons Dijon-style mustard, and 1/2 teaspoon finely minced garlic. Cook over medium heat 5 minutes. Remove from the heat and mix in 1/4 cup pineapple juice. Alternate ham and pineapple chunks on skewer.

ORIENTAL MARINADES

Consult the Chinese or Japanese Glossary for information on any unfamiliar items called for in these marinades.

FIVE-SPICE POWDER MARINADE Combine 1/4 cup soy sauce; 3 tablespoons sake, dry sherry, or whiskey; 2 tablespoons corn oil; 2 garlic cloves, minced; 3 slices ginger root, minced; and 1/2 teaspoon *each* five-spice powder and softened and minced dried tangerine peel.

HOISIN MARINADE Combine 1/3 cup hoisin sauce; 2 teaspoons soy sauce; 3 tablespoons Chinese rice wine or dry sherry; 3 garlic cloves, finely minced; 1 teaspoon finely minced ginger root; and 2 green onions, minced. Especially good with pork.

INDONESIAN-STYLE SATAY MARI-NADE Combine 3 garlic cloves, pressed; 1 small onion, chopped; 2 teaspoons brown sugar; 1-1/2 tablespoons fresh lemon juice; and 2 tablespoons dark soy sauce. Especially good with lamb; serve with Peanut Sauce with Chili.

OYSTER SAUCE MARINADE Combine 3 tablespoons oyster sauce, 2 tablespoons *each* corn oil and chopped green onion, 1 tablespoon soy sauce, and 1 teaspoon minced garlic.

SESAME SEED MARINADE Combine 1/3 cup soy sauce; 1 tablespoon *each* granulated sugar and cider vinegar; 3 tablespoons minced green onion and tops; 2 garlic cloves, minced; 2 slices ginger root, minced; 1/4 teaspoon black pepper; and 2 to 3 teaspoons lightly toasted sesame seeds, crushed.

SWEET-SOUR MARINADE Combine 1/3 cup soy sauce; 2 tablespoons granulated sugar; 2 tablespoons cider vinegar; 2 or 3 garlic cloves, pressed or finely minced; 1 to 2 teaspoons finely minced ginger root; and 1/2 teaspoon Oriental sesame oil. Baste with corn oil and sake or dry sherry.

TERIYAKI MARINADE I Combine 1/4 cup mirin or sweet sherry (or 1/4 cup sake and 1 teaspoon granulated sugar), 1/4 cup soy sauce, and 1/4 cup chicken stock. Reserve 1/4 cup of the mixture and add to it 1 teaspoon cornstarch dissolved in 1 tablespoon water and 1 teaspoon granulated sugar. Baste with this mixture to form a glaze.

TERIYAKI MARINADE II Combine 1/3 cup sake; 3 tablespoons soy sauce; 3 tablespoons corn oil; 2 large garlic cloves, minced; 3 slices ginger root, minced; and 2 green onions and tops, chopped.

THAI-STYLE SATAY MARINADE Combine 3 garlic cloves, pressed, 1 small onion, chopped; 1 tablespoon brown sugar; 2 to 3 tablespoons Thai fish sauce (available in Asian markets); 3 tablespoons fresh lime juice; and 2 tablespoons peanut oil. Good with chicken, pork, or beef; serve with Peanut Sauce with Chili.

YAKITORI MARINADE Combine 1/3 cup sake; 2 tablespoons soy sauce; and 1 tablespoon granulated sugar. Arrange the cooked skewers (chicken is best) on a bed of shredded daikon sprinkled with a little ground ginger and white pepper.

CHAFING DISH

The chafing dish allows the busy host or hostess to relax, for the only concern is to make sure the food is replenished and the water in the lower pan doesn't boil away. All that is needed for this elegant form of entertaining is a sauce on the side for dipping, if called for, and a small silver or ceramic mug with cocktail picks for spearing the hot morsels.

If you do not own a chafing dish, rental stores can provide what you need. Just be sure to use one that has a water pan. The type of chafing dish that has only a flame is apt to burn the food if not constantly attended.

MEATBALLS

GENERAL INSTRUCTIONS FOR MEATBALLS

Always one of the most sought-after items on the menu, meatballs are a must at a large party because they are delicious and substantial. Many of the sauces that accompany meatballs should be made the day of the party, but since meatballs can generally be made ahead, this will not put too much pressure on the cook.

The meatball mixture should be refrigerated several hours until firm enough to form into balls. Form the mixture into balls about 1 inch in diameter, using your palms to create even spheres.

To cook meatballs, arrange the balls on a rack in a shallow baking dish, not touching, and bake in a preheated 400° F oven 12 to 15 minutes, turning once. Alternatively, arrange meatballs on tiers of a large steamer and steam 10 minutes, or until meatballs are cooked through (see Steaming).

Meatballs may also be steamed in a large shallow dish, in several batches, in which case the juices can be saved. The meatballs steamed either way will have a softer texture and will be more moist.

Uncooked balls may be refrigerated for up to 2 days, or sheet frozen for up to 2 months, in which case they should be defrosted before cooking. Cooked unsauced meatballs may also be refrigerated and frozen in the same manner, then defrosted and reheated with their sauce or with a little stock in a covered nonstick skillet, a double boiler, or a microwave oven.

Unless you have meatballs left over from a party, do not freeze cooked balls in their sauce. They tend to break easily when stirred during the reheating process. Steamed meatballs are especially sensitive to reheating because of their softer texture. If you must reheat them, do it slowly and stir them carefully.

Unsauced cooked meatballs that have been refrigerated or frozen will need to have a little stock added to the pan when they are reheated. Check them frequently while they are heating so they do not dry out.

If the meatballs remain in the chafing dish for a number of hours, the constant warming will dry out unsauced meatballs or overthicken the sauce of sauced ones. Add a little stock to the unsauced ones, and more stock, cream, or other complementary liquid to the sauced ones. Always make sure that the chafing dish contains sufficient meatballs; if there are too few, they will dry out very quickly and the dish will look unattractive.

If making the accompanying sauce in advance, reheat gently, adding more liquid as needed. Stir frequently, and especially in the case of sauces with cream, watch carefully so the sauce does not scorch. If you are making a large recipe and keeping the sauce hot on the stove before transferring it to the chafing dish, again add liquid as needed to thin to sauce consistency.

CLAM AND PORK SAUSAGE MEATBALLS ●■

The unusual combination of clams and pork sausage is enhanced by the delicate dill sauce. If making the meatballs in advance, freeze the clam juice separately and then defrost it on party day so that it can be used to make the sauce.

Makes Approximately Four Dozen
Two 7-1/2-ounce cans minced
   clams
1 egg
2 tablespoons fine fresh bread
   crumbs
2 tablespoons reserved clam
   liquid
1 tablespoon minced fresh
   parsley
1/2 teaspoon crumbled dried sage
1/4 teaspoon freshly ground
   black pepper
1 pound mild pork sausage meat
Clam-Dill Sauce, following

Drain clams and reserve liquid for making sauce; set clams aside. In a mixing bowl, beat egg lightly and add clams, 2 tablespoons liquid, bread crumbs, parsley, sage, and pepper. With hands, mix in sausage meat. Pinch off a small portion of mixture and sauté until cooked through. Taste and adjust seasonings.

Chill meatball mixture 1 hour and form into balls about 1 inch

in diameter. Cook meatballs as directed in General Instructions for Meatballs.

While the meatballs are cooking, make the sauce. Add the meatballs to the sauce and transfer to a chafing or equivalent dish.

CLAM-DILL SAUCE

Makes Approximately Two Cups
3 tablespoons butter
3 tablespoons unbleached flour
1/2 cup reserved clam liquid,
   or as needed
1-1/3 cups light cream or milk,
   or as needed
1 tablespoon minced fresh dill
1 to 2 tablespoons dry sherry
1 tablespoon minced fresh chives
Salt and freshly ground white
   pepper to taste

In a large nonstick skillet, melt butter until bubbly, sprinkle with flour, and cook, stirring, 3 minutes. Gradually add clam liquid and cream; cook and stir until smooth and thickened. Add dill and just before serving blend in sherry and chives, adding additional clam liquid or cream if sauce has thickened too much. Taste and adjust seasonings.

LAMB MEATBALLS ●■

A trio of interesting meatball preparations are possible with this one recipe. Twelve dozen seems like a goodly amount, but the number is ideal for a large party, or for making ahead and freezing to have on hand.

The recipe can be easily broken down into three recipes, however. Simply take one-third of the ground lamb ingredients and add one of the seasoning mixtures.

Makes Approximately Twelve Dozen
3 pounds ground lean lamb
1 large onion, grated
6 large garlic cloves, very
    finely minced
3 eggs, lightly beaten
3 tablespoons fresh lemon juice
3/4 cup fine dry bread crumbs
1/2 cup minced fresh Italian
    parsley
2 teaspoons salt
3/4 teaspoon freshly ground
    black pepper

SEASONING MIXTURE I
1/2 tablespoon minced fresh
    basil
1 teaspoon very finely minced
    fresh rosemary
1 cup well-drained finely chopped
    cooked spinach

SEASONING MIXTURE II
1/4 teaspoon celery salt
1/4 teaspoon ground ginger
1/4 teaspoon curry powder
1/8 teaspoon ground cardamom

SEASONING MIXTURE III
1/4 cup chopped ripe olives
1 teaspoon freshly grated lemon
    peel
1/4 teaspoon ground allspice

SUGGESTED DIPS
Yoghurt Sauce
Sour cream and caraway seeds
    to taste
Garlic Mayonnaise

In a large mixing bowl, combine lamb, onion, garlic, eggs, lemon juice, bread crumbs, parsley, salt, and pepper. Divide mixture into 3 portions. To one portion, add seasoning mixture I: basil, rosemary, and spinach. To the second portion, add seasoning mixture II: celery salt, ginger, curry, and cardamom. To the third portion, add seasoning mixture III: olives, lemon peel, and allspice.

Pinch off a small portion of each mixture and sauté until cooked through. Taste and adjust seasonings. Chill mixtures 1 hour and form into balls about 1 inch in diameter.

Cook the meatballs as directed in General Instructions for Meatballs. Reheat with the cooking juices and/or stock if moisture is

needed and transfer to a chafing or equivalent dish. Serve with any or all of the dipping sauces.

MINTED LAMB MEATBALLS ●■

Makes Approximately Four Dozen
1 egg
1/4 cup minced green onion
    and tops
3 tablespoons minced fresh mint
3 tablespoons minced fresh
    parsley
3 tablespoons fine dry bread
    crumbs
3 tablespoons Chili Sauce
1 teaspoon salt
1/2 teaspoon ground cumin
1/4 teaspoon freshly ground
    black pepper
1 pound ground lean lamb
Yoghurt Sauce

In a mixing bowl, beat egg lightly. Add onion, mint, parsley, bread crumbs, chili sauce, salt, cumin, and pepper. With hands, mix in lamb. Pinch off a small portion of mixture and sauté until cooked through. Taste and adjust seasonings. Chill mixture 1 hour and form into balls about 1 inch in diameter.

Cook meatballs as directed in General Instructions for Meatballs. Reheat with the cooking juices and/or stock if needed and transfer to a chafing or equivalent dish. Serve the sauce in a bowl on the side.

POLPOTTE
(Italian Meatballs) ●■

Makes Approximately Four Dozen
1 egg
1/2 cup well-drained finely
  chopped cooked spinach
2 tablespoons minced fresh
  Italian parsley
1/2 tablespoon minced fresh
  basil
1 teaspoon minced fresh oregano
1 tablespoon freshly grated
  lemon peel
2 large garlic cloves, finely
  minced
1/2 teaspoon salt
1/4 teaspoon freshly ground
  black pepper
2 tablespoons fine dry bread
  crumbs
1/2 pound ground lean beef
1/2 pound ground lean veal
1/4 pound sweet Italian sausage,
  removed from casing and
  crumbled
1/4 cup beef stock, or as needed

In a mixing bowl, beat egg
lightly. Add spinach, parsley,
basil, oregano, lemon peel, garlic,
salt, pepper, and bread crumbs
and mix well. With hands, mix
in beef, veal, and sausage. Pinch
off a small portion of mixture
and sauté until cooked through.
Taste and adjust seasonings. Chill
mixture 1 hour and form into
balls about 1 inch in diameter.
  Cook meatballs as directed in
General Instructions for Meatballs. Reheat with cooking juices
and/or stock if needed and transfer
to a chafing or equivalent dish.

PORK SAUSAGE AND
BEEF MEATBALLS ●■

If the pork sausage available in
your market is not highly seasoned, add freshly ground black
pepper, crumbled dried oregano,
and Tabasco sauce to this list of
ingredients.

Makes Approximately Six Dozen
1 egg
3 tablespoons whole-wheat
  bread crumbs
3 tablespoons Chili Sauce
1 teaspoon dry mustard
1 pound highly seasoned pork
  sausage meat
1/2 pound ground lean beef
1/2 cup rich beef stock,
  or as needed
Chili Sauce for dipping
Assorted mustards

In a large mixing bowl, beat egg
lightly and stir in bread crumbs,
chili sauce, and dry mustard.
With hands, work in sausage and
beef. Pinch off a small portion
and sauté until cooked through.
Taste and adjust seasonings. Chill
mixture for 1 hour and then
form into balls 1 inch in diameter.
  Cook meatballs as directed in
General Instructions for Meatballs.
Reheat with the cooking juices
and/or stock if needed and transfer to a chafing or equivalent
dish. Serve the chili sauce and
mustards in bowls on the side.

SWEET-AND-SOUR MEATBALLS ●■

The quick sweet-and-sour sauces included here should only be prepared when the cook is too busy to make a sauce from scratch. All of the sauces, however, may be assembled ahead of time and then gently reheated.

Makes Approximately Eight Dozen
1 egg
1 large onion, grated
3 large garlic cloves, finely
   minced
2 tablespoons Chili Sauce
2 teaspoons soy sauce
1 teaspoon Worcestershire sauce
1 tablespoon Dijon-style mustard
1/2 cup fine dry bread
   crumbs
2 tablespoons milk
3/4 teaspoon salt
1/2 teaspoon freshly ground
   black pepper
1-1/2 pounds ground lean beef
1/2 pound ground lean pork
One 8-ounce can water
   chestnuts, drained and very
   finely minced to measure
   approximately 1 cup
One 8-ounce jar small pimiento-
   stuffed olives
Sweet-and-Sour Sauce, following

In a large mixing bowl, beat egg lightly and stir in onion, garlic, chili sauce, soy sauce, Worcestershire sauce, mustard, bread crumbs, milk, salt, and pepper. With hands, mix in beef, pork, and water chestnuts. Pinch off a small portion of mixture and sauté until cooked through. Taste and adjust seasonings. Chill mixture 1 hour.

Drain olives and form a portion of meat around each olive to make a ball approximately 1-1/4 inches in diameter. Cook meatballs as directed in General Instructions for Meatballs.

While the meatballs are cooking, make the sauce. Add meatballs to sauce and transfer to a chafing or equivalent dish.

SWEET-AND-SOUR SAUCE

Makes Approximately Three Cups
3/4 cup granulated sugar
3/4 cup white rice vinegar
3/4 cup catsup
3/4 cup water, or as needed
1 tablespoon arrowroot
1 tablespoon soy sauce, or to
   taste
5 large garlic cloves, finely
   minced
5 large slices ginger root,
   finely minced

In a saucepan, combine sugar, vinegar, catsup, water, arrowroot, soy sauce, garlic, and ginger root. Stir to dissolve arrowroot. Place pan over medium heat and cook, stirring often, until sauce thickens.

If making ahead, reheat, adding additional water as needed to make sauce consistency.

THREE QUICK SWEET-AND-SOUR SAUCES

For 2-1/2 to 3 cups of sauce, combine and heat, stirring to melt jelly, one of the following:
● One 12-ounce bottle chili sauce, one 10-ounce jar grape jelly, and 1/4 cup fresh lemon juice, or to taste.
● One 12-ounce bottle chili sauce, 1/2 cup hot pepper (jalapeño) jelly, 1/2 cup water, 2 to 3 tablespoons fresh lemon juice, and Tabasco sauce to taste.
● 2 cups catsup, 1 cup red currant jelly, 2 tablespoons Worcestershire sauce, and 1/4 teaspoon Tabasco sauce.

TURKEY TOFU BALLS ●■

Because this meatball mixture is very soft, compact balls are difficult to form. The cooking juices are especially tasty, so the meatballs are best steamed in a shallow dish. Transfer the balls to a chafing or equivalent dish, stir the juices well, and pour them over the meatballs.

Makes Approximately Four Dozen
1/2 cup finely minced water
    chestnuts, or
    1/4 cup *each* finely minced
    water chestnuts and finely
    minced bamboo shoots
1/2 cup finely minced green
    onion and tops
2 large garlic cloves, finely
    minced
1 teaspoon salt
1/2 teaspoon ground ginger
1/4 teaspoon freshly ground
    white pepper
3 tablespoons fine fresh bread
    crumbs
1/4 cup *soft* tofu (bean curd)
1 pound ground turkey

In a large mixing bowl, combine water chestnuts, onion, garlic, salt, ginger, pepper, bread crumbs, and tofu. With hands, work in turkey. Pinch off a small portion and sauté until cooked through. Taste and adjust seasonings. Chill mixture 2 hours and form into balls 1 inch in diameter.

Steam meatballs in a shallow dish as directed in General Instructions for Meatballs and transfer the meatballs and juices to a chafing or equivalent dish.

MEATBALLS WITH CHILI PEPPERS AND CHEESE ●■

*Makes Four to Four and
One-half Dozen*
1 egg
1/3 cup finely minced onion
2 large garlic cloves, finely
    minced
2 teaspoons minced fresh oregano
1 teaspoon fresh lemon juice
1/2 teaspoon salt
1/4 teaspoon freshly ground
    black pepper
2 tablespoons fine dry bread
    crumbs
1/2 pound ground lean beef
1/2 pound ground lean pork
One 4-ounce can diced jalapeño
    peppers
4 ounces Monterey Jack cheese
1/4 cup beef or pork stock,
    or as needed

In a mixing bowl, beat egg lightly. Add onion, garlic, oregano, lemon juice, salt, pepper, and bread crumbs and mix well. With hands, mix in beef and pork. Pinch off a small portion of mixture and sauté until cooked through. Taste and adjust seasonings. Chill mixture 1 hour.

Drain peppers. Cut cheese into 1/4-inch cubes. Pinch off about 1-1/2 tablespoons of the meat mixture and form it into a ball with a pepper dice and a cheese cube in the center. The ball should be about 1-1/4 inches in diameter.

Cook meatballs as directed in General Instructions for Meatballs. Reheat with juices and/or stock and transfer to a chafing or equivalent dish.

VEAL AND BEEF MEATBALLS ●■

Makes Approximately Four Dozen
1 egg
1/2 cup cooked brown rice
2 tablespoons minced fresh
   Italian parsley
1 tablespoon freshly grated
   lemon peel
1 teaspoon crumbled dried
   oregano
1 teaspoon salt
1/2 teaspoon freshly ground
   black pepper
1/2 pound ground veal
1/2 pound ground lean beef
Sorrel Sauce, following

In a large mixing bowl, beat egg
lightly and stir in rice, parsley,
lemon peel, oregano, salt, and
pepper. With hands, work in
veal and beef. Pinch off a small
portion and sauté until cooked
through. Taste and adjust seasonings. Chill mixture 1 hour and
form into balls 1 inch in diameter.

   Cook meatballs as directed in
General Instructions for Meatballs.
While the meatballs are cooking,
make the sauce. Add meatballs
to sauce, turn gently to coat,
and transfer to a chafing or
equivalent dish.

SORREL SAUCE

Makes Approximately Two Cups
1/2 cup minced green onion
   and tops
2 large garlic cloves, finely
   minced
2 tablespoons butter
2 tablespoons unbleached flour
1/2 cup dry white wine
1/2 cup light cream
1/2 cup rich chicken stock,
   or as needed
4 ounces sorrel
1 tablespoon fresh lemon juice
Salt and freshly ground
   white pepper to taste

In a covered nonstick skillet,
cook onion and garlic in butter
over medium heat 5 minutes.
Sprinkle with flour and cook,
stirring, 2 minutes. Gradually
add wine, cream, and stock.
Cook and stir until smooth and
thickened.

   Trim tough stems from sorrel
and finely chop leaves to measure
approximately 3/4 cup firmly
packed. Add sorrel to sauce with
lemon juice, salt, and pepper.
Cook over medium heat, stirring,
5 minutes, adding additional
chicken stock if sauce needs
thinning.

OTHER CHAFING DISHES

CRAB MELBA

When retesting this elegant dish,
I was loathe to use the prohibi-
tively high-priced crab for which
it is named. Steamed pollack
fillets made a most remarkable
substitute; guests could not tell
the difference. Steamed monkfish
made an excellent stand-in for
the equally high-priced lobster.
For directions on preparing these
fish for use in this dish, see Basics.

   This seafood melba should be
rather thick; provide several small
broad-bladed knives so guests
can spread the mixture on crackers
or melba toast rounds. Check
the mixture frequently after transferring it to the chafing dish to
make sure it does not thicken
too much, but stir as little as
possible so as not to break up
the seafood.

Approximately Forty Servings
6 tablespoons butter
4 ounces mushrooms, very finely
   minced (do not mince in a
   blender or processor)
1/4 cup minced green onion
   and tops
2 large garlic cloves, very finely
   minced
1/4 cup unbleached flour

2 cups light cream, or as needed
2 tablespoons catsup, or
   1 tablespoon tomato paste or
   Pumate Purée
1/2 cup grated sharp Cheddar or
   shredded Gruyère cheese
1 teaspoon paprika
1/4 teaspoon salt
1/4 teaspoon freshly ground
   white pepper
1/8 teaspoon cayenne pepper
1 tablespoon fresh lemon juice
2 tablespoons dry sherry
12 ounces flaked cooked crab
   meat
12 ounces minced cooked lobster
   or shrimp
3 tablespoons minced drained
   pimiento or Roasted Pepper
Minced fresh parsley
Unsalted crackers and/or Melba
   Toast rounds

In a large saucepan or skillet, melt butter until bubbly. Add mushrooms and onion and cook over medium heat 2 minutes. Add garlic and cook 1 minute. Sprinkle with flour and cook, stirring with a fork, 3 minutes. Gradually stir in cream, then cook and stir until sauce is thickened. Stir in tomato paste, cheese, paprika, salt, white and cayenne peppers, and lemon juice. Cook, stirring constantly, just until cheese is melted. At this point, the sauce may be cooled, covered, and refrigerated for up

to 2 days. Bring to room temperature and reheat gently before proceeding.

With a fork, carefully stir sherry, crab, lobster, and pimiento into sauce. Reheat without boiling, taste, and adjust seasonings. If sauce appears too stiff, thin with a little additional cream.

Transfer the mixture to a chafing or equivalent dish and sprinkle lightly with minced parsley. Serve with crackers and/or melba rounds.

PORK BITS O

The quality of pork is important for the success of this chafing dish presentation. Purchase a pork loin and cut the meat into cubes, discarding any visible fat. (An even more delicious choice is loin of young wild boar, though finding it will depend on your knowing a hunter.) Brown the bones and scraps in a 350° F oven and save for making stock. Be careful the pork bits do not dry out during baking or while they are being kept hot in the chafing dish. Add additional stock as needed to maintain proper moisture.

Approximately Four Dozen Pork Bits
One 1-1/2-pound lean center-cut
   pork loin
1 tablespoon soy sauce
1 tablespoon fresh lemon juice
1 tablespoon peanut oil
1/2 teaspoon granulated sugar
1/4 teaspoon freshly ground
   black pepper
2 large garlic cloves, minced
Two 1-inch slices ginger root,
   minced
1/3 cup pork or chicken stock,
   or as needed
Assorted mustards

Cut the pork into bite-size pieces approximately 3/4 inch square. Place the pieces in a nonmetallic container. Combine soy sauce, lemon juice, oil, sugar, pepper, garlic, and ginger root. Toss pork with soy mixture to coat pieces evenly, cover, and refrigerate 8 hours, or overnight, turning occasionally.

Preheat oven to 325° F. Spread the pork bits and marinade in a single layer in a shallow baking pan. Pour stock over and bake in the preheated oven 30 to 35 minutes, or until pork bits are just cooked through. Stir occasionally and add more stock if needed for moisture.

Transfer pork bits and stock to a chafing or equivalent dish and serve with cocktail picks. Place bowls of assorted mustards alongside for dipping.

PORK LINK SAUSAGES WITH RUM OR CRANBERRY SAUCE ●■

Convenient to prepare, this sausage dish is best when made ahead and reheated. The links become totally infused with the flavor of the sauce during the second warming.

There are two sauces from which to choose, one rum-based and the other made with cranberry sauce. Cocktail franks or regular frankfurters, turkey link sausages, kielbasa, or Portuguese linguica sausage may also be prepared in these sauces.

Approximately Six Dozen Servings
2 pounds pork link sausages

SAUCE I
1 cup firmly packed dark or
   light brown sugar
1 cup dark rum

SAUCE II
8 ounces jellied cranberry sauce
One 12-ounce jar chili sauce
2 tablespoons fresh lemon juice
1 lemon, thinly sliced
Cayenne pepper to taste

Preheat oven to 325° F. Prick sausages with tines of a fork in several places. Place sausages on rack in broiler pan and bake, turning once to brown evenly,

40 minutes. Cool and cut each sausage crosswise into 3 pieces.

If preparing sauce I, combine sugar and rum in a skillet and place over medium heat. Heat, stirring constantly, to dissolve sugar. Add the sausage pieces and cook, covered, over medium-low heat 1 hour. Stir occasionally to coat sausages with sauce. Transfer to a chafing or equivalent dish and serve with cocktail picks.

If preparing sauce II, combine cranberry sauce, chili sauce, lemon juice, and lemon slices in a skillet. Place over medium heat and heat, stirring to melt jelly. Season with cayenne pepper. Add sausage pieces and cook and serve as for sauce I.

The sausages and sauce may be cooked and refrigerated for up to 2 days, or frozen for up to 1 month. Reheat gently.

CHICKEN LIVERS AND GIZZARDS

Those who generally abstain from eating chicken livers and gizzards will quickly become converts once they have sampled this dish. That is, if those in the know don't eat it all before the others get the chance.

This is a perfect offering for a brunch buffet. Turkey link sausages may be used in place of the pork sausages.

Approximately Forty Servings
1/2 pound chicken livers, cut
   into bite-sized pieces
1/2 pound chicken gizzards,
   scored and then cut into slices
   1/8 inch thick
2 tablespoons butter
2 tablespoons corn or safflower
   oil
2 teaspoons finely minced garlic
1 pound pork link sausages,
   cooked and cut into thirds
1/2 cup sliced water chestnuts
3/4 cup diagonally sliced celery
2 teaspoons finely minced
   ginger root
1 cup rich pork or chicken stock
1 to 2 tablespoons soy sauce
1/2 teaspoon salt
1/4 teaspoon freshly ground
   black pepper
1 teaspoon arrowroot, dissolved
   in 3 tablespoons water
Minced fresh parsley or
   coriander sprigs

In a large skillet, brown chicken livers and gizzards in butter and oil, adding the garlic the last 2 minutes. Add sausage, water chestnuts, celery, ginger root, stock, soy sauce, salt, and pepper. Cover and cook over medium heat 10 minutes. Add arrowroot mixture and cook, stirring, until thickened. Taste and adjust seasonings.

Transfer liver mixture to a chafing or equivalent dish. Sprinkle with minced parsley or garnish with coriander sprigs. Serve with cocktail picks.

LAMB KIDNEYS IN MADEIRA SAUCE

Approximately Five Dozen Servings
2 pounds lamb kidneys
Madeira to cover
1-1/4 cups minced onion
1/2 tablespoon finely minced garlic
1 large bay leaf, broken
6 tablespoons olive oil
2 tablespoons unbleached flour
2/3 cup rich lamb or chicken stock, or as needed
3 tablespoons minced fresh parsley
3 tablespoons ground cooked ham (optional)
1/2 teaspoon salt
1/4 teaspoon freshly ground black pepper
1/2 cup Madeira

If the butcher has not already trimmed the kidneys, remove any fat and membrane. Slice kidneys in half lengthwise, then slice each half across in 5 or 6 bite-size pieces. Place kidney pieces in a nonmetallic container and pour Madeira over. Cover and refrigerate 3 hours, or overnight.

Drain the kidney pieces and transfer to a saucepan. Cover with cold water and bring to a boil. Remove from heat and let stand 1 minute. Drain, rinse with running cold water, and then let stand in the strainer until almost dry.

In a covered nonstick skillet placed over medium heat, cook onion, garlic, and bay leaf in 4 tablespoons of the oil 5 minutes, or until onion is soft. Sprinkle with flour, cook and stir 2 minutes, and gradually add stock. Cook, stirring, until smooth and thickened. Stir in parsley and set onion sauce aside.

In a large skillet, heat the 2 remaining tablespoons oil and quickly sauté kidneys 5 minutes, or until evenly browned; do not overcook. Sprinkle the kidneys with salt and pepper as they cook. Add 1/2 cup Madeira, scrape up any brown bits on bottom of skillet, and add reserved onion sauce. Reheat, adding additional stock if sauce is too thick. Taste and adjust seasonings.

Transfer to a chafing or equivalent dish. Serve with cocktail picks.

SWEETBREADS AND MUSHROOMS

Approximately Forty Servings
1/2 pound sweetbreads, cooked (see Basics) and broken or sliced into bite-size pieces
1/2 pound fresh button mushrooms
4 tablespoons butter
1/2 teaspoon ground oregano
1/2 teaspoon garlic powder
1/2 teaspoon salt
1/4 teaspoon freshly ground white pepper
Dash cayenne pepper
1/4 cup dry sherry
1/2 cup rich chicken stock and/or stock from cooking sweetbreads
1/2 cup Crème Fraîche
Fried Bread rounds

In a large skillet, sauté sweetbreads and mushrooms in butter until lightly browned, sprinkling with oregano, garlic powder, salt, and peppers as they cook. Raise heat slightly, add sherry, and cook and stir until sherry has almost evaporated and sweetbreads and mushrooms are lightly glazed. Add chicken stock and crème fraîche and heat, stirring, to serving temperature.

Transfer sweetbreads and mushrooms to a chafing or equivalent dish and serve with fried bread rounds on the side. Guests spear morsels with cocktail picks and place them on the bread.

CHARCUTERIE & MOLDS

In France, the term *pâté* specifically refers to a pastry-lined meat, poultry, or fish dish that is baked and served hot or cold. A terrine, which is always served cold, is made of these same ingredients and is baked, but the vessel, which is oval or rectangular and is also termed a terrine, is lined with fresh pork fatback (sliced paper thin and called bards or barding fat) rather than pastry. Finally, there is the galantine, boned poultry or meat that is spread with forcemeat and fingers of meat, and then rolled and poached.

With these distinctions made, it must be understood that these terms, especially pâté, are seldom used so restrictively in the United States. For example, my Chicken Liver Pâté is neither encased in pastry nor baked, but since the majority of cooks and eaters would term it a pâté, I have too. Today, layered vegetable "terrines" and complex fish terrines are popular buffet table offerings, but they are not larded as the classic meat terrines are, nor are they always prepared in the traditionally shaped mold. So the term terrine, like pâté, has taken on a much broader meaning.

PATES

PORK PATE WITH SAVORY ○

Approximately Forty Servings
1 pound ground lean pork
1 cup coarsely grated onion
2 tablespoons heavy cream or evaporated milk
1/2 teaspoon salt
1/2 teaspoon ground savory or sage
1/2 teaspoon paprika
1/4 teaspoon freshly ground black pepper
1/3 cup sour cream
2 teaspoons fresh lemon juice

PRESENTATION
Slivers of gherkin
1 lemon, thinly sliced
Pickle Fans
Parsley sprigs
Crusty sourdough bread slices

In the top pan of a double boiler placed over gently boiling water, combine pork, onion, cream, salt, savory, paprika, and pepper and cook for 2 hours. Check the water in the lower pan occasionally to make sure it doesn't boil away.

Strain mixture and purée in a blender or food processor. Add sour cream and lemon juice and whirl just to mix. Taste and adjust seasonings.

Oil a 3- to 4-cup mold with Lecithin Oil. Mound pork mixture into mold and level with a spatula or back of a wooden spoon. Cover tightly and refrigerate at least 6 hours or overnight.

To serve, unmold pâté (see General Instructions for Molds) onto a serving platter and decorate with slivers of gherkin. Arrange lemon slices, pickle fans, and parsley sprigs around pâté on platter. Place a basket of bread alongside.

CHICKEN LIVER PATE O

This basic chicken liver pâté recipe with a number of variations is uncomplicated and not at all difficult. It can be halved or doubled, and is designed to serve as the guide in creating your own pâté from what you may have on hand or have accumulated in the freezer. It is best with melba toast or dark rye bread, but can be served with crackers.

For a more elegant presentation, coat the pâté with aspic before and/or after decorating (see Coating Foods with Aspic Jelly).

Approximately Forty Servings

1 pound chicken livers, trimmed of fat and cut up
Dry sherry to cover
1 cup chopped onion
2 large garlic cloves, chopped
3 tablespoons rendered chicken fat
5 tablespoons butter
1 teaspoon salt
1/4 teaspoon freshly ground white pepper
1/4 teaspoon ground turmeric
1/4 teaspoon paprika
1/4 teaspoon freshly grated nutmeg
3 tablespoons brandy or dry sherry

PRESENTATION

1 hard-cooked egg, yolk and white sieved separately
Minced ripe olives
Parsley leaves
Aspic Cutouts and Chopped Aspic (optional)
Melba Toast rounds or rye bread

Marinate livers in sherry 4 hours or overnight. Drain, pat dry with paper toweling, and set aside.

In a covered nonstick skillet, cook onion and garlic over medium heat in rendered chicken fat and 3 tablespoons of the butter 5 minutes, or until soft. Raise heat slightly, add livers, sprinkle with seasonings, and cook, stirring often, 5 minutes, or until livers have stiffened and are almost cooked through. They should still be slightly pink inside.

Lightly oil a 3-cup mold or round-bottomed bowl with Lecithin Oil.

In a blender or food processor, purée liver mixture until smooth. With motor running, gradually add remaining 3 tablespoons butter, whirling until completely incorporated. Add brandy and whirl briefly. Taste and adjust seasonings. Pack mixture into prepared mold, cover with plastic wrap, and refrigerate at least 6 hours, or for up to 2 days.

To serve, unmold pâté (see General Instructions for Molds) on a serving plate and decorate with eggs, olives, parsley, and aspic cutouts. Serve with melba toast rounds or rye bread slices.

VARIATIONS

• Season liver mixture to taste with one of the following: dry mustard, ground or minced fresh thyme, Worcestershire sauce, chili powder, paprika, minced fresh or crumbled dried dill or tarragon, fresh lemon juice, ground cloves, or ground ginger.
• Cook 6 to 8 chicken gizzards in rich chicken stock to cover with 1 bay leaf about 30 minutes, or until very tender. Drain well and purée with liver mixture.
• Reduce amount of chicken livers to 12 ounces. Add 8 ounces mushrooms, finely minced, to the skillet with the livers. Proceed as directed.
• Before packing liver mixture into mold, mix in 1/2 cup shelled green pistachios or other nuts, finely chopped. (Do not chop nuts in a blender or food processor.)
• Before packing liver mixture into mold, mix in 1/2 cup chopped ripe olives (in which case your guests will think they are eating truffles), hard-cooked egg, or cooked ham, or 1/3 cup crumbled crisply cooked bacon.

BAKED
CHICKEN LIVER PATE ○

Makes Approximately Forty Servings
1 pound chicken livers, trimmed
  of fat and cut up
Dry sherry to cover
1/2 cup minced onion
1 garlic clove, minced
2 tablespoons rendered chicken
  fat
2 tablespoons butter
1/2 tablespoon minced fresh
  tarragon
1/4 teaspoon salt
1/4 teaspoon freshly ground
  white pepper
1/4 cup heavy cream

PRESENTATION
Chopped hard-cooked eggs
Parsley or watercress sprigs
Melba Toast rounds or crackers

Marinate livers in sherry 4 hours
or overnight. Drain, pat dry with
paper toweling, and set aside.

In a covered nonstick skillet,
cook the onion and garlic over
medium heat in rendered chicken
fat and butter 5 minutes, or
until soft. Raise heat slightly,
add livers and tarragon, and
sprinkle with seasonings. Cook,
stirring often, 5 minutes, or
until livers have stiffened and
are almost cooked through. They
should still be a little pink
inside.

In a blender or food processor,
combine liver mixture and cream
and purée until smooth. Taste
and adjust seasonings.

Preheat oven to 325° F. Lightly
oil a 4-cup mold or round-
bottomed bowl with Lecithin
Oil. Have a kettle of boiling
water ready.

Spoon puréed mixture into
prepared mold and cover tightly
with aluminum foil. Set dish in a
baking pan and fill pan with
boiling water to come two-thirds
up the sides of dish. Place pan in
the preheated oven and bake
1-1/4 to 1-1/2 hours, or until
pâté is firm. To test for doneness,
insert a cake tester or slender
metal skewer in center; it should
come out clean and feel hot to
the touch. A second test is to
tap the mold; the pâté should
not tremble.

Remove dish to a cooling
rack, uncover, and discard foil.
Cool, cover with plastic wrap,
and refrigerate at least 6 hours,
or for up to 2 days.

To serve, unmold pâté (see
General Instructions for Molds)
onto a serving plate and decorate
with eggs. Garnish with parsley
and serve with melba rounds or
crackers.

SPICY BAKED
CHICKEN LIVER PATE ○

Approximately Twenty-Four Servings
1/2 pound chicken livers, trimmed
  of fat and cut up
Dry white port or brandy
  to cover
1 egg
1/2 cup diced onion
2 garlic cloves, minced
2 tablespoons butter, at room
  temperature
2 tablespoons unbleached flour
1/2 cup heavy cream
1 teaspoon salt
1/4 teaspoon freshly ground
  white pepper
1/4 teaspoon ground ginger
1/8 teaspoon ground cinnamon
1/8 teaspoon ground cloves
1/8 teaspoon freshly grated
  nutmeg
Tiny piece of bay leaf, crumbled

PRESENTATION
Chopped Aspic
Green Onion Brushes
Black bread slices

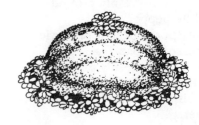

Marinate livers in sherry 4 hours or overnight. Drain and pat dry with paper toweling.

In a blender or food processor, combine marinated livers, egg, onion, garlic, butter, flour, cream, salt, pepper, spices, and bay leaf and purée until smooth. Spoon a small portion of liver mixture into a nonstick skillet and cook briefly. Taste and adjust seasonings.

Preheat oven to 325° F. Lightly oil a 3-cup, round-bottomed baking dish with Lecithin Oil. Have a kettle of boiling water ready.

Spoon liver mixture into prepared mold, cover tightly, and proceed as directed in the preceding recipe for Baked Chicken Liver Pâté. Decorate serving plate with chopped aspic and green onion brushes. Place a basket of sliced black bread alongside.

CHICKEN PATE WITH SPINACH ●

The addition of tofu and the method of cooking transform this simple chicken mixture into a delicate pâté flecked with green and silvery white.

Ground chicken can be purchased in most poultry markets or in the poultry section of your supermarket.

Approximately Fifty Servings
1 egg
1/2 cup cooked brown rice
1/2 cup very finely chopped raw spinach
2 tablespoons very finely minced green onion tops
2 tablespoons very finely minced fresh parsley
2 tablespoons grated onion
2 large garlic cloves, grated or pressed
2 tablespoons Chili Sauce
1/3 cup *soft* tofu (bean curd)
1 teaspoon salt
1/2 teaspoon freshly ground white pepper
1/8 teaspoon freshly grated nutmeg
3/4 cup fine fresh bread crumbs
1 pound ground chicken
Parsley sprigs
Sourdough baguettes

In a large mixing bowl, beat egg lightly. With a fork, stir in rice, spinach, green onion tops, parsley, grated onion, garlic, chili sauce, tofu, salt, pepper, nutmeg, and bread crumbs.

With your hands, mix in chicken until well blended. Pinch off a small portion and sauté until cooked through. Taste and adjust seasonings.

Oil a 7-1/2-by-3-1/2-by-2-1/4-inch loaf pan with Lecithin Oil. Pack chicken mixture into the pan, patting down with fingertips to make the loaf even. Wrap the lid of a large steamer or equivalent saucepan in a kitchen towel. Place loaf on a rack over boiling water in the steamer, cover, and steam 40 minutes, or until pâté has pulled away slightly from sides of pan. Remove to a cooling rack and let cool 15 minutes. Pour off accumulated juices (save for stock), turn pâté out onto wire rack, and let cool completely. Wrap in plastic wrap and refrigerate 2 hours, or for up to 2 days.

To serve, cut 6 or 8 thin slices from the pâté with a sharp knife. Cut the slices in half crosswise, and arrange alongside the pâté. Garnish the plate with parsley sprigs and serve with baguettes. Guests help themselves to the slices, or cut their own.

TERRINES

GENERAL INSTRUCTIONS FOR TERRINES

Terrines, which have been defined in the introduction to this chapter, are time-consuming to prepare but make beautiful presentations. Because of their labor-intensive nature, they deserve superior ingredients and careful preparation.

The quality of the pork fatback, which moistens meat terrines with richness and flavor, is especially important. Purchase pieces without any ribbons of meat running through them. Fresh fatback is preferable, but salted fat may be used if it is first blanched 5 minutes. Both may be purchased in most butcher shops.

Fatback is used in three forms in terrines (and galantines, which follow): lardoons, 1/4-inch-square strips that are layered with the strips of poultry or meat; dice, 1/4-inch cubes that are mixed with the forcemeat or are rendered to produce fat for sealing the terrine; and bards (barding fat), very thin sheets used for lining the mold.

For ease of cutting, chill the fatback until very firm. Lay the fat flat on a work surface rind side down and cut the fat in a single piece away from the rind. *To form lardoons,* slice the fatback into 1/4-inch-square strips the length of the piece of fat. *To make fatback dice,* form a bundle of lardoons and slice crosswise into 1/4-inch cubes. *To prepare bards,* freeze the fatback about 1 hour and then slice very thinly (no more than 1/8 inch thick, and preferably 1/16 inch) and evenly. Caul fat (the fatty membrane from pig's stomach) may be used in place of the bards, but it is almost impossible to purchase.

Forcemeat is simply the ground or finely minced meat or fowl mixture that comprises the base to "encase" the strips of meat and fatback dice or lardoons. It is the backdrop for the design you create within the terrine.

LINING AND FILLING TERRINE MOLDS Completely cover the bottom and sides of the mold with bards, overlapping the sheets and allowing any long ends to hang over the rim of the vessel. Gently press the fat against the sides of the mold as you work, patching any gaps that form. Save enough bards to cover the top of the terrine once it is filled.

Layer the terrine ingredients as directed in the recipes, mounding the center about 1/2 inch above the level of the rim to allow for shrinkage. As you fill the mold, tap it occasionally on the work surface so the filling settles to the bottom.

When all of the ingredients are in the mold, fold any bard ends up and over the filling, then completely cover the surface of the terrine with the reserved bards.

COVERING AND COOKING TERRINES Cut a piece of waxed paper or parchment paper slightly larger than the surface of the terrine and lightly butter a portion in the center the same dimension as the top of the terrine. Place paper buttered side down over the terrine and then cover the mold with heavy-duty aluminum foil, crimping edges well to make a tight lid. Prick the covers in 3 or 4 places with a cake tester to allow some of the steam to escape.

Place the readied terrine on a low rack, folded towel, or several layers of newspaper in a roasting pan. Fill the roasting pan with boiling water to come three-fourths up the sides of the mold. This water bath, or *bain-marie,* helps to ensure even heat and texture. Bake in a preheated oven as directed in recipes. To test for doneness, insert a cake tester or slender metal skewer in center; it should come out clean and feel hot to the touch. The terrine will have shrunk slightly away from the sides of the vessel. A terrine baked in a deep vessel will take slightly longer to cook than one baked in a long, shallow vessel.

WEIGHTING THE TERRINE Most terrines must be weighted to compact the ingredients. A board of the same dimensions as the inside rim of the vessel in which the terrine was cooked is an ideal platform for holding the weights. Such a board is not always possible to locate, in which case you must improvise. Cut several pieces of heavy cardboard to size, stack them, and then wrap the stack in aluminum foil.

The weights themselves can be unopened canned goods, paper weights, scale weights, or any other dense, heavy objects you have on hand. If you have a brick that is the correct size, wrap it in aluminum foil to form a platform and weight all in one. This arrangement is too heavy for vegetable or fish terrines, however.

Remove the baked terrine from the oven and place it on a wire rack; let stand, covered, for 20 minutes. Place the platform on the terrine and set the weights on the board. Refrigerate the terrine 3 or 4 hours, then remove weights and platform. Return terrine to the refrigerator for time specified in each recipe.

TERRINE OF PORK, PORK LIVER, AND VEAL ○

Approximately Forty Servings
1/2 tablespoon ground sage
8 ounces pork liver, cut
    into 1-inch pieces
2 tablespoons butter
1/3 cup chopped onion
4 large garlic cloves, cut up
1 pound lean pork
1 pound lean veal
1/2 pound pork fatback dice
1/4 cup high-quality bourbon
    or brandy
1 teaspoon salt
3/4 teaspoon ground allspice
1/2 teaspoon ground mace
1/2 teaspoon freshly ground
    black pepper
1 egg, lightly beaten
Approximately 3/4 pound pork
    fatback bards
3 bay leaves, or 6 fresh tarragon
    leaves
1 cup rendered pork fat, or
    as needed

PRESENTATION
Shredded lettuce
Sage leaves
Egg-Aspic Cutouts
Parsley sprigs
Lemon Twists
Pumpernickel slices

Sprinkling with sage while cooking, sauté liver in butter until stiffened and almost cooked through. Remove from the heat and let cool.

Using the finest blade of a meat grinder, grind together liver, onion, and garlic. Using coarsest blade, grind together pork, veal, and fatback dice. Combine both mixtures with bourbon, salt, allspice, mace, pepper, and egg. Let stand 1 to 2 hours to blend flavors. Pinch off a small portion and sauté until cooked through. Taste and adjust seasonings.

Following directions for Lining and Filling Terrine Molds, line a 1-1/2- to 2-quart terrine, loaf pan, or pâté mold with bards. Pack meat mixture into terrine, mounding slightly, and arrange bay leaves on top. Tap terrine on the work surface to settle the ingredients.

Preheat oven to 325° F. Following directions for Covering and

Cooking Terrines, cover mixture with bards, waxed paper, and aluminum foil. Bake in the preheated oven 2 to 2-1/2 hours. Check for doneness after 2 hours.

Remove terrine from roasting pan, let cool 20 minutes, and weight as directed in Weighting the Terrine. Remove weights and refrigerate 48 hours, or for up to 3 days.

To serve, loosen the terrine from the vessel with a small spatula and turn out onto a plate. Wash vessel and re-place the terrine in it. Melt rendered pork fat and *slowly* pour melted fat over the terrine to cover completely. You must pour slowly to allow time for the fat to seep down to the bottom of the terrine. Cover the terrine with foil and refrigerate for 48 hours, or for up to 3 days.

To serve, run a thin-bladed knife around edges of container and gently ease the terrine out of the container, turning it out onto a bed of shredded lettuce on a serving platter. With a small spatula, smooth the fat and decorate the top of the terrine with sage leaves and egg-aspic cutouts. Surround the terrine with parsley sprigs and tuck lemon twists in the parsley. Serve with pumpernickel.

TERRINE OF RABBIT, VEAL, AND HAM O

Approximately Thirty Servings
1 rabbit, approximately 3 pounds
12 ounces veal cut from leg
8 ounces cooked ham
6 ounces pork fatback lardoons
Approximately 12 ounces pork fatback bards

MARINADE
1/2 cup brandy
2 thyme sprigs
2 oregano sprigs
1 rosemary sprig
1 tablespoon fresh lemon juice
1 teaspoon salt
1/2 teaspoon freshly ground white pepper

STOCK
2 veal knuckles, cracked
1 large onion, unpeeled and cut up
1 large carrot, cut up
2 small leeks, white and a little green, sliced
4 parsley sprigs
4 small thyme sprigs
2 rosemary sprigs
2 oregano sprigs
2 bay leaves, broken
6 black peppercorns, lightly crushed
3/4 cup dry white wine
2 cups veal or chicken stock
1 tablespoon fresh lemon juice
1/2 teaspoon salt

FORCEMEAT
1 egg
1/4 cup fine dry bread crumbs
1/2 teaspoon finely minced fresh oregano
1/4 teaspoon finely minced fresh thyme
1/4 teaspoon finely minced fresh rosemary
2 teaspoons fresh lemon juice
1/2 teaspoon salt
1/4 teaspoon freshly ground white pepper

PRESENTATION
Aspic Cutouts
Chopped Aspic
Parsley sprigs
Lemon Twists
Baguette and/or buffet rye or black bread

Cut the meat from the rabbit, discarding all visible fat, and keeping pieces as large as possible. Place the bones in a shallow baking dish and brown in a 350° F oven for approximately 40 minutes.

While the bones are browning, cut the rabbit meat into strips 1/4-inch square. Place in one corner of a nonmetallic container. Cut the veal and ham in the same manner and add to the container, keeping the meats separate. Place the fatback lardoons in another corner of the container.

To prepare the marinade, combine brandy, herbs, lemon juice, salt, and white pepper in a mixing bowl and stir well. Pour marinade over meats and fat. Cover and refrigerate overnight, turning several times to distribute marinade evenly. Be careful to keep the meats separate.

To prepare the stock, transfer the browned bones to a soup kettle and set aside. Put veal knuckles in a saucepan and add cold water to cover. Bring to a rolling boil and boil 2 minutes. Remove from the heat and rinse bones under running cold water. Add to clean soup kettle with browned bones and all remaining stock ingredients. Cover kettle, bring to a boil, lower heat, and simmer 1-1/2 hours. Strain stock into a clean saucepan and bring to a boil. Boil gently until stock is reduced by approximately half. Taste and adjust seasonings. Strain, jar, cool, cover, and refrigerate overnight.

The next day, prepare the forcemeat. Transfer about two-thirds of the rabbit, veal, and ham and 6 to 8 of the lardoons with any of the marinade liquid that clings to the pieces to a food processor with metal blade in place, or to a meat grinder. Grind coarsely and combine with egg and all remaining forcemeat ingredients. Pinch off a small portion and sauté until cooked through. Taste and adjust seasonings. Set aside.

Oil a 2-quart terrine, loaf pan, or pâté mold with Lecithin Oil and line it with a double thickness of cheesecloth. Following directions for Lining and Filling Terrine Molds, line the terrine with bards. Press one-third of the forcemeat into the mold and arrange half the veal, ham, and lardoons lengthwise on top of the forcemeat in the following order: veal, lardoons, ham, lardoons, veal. Press half of the remaining forcemeat on the strips and layer remaining ham, veal, and lardoons on top in reverse order: ham, lardoons, veal, lardoons, ham. Cover with remaining forcemeat and press firmly, tapping the terrine on the work surface to settle the ingredients.

Preheat oven to 325° F. Lift off and discard any fat from the reserved stock and heat to a simmer. *Slowly* pour the stock into the filled terrine *just* until the stock shows at the top. You must pour slowly to allow time for liquid to seep down through the layers. Cool and refrigerate excess stock. Cover the rabbit mixture with the reserved bards.

Following directions for Covering and Cooking Terrines, cover the terrine mixture with bards, waxed paper, and aluminum foil. Bake in the preheated oven 2-1/2 hours. Check for doneness after this time and continue baking if necessary.

Remove terrine from the roasting pan, let cool 20 minutes, and weight as directed in Weighting the Terrine. Remove weights and refrigerate at least 24 hours, or for up to 2 days.

To make Aspic Cutouts and Chopped Aspic, see Garniture Suggestions. Check the gelling quality of the reserved stock and add gelatin if needed (see To Prepare Aspic Jelly). Do not cut the aspic until you are ready to garnish the terrine.

To serve, ease the terrine out of its container with the help of the cheesecloth, turning it out onto a serving plate. Carefully remove and discard cheesecloth. Decorate terrine with aspic cutouts and garnish the plate with chopped aspic and parsley sprigs. Tuck lemon twists into the parsley. Serve with baguettes and/or buffet rye or black bread.

TERRINE OF TONGUE AND SWEETBREADS ○

You will need to allow three days for assembling and baking this very special terrine. On the first day, cook the sweetbreads and tongue, then refrigerate them overnight in their cooking liquids.

Approximately Fifty Servings
6 dried shiitake mushrooms
1 pound veal sweetbreads, cooked (see Basics)
5 ounces cooked tongue (see Meats), cut into 1/4-inch-thick strips
6 ounces fat-free veal, cut into small cubes
6 ounces fat-free pork, cut into small cubes
6 ounces pork fatback dice
Approximately 1 pound pork fatback bards
3 bay leaves, broken

MARINADE
1/2 cup brandy
6 thyme sprigs
6 parsley sprigs
4 large garlic cloves, chopped

FORCEMEAT
1 egg
1/2 tablespoon salt
1/2 teaspoon freshly ground black pepper
1/2 teaspoon dry mustard
1/4 teaspoon ground thyme
1/2 cup fine dry bread crumbs
1/3 cup stock reserved from cooking sweetbreads

PRESENTATION
1/2 lemon or lime
Thyme sprigs
Sliced black bread or baguettes and/or Melba Toast rounds

Soak the mushrooms in warm water to cover 10 minutes, or until softened. Drain mushrooms and cut off and discard tough stems. Mince mushroom caps and place in one corner of a large shallow nonmetallic container.

Slice the sweetbreads 1/4 inch thick and place in the container with the mushrooms. Keeping all ingredients separate, place tongue, veal, pork, and fatback dice in the container.

To prepare the marinade, combine brandy, thyme and parsley sprigs, and garlic cloves in a mixing bowl and pour over sweetbreads, meats, and fatback dice. Cover and refrigerate overnight, turning several times to distribute the marinade evenly. Be careful to keep the meats separate.

The next day, transfer the veal and pork with any of the marinade liquid that clings to the pieces to a food processor with metal blade in place, or to a meat grinder, and coarsely grind. Remove sweetbreads and tongue from marinade and set aside. Remove mushrooms and fatback dice to a strainer.

To prepare the forcemeat, break the egg into a mixing bowl and beat lightly with a fork. Stir in reserved drained mushrooms and fatback dice, salt, pepper, mustard, thyme, bread crumbs, and stock. Add the ground veal and pork and work in thoroughly. Pinch off a small portion and sauté until cooked through. Taste and adjust seasonings.

Following directions for Lining and Filling Terrine Molds, line a 2-quart terrine, loaf pan, or pâté mold with bards. Press one-third of the forcemeat into the mold and layer the sweetbreads on top of the forcemeat. Cover with half the remaining forcemeat, then layer the tongue on top, arranging the strips lengthwise. Cover with remaining forcemeat, mounding slightly, and tap the terrine on the work surface to settle the ingredients. Place bay leaves on top of the mixture.

Preheat the oven to 325° F. Following directions for Covering and Cooking Terrines, cover the terrine mixture with bards, waxed paper, and aluminum foil. Bake in the preheated oven 2 to 2-1/2 hours. Check for doneness after 2 hours.

Remove the terrine from the roasting pan and let cool 20 minutes. Weight as directed in Weighting the Terrine. Remove weights and refrigerate at least 24 hours, or for up to 3 days.

To serve, loosen the terrine from the vessel with a small spatula and turn out onto a serving platter. To form the garnish with the lemon half and thyme sprigs, see Citrus Flowers. Set the flower on the platter and surround with black bread, baguettes, and/or melba toast rounds.

FISH TERRINES

Fish terrines do not keep well, so plan on serving them the day after they have been made, and then keep them no longer than two days.

There are two basic methods for preparing fish terrines, one in which the egg whites and cream are whipped until stiff and then folded into the fish mixture and one in which the egg whites and cream are simply mixed with the fish. An example

of each method follows. In both cases, however, it is important that the terrine go into the oven the moment it is assembled. Before beginning the assembly, carefully read Covering and Cooking Terrines so that everything is properly readied.

TERRINE OF POLLACK, SHRIMP, AND SMOKED SALMON O

This delicate and colorful terrine must be sliced with a very sharp knife so that the layers do not separate. A small silver spatula will facilitate positioning the slices on the crackers or bread.

Approximately Thirty Servings
1/3 cup minced shallots
1/2 tablespoon butter
1/4 cup parsley leaves
1/4 cup chopped fresh dill
2 tablespoons chopped fresh chives
8 ounces pollack or other firm white fish, cut into small pieces and chilled
8 ounces shrimp, shelled, deveined, cut into pieces, and chilled
1 teaspoon dry mustard
1 teaspoon salt
1/2 teaspoon freshly ground white pepper

4 drops Tabasco sauce
1 egg, separated and chilled
2 egg whites, chilled
1 cup heavy cream, chilled
1 pound spinach, tough stems discarded
1/3 cup Crème Fraîche, chilled
1/4 teaspoon freshly grated nutmeg
2 tablespoons fresh bread crumbs
1 cup finely minced smoked salmon (about 5 ounces), chilled

PRESENTATION
Tomato Roses
Watercress sprigs
Plain crackers and/or sliced baguette and buffet rye

In a small covered nonstick skillet, cook shallots in butter 3 minutes. Remove from heat and set aside.

In a blender or food processor, finely mince parsley, dill, and chives. Add pollack and shrimp and whirl until finely minced. Add mustard, salt, 1/4 teaspoon of the pepper, Tabasco sauce, and reserved shallot mixture and whirl briefly. With motor running, add egg yolk, mix a few seconds, and add egg whites, one at a time. Gradually pour in cream, stop to scrape down sides of blender or processor bowl, and then whirl until well mixed. Sauté a small amount of the mixture, taste, and adjust seasonings. Transfer the mixture to a bowl nested in a bowl of crushed ice, cover, and refrigerate.

Select a terrine or other vessel 6 inches by 4 inches by 3 inches. The vessel will eventually be lined with a single layer of spinach leaves, so at this point figure out how many spinach leaves you will need by arranging them in the vessel. Now, place those leaves on a rack over boiling water. Cover pot and steam until leaves are limp. With tongs, remove leaves to a plate lined with paper toweling, arranging them flat. Add remaining spinach leaves to the steamer and steam until cooked through. With tongs, transfer leaves to a blender or food processor. (Press out as much water as possible with the tongs.) Purée spinach leaves and then spoon into a sieve; press all moisture from the spinach with the back of a wooden spoon. Place spinach in a mixing bowl and add crème fraîche, bread crumbs, nutmeg, and remaining pepper. Taste, adjust seasonings, cover, and refrigerate until well chilled.

To assemble the terrine, oil the vessel with Lecithin Oil and line it with the reserved spinach leaves. Preheat the oven to 350° F. Have the roasting pan ready and the water boiling.

Spread one-third of the shrimp-pollack mixture on the spinach leaves in the bottom of the terrine. Top with a layer of half the spinach mixture and cover with a layer of 1/2 cup of the smoked salmon. Carefully spread half the remaining shrimp-pollack mixture over the salmon and tap terrine on work surface to settle the ingredients. Repeat with remaining spinach mixture, smoked salmon, and shrimp mixture. Again tap the terrine on the work surface to settle ingredients.

Following directions for Covering and Cooking Terrines, cover terrine with waxed paper and aluminum foil. Bake in the preheated oven 1 hour and 10 minutes, or until a cake tester inserted in center comes out clean and feels warm to the touch. The terrine should have pulled away slightly from the sides of the vessel.

Remove terrine from roasting pan and place on a rack. Let cool 20 minutes, and lightly weight as directed in Weighting the Terrine. Remove weights and refrigerate overnight.

To serve, loosen the edges of the terrine with a thin spatula or knife and ease it out of the vessel, inverting it onto a serving plate. Garnish the plate with tomato roses and watercress sprigs. Cut a 1/4-inch-thick slice from the terrine and then cut the slice

into 3 pieces crosswise and arrange on the platter. Let guests cut the remainder of the terrine. Serve with crackers and/or breads.

TERRINE OF SALMON ○

Stunningly colorful and absolutely delicious describe this exquisite salmon terrine. It is equally good when made with a white fish such as lingcod, sole, or pollack.

The terrine must be sliced with care, so it will be best if you cut the first few slices for your guests. Divide each slice into three equal pieces—the perfect size to balance on a small soda cracker.

Approximately Thirty Servings
1/4 cup finely minced white
   of green onion
1/2 tablespoon butter
3 ounces sorrel, ribs removed
   and leaves chopped
1/3 cup firmly packed fresh
   parsley leaves
2 tablespoons minced green
   onion tops
2 tablespoons minced fresh
   tarragon
8 ounces cooked salmon, flaked
   (approximately 2 cups firmly
   packed)
1/3 cup Crème Fraîche or
   sour cream
2 eggs, separated and
   at room temperature

2 tablespoons fine dry bread
  crumbs
2 teaspoons fresh lemon juice
3/4 teaspoon salt
1/4 teaspoon freshly ground
  white pepper
1/8 teaspoon cream of tartar
1/2 cup heavy cream, chilled

PRESENTATION
Sliced hard-cooked eggs
Paprika
Citrus Cups
Parsley sprigs
Soda crackers, such as Bremner
  Wafers

In a small covered nonstick skillet, cook onion in butter 3 minutes. Remove from heat and let cool.

Place onion mixture, sorrel, parsley, onion tops, and tarragon in a blender or food processor and whirl until minced. Add salmon and whirl just until mixed. Add crème fraîche, egg yolks, bread crumbs, lemon juice, salt, and pepper and whirl just until mixture is well blended. Taste, adjust seasonings, and transfer to a large mixing bowl. Cover and refrigerate.

Preheat oven to 350°F. Select a terrine or other vessel that is 6 by 4 by 3 inches and oil it with Lecithin Oil. Line the terrine with plastic wrap or cheesecloth and brush the liner with additional lecithin oil. Have the roasting pan ready and the water boiling.

Whip the egg whites and cream of tartar until stiff peaks form; set aside. In a separate bowl and with clean beaters, whip the cream until stiff. Fold 1/2 cup of the whipped cream into salmon mixture to lighten it, then fold in remaining whipped cream. Carefully fold in egg whites and mound mixture into prepared terrine.

Following directions for Covering and Cooking Terrines, cover the terrine with waxed paper and aluminum foil. Bake in the preheated oven 1 hour, or until a cake tester inserted in center comes out clean. The terrine should feel firm to the touch and have pulled away slightly from sides of vessel.

Remove terrine from roasting pan, let cool 20 minutes, and *lightly* weight as directed in Weighting the Terrine. Remove weights and refrigerate overnight.

To serve, ease the terrine out of the vessel with the help of the plastic wrap and invert onto a serving plate. Garnish the terrine with egg slices and sprinkle with paprika. Garnish the plate with citrus cups. Serve with soda crackers.

THREE VEGETABLE TERRINE O

I have chosen green beans, carrots, and mushrooms to make this colorful terrine, but other vegetables—cauliflower, peas, broccoli, spinach, or swiss chard—can be prepared in the same manner, using the same proportions of other ingredients. Season them with complementary herbs and spices and keep color contrast in mind.

This terrine should be served at a large party, since it does not keep well. The purées can be prepared a day ahead and refrigerated until you are ready to assemble and bake the terrine.

Approximately Forty Servings

BEAN PUREE
12 ounces green beans, cut
  into small pieces
1/3 cup chopped onion
1/2 teaspoon crumbled dried
  tarragon
1 teaspoon salt
1/4 teaspoon freshly ground
  white pepper
1/2 tablespoon butter
1 tablespoon rich chicken or
  beef stock
1 tablespoon Crème Fraîche
3 tablespoons fine fresh bread
  crumbs
2 eggs

CARROT PUREE

1 pound carrots
1/3 cup chopped onion
1-1/2 tablespoons minced fresh mint
3/4 teaspoon salt
1/4 teaspoon freshly ground white pepper
1/4 teaspoon ground cloves
1 tablespoon butter
1 tablespoon rich chicken or beef stock
1 tablespoon Crème Fraîche
2 tablespoons fine fresh bread crumbs
2 eggs

MUSHROOM PUREE

4 large garlic cloves, minced
1/3 cup minced shallots
1/3 cup minced white of green onion
1 tablespoon butter
1 tablespoon rich chicken or beef stock
1 pound mushrooms, minced
1/2 teaspoon salt
1/2 teaspoon freshly ground white pepper
1 teaspoon crumbled dried oregano
Dash cayenne pepper
1 teaspoon fresh lemon juice
1 tablespoon Crème Fraîche
3 tablespoons fine fresh bread crumbs
2 eggs

1/3 cup chopped pine nuts or walnuts (optional)
1/3 cup very finely minced fresh parsley

1 cup very tiny broccoli florets
2 green onion tops, blanched, drained, and patted dry

PRESENTATION

1 hard-cooked egg, white and yolk sieved separately
Green Onion Brushes
Unsalted crackers

To prepare the bean purée, steam beans on a rack over boiling water 10 minutes, or until very soft. Remove beans to a blender or food processor; reserve the steaming water in the steaming vessel. In a covered nonstick skillet, cook onion, tarragon, salt, and pepper in butter and stock 5 minutes, or until onion is soft. Remove lid and let any remaining liquid cook away.

Add the onion mixture to the beans and purée until smooth. Add crème fraîche, bread crumbs, and eggs. Whirl until well blended, scraping down sides of container several times. Taste, adjust seasonings, and transfer to a bowl. Cover and refrigerate.

To prepare the carrot purée, slice the carrots about 1/8 inch thick. Place all but 16 of the carrot slices in the water in which the beans were steamed.

Place the reserved slices and the broccoli florets on the rack above the water, cover steamer, and bring liquid to a boil. Steam the broccoli florets 2 minutes, remove from the rack, refresh under cold running water, and set aside. Steam the carrot slices 3 minutes longer, or until just starting to soften, remove from the rack, and set aside. Continue to boil the carrot slices 10 minutes, or until very soft. Drain the carrots (reserve liquid for soup stock) and place in a blender or food processor.

To continue preparing the carrot purée, cook onion, mint, salt, pepper, and cloves in butter and stock in a large covered skillet 5 minutes, or until onion is soft. Remove lid and let any remaining liquid cook away.

Add onion mixture to carrots in blender and purée until smooth. Add crème fraîche, bread crumbs, and eggs and whirl until well blended. Taste, adjust seasonings, and transfer to a bowl. Cover and refrigerate.

To prepare the mushroom purée, cook garlic, shallots, and green onion in butter and stock in a large covered skillet 3 minutes. Add mushrooms and sprinkle with salt, white pepper, oregano, cayenne pepper, and lemon juice. Cover and cook, stirring occasionally, 5 minutes, or until mushrooms are soft. Remove lid and let any remaining liquid cook away.

Transfer mushroom mixture to a blender or food processor and purée until smooth. Add crème fraîche, bread crumbs, and eggs. Whirl until well blended. Remove to a bowl and stir in pine nuts and parsley. Taste, adjust seasonings, cover, and refrigerate at least 1 hour.

To assemble the terrine, oil a 4- to 6-cup terrine generously with Lecithin Oil. Preheat oven to 350° F. Have the roasting pan ready and a kettle of water boiling.

Cut the reserved steamed carrot slices into fanciful shapes with tiny hors d'oeuvre cutters. Arrange the carrot cutouts in flower patterns on the bottom of the terrine. Make flower "stems" and "leaves" from the blanched green onion tops. Gently spoon bean purée into the terrine, being careful not to disturb the pattern. Spoon half the carrot purée over the layer of bean purée and set the reserved broccoli florets on top in 2 or 3 lengthwise rows. Carefully spoon remaining carrot purée over the broccoli florets, then cover with the mushroom purée. Tap the

terrine lightly several times on the counter to settle the ingredients.

Following directions for Covering and Cooking Terrines, cover the terrine with waxed paper and aluminum foil. Bake in the preheated oven 1 hour and 20 minutes, or until a cake tester inserted in the center comes out clean. The terrine should feel firm to the touch and have pulled away slightly from sides of vessel.

Remove terrine from roasting pan, let cool 20 minutes, and *lightly* weight as directed in Weighting the Terrine. Remove weights and refrigerate overnight.

To serve, loosen the edges of the terrine with a small spatula and invert onto a serving plate. Make a mound of sieved egg white on a corner of the plate and surround it with a ring of sieved yolk. Tuck green onion brushes around the mound in a spoke pattern. Serve with unsalted crackers.

GALANTINES

GENERAL INSTRUCTIONS FOR GALANTINES

Galantines can be true works of art, for not only do they lend themselves to creative surface decorating as canapés do, but their internal structure can be designed so that new beauty is revealed as they are sliced. A real challenge to the artist-sculptor-cook, galantines are complex only in their lengthy preparation, not in the simple steps involved.

The ancient origin of galantines is obscure, but undoubtedly related to the Latin verb *gelare,* to freeze, for they are dishes of rolled boned meat, poultry, or fish filled with forcemeat and strips of meat, cooked in rich stock, wrapped, pressed, and served cold, coated with aspic jelly. Chaucer knew them well, for he claimed never to be walled and wound in "galauntyne" as he was in love.

You will need to refer to the General Instructions for Terrines for information on pork fatback and for directions on weighting the galantine, and to Aspic Jellies for an explanation of coating and garnishing with aspic. Instructions for wrapping and poaching galantines appear here.

WRAPPING THE GALANTINE Once you have formed the galantine ingredients into a cylinder, roll the cylinder into the towel on which you have been working. Place the wrapped galantine seam side down on work surface. Secure the ends of the towel with kitchen twine, giving the roll a "sausage look." Cut 4 or 5 strips of sheeting 2 inches wide and about 18 inches long and tie the cylinder at 4 or 5 intervals to keep the roll snug and even. Do not make the bands too tight; they should be just tight enough to hold the cylinder firmly without cutting into it.

POACHING THE GALANTINE
Choose a saucepan or kettle in which the galantine will fit snugly. Place a rack on the bottom of the vessel and add the reserved stock. Cover and bring to a boil. Lower the galantine into the boiling stock (it should just cover it; add water if needed), bring back to a slow boil, cover vessel with a slightly tilted lid, and poach the galantine at a gentle boil 1 hour and 50 minutes, or until it feels firm to the touch.

GALANTINE OF TURKEY O ■

Approximately Forty Servings
1 large turkey breast
    (approximately 6 pounds)
Herb salt
6 ounces cooked smoked tongue,
    cut into 1/4-inch-square strips
8 ounces pork fatback lardoons
8 to 10 medium pitted ripe olives
1 recipe Sour Cream Aspic Jelly,
    made from reserved stock
1 cup aspic jelly, made from
    reserved stock
Garnitures for Lined Molds

MARINADE
1 cup brandy
6 parsley sprigs, coarsely chopped
10 black peppercorns, lightly
    crushed
10 allspice berries, lightly
    crushed

STOCK
2 veal knuckles, cracked
1 large pig's foot
Bones from turkey breast
1 large carrot, cut up
1 celery rib, cut up
1 unpeeled onion, stuck with
    3 whole cloves
1 leek with a little green,
    chopped
6 parsley sprigs
3 thyme sprigs
3 quarts water

FORCEMEAT
1 pound lean veal, cut into
    1/2-inch cubes
2 ounces pork fatback, cut into
    1/2-inch cubes
1 egg, lightly beaten
1/4 cup reserved marinade,
    strained
1 teaspoon salt
1/4 teaspoon freshly ground
    black pepper
1/4 teaspoon ground allspice
2 tablespoons fine dry bread
    crumbs
1/4 cup minced fresh parsley

PRESENTATION
Chopped Aspic (from approxi-
    mately 2 cups aspic jelly)
Parsley or watercress sprigs
French or other crusty bread
    slices

Bone the turkey breast (see Basics), being careful not to pierce the skin. Place the bones, any loose skin, and fatty trimmings in a baking pan, sprinkle with herb salt, and bake in a 350° F oven until nicely browned, about 45 minutes.

While bones are browning, lay the turkey breast skin side down on a cutting board and carefully trim away the flesh to leave a layer on the skin about 1/4 inch thick. If the flesh pulls away from the skin completely, the hollows can be filled in later. Place the skin and the loose pieces of flesh in a nonmetallic container. Add the veal and fatback cubes (see forcemeat ingredients), tongue, and lardoons, keeping all the ingredients separate.

To prepare the marinade, combine brandy, parsley, peppercorns, and allspice berries in a mixing bowl and stir well. Pour all but 1/4 cup of the marinade over all of the meats. Cover and marinate overnight, turning occasionally. Be careful to keep the meats separate. Cover the reserved 1/4 cup marinade and refrigerate.

To make the stock, transfer the browned bones to a soup kettle and set aside. Combine veal knuckles and pig's foot in a saucepan and add cold water to cover. Bring to a rolling boil and boil 2 minutes. Remove from heat and rinse the bones under running cold water. Add the bones to the soup kettle containing the browned turkey bones with carrot, celery, onion, cloves, leek, parsley and thyme sprigs, and water. Cover kettle, bring to a boil, lower heat, and simmer 2 hours. Taste and adjust seasonings. Strain, jar, cover, cool, and refrigerate overnight.

The next day, prepare the forcemeat. Remove the veal and fatback cubes from the marinade and grind in a food processor or meat grinder. Transfer to a mixing bowl and add egg, reserved 1/4 cup marinade, salt, pepper, allspice, bread crumbs, and parsley. Pinch off a small portion and sauté until cooked through. Taste and adjust seasonings. Cover and refrigerate.

Place a muslin towel, folded crosswise (about 1-1/2 feet by 2 feet), on work surface. Remove the turkey skin from the marinade and spread it out, meat side up, on the towel. Remove the pieces of turkey from the marinade and trim about half the meat into slices 1/4 inch thick. Cover the skin and flesh attached to it with the turkey slices and any smaller pieces to make an even layer about 1/2 inch thick, filling in hollows with small pieces as needed. Cut the remaining large pieces of turkey into 1/4-inch-square strips and set aside. Cut the remaining small pieces into 1/4-inch cubes and mix into the forcemeat.

To assemble the galantine, spread half the forcemeat evenly over the turkey skin and flesh, leaving a 1/2-inch border on all sides. Alternating them, arrange the strips of tongue, turkey, and

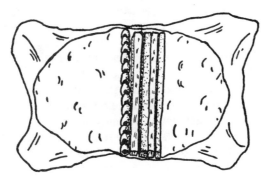

lardoon crosswise in a single layer over the forcemeat. Being careful not to disturb the pattern, spread remaining forcemeat over all. Make a row of olives across the middle of the forcemeat, arranging them lengthwise so when the galantine is cut they will be sliced crosswise. The row should be in the same direction as the meat and fat strips.

Fold the uncovered portion of the skin on the long sides over the forcemeat. With the help of the towel, lift one short end of the turkey breast, rolling and folding it into the center; lift the other side to meet the first at the center, pulling the skin tightly over the top to form a cylinder. Following General Instructions for Galantines, wrap the cylinder into the towel and poach the galantine.

Remove vessel from the heat and cool stock and galantine to lukewarm. Lift roll out onto a shallow dish or platter. Weight (see Weighting the Terrine) with moderately heavy weights—the galantine should be firm but all liquid should not be pressed out—and let cool completely. Refrigerate the weighted galantine 4 hours, then remove weights. Continue to refrigerate galantine overnight.

Reheat stock and strain into a saucepan, bring to a boil, and boil until reduced by one-third.

Clarify (see To Clarify Stock), jar, cool, cover, and refrigerate. Remove and discard any hardened fat from top before using.

The next day, remove galantine from towel and rewrap in plastic wrap and then aluminum foil. Refrigerate at least 1 day, or for up to 3 days. Several days of mellowing will improve the flavor. At this point, the galantine may be frozen for up to 1 month.

The morning of the day the galantine is to be served, prepare the sour cream aspic jelly and the aspic jelly, using the reserved clarified stock. Carefully cut about one-third of the galantine into 1/8-inch-thick slices. Following directions for Coating Foods with Aspic, coat the uncut portion of the galantine with 4 or 5 layers of sour cream aspic jelly. Decorate with garnitures and finish with several coatings of clear aspic jelly. Chill to set firmly. Coat the slices with clear aspic jelly and refrigerate.

To serve, cover a serving platter with chopped aspic (made with the reserved clarified stock) and arrange the decorated galantine on the aspic. Place the slices in front and around it and garnish the platter with parsley sprigs. Place a basket of french or other crusty bread slices next to the platter.

GALANTINE OF CHICKEN O■

Approximately Thirty Servings
One 4- to 4-1/2-pound chicken
12 ounces ham, cut into
    1/4-inch-square strips
8 ounces pork fatback lardoons
6 parsley sprigs
1/3 cup lightly toasted finely
    chopped walnuts
1 cup Madeira Aspic Jelly,
    made from reserved stock
Garnitures for Lined Molds

MARINADE
1 cup Madeira
10 whole cloves
1/4 teaspoon freshly grated
    nutmeg
8 coriander seeds, lightly crushed
6 black peppercorns, lightly
    crushed

STOCK
See Galantine of Turkey (pre-
    ceding), substituting chicken
    bones for the turkey bones

FORCEMEAT
8 ounces lean pork, cut into
    1/2-inch cubes
8 ounces lean veal, cut into
    1/2-inch cubes
2 ounces pork fatback, cut into
    1/2-inch cubes
2 chicken livers, halved
1 tablespoon butter
1/4 cup strained reserved
    marinade
1 egg, lightly beaten

1/3 cup fine dry bread crumbs
1 teaspoon salt
1/2 teaspoon freshly ground
   black pepper
1/4 teaspoon ground cloves
1/8 teaspoon freshly grated
   nutmeg
1/8 teaspoon ground coriander

PRESENTATION
Aspic Cutouts (from approxi-
   mately 1 cup aspic jelly)
Watercress sprigs
Green Onion Brushes
Homemade-style light rye bread
   slices

Bone the chicken (see Basics)
and brown the bones as in
Galantine of Turkey (preceding).

While bones are browning,
lay the chicken, skin side down,
on work surface. With a sharp
knife, separate all of the flesh
from the skin, being careful not
to pierce the skin. Wrap the
skin in plastic wrap and refrigerate. Place the chicken meat in a
nonmetallic container. Add the
pork, veal, and fatback cubes
(see forcemeat ingredients), ham,
and lardoons, keeping all the
meats separate. Lay the parsley
sprigs on top.

To prepare the marinade, combine Madeira, cloves, nutmeg,
coriander, and peppercorns. Pour
all but 1/4 cup of the marinade
over the meats. Cover and refrigerate overnight, turning occasionally. Be careful to keep the
meats separate. Cover and refrigerate the reserved 1/4 cup marinade.

To prepare and store the
stock, follow directions in Galantine of Turkey.

The next day, prepare the
forcemeat. Remove the pork,
veal, and fatback cubes from the
marinade and grind in a food
processor or meat grinder. Transfer to a mixing bowl and set
aside. In a small skillet, sauté
chicken livers in butter until
they stiffen. Mince the parsley
from the marinade and add to
the meat mixture in the mixing
bowl. When livers are cool enough
to handle, chop coarsely and add
to the bowl. Mix in egg, reserved
1/4 cup marinade, bread crumbs,
salt, pepper, cloves, nutmeg, and
coriander. Pinch off a small portion and sauté until cooked
through. Taste and adjust seasonings. Cover and refrigerate.

Place a muslin towel, folded
crosswise (about 1-1/2 feet by 2
feet), on work surface. Unwrap
the chicken skin and spread it
out on the towel, inside up.
Remove the chicken meat from
the marinade and trim the large
pieces into slices about 1/4 inch

thick. Arrange the slices on the
skin to make an even layer
about 1/4 inch thick, filling in
hollows with small pieces of
chicken as needed. Cut remaining
chicken into 1/4-inch cubes and
add to the forcemeat.

To assemble the galantine,
spread half the forcemeat evenly
over the chicken layer, leaving a
1/2-inch border on all sides.
Alternating them, arrange the
ham strips and lardoons crosswise
over the forcemeat. Bring careful
not to disturb the pattern, spread
remaining forcemeat over all.
Make a row of the walnuts
across the middle of the forcemeat
in the same direction as the ham
strips and lardoons.

Fold the uncovered portion
of the skin over the forcemeat
on the long sides. Following
directions in Galantine of Turkey,
form into a cylinder, wrap, poach,
and weight the galantine. Refrigerate the weighted galantine
4 hours, then remove weights.
Continue to refrigerate galantine
overnight.

Reheat stock and strain into a
saucepan, bring to a boil, and
boil until reduced by one-third.
Clarify (see To Clarify Stock),
jar, cool, cover, and refrigerate.
Remove and discard any hardened
fat from top before using.

The next day, remove galantine
from towel and rewrap in plastic

wrap and then aluminum foil. Refrigerate at least 1 day, or for up to 3 days. Several days of mellowing will improve the flavor. At this point, the galantine may be frozen for up to 1 month.

The morning of the day the galantine is to be served, prepare the Madeira aspic jelly, using the reserved clarified stock. Carefully cut about 1/3 of the galantine into 1/8-inch-thick slices. Following directions for Coating Foods with Aspic, coat the uncut portion of the galantine with 2 or 3 layers of aspic jelly. Decorate with garnitures and finish with 2 or 3 more coatings of aspic jelly. Chill to set firmly. Coat the slices of galantine with aspic jelly and refrigerate.

To serve, place the uncut galantine on a serving platter and surround with the slices, tucking watercress sprigs in between the slices. Cluster the green onion brushes at the uncut end of the galantine and place a basket of rye bread next to the platter.

GALANTINE OF VEAL ○■

Approximately Thirty Servings

One 4-pound breast of veal (or two 2-pound breasts)
8 ounces cooked smoked tongue, cut into 1/4-inch-square strips
8 ounces pork fatback lardoons
1/3 cup unsalted pistachio nuts
1 cup aspic jelly, made from reserved stock and dry vermouth
Garnitures for Lined Molds

MARINADE

1 cup dry vermouth
2 tablespoons fresh lemon juice
1/2 teaspoon ground thyme
1/4 teaspoon ground mace
1 large bay leaf, broken
3 large garlic cloves, finely minced
6 parsley sprigs, chopped

STOCK

See Galantine of Turkey (preceding), substituting veal bones for the turkey bones and decreasing the water measurement to 2-1/2 quarts

FORCEMEAT

4 ounces lean pork, cut into 1/2-inch cubes
4 ounces veal, cut into 1/2-inch cubes
4 ounces ham, cut into 1/2-inch cubes

2 ounces pork fatback, cut into 1/2-inch cubes
2 veal kidneys, halved
1 tablespoon butter
1 egg, lightly beaten
1/4 cup fine dry bread crumbs
1/4 cup minced fresh parsley
1/4 cup strained reserved marinade
1 teaspoon salt
1/4 teaspoon freshly ground black pepper
1/4 teaspoon ground thyme
1/4 teaspoon ground mace

PRESENTATION

Chicory, coarsely broken
Egg-Aspic Cutouts
Tomato Roses
Homemade-style dark rye bread slices

Carefully bone the breast(s) of veal, keeping in 1 (or 2) pieces, then scrape all remaining meat from the bones. Brown the bones as in Galantine of Turkey.

While bones are browning, place the breast(s) and any bits of meat in a shallow nonmetallic container. Add the pork, veal, ham, and fatback cubes (see forcemeat ingredients), tongue, and lardoons, keeping all meats separate.

To prepare the marinade, combine vermouth, lemon juice, thyme, mace, bay, garlic, and parsley. Pour all but 1/4 cup of the marinade over all the meats, cover, and refrigerate overnight, turning occasionally. Be careful to keep the meats separate. Cover and refrigerate the reserved 1/4 cup marinade.

To prepare and store the stock, follow directions in Galantine of Turkey.

The next day, prepare the forcemeat. Remove the pork, veal, ham, and fatback cubes from the marinade and grind in a food processor or meat grinder. Transfer mixture to a mixing bowl and set aside. In a small skillet, sauté kidneys in butter over medium-high heat 5 minutes, or until they are almost cooked through. When cool enough to handle, chop finely and add to the bowl. Mix in egg, bread crumbs, parsley, reserved 1/4 cup marinade, salt, pepper, thyme, and mace. Pinch off a small portion and sauté until cooked through. Taste and adjust seasonings, adding thyme and mace if needed. Cover and refrigerate.

Place a muslin towel, folded crosswise (about 1-1/2 feet by 2 feet), on work surface. Remove veal breast(s) from marinade and lay flat on the towel (if using 2 small breasts, overlap them by about 3/4 inch). If the thickness of the breast(s) is not uniform, fill in any hollows with the reserved marinated pieces of veal breast.

To assemble the galantine, spread half the forcemeat over the veal, leaving a 1/2-inch border on all sides. Alternating them, arrange the tongue, lardoons, and any remaining pieces of veal crosswise on the forcemeat. Sprinkle pistachio nuts evenly over. Being careful not to disturb the pattern, spread remaining forcemeat over all.

With the help of the towel, lift one short end of the breast and carefully roll into a cylinder. Following directions in Galantine of Turkey, wrap, poach, and weight the galantine. Refrigerate the weighted galantine 4 hours, then remove weights. Continue to refrigerate galantine overnight.

Reheat stock and strain into a saucepan, bring to a boil, and boil until reduced by one-third.

Clarify (see To Clarify Stock), jar, cool, cover, and refrigerate. Remove and discard any hardened fat from top before using.

The next day, remove galantine from towel and rewrap in plastic wrap and then aluminum foil. Refrigerate at least 1 day, or for up to 3 days. Several days of mellowing will improve the flavor. At this point, the galantine may be frozen for up to 1 month.

The morning of the day the galantine is to be served, prepare the aspic jelly, using the reserved clarified stock. Carefully cut about one-third of the galantine into 1/8-inch-thick slices. Following directions for Coating Foods with Aspic, coat the uncut portion of the galantine with 2 or 3 layers of aspic jelly. Decorate with garnitures and finish with 2 or 3 more coatings of aspic jelly. Chill to set firmly. Coat the slices of galantine with aspic jelly and refrigerate.

To serve, line a platter with chicory. Place the uncut galantine on the bed of chicory and surround with the slices. Garnish the platter with egg-aspic cutouts and tomato roses. Place a basket of dark rye bread next to the platter.

MOLDS

GENERAL INSTRUCTIONS FOR MOLDS

The term "mold" can be a confusing one, for it refers to both the container and its contents. A mold in the latter sense is a preparation in which gelatin, cream, and/or egg whites are used to bind the ingredients. Savory mousses fit into this definition, as do a whole array of spectacular-looking dishes that are simply called "molds." Included here are ones made with creamy Gorgonzola, luxurious red caviar, and robust Braunschweiger.

Selection of the mold form can be crucial. The form can be deep or shallow, depending upon the stiffness and weight of the ingredients. It can be shaped like a fish, a fruit, or a chicken, or can be a fluted pie tin, baking pan, or bowl. Metal containers without intricate designs, sharp corners, or ridges are better than glass, plastic, and ceramic because the metal permits quick cooling and warming of the mold's surface without ruining its shape.

Once you have combined the mold ingredients, brush the inside of the chosen container with Lecithin Oil. Spoon in the mold mixture, cover with plastic wrap, and refrigerate at least six hours or overnight.

The *unmolding* can be done the morning of the party. Hold the container in hot water up to the rim for several seconds, or *just* until the edges of the gelatin start to melt. Remove the container from the water and dry the outside with a towel. Run a thin-bladed knife or spatula lightly around the edges of the mold to help release it. Invert a chilled plate or platter on top of the mold. (If the plate has been rinsed in cold water first, the mold can be easily slid into a more accurate position on the plate once it is unmolded.) Turn the mold upside down with the plate in place, and give a sharp shake before lifting the container straight up and off the mold. Wipe the plate clean. Cover the mold with plastic wrap and refrigerate immediately.

For large molds or multiple molds on a single platter, or when the mold is to be served on a bed of shredded lettuce or other greens, the hot-water dipping method is not feasible. Containers should be inverted cold onto the plate and then warmed with hot damp towels, repeating until the container lifts free.

Serve the molds with plain crackers, various breads, and/or sliced raw vegetables. Provide several small broad-bladed knives so guests can spread the preparation onto the crackers.

BLUE CHEESE MOLD O

Approximately Thirty Servings
1 envelope (2 teaspoons)
    unflavored gelatin
3 tablespoons cold water
6 ounces blue cheese, crumbled
    (1-1/2 cups)
4 ounces cream cheese,
    at room temperature
3/4 cup heavy cream
1 teaspoon grated onion
1 teaspoon minced fresh chives
1 teaspoon minced fresh dill
1/4 teaspoon freshly ground
    white pepper, or to taste
1 egg white, at room temperature
20 to 30 pimiento-stuffed olives
Pumpernickel slices

Sprinkle gelatin over water in a small dish, let stand 10 minutes until softened, set dish in a saucepan of hot water, and stir until gelatin is dissolved. Let cool briefly.

Oil a 3-cup mold with Lecithin Oil. Put blue and cream cheeses in a mixing bowl, and with a fork, mash to combine and soften. Stir in cream, onion, herbs, pepper, and dissolved gelatin until well blended and smooth. Taste and adjust seasonings.

Beat egg white until stiff peaks form, then gently fold into cheese mixture. Mound mixture into prepared mold, packing gently and leveling with a spatula or back of a wooden spoon. Cover with plastic wrap and refrigerate at least 6 hours, or overnight.

To serve, turn mold out onto a serving platter as directed in General Instructions for Molds. Slice some of the olives crosswise and decorate the top of the mold. Mince the remaining olives and use them to form a border on the platter around the mold. Serve with pumpernickel.

AVOCADO MOLD O

Approximately Forty Servings
2 large ripe avocados
1/4 cup fresh lemon or lime juice
1/4 cup Garlic Olive Oil
1 envelope (2 teaspoons)
    unflavored gelatin
1/4 cup cold water
2 teaspoons grated onion
1/4 cup commercial mayonnaise
1/4 teaspoon salt, or to taste
1/4 teaspoon freshly ground
    white pepper, or to taste
1/2 teaspoon Worcestershire sauce
4 drops Tabasco sauce, or to taste
12 ounces cooked shrimp, very
    finely minced, or 6 ounces
    smoked salmon, very finely
    minced
1 cup heavy cream

PRESENTATION
Watercress sprigs
Thin slices of lemon, halved
Salmon roe
Melba Toast rounds

Peel, pit, and dice avocados and place in a glass or ceramic bowl. Add lemon juice and oil and let stand 2 hours. Sprinkle gelatin over water in a small dish, let stand 10 minutes until softened, set dish in a saucepan of hot water, and stir until gelatin is dissolved. Let cool briefly.

Oil a 3- to 4-cup mold with Lecithin Oil. In a blender or food processor, purée avocado and marinade, dissolved gelatin, onion, mayonnaise, and seasonings. Add shrimp and whirl just until mixed. Transfer avocado mixture to a large bowl. Whip cream until stiff and gently fold into avocado mixture. Taste and adjust seasonings. Mound mixture into prepared mold, packing gently and leveling with a spatula or back of a wooden spoon. Cover with plastic wrap and refrigerate at least 6 hours, or overnight.

To serve, turn mold out onto serving platter as directed in General Instructions for Molds and garnish with watercress and lemon slices. Place salmon roe in a small crystal bowl alongside. Serve with melba rounds.

HERBED
FETA CHEESE MOLD ○

Approximately Twenty-five Servings
1/2 tablespoon unflavored gelatin
3 tablespoons water
1/4 cup firmly packed fresh
    parsley leaves
2 tablespoons firmly packed
    fresh basil leaves
1 teaspoon firmly packed fresh
    rosemary leaves
1/3 cup chopped onion
1/4 cup chopped green bell
    pepper
1 large garlic clove, minced
1/4 pound unsalted butter, cut
    into bits and at room
    temperature
2 ounces cream cheese,
    at room temperature
8 ounces feta cheese, crumbled
    (1-3/4 cups)
2 tablespoons heavy cream
1/4 teaspoon freshly ground
    white pepper

PRESENTATION
6 Mediterranean-style ripe olives,
    slivered
4 basil leaves
Rosemary sprigs
Crudités
Unsalted crackers

Sprinkle gelatin over water in a
small dish. Set dish in a saucepan
of hot water and stir until gelatin
is dissolved. Let cool briefly.

In a blender or food processor,
whirl parsley, basil, and rosemary
leaves until minced. Add onion,
bell pepper, and garlic. Whirl
until finely minced. Add butter
and cream cheese; mix well.
Blend in feta cheese, cream, and
white pepper. Add dissolved gelatin and whirl just until mixed.
Taste and adjust seasonings.

Oil a decorative 3-cup mold
with Lecithin Oil. Pack cheese
mixture into the prepared mold,
cover with plastic wrap, and
refrigerate at least 6 hours, or
overnight.

To serve, turn mold out onto
a serving plate as directed in
General Instructions for Molds.
Decorate mold with olive slivers
and garnish the plate with basil
leaves and rosemary sprigs. Surround the mold with crudités
and place a basket of unsalted
crackers nearby.

WATERCRESS
CREAM MOLD ○

Approximately Thirty Servings
1 teaspoon unflavored gelatin
2 tablespoons cold water
1 large bunch watercress
    (approximately 7 ounces)
8 ounces cream cheese,
    at room temperature
2 ounces blue cheese,
    crumbled (1/2 cup)
2 tablespoons prepared
    horseradish
1/2 cup mayonnaise
3 tablespoons fresh lemon juice
1/2 teaspoon freshly grated
    lemon peel
1/2 teaspoon dry mustard
1/4 teaspoon freshly ground
    white pepper
1 cup heavy cream
Shredded lettuce
Plain crackers

Sprinkle gelatin over water in a
small dish, let stand 10 minutes
until softened, set dish in a
saucepan of hot water, and stir
until gelatin is dissolved. Let
cool briefly.

Oil a 4-cup mold with Lecithin
Oil. Set aside several of the best
watercress sprigs. Mince (do not
use blender or food processor)
enough of the remaining leaves
to measure 1-1/2 cups, firmly
packed. Put cream and blue

cheeses in a large mixing bowl, and with a fork, mix to combine and soften. Stir in horseradish, mayonnaise, lemon juice, lemon peel, mustard, and pepper, then mix in minced watercress and gelatin mixture. Whip cream until stiff and gently fold into watercress mixture. Mound mixture in prepared mold, packing gently and leveling with a spatula or the back of a wooden spoon. Cover with plastic wrap and refrigerate at least 6 hours, or overnight.

To serve, line a serving platter with shredded lettuce and turn mold out as directed in General Instructions for Molds. Garnish with watercress sprigs and serve with crackers.

SHRIMP AND CHEESE MOUSSE O

This airy yet rich mousse is especially attractive chilled in a fish-shaped mold. The full-flavored shrimp and cheese make additional seasonings unnecessary.

Approximately Forty Servings
8 ounces shrimp
1-1/2 quarts water
1 large ripe tomato, chopped
1 tablespoon pickling spice
Peel of 1 lemon
2 tablespoons fresh lemon juice
1 tablespoon salt

1 envelope (2 teaspoons) unflavored gelatin
1/3 cup fresh parsley leaves
1/4 cup chopped green onion tops
One 4-ounce package Rondale cheese, at room temperature
1/4 cup mayonnaise
1/4 teaspoon freshly ground white pepper
1/2 cup heavy cream, chilled

PRESENTATION
1 slice ripe olive (slice crosswise)
Tarragon leaves
Parsley sprigs
Light rye bread and/or unsalted crackers

Wash the shrimp and remove and reserve the shells. Devein the shrimp and set aside. Place the shells in a large saucepan and add water, tomato, pickling spice, lemon peel and juice, and salt. Bring to a rolling boil, add shrimp, bring back to a rapid boil, and boil 1-1/2 minutes, or until shrimp turn pink and are just barely cooked. Drain shrimp, reserving liquid. Remove shrimp from strainer, cool, and refrigerate. Discard anything that remains in strainer. Measure 1/3 cup of

the liquid into a small dish and refrigerate until cold. Save the remaining strained cooking liquid to use as a base for fish stock.

Sprinkle gelatin over the chilled liquid, let stand 10 minutes until softened, set dish in a saucepan of hot water, and stir until gelatin is dissolved. Let cool briefly.

In a blender or food processor, whirl parsley and onion tops until finely minced. Coarsely chop the reserved shrimp and add to blender, whirling just until shrimp are minced. Add the softened gelatin, cheese, mayonnaise, and pepper and whirl until well blended. Taste, adjust seasonings, and transfer to a large mixing bowl.

Oil a 3- to 4-cup mold with Lecithin Oil; set aside. Whip cream until stiff and stir about 1/2 cup of the cream into the shrimp mixture to lighten it. Fold in remaining cream and spoon into prepared mold. Cover mold with plastic wrap and refrigerate at least 6 hours, or overnight.

To serve, turn mold out onto an oval serving platter as directed in General Instructions for Molds. Decorate the fish, using the olive slice as an eye and tarragon leaves as gills. Tuck parsley sprigs around the fish and serve with rye bread and/or crackers.

CHICKEN MOUSSE WITH ALMONDS ○

Vary this mousse by substituting cooked turkey for the chicken, or by using half chicken or turkey and half ground cooked ham. If using ham, reduce the salt measurement.

Approximately Twenty Servings
1 envelope (2 teaspoons) unflavored gelatin
3 tablespoons dry white wine
1-1/4 cups rich chicken stock, heated
1-1/2 cups coarsely ground or finely chopped cooked chicken
1 tablespoon brandy
1/2 teaspoon salt
1/4 teaspoon paprika
1/4 teaspoon freshly ground white pepper
1/8 teaspoon freshly grated nutmeg
1/3 cup lightly toasted, finely chopped blanched almonds
1/2 cup heavy cream
Parsley sprigs
Light and dark rye bread slices

Sprinkle gelatin over wine in a small dish and let stand 10 minutes until softened. Spoon into heated stock and stir to dissolve.

Oil a 3-cup mold with Lecithin Oil. In a blender or food processor, purée chicken with 1/2 cup of the stock. Transfer to a mixing bowl and add remaining stock, brandy, seasonings, and almonds. Taste and adjust seasonings. Chill the chicken mixture until almost set, stirring occasionally. Do not allow to harden.

Whip cream until stiff and gently fold into chicken mixture. Mound mixture in prepared mold, packing gently and leveling with a spatula or back of a wooden spoon. Cover with plastic wrap and refrigerate at least 6 hours, or overnight.

To serve, turn mold out onto serving plate as directed in General Instructions for Molds and garnish with parsley sprigs. Serve with rye bread.

BLACK CAVIAR MOLD ○

Approximately Forty Servings
1 envelope (2 teaspoons) unflavored gelatin
3 tablespoons cold water
2 eggs, separated
1/2 cup plus 2 tablespoons heavy cream
4 ounces cream cheese, cut into bits and at room temperature
2 tablespoons fresh lemon juice
1 tablespoon freshly grated lemon peel
1 teaspoon Worcestershire sauce
One 3-3/4-ounce jar lumpfish caviar

PRESENTATION
One 3-3/4-ounce jar lumpfish caviar, or
20 black olives, quartered lengthwise
2 hard-cooked eggs, whites and yolks sieved separately
Black bread slices

Sprinkle gelatin over water in a small dish, let stand 10 minutes until softened, set dish in a saucepan of hot water, and stir until gelatin is dissolved. Let cool briefly.

In a large saucepan, beat together egg yolks and 2 tablespoons heavy cream. *Stirring constantly,* cook over medium-low heat *just* to heat. Add cheese and stir until cheese melts. Remove saucepan from heat. Stir in lemon juice, lemon peel, Worcestershire sauce, caviar, and gelatin mixture.

Oil a 4-cup mold with Lecithin Oil. Whip egg whites until stiff peaks form. In a separate bowl, whip the remaining 1/2 cup cream until stiff. Fold the egg whites into the caviar mixture, and then gently fold in the whipped cream. Mound mousse into prepared mold, leveling with a spatula or back of a wooden spoon. Cover with plastic wrap and refrigerate at least 6 hours, or overnight.

To serve, turn mold out onto a serving plate as directed in General Instructions for Molds and decorate with caviar or black olive slivers and hard-cooked eggs. Serve with black bread.

RED CAVIAR MOUSSE O

The quality of the caviar is crucial in this recipe, so don't skimp when you go to purchase the jar.

Approximately Twenty-five Servings
1 envelope (2 teaspoons) unflavored gelatin
2 tablespoons fresh lemon juice
2 tablespoons water
1/2 cup Crème Fraîche or sour cream
1/2 teaspoon Worcestershire sauce
3 drops Tabasco sauce
1 teaspoon grated onion
2 tablespoons minced fresh parsley
2 tablespoons minced fresh chives or green onion tops
1/4 teaspoon salt
1/4 teaspoon freshly ground white pepper
1 hard-cooked egg
One 2-ounce jar red caviar
1/2 cup heavy cream

PRESENTATION
hard-cooked eggs, whites and yolks sieved separately
finely minced fresh parsley
Melba Toast rounds

Sprinkle gelatin over lemon juice and water in a small dish, let stand 10 minutes until softened, set dish in a saucepan of hot water, and stir until gelatin is dissolved. Let cool briefly.

Oil a 2-cup mold with Lecithin Oil. In a large mixing bowl, combine crème fraîche, Worcestershire and Tabasco sauces, onion, parsley, chives, salt, pepper, and dissolved gelatin. Sieve the egg and stir into the mixture with the caviar. Whip cream until stiff and gently fold into the mixture. Mound mousse in prepared mold, packing gently and leveling with a spatula or back of a wooden spoon. Cover with plastic wrap and refrigerate at least 6 hours, or overnight.

To serve, turn mold out onto a serving plate as directed in General Instructions for Molds. Decorate with sieved whites and yolks and minced parsley. Accompany with melba toast rounds.

CHICKEN LIVER MOUSSE WITH BRANDY O

Approximately Fifty Servings
1 envelope (2 teaspoons) unflavored gelatin
3 tablespoons cold water
1-1/2 cups Chicken Liver Pâté, at room temperature
1 tablespoon brandy, or to taste
3 tablespoons minced ripe olives
1/2 cup heavy cream
Ripe olives, halved
Rye bread slices

Sprinkle gelatin over water in a small dish, let stand 10 minutes until softened, set dish in a saucepan of hot water, and stir until gelatin is dissolved. Let cool briefly.

Oil a 3-cup mold with Lecithin Oil. In a mixing bowl, combine pâté and brandy and beat with a wooden spoon until smooth. Stir in dissolved gelatin and olives. Whip cream until stiff and gently fold into pâté mixture. Mound mixture into prepared mold, leveling gently with a spatula or back of a wooden spoon. Cover with plastic wrap and refrigerate at least 6 hours, or overnight.

To serve, turn out onto a serving plate as directed in General Instructions for Molds and decorate with olive halves. Accompany with rye bread.

PARSLIED HAM IN ASPIC ○

The flavor of the aspic and the quality of the ham are critical to the success of this lovely presentation. For added eye appeal and texture, encase sliced hard-cooked eggs and tarragon leaves in a layer of aspic jelly in the bottom of the mold before layering the ham and parsley (see Lining Containers with Aspic Jelly and Garnishing Aspic-lined Molds).

Approximately Thirty Servings
12 ounces cooked ham, *very* finely shredded
3 tablespoons brandy
1 cup very finely minced fresh parsley
6 black peppercorns, lightly crushed
6 allspice berries, lightly crushed
3 cups Madeira Aspic Jelly

PRESENTATION
Parsley leaves
Mustard Mayonnaise
Sourdough Melba Toast rounds

In a nonmetallic container, combine ham, brandy, 2 tablespoons of the parsley (wrap the remainder in paper toweling, place in a plastic bag, and refrigerate), peppercorns, and allspice berries.

Cover and marinate in the refrigerator, turning frequently, 3 hours or overnight.

Make jelly and keep at room temperature without allowing to set. Oil a 6- or 7-inch soufflé dish or other mold with Lecithin Oil. Sprinkle the remaining parsley over the bottom of the mold, then carefully cover with the ham mixture. Slowly pour in jelly, being careful not to disturb the parsley and ham layers. Cover with plastic wrap and refrigerate at least 6 hours, or overnight.

To serve, turn mold out onto a serving plate as directed in General Instructions for Molds. Surround mold with parsley leaves and accompany with a dish of mayonnaise and a basket of melba toast rounds.

BRAUNSCHWEIGER MOLD WITH CAVIAR ●

This Braunschweiger mold and the one that follows are not true molds, for they have no gelatin, egg white, or whipped cream. They are held together by the liver sausage, the cheese, and the chilling. These mock molds appear here because they are similar in texture to and have the appearance of molds without having to work with as many ingredients as the true versions demand.

Approximately Twenty-five Servings
8 ounces Braunschweiger (liver sausage)
3 ounces cream cheese, at room temperature
1 tablespoon dry vermouth
Light cream as needed
One 3-3/4-ounce jar lumpfish caviar
2 hard-cooked eggs, whites and yolks sieved separately
Baguette slices

Oil a 2-cup round-bottomed bowl with Lecithin Oil and place 2 broad strips of cheesecloth overlapping in a crisscross pattern in the center of the mold. The strips should overhang the bowl by about 1 inch so that they can be used to ease the mold out of the bowl once it has been chilled.

In a mixing bowl, mash the Braunschweiger with a fork and press firmly into prepared bowl. Cover with plastic wrap and chill at least 2 hours. Carefully ease the Braunschweiger from the mold with the help of the cheesecloth, turning it upside down on a round serving plate and carefully removing the cheesecloth.

In a mixing bowl, combine the cream cheese and vermouth and beat with a wooden spoon until smooth, adding cream as needed to make spreading consistency. Spread the cheese mixture evenly over the mound of Braunschweiger. Cover the mound with caviar and garnish with a ring of hard-cooked eggs. Serve with baguettes.

BRAUNSCHWEIGER CREAM CHEESE MOLD ●

Approximately Fifty Servings
12 ounces Braunschweiger
    (liver sausage)
8 ounces cream cheese, at room
    temperature
3 tablespoons finely minced
    green onion and tops
1 tablespoon fresh lemon juice
1/2 tablespoon Worcestershire
    sauce
6 drops Tabasco sauce,
    or to taste
1/4 teaspoon salt
1/4 teaspoon freshly ground
    white pepper
1/4 teaspoon garlic powder,
    or to taste

PRESENTATION
8 ounces cream cheese,
    at room temperature
1 tablespoon light cream,
    or as needed
1/2 cup lightly toasted halved
    almonds, cut into slivers
10 small pimiento-stuffed olives,
    sliced crosswise
Rye and black bread slices

Oil a 6-cup mold with Lecithin Oil and place 2 broad strips of cheesecloth overlapping in a criss-cross pattern in the center of the mold. The strips should overhang the edge of the mold by about 1 inch so that they can be used to ease the Braunschweiger mixture out once it has chilled.

In a mixing bowl, mash Braunschweiger with a fork and blend in 8 ounces cream cheese, green onion, lemon juice, Worcestershire and Tabasco sauces, salt, pepper, and garlic powder. Mixture should be well mixed and smooth. Taste and adjust seasonings. Pack firmly into prepared mold, smoothing with a spatula or back of a wooden spoon. Tap the mold on the counter several times to help settle the mixture. Cover with plastic wrap and chill at least 4 hours, or overnight.

To serve, ease Braunschweiger mixture out of the mold with the help of the cheesecloth, turning it upside down onto a large round plate and carefully removing the cheesecloth. In a mixing bowl, combine 8 ounces cream cheese and 1 tablespoon cream and stir with a fork or wooden spoon until smooth and well blended, adding more cream as needed to make spreading consistency. Spread cheese mixture evenly on top and sides of Braunschweiger mold and decorate with almond slivers and olive slices. Serve with rye and black bread slices.

PASTRIES

Many an experienced cook is made nervous at the mention of making pastry dough. The anxious response is unnecessary, for making pastry can be easy and fun, especially when you use a food processor to mix the dough.

The pastry dough recipes that follow give directions for preparing the dough by hand, but all of them, with the exception of Short Crust Pastry, go together beautifully in a processor. Once the dough is mixed, follow the simple, thorough directions for rolling out the dough, cutting it into shapes, and filling it. The steps have been outlined with conservative estimates on how many pastries to assemble at one time. For example, initially you may be able to handle only ten pastry rounds, but as you become more proficient and are able to work faster, the number will increase.

No yields are given for the pastry doughs, as each is geared to specific filling recipes. Each quiche, however, uses only one pie-sized shell, even though the dough recipe may make two. Rather than make a half recipe, line two pans with pastry and freeze one of them for a future date.

Once you feel comfortable making pastry, you will find yourself looking forward to the opportunity to work with dough. Pastries are most easily made in large quantities, and because they freeze well, they can be kept on hand for serving any size group. They are perfect to bring out when unexpected guests arrive or to preface a last-minute dinner party.

A wide range of choices appear here: pastry rounds and spirals, empanaditas, piroshki, quiches, tartlets, bouchées, barquettes, phyllo triangles, and choux. Set aside a day to prepare one or more of these, then sit back and relax on the day of your party.

GENERAL INSTRUCTIONS FOR PASTRY

MAKING DOUGH IN A FOOD PROCESSOR

Combine dry ingredients in the bowl of the processor and pulse once or twice to mix. Strew the butter and/or lard evenly in bowl, and with on/off pulses, process until mixture is the consistency of coarse cornmeal. Rub the mixture between your fingertips to check for proper consistency. With processor motor running, add liquid and process *just* until dough *begins* to gather on one side of bowl. Do not overprocess or the dough will toughen. It is better to undermix than to overmix.

Remove dough from bowl, lightly form into a loose ball, gathering all the stray bits from the sides of the bowl, and, if recipe so indicates, divide the ball in half. Form the loose ball (or each half) into a rough ball, then gently flatten the ball into a disc about 1/2-inch thick. Do not handle too much; the disc need not be compact and too much handling will toughen the dough. Wrap disc(s) in waxed paper, place in a plastic bag, and refrigerate at least 1 hour, or up to 1 day, before rolling out.

ROLLING THE DOUGH

Remove one disc of dough at a time from the refrigerator and let stand 3 to 4 minutes at room temperature (up to 10 minutes if dough has been refrigerated more than 1 hour) before proceeding. If the dough is too cold, it will crack as you roll it out; if it is too warm, it will become sticky when rolled and added flour will toughen it. Place dough on a lightly floured surface, preferably of marble, though wood is the second choice. Using a lightly floured long, slender rolling pin, roll from the center of the disc outward, pressing gently rather than sliding across the surface of the dough. Always roll from the center of the disc outward, and as you roll, gradually radiate the strokes around the entire disc.

When the pastry round is about 8 inches in diameter, carefully slip a long, thin-bladed, flexible metal spatula under it, lift up, flip the round over onto your hand and forearm, lightly flour the work surface, and then slip the dough back onto it so the surface of the round on which you were rolling is now facing the marble slab. Continue rolling out the dough in the same manner, always remembering not to force it by applying too much pressure and to begin all of the strokes at the center. Loosen the round and flip as many times as are necessary to prevent it from sticking. The final round should be 1/8 to 1/16 inch thick, depending upon the recipe.

Line a quiche pan with the round as described below, or cut the dough into rounds or other shapes as specified in individual recipes. As you cut, place the rounds on a baking sheet and cover loosely with a tea towel to prevent them from drying out. Gather the scraps, form into a loose ball, wrap in waxed paper, and refrigerate 10 minutes or so. Then roll out and cut additional rounds as described above. For using the final scraps, see Rolling Pastry Scraps.

LINING QUICHE PANS

To line a quiche pan, the pastry round or rectangle should be about 1 inch larger than the pan. (See General Instructions for Quiches for information on quiche pans.) When the pastry round is the proper size, carefully fold it in half, gently lift from the board, and set it down on one-half of the pan. Unfold the round and center it on the pan. Lifting the edges of the round as you work, gently press the dough to the sides of the pan.

With kitchen shears, trim the edges evenly to leave a 1/4-inch overhang. (Gather the scraps into a rough ball, wrap in waxed paper, place in a plastic bag, and refrigerate. See Rolling Pastry Scraps for how to work with them.) Gently but firmly press the edges of the dough to make a narrow rim around the top of the pan, folding under the overhang and forming a nice flute around the rim with your fingertips. The flute should be about 1/4 inch higher than the rim of the pan to allow for shrinkage of the dough during baking. Chill at least 30 minutes before baking.

If time allows, wrap the pastry-lined pan in plastic wrap and freeze several hours; defrost in the refrigerator 15 minutes before baking. This freezing will result in a flakier crust.

MAKING TARTLETS AND BARQUETTES

Use Lemon Egg White, Short Crust, Cream Cheese, or Cheddar-Parmesan Cheese Pastry for forming tartlets and barquettes. Roll the dough as directed (see Rolling the Dough) and cut into rounds as close to 2-5/16 inches in diameter as possible. Carefully and gently press the rounds into muffin-tin wells 1-3/4 inches wide and 7/8 inch deep. (You can line small oyster, scallop, or clam shells in place of the muffin tins.)

For barquettes, you will need barquette tins, which are small, boat-shaped molds. Using one of the molds as a guide, cut out ovals about 1/2 inch greater in size than the mold, and then gently press the pastry ovals into the tins.

Refrigerate the tartlet and barquette shells at least 30 minutes before baking, or wrap and freeze for several hours as for a quiche shell.

Unless otherwise specified, these shells are fully baked before filling. For best results, weight and bake the shells as explained in the section on fully baked pastry shells that follows, but reduce the baking time for the first step to 5 minutes and for the second step to 5 to 8 minutes. Alternatively, do not weight the shells. Prick the bottoms well with the tines of a fork and bake in a preheated 350° F oven 12 to 15 minutes, or until lightly golden. Cool on a wire rack before filling. To remove from the wells or molds, slip the tip of a thin-bladed knife or tines of a fork along the edge of the pastry and gently lift out.

ROLLING PASTRY SCRAPS

The second batch of scraps that results from rolling out pastry cannot be used for making hors d'oeuvres. Gather the scraps together, form them into a disc about 1/2 inch thick, wrap in waxed paper, and refrigerate at least 20 minutes.

Roll the dough out as best you can. Spread the dough with softened butter, sprinkle with freshly grated Parmesan cheese or sugar and cinnamon, cut into rough squares, and place on a baking sheet. Bake in a preheated 375° F oven 10 minutes, or until golden. Cool on a rack and store in an airtight container for up to 2 days, or freeze in the container for up to 3 weeks. These scraps lack eye appeal, but they taste marvelous.

PASTRY SHELLS

PREBAKING PASTRY SHELLS Preheat oven to 400° F. Carefully line the quiche shell with a sheet of lightweight aluminum foil large enough so that it can be easily lifted out. Fill the foil-lined shell with metal pie weights or with raw rice or legumes halfway up the sides of the shell. Crimp the foil so that it covers the exposed rim of the crust to prevent burning.

Bake the weighted shell in the preheated oven 10 minutes. Remove from the oven, lift out the foil and weights, prick the entire bottom surface of the shell with the tines of a fork, and return the shell to the oven. Bake an additional 5 minutes, then remove from the oven, place on a wire rack, and let cool completely before filling.

FULLY BAKING PASTRY SHELLS Proceed as directed for Prebaking Pastry Shells. After removing the weights and pricking the shell, lower oven heat to 350° F and bake shell 15 to 20 minutes, or until golden. Cool on wire rack.

STORING UNBAKED PASTRY DOUGHS AND BAKED AND UNBAKED SHELLS The disc formed once the dough has been mixed can be wrapped in waxed paper, placed in a plastic bag, and refrigerated up to 24 hours before rolling out. Only in an emergency should the disc be frozen, in which case wrap it in aluminum foil and freeze no more than 2 weeks. Defrost the disc in the refrigerator and be patient when rolling out the dough, for it will be much more difficult to work with than freshly made pastry dough.

Rolled-out rounds may be sheet frozen up to 1 month. Defrost in a single layer in the refrigerator. As with the frozen discs, the dough will have dried out a bit in freezing, making it harder to work with.

If you have prebaked or fully baked a shell, it will keep at room temperature for 6 hours before filling. Unbaked, prebaked, and fully baked shells may be wrapped in plastic wrap or aluminum foil and frozen for up to 3 to 4 weeks. They will defrost quickly in or out of the refrigerator.

CREAM CHEESE PASTRY ●

1 cup plus 2 tablespoons
    unbleached flour
3/4 teaspoon salt
1/4 pound butter, cut into
    16 bits and chilled
4 ounces cream cheese, cut into
    8 pieces and chilled
1 egg, lightly beaten

In a mixing bowl, combine flour and salt. With fingertips, pastry blender, or 2 knives, crumble butter and cream cheese into flour mixture until the consistency of coarse cornmeal. With a fork, blend in beaten egg just until moistened. (Or mix dough in a food processor as explained in General Instructions for Pastry.)

With fingers, gently gather the dough into a loose ball; do not "pack" the dough. Flatten ball into a disc about 1-1/2 inches thick, wrap disc in waxed paper, place disc in a plastic bag, and refrigerate at least 1 hour.

COTTAGE CHEESE PASTRY ●

1-1/4 cups unbleached flour
1/2 teaspoon salt
1/4 teaspoon ground mace
    (optional)
1/4 pound butter, cut into
    16 bits and chilled
2 tablespoons milk
1/2 cup low-fat small-curd
    cottage cheese

In a mixing bowl, combine flour, salt, and mace. With fingertips, pastry blender, or 2 knives, crumble butter into flour mixture until the consistency of coarse cornmeal. With a fork, blend in milk and cottage cheese just until moistened. (Or mix dough in a food processor as explained in General Instructions for Pastry.)

With fingers, gently gather the dough into a rough ball; do not "pack" the dough. Flatten ball into a disc about 1-1/2 inches thick, wrap disc in waxed paper, place disc in a plastic bag, and refrigerate at least 1 hour.

SOUR CREAM PASTRY ●

1 cup unbleached flour
1/8 teaspoon salt
4 tablespoons butter, cut into
    8 bits and chilled
1/2 cup sour cream

In a large mixing bowl, combine flour and salt. With fingertips, pastry blender, or 2 knives, crumble butter into flour mixture until the consistency of coarse cornmeal. With a fork, stir in sour cream until just moistened. (Or mix dough in a food processor as explained in General Instructions for Pastry.)

With fingers, gently gather the dough into a loose ball; do not "pack" the dough. Flatten ball into a disc about 1-1/2 inches thick, wrap disc in waxed paper, place disc in a plastic bag, and refrigerate at least 1 hour.

SHORT CRUST PASTRY ●

If you wish to use the processor for this recipe, combine and mix the ingredients as directed for an electric mixer. Do not follow the general directions for making dough in a processor.

1 cup lard, at room temperature
1/3 cup boiling water
1 tablespoon milk
2-1/2 cups unbleached flour, mixed with 1 teaspoon salt

In the large bowl of an electric mixer, beat lard until smooth and creamy. Beat in water and milk until liquid is well blended into lard. With a fork, stir in flour mixture.

With fingers, gently gather the dough into a loose ball. Divide ball in half and form each half into a rough ball; do not "pack" the dough. Flatten each ball into a disc about 1-1/2 inches thick, wrap each disc in waxed paper, place discs in a plastic bag, and refrigerate at least 1 hour.

LEMON EGG WHITE PASTRY ●

2 cups unbleached flour
1/2 teaspoon salt
1/2 teaspoon ground thyme, savory, or marjoram (optional)
4 tablespoons butter, cut into 8 bits and chilled
4 tablespoons lard, cut into 8 bits and chilled
2 egg whites (unbeaten), chilled
Approximately 1/4 cup fresh lemon juice, chilled

In a large mixing bowl, combine flour, salt, and thyme. With fingertips, pastry blender, or 2 knives, crumble butter and lard into flour mixture until the consistency of coarse cornmeal. Place egg whites in a measuring cup and add lemon juice to measure 1/2 cup. With a fork, quickly stir liquid into flour-butter mixture until just moistened. (Or mix dough in a food processor as explained in General Instructions for Pastry.)

With fingers, gently gather the dough into a loose ball. Divide ball in half and form each half into a rough ball; do not "pack" the dough. Flatten each ball into a disc about 1-1/2 inches thick, wrap each disc in waxed paper, place discs in a plastic bag, and refrigerate at least 1 hour.

CHEDDAR-PARMESAN CHEESE PASTRY ●

1-1/4 cups unbleached flour
1/2 teaspoon salt
1/8 teaspoon cayenne pepper (optional)
1/4 pound butter, cut into 16 bits and chilled
1 cup finely shredded or grated sharp Cheddar cheese
1 cup freshly grated Parmesan cheese
3 tablespoons ice water, or as needed

In a large mixing bowl, combine flour, salt, and cayenne pepper. With fingertips, pastry blender, or 2 knives, crumble butter into flour mixture until the consistency of coarse cornmeal. Toss in cheeses and mix well. With a fork, quickly stir in ice water, adding only enough to moisten the mixture. (Or mix dough in a food processor as explained in General Instructions for Pastry.)

With fingers, gently gather the dough into a loose ball; do not "pack" dough. Flatten the ball into a disc about 1-1/2 inches thick, wrap disc in waxed paper, place disc in a plastic bag, and refrigerate at least 1 hour.

LITTLE PASTRIES

GENERAL INSTRUCTIONS FOR PASTRY ROUNDS

Pastry rounds are dough circles topped with a filling and then capped with a second circle and baked. They can be made well in advance and frozen until serving day.

To make pastry rounds, roll out dough as described in General Instructions for Pastry and cut into 1-1/2-inch rounds. Working with 10 rounds at a time, and keeping remaining rounds covered with a tea towel, place 1/2 teaspoon filling in the center of 5 of the rounds. Top with the remaining 5 rounds and press edges gently to seal. With the tines of a fork, press along the rim of each filled pastry round to make a tiny border and to seal securely.

Arrange the filled rounds, not touching, on a baking sheet. Cover the rounds with a tea towel to prevent them from drying out and repeat with remaining dough and filling. When all rounds are finished, cover the baking sheets with plastic wrap, securing it well, and refrigerate until about 20 minutes before baking, but no longer than 4 hours.

Preheat oven to 375° F. Brush rounds lightly with Egg Wash and bake in the preheated oven for 15 to 20 minutes, or until pastry is golden. Serve at once.

Unbaked filled pastry rounds may be sheet frozen up to 2 months. Defrost in the refrigerator before proceeding.

Do not be restricted to the fillings that follow. Sometimes you may run out of filling before you have stuffed all the pastries. Then, too, you may want to use up pastry dough left over from making a recipe for one of the quiches. Use one of the Potted Cheeses for filling the pastry rounds. Since the number of rounds you will be working with will vary, it is impossible to give an amount for the cheese; just figure on 1/2 teaspoon of filling for each round.

CHEESE ROUNDS ■

Makes Approximately
Four and One-half Dozen
1 recipe Short Crust Pastry

FILLING
1 cup crumbled Gorgonzola or
   other blue cheese (4 ounces), or
1 cup shredded Gruyère cheese

4 tablespoons butter, at room
   temperature
1 egg, lightly beaten
1/2 tablespoon water
3 tablespoons finely minced
   green onion and tops
2 tablespoons minced fresh
   parsley
1/4 teaspoon freshly ground
   white pepper
1/4 teaspoon Worcestershire
   sauce, or to taste
2 drops Tabasco sauce,
   or to taste

Prepare the pastry dough and chill discs as directed.

To make the filling, combine Gorgonzola and butter in a large mixing bowl and mix with a fork or wooden spoon until soft. Stir in half the egg. To the remaining half of the egg add water and whisk until blended. Cover egg-water mixture and refrigerate.

Add onion, parsley, pepper, and Worcestershire and Tabasco sauces to the cheese-butter mixture and stir to mix well. Cover and refrigerate at least 30 minutes, or for up to 1 day.

Working with 1 disc at a time, roll dough out and proceed as directed in General Instructions for Pastry Rounds. Use the reserved egg-water mixture in place of the egg wash called for in the general instructions.

CREAM CHEESE–ANCHOVY ROUNDS ■

Makes Approximately Three Dozen
1 recipe Cream Cheese Pastry
Egg Wash

FILLING
5 ounces cream cheese,
    at room temperature
2 tablespoons heavy cream or
    Crème Fraîche
2 teaspoons anchovy paste,
    or to taste
1 tablespoon finely minced fresh
    chives
1/4 teaspoon freshly ground
    white pepper, or to taste

Prepare the pastry dough and
chill disc as directed.
    To make the filling, combine
cheese and heavy cream in a
mixing bowl and mix until smooth
with a fork or wooden spoon.
Stir in anchovy paste, chives,
and pepper. Taste and adjust
seasonings. Cover and chill at
least 20 minutes.
    Roll dough out and proceed
as directed in General Instructions
for Pastry Rounds.

SHRIMP-WATER CHESTNUT ROUNDS ■

*Makes Approximately
Four and One-half Dozen*
1 recipe Short Crust Pastry
Egg Wash

FILLING
1 cup finely minced cooked
    shrimp
3 tablespoons finely minced
    green onion and tops
3 tablespoons finely minced
    water chestnuts
1 teaspoon Dijon-style mustard
3 tablespoons commercial
    mayonnaise
1/2 teaspoon Worcestershire
    sauce
1/4 teaspoon salt
1/4 teaspoon freshly ground
    white pepper
1/4 teaspoon crumbled dried
    basil
2 teaspoons fresh lemon juice

Prepare the pastry dough and
chill discs as directed.
    To make the filling, combine
shrimp, onion, water chestnuts,
mustard, mayonnaise, Worcestershire sauce, salt, pepper, basil,
and lemon juice in a large mixing
bowl and mix well with a fork.
Taste and adjust seasonings.
    Working with 1 disc at a
time, roll dough out and proceed
as directed in General Instructions
for Pastry Rounds.

RICOTTA CHEESE ROUNDS ■

Makes Approximately Six Dozen
2 recipes Cottage Cheese Pastry
Egg Wash

FILLING
1 egg
2/3 cup low-fat ricotta cheese
2/3 cup finely shredded Monterey
    Jack or freshly grated
    Parmesan cheese
1/4 cup finely minced green
    onion and tops
3 tablespoons finely minced
    fresh parsley
1/4 teaspoon salt, or to taste
1/4 teaspoon freshly ground
    white pepper, or to taste
Tabasco sauce to taste

Prepare the pastry dough (if
making in a food processor, do
in 2 batches for ease of mixing)
and chill discs as directed.
    Lightly beat egg in a large
mixing bowl and stir in ricotta,
Monterey Jack, onion, parsley,
salt, pepper, and Tabasco sauce.
Cover and chill at least 1 hour.
    Working with 1 disc at a
time, roll dough out and proceed
as directed in General Instructions
for Pastry Rounds.

LEMONY MUSHROOM ROUNDS ■

Makes Approximately Four Dozen
1 recipe Egg White Pastry
Egg Wash

FILLING
3/4 pound mushrooms
1 cup water
4 teaspoons fresh lemon juice
3/4 teaspoon salt
4 tablespoons butter
1/2 cup finely minced green
   onion and tops
3 tablespoons minced fresh
   parsley
2 tablespoons minced shallot
1 teaspoon finely minced garlic
1/2 teaspoon paprika
8 drops Tabasco sauce
2 tablespoons unbleached flour
1/2 cup sour cream

Prepare the pastry dough and chill discs as directed.

To make the filling, trim discolored ends from mushrooms and clean caps and stems with a soft-bristled brush. Snap off stems and set aside. Finely mince the caps and set aside.

In a saucepan, combine stems with water, 1 teaspoon of the lemon juice, and 1/4 teaspoon of the salt. Bring to a boil and simmer, uncovered, 30 minutes. Drain and discard stems; reserve liquid.

In a skillet melt butter and sauté onion, parsley, shallot, garlic, and reserved minced caps 5 minutes. Season with remaining 1/2 teaspoon salt, remaining 3 teaspoons (1 tablespoon) lemon juice, paprika, and Tabasco. Sprinkle with flour and cook and stir 3 minutes. Gradually add 1/2 cup of the reserved mushroom liquid; cook and stir until thickened. Blend in sour cream and cook without boiling 2 minutes. Taste and adjust seasonings. Let filling cool.

Working with 1 disc at a time, roll dough out and proceed as directed in General Instructions for Pastry Rounds.

SAUSAGES WRAPPED IN PASTRY ■

These hearty pastry-wrapped sausages are a hit at every gathering. Substitute puff pastry for the cream cheese pastry, if preferred.

Makes Approximately Five Dozen
1 recipe Cream Cheese Pastry
2-1/2 pounds link pork sausages
Egg Wash

Prepare the pastry dough and chill disc as directed.

Preheat oven to 350° F. With a cake tester or thin skewer, lightly prick sausages in several places and arrange on a rack in a baking pan. Bake 20 minutes or until sausages are slightly browned. Drain on paper toweling and, when cool enough to handle, cut into pieces about 1 inch long; set aside.

Roll out dough (see Rolling the Dough). Cut pastry into 1-1/4-inch squares. Place a piece of sausage across one corner of a pastry square and roll the sausage up into the pastry; the sausage will protrude from either end of the pastry "blanket." Place seam side down on a baking sheet. Cover baking sheet tightly with plastic wrap and chill 1 hour, or for up to 4 hours.

Preheat oven to 375 ° F. Brush the top of the pastry with egg wash and bake 15 minutes, or until pastry is golden. Cool briefly before serving, as the sausages retain heat.

Wrapped sausages may be sheet frozen for up to 2 months. Defrost in the refrigerator before baking.

PASTRY BALLS ∎

These balls are an excellent way to use up excess pastry or pastry scraps or small amounts of meats or cheeses. Wrap a small Steak Tartare Ball, a cube of cooked veal, a pitted olive, a small cube of chèvre, feta, Monterey Jack, Cheddar, or other firm cheese. Any of the pastry recipes in this chapter will work well.

Roll out dough (see Rolling the Dough). Cut dough into 1-1/2-inch rounds. Place a morsel in the center of the round and, with fingers, bring the dough up and around the morsel to cover it completely. To encase the morsel evenly in the dough and to seal the seam, gently roll the ball in the palms of your hands to make a smooth sphere.

Arrange balls 1 inch apart on a baking sheet, cover tightly with plastic wrap, and refrigerate at least 30 minutes, but no more than 6 hours.

Preheat oven to 375° F. Brush balls with Egg Wash and bake 15 minutes, or until golden. Cool briefly before serving, as the balls retain heat.

Pastry balls may be sheet frozen for up to 2 months. Defrost in the refrigerator before baking.

PORK AND CRAB PASTRY SPIRALS ∎

Approximately Six Dozen Servings
2 recipes Lemon Egg White
   Pastry
Egg Wash

FILLING
1 pound ground lean pork
1/2 cup finely flaked crab meat
   or chopped cooked shrimp
1/2 teaspoon salt
1/2 cup finely minced water
   chestnuts
1/4 cup finely minced bamboo
   shoots
2 tablespoons minced green
   onion and tops
2 teaspoons finely minced
   ginger root
1 teaspoon finely minced garlic
2 tablespoons soy sauce
1 egg, lightly beaten
1/4 cup fine dry bread crumbs,
   or as needed
1/2 teaspoon Oriental sesame oil

Prepare pastry (if making in a food processor, do in 2 batches for ease of mixing) and chill discs as directed.

To make the filling, place the pork in a large nonstick skillet and cook it until it loses its color. Use a fork to crumble it evenly and finely; do not brown. Add crab, salt, water chestnuts, bamboo shoots, onion, ginger root, garlic, soy sauce, egg, bread crumbs, and sesame oil. Stir to mix well.

Sauté a small portion of the pork mixture until cooked through. Taste and adjust seasonings. Add more bread crumbs if mixture appears too runny. Cover and refrigerate while rolling the dough.

Working with 1 disc at a time and keeping remaining discs refrigerated, roll dough out (see Rolling the Dough) into a rectangle about 9 by 12 inches and 1/16 inch thick. Cut rectangle in half lengthwise and spread each half with one eighth of the filling, leaving a 1/4-inch border on all 4 sides. Starting from a long edge, roll each half up tightly like a jelly roll, seal seam with a little cold water, and place roll seam side down on a baking sheet. Repeat with remaining dough portions, cover baking sheet tightly with plastic wrap, and refrigerate at least 30 minutes, but no longer than 2 hours.

Preheat oven to 375° F. Brush rolls with egg wash and bake in the preheated oven 15 to 20 minutes, or until pastry is golden. Remove from the oven, let cool 3 or 4 minutes, and cut into 1-inch slices on the diagonal with a sharp knife. Serve immediately.

Unbaked rolls may be sheet frozen for up to 1 month. Defrost in the refrigerator before baking.

GENERAL INSTRUCTIONS FOR RUSSIAN PIROSHKI AND LATIN AMERICAN EMPANADITAS

These two filled pastries are miniature versions of classic preparations, adapted to my pastry recipes and my taste in seasonings. They are both formed into a half-moon shape, but the piroshki are placed upright on the baking sheet, while the empanaditas are positioned on their sides. These pastries, like the pastry rounds, may be prepared well in advance of baking.

To make piroshki and empanaditas, roll out dough as described in General Instructions for Pastry and cut into 2-5/16-inch rounds (or as near to that size as possible). Working with 20 rounds at a time, and keeping remaining rounds covered with a tea towel, place 3/4 teaspoon filling slightly off center on each round. Fold round over to make a half-moon shape. With the tines of a fork, press along the rim of each filled pastry to make a tiny border and to seal securely.

Arrange the filled pastries, not touching, on a baking sheet. Stand the piroshki seam side up, flattening bottoms slightly; lay the empanaditas on their sides. Cover the pastries with a tea towel to prevent them from drying out and repeat with remaining dough and filling. When all the rounds are filled, tightly cover the baking sheets with plastic wrap and refrigerate about 20 minutes before baking, but no longer than 4 hours.

Preheat oven to 375° F. Brush rounds lightly with Egg Wash and bake in the preheated oven 15 to 20 minutes or until golden. Serve hot.

Unbaked filled piroshki and empanaditas without hard-cooked egg may be sheet frozen up to 2 months. Those with egg should be frozen no more than 2 weeks. Defrost in the refrigerator before baking.

CHICKEN PIROSHKI ■

Makes Approximately Four Dozen
1 recipe Cottage Cheese or
    Sour Cream Pastry
Egg Wash

FILLING
1/2 cup finely minced
    mushrooms
1/4 cup minced onion
2 tablespoons butter
1 cup finely minced cooked
    chicken
1/2 cup cooked white rice
1/2 teaspoon salt
1/4 teaspoon freshly ground
    white pepper
1/4 teaspoon ground savory
1/4 teaspoon paprika
2 hard-cooked eggs, finely
    chopped

Prepare the pastry dough and chill disc as directed.

To make the filling, sauté mushrooms and onion in butter in a large skillet about 5 minutes, or until onion is soft. Add chicken, raise heat, and cook until chicken is lightly browned, stirring often. With a fork, mix in rice and seasonings. Remove from the heat, and gently stir in eggs. Taste and adjust seasonings. Let mixture cool.

Roll dough out and proceed as directed in General Instructions for Russian Piroshki.

BEEF PIROSHKI ∎

Makes Approximately Four Dozen
1 recipe Cottage Cheese or
    Sour Cream Pastry
Egg Wash

FILLING
3/4 pound ground lean beef
2 tablespoons beef stock
1 tablespoon unbleached flour
1/2 cup finely minced onion
2 tablespoons butter
1 tablespoon minced fresh dill
1/2 teaspoon salt
1/4 teaspoon freshly ground
    black pepper
1/4 teaspoon paprika
3 hard-cooked eggs, finely
    chopped

Prepare the pastry dough and
chill disc as directed.

    To make the filling, combine
beef and stock in a large skillet
and cook over medium heat
until meat loses its color; do not
brown. As the meat cooks, stir it
with a fork so that it breaks
apart finely and evenly. Sprinkle
meat with flour and cook and
stir 3 minutes. Remove from the
heat and set aside.

    In a separate skillet, sauté
onion in butter about 5 minutes,
or until soft. Add dill, salt,
pepper, and paprika to

cooked meat. With a fork, gently
stir in eggs. Taste and adjust
seasonings. Let mixture cool.

    Roll dough out and proceed
as directed in General Instructions
for Russian Piroshki.

BEEF EMPANADITAS ∎

Makes Approximately Four Dozen
1 recipe Cream Cheese Pastry
Egg Wash

FILLING
3/4 pound ground lean beef
1/4 cup water
1/4 cup minced onion
1 teaspoon minced garlic
1/2 teaspoon salt
1/2 teaspoon crumbled dried
    oregano
1 tablespoon tomato paste
6 drops Tabasco sauce
1/2 teaspoon Worcestershire
    sauce
1 medium-size ripe tomato,
    finely chopped and drained
3 tablespoons freshly grated
    Parmesan cheese
1/3 cup finely shredded sharp
    Cheddar cheese

Prepare the pastry dough and
chill disc as directed.

    To make the filling, brown
beef in a large skillet, stirring
with a fork to crumble the meat
finely and evenly. Add water,
onion, garlic, salt, oregano, tomato
paste, Tabasco and Worcester-

shire sauces, and tomato. Blend
well and simmer, stirring occasionally, 30 minutes, or until
moisture has evaporated. Let
cool and toss in cheeses. Taste
and adjust seasonings.

    Roll dough out and proceed
as directed in General Instructions
for Latin American Empanaditas.

CHILI-CHEESE
EMPANADITAS ∎

Makes Approximately Four Dozen
1 recipe Cream Cheese or
    Cheddar-Parmesan Cheese
    Pastry
Egg Wash

FILLING
1 cup finely shredded sharp
    Cheddar cheese
2 tablespoons butter, at room
    temperature
2 to 4 tablespoons seeded and
    finely minced canned jalapeño
    chili peppers (or less if using
    fresh peppers)
1/4 cup finely chopped ripe
    olives
1/4 cup finely chopped green
    onion and tops
1/2 teaspoon crumbled dried
    oregano
1/4 teaspoon salt
1/4 teaspoon freshly ground
    black pepper

Prepare the pastry dough and chill disc as directed.

To make the filling, combine cheese, butter, chili peppers, olives, onion, oregano, salt, and pepper in a mixing bowl. Taste and adjust seasonings.

Roll dough out and proceed as directed in General Instructions for Latin American Empanaditas.

BUTTERY CHEDDAR "COOKIES" ■

Keep these scrumptious treats on hand in the freezer for last-minute entertaining.

Makes Approximately Three Dozen
1/2 cup unbleached flour
1/8 teaspoon salt
1/8 teaspoon freshly ground white pepper
1/4 teaspoon ground oregano
4 tablespoons butter, cut into 8 bits and chilled
1/2 cup finely shredded sharp Cheddar cheese
Approximately 1-1/2 tablespoons dry white wine or water

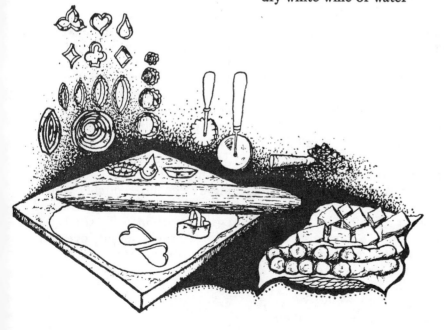

In a mixing bowl, combine flour, salt, pepper, and oregano. With fingertips, pastry blender, or 2 knives, crumble in butter until the consistency of coarse cornmeal. Toss in cheese and mix well. With a fork, stir in wine until just moistened. (Or mix dough in a food processor as explained in General Instructions for Pastry.) The dough will have a crumbly texture. As you work with it, the cheese will help it to adhere.

With fingers, gently gather the dough into a loose ball; do not "pack." Flatten ball into a disc about 1-1/2 inches thick, wrap disc in waxed paper, place disc in a plastic bag, and refrigerate at least 1 hour.

Roll dough out (see Rolling the Dough) and with canapé or cookie cutters, cut into desired shapes. Arrange, not touching, on a baking sheet, cover tightly with plastic wrap, and refrigerate at least 20 minutes, or for up to 3 hours.

Preheat oven to 375° F. Bake cheese cutouts in the preheated oven 10 minutes, or until crisp and lightly golden. Remove to wire rack and let cool.

Serve cookies immediately, or store in an airtight container for up to 2 days, or freeze for up to 2 months. Unbaked cookies may also be sheet frozen for up to 2 months. Defrost in the refrigerator before baking.

QUICHES AND TARTS

GENERAL INSTRUCTIONS FOR QUICHES

There are basically two kinds of fillings for quiche, one in which the ingredients are layered and one in which the ingredients are mixed together. Regardless of which type you make, you will need to fill the pie shell three-fourths full, which means 2-1/2 to 3 cups filling for an 8- or 9-inch quiche and 3-3/4 cups filling for a 10-inch quiche. For a quiche that is to be served as an hors d'oeuvre, the filling ingredients should be finely minced to facilitate easy cutting of the baked quiche.

Quiche or flan pans, either round or rectangular, are shallow springform pans with fluted rings set on a removable bottom. This arrangement allows you to remove the baked quiche from the pan intact. The quiche can be left on the bottom sheet of the pan and placed on a serving plate, or it can be carefully removed from the bottom sheet by loosening with a flexible spatula and easing it off onto the serving plate. It is then cut into wedges or squares, in the case of a round pan (see Kitchen Hints), or squares, in the case of a rectangular pan.

Following General Instructions for Pastry, prepare, chill, and roll out pastry dough and then line the quiche pan with it (see Lining Quiche Pans). Be especially careful that there are no tears in the pastry lining; if there are, the egg and cream mixture will leak out while the quiche is baking. Chill the lined pan for 30 minutes, then follow directions for prebaking shells. Cool before filling.

The cooled prebaked crust will stay crisper if it is brushed lightly with Egg Wash before it is filled, and then sprinkled with freshly grated Parmesan cheese or the cheese called for in the recipe. (When recipes call for Gruyère cheese, try Emmenthaler, Samsoe, or Jarlsberg for variety.)

The quiche recipes call for 1 prebaked shell. Use the rest of the pastry for other recipes such as Pastry Rounds or Balls, or roll it out, line a pie plate, and freeze for a future pie. Lemon Egg White and Short Crust pastries are preferred for quiches.

Quiches may be prepared and baked 3 or 4 hours prior to serving. Cover with plastic wrap and place in a cool area, then bring to room temperature before setting out for guests. To serve, place a flexible metal spatula alongside the dish for guests to help themselves. Alternatively, cut the quiche in the kitchen and arrange the pieces on a garnished serving plate.

MINIATURE QUICHES

The quiche recipes may all be made in tiny muffin-tin wells. Prepare pastry following General Instructions for Pastry. After chilling pastry disc, roll out pastry and line 3 or 4 dozen tiny muffin-tin wells as directed in Making Tartlets and Barquettes, then prebake shells.

Brush prebaked shells with Egg Wash, let dry, and sprinkle with a little bit of the cheese. Instead of mixing the filling ingredients with the egg and cream, combine the ingredients and spoon a little of the mixture into the prepared tartlet shells. Then combine the eggs and cream and pour through a fine-mesh sieve into a pitcher with a spout. Now carefully pour the egg mixture into the shells. Sprinkle cheese evenly over surface of filling.

Bake miniature quiches as directed for regular-size quiches, but reduce baking time by 5 to 10 minutes. Remove pans to a wire rack and cool 5 minutes. With the tip of thin-bladed knife or the tines of a fork, ease the quiches out of the wells and serve warm or at room temperature.

Miniature quiches may also be filled with the mixtures normally used for making frittatas (see Eggs). In this case, the eggs and other ingredients can be combined before filling the pastry shells. It is important, however, that the filling mixture be well stirred each time before spooning it into a shell. Bake and serve as for miniature quiches.

CRAB QUICHE

If you don't want to pay the high price that crab commands, substitute steamed pollack (see Basics) for an equally delicious result.

Approximately Forty Servings

One 10-inch prebaked pastry
   shell
Egg Wash
1/3 cup freshly grated Parmesan
   cheese
1/2 cup finely minced white of
   green onion
1/4 cup finely minced celery

2 tablespoons finely minced
   shallots
1 teaspoon finely minced garlic
2 tablespoons butter
2-1/2 cups finely flaked crab
   meat
1/2 teaspoon freshly grated
   lemon peel
2 tablespoons minced fresh
   parsley
2 tablespoons finely minced
   green onion tops
1 cup finely shredded Gruyère
   cheese
3 eggs
1-1/2 cups light cream
1/4 teaspoon salt
1/4 teaspoon freshly ground
   white pepper
1/4 teaspoon freshly grated
   nutmeg
1/8 teaspoon cayenne pepper
Paprika
Cherry tomatoes or tomato
   wedges
Watercress sprigs

Following General Instructions for Quiches, brush prebaked pastry shell with egg wash and let dry. Sprinkle shell evenly with Parmesan cheese and refrigerate.

In a large covered nonstick skillet, cook onion, celery, shallots, and garlic in butter over medium heat 5 minutes, or until onion is soft. Cool briefly.

Preheat oven to 375° F. Toss crab meat with lemon peel, parsley, green onion tops, and 1/2 cup of the Gruyère cheese. With a fork, stir crab mixture into reserved onion mixture and spoon into prepared pastry shell.

In a mixing bowl, beat eggs lightly with cream, salt, white pepper, nutmeg, and cayenne pepper. Pour the egg mixture through a fine-mesh sieve into the crab mixture and sprinkle evenly with remaining 1/2 cup Gruyère cheese. Dust with paprika and place in the preheated oven.

Bake quiche 25 to 30 minutes, or until a cake tester inserted in center comes out clean. Remove quiche to a wire rack and cool at least 10 minutes.

To serve, remove the quiche from the pan by pushing the pan bottom up through the rim of the pan. Transfer quiche to a serving plate, and garnish plate with cherry tomatoes and watercress sprigs.

MUSHROOM QUICHE

Approximately Forty Servings
One 10-inch prebaked pastry
    shell
Egg Wash
1 cup finely shredded
    Gruyère cheese
1/4 cup finely minced green
    onion and tops
1 teaspoon finely minced garlic
3 tablespoons butter
1 pound fresh mushrooms,
    finely minced
1/2 teaspoon ground oregano
1/2 teaspoon salt
1/4 teaspoon freshly ground
    white pepper
1/8 teaspoon granulated sugar
Dash cayenne pepper
1 teaspoon fresh lemon juice
1/4 cup finely minced fresh
    parsley
3 eggs
1-1/2 cups light cream
Paprika
Parsley sprigs

Following General Instructions
for Quiches, brush prebaked pie
shell with egg wash and let dry.
Sprinkle shell evenly with 1/4
cup of the cheese and refrigerate.

In a large covered nonstick
skillet, cook onion and garlic in
butter over medium heat 5 minutes, or until soft. Remove lid
and add mushrooms. Sprinkle
with oregano, salt, white pepper,
sugar, and cayenne pepper. Raise
heat slightly and sprinkle with
lemon juice. Stirring almost constantly, cook mushrooms until
they are lightly browned and all
moisture has evaporated. Remove
from heat, stir in parsley, and
cool briefly.

Preheat oven to 375° F. In a
mixing bowl, beat eggs lightly
with cream. Toss 1/2 cup of the
remaining cheese with the mushroom mixture and pour the egg
and cream mixture through a
fine-mesh sieve into the mushroom mixture. Stir to combine
all ingredients thoroughly and
pour into the prepared pastry
shell. Sprinkle evenly with remaining 1/4 cup cheese and dust with
paprika.

Bake quiche in the preheated
oven 25 to 30 minutes, or until
a cake tester inserted in center
comes out clean. Remove quiche
to a wire rack and cool at least
10 minutes.

To serve, remove the quiche
from the pan by pushing the pan
bottom up through the rim.
Transfer quiche to a serving
plate, and garnish plate with
parsley sprigs.

VARIATIONS Before pouring
mushroom mixture into prepared
shell, strew shell with 1/4 cup
crumbled crisply cooked bacon
or 1/3 cup minced ham and 2
tablespoons minced fresh parsley.

SPINACH QUICHE WITH SHALLOTS

Approximately Thirty Servings
One 8-inch prebaked pastry shell
Egg Wash
1/4 cup freshly grated Parmesan
    cheese
1 large bunch fresh spinach
    (one 10-ounce package frozen
    chopped spinach)
1/4 cup very finely minced
    shallots
1 teaspoon very finely minced
    garlic
2 tablespoons butter
2 eggs
3/4 cup light cream
1/4 cup reserved spinach cooking
    liquid
1/2 teaspoon salt
1/4 teaspoon freshly ground
    black pepper
1/4 teaspoon freshly grated
    nutmeg
1/2 cup finely shredded
    Gruyère cheese
Paprika
Lemon Twists

Following General Instructions
for Quiches, brush prebaked
pastry shell with egg wash and
let dry. Sprinkle shell evenly
with Parmesan cheese and refrigerate.

In a covered saucepan, cook spinach with washing water clinging to its leaves 5 minutes, or until limp. Transfer to a sieve placed over a mixing bowl and press out all moisture. Finely chop the spinach and return to sieve. Again press out all moisture and measure 1 cup of the spinach; set aside. Measure 1/4 cup of the cooking liquid and set aside. (Reserve any remaining spinach or liquid for soup.)

In a covered nonstick skillet, cook shallots and garlic in butter over medium heat 5 minutes, or until soft; do not brown. Cool briefly.

Preheat oven to 375° F. In a mixing bowl, beat eggs lightly and add cream, reserved 1/4 cup cooking liquid, salt, pepper, nutmeg, and reserved spinach and shallot mixtures. Mix well and pour into prepared shell. Sprinkle evenly with Gruyère cheese and dust with paprika.

Bake quiche in the preheated oven 25 to 30 minutes, or until a cake tester inserted in center comes out clean. Remove quiche to a wire rack and cool at least 10 minutes.

To serve, remove the quiche from the pan by pushing the pan bottom up through the rim. Transfer quiche to a serving plate, and garnish plate with lemon twists.

VARIATIONS Reduce salt measurement to 1/4 teaspoon and add to spinach-egg mixture 1/2 to 2/3 cup drained minced canned clams, minced bay shrimp, finely flaked crab meat, crumbled crisply cooked bacon, or crumbled feta cheese.

QUICHE LORRAINE
(Cheese and Bacon Quiche)

Approximately Forty Servings
One 9-inch prebaked
    pastry shell
Egg Wash
1/2 cup freshly grated
    Parmesan cheese
3 eggs
1 egg yolk
1-1/2 cups heavy cream
1-1/4 cups shredded
    Gruyère cheese
1/2 teaspoon salt
1/4 teaspoon freshly ground
    white pepper
1/8 teaspoon freshly grated
    nutmeg
8 lean strips bacon, crisply
    cooked and crumbled
1 tablespoon butter, cut into
    tiny pieces
Paprika
Watercress sprigs

Following General Instructions for Quiches, brush prebaked pastry shell with egg wash and let dry. Sprinkle shell evenly with Parmesan cheese and refrigerate.

Preheat oven to 375° F. In a mixing bowl, beat eggs and egg yolk lightly and add cream, Gruyère cheese, salt, pepper, nutmeg, and bacon. Mix well and pour into prepared shell. Dot cheese mixture with butter and sprinkle lightly with paprika.

Bake quiche in the preheated oven 30 to 35 minutes, or until a cake tester inserted in center comes out clean. Remove quiche to a wire rack and cool at least 10 minutes.

To serve, remove the quiche from the pan by pushing the pan bottom up through the rim. Transfer quiche to a serving plate, and garnish plate with watercress sprigs.

VARIATION Substitute 3/4 cup very finely minced ham for the bacon and use Emmenthaler cheese in place of the Gruyère.

PISSALADIERE
(Provençal Onion Tart)

Treat this pizzalike tart as you would a quiche, but don't pre-bake the shell. Complete the first steps of preparation and then refrigerate or freeze. If freezing, let thaw overnight in the refrigerator.

This tart is so beautiful that it should be brought to the table in its uncut form. It needs no garnish.

Approximately Thirty Servings

1 recipe Lemon Egg White or Short Crust Pastry
2 tablespoons finely minced parsley
Egg Wash
1/4 cup freshly grated Parmesan cheese
1/4 cup finely shredded Gruyère cheese
1-1/2 cups minced onion
2 tablespoon butter
1 teaspoon finely minced garlic
2 teaspoons olive oil
4 large ripe tomatoes, peeled and chopped
3 rosemary sprigs
1/2 teaspoon sugar
1/2 teaspoon Worcestershire sauce
1/2 teaspoon salt
1/4 teaspoon freshly ground black pepper
3 drops Tabasco sauce
Paste of 1 teaspoon butter and 2 teaspoons unbleached flour, if needed
Two 2-ounce cans anchovy fillets
20 to 30 medium-size pitted black olives, halved
1 tablespoon olive oil

Prepare pastry, adding the parsley when combining the flour and salt. Chill, roll, and line a 10-inch quiche pan as directed in General Instructions for Pastry. (See General Instructions for Quiches for a description of a quiche pan.) Brush shell with

egg wash and let dry. Sprinkle bottom evenly with Parmesan and Gruyère cheeses. Cover with plastic wrap and refrigerate.

In a small covered nonstick skillet, cook the onion in butter over medium heat 5 minutes, or until soft. Remove cover and let moisture cook away without browning the onions. Let cool briefly.

In a large skillet, sauté garlic in oil 3 minutes. Add tomatoes, rosemary sprigs, sugar, Worcestershire sauce, salt, pepper, and Tabasco sauce. Cook over medium heat, stirring occasionally, until mixture is reduced to 1-3/4 cups. Discard rosemary sprigs and purée mixture in a blender or food processor.

Return sauce to skillet, reheat over medium heat, taste, and adjust seasonings. Sauce should be thick but not stiff. If tomatoes were very juicy, the sauce may be runny, in which case it will need to be thickened. Make a paste by working the butter and flour together with your fingers until it forms tiny beads. Stir the beads into the sauce and cook, stirring often, 10 minutes. The sauce should now be properly thickened. Remove the sauce from the heat and let cool.

Strew reserved onion mixture evenly over the cheese in the prepared pan. Pour cooled tomato sauce over onions. At this point, the tart may be covered and refrigerated for up to 2 hours, or frozen for up to 1 month. Defrost in the refrigerator before proceeding.

Preheat oven to 450° F. Decorate the top of the sauced shell with anchovy fillets and olive halves in a spoke pattern for a round tart or a crisscross pattern for a rectangle. Carefully brush olives and anchovies with olive oil and place tart in the preheated oven. Bake 25 minutes, or until crust is golden and filling is set. Remove to a wire rack and let stand 10 minutes.

To serve, remove the tart from the pan by pushing the pan bottom up through the rim of the pan. Transfer pissaladière to a serving platter. Place a broad-bladed knife alongside for guests to cut their own wedges or squares.

The pissaladière may be prepared and baked 2 or 3 hours prior to serving. Cover with plastic wrap and place in a cool area until serving time.

CHOUX

The French word *chou* has two meanings. It means "cabbage," and it refers to the light airy pastry most widely recognized as the shell for cream puffs. This basic chou pastry dough, however, is for holding hot or cold savory mixtures; a dessert version appears in the American Buffet.

CHOUX DOUGH ●■

Makes Approximately Eighty Choux
1 cup water
1/4 pound butter
1/2 teaspoon salt
1/8 teaspoon freshly grated
    nutmeg
1/4 teaspoon freshly ground
    white pepper
1 cup unbleached flour
4 eggs
Egg Wash
Filling of choice, following

To prepare the chou dough, combine water, butter, salt, nutmeg, and pepper in a heavy saucepan and place over medium heat until butter melts. Now bring the mixture to a rolling boil, add the flour all at once, and immediately remove the pan from heat. Stir the mixture vigorously with a wooden spoon until the batter is smooth and pulls away from the sides of the saucepan. Cool 2 minutes.

One at a time, beat in the eggs, blending well after each addition. Let dough rest 15 minutes, or cover and refrigerate for up to 4 days.

Preheat oven to 400° F. On greased baking sheets, form tiny mounds of dough with a spoon or a pastry bag fitted with a plain tube (see General Instructions for Piping). Each mound should be about 1 inch in diameter and 1/2 inch high. Lightly brush tops of choux with egg wash. Place baking sheets in the preheated oven and bake 10 minutes. Reduce heat to 325° F, and bake 15 minutes more, or until golden.

Remove baking sheets from the oven and immediately prick an edge of each chou with the tines of a small fork to release air. Shut off oven heat and return choux to oven for 5 minutes with door open. Remove choux from baking sheets and cool on racks.

Depending upon the humidity, choux will stay crisp at room temperature for several hours. They may also be sheet frozen for up to 2 months and then defrosted at room temperature. Should they soften in either of these cases, crisp them in a 350° F oven, then cool and fill. If the filled choux are to be served cold, *do not fill until shortly before serving.*

To serve choux hot, fill with room-temperature mixture and place in a preheated 350° F oven 10 minutes, or until heated through.

Filled choux to be served hot may be sheet frozen for up to 2 weeks and then defrosted in the refrigerator. To reheat, make an aluminum foil "box" for the choux, leaving the foil slightly open at the top to expose the pastries. Defrost at room temperature and bake in a preheated 400° F oven 10 minutes.

CHOU DOUGH VARIATIONS
• Use bottled clam juice or milk in place of 1/2 cup of the water. Omit nutmeg and season with 1/4 teaspoon *each* crumbled dried dill and thyme and 1 teaspoon minced fresh chives.
• Add 1/3 cup grated Gruyère cheese after adding the eggs. (This cheese-flavored dough is used to make a special chou called *gougère.*)

FILLINGS FOR COLD CHOUX

• Combine 1/2 cup finely minced raw mushrooms, 1-1/2 cups minced cooked chicken or turkey, and 1/2 cup finely chopped blanched almonds. Bind with mayonnaise and season to taste with freshly grated nutmeg, salt, and freshly ground white pepper.
• Combine 2 cups ground cooked ham, 1/2 cup finely chopped walnuts, 3 tablespoons Chili Sauce, mayonnaise to bind, and Tabasco sauce to taste.
• Peel, pit, and mash 2 large ripe avocados with 1 tablespoon fresh lemon juice and blend in 1/2 cup sour cream or Crème Fraîche. Season to taste with grated onion, minced drained Pumate, salt, white pepper, and Tabasco sauce.
• Season 2 cups Crème Fraîche or sour cream with grated onion and white pepper to taste. Fill each chou just to rim and top with a dab of lumpfish caviar and a tiny lemon peel.
• Combine 1-1/2 cups finely minced crab meat or cooked shrimp with 1/2 cup Lemon or Lime Mayonnaise. Add 1 to 2 teaspoons drained capers and/or minced gherkins and dry mustard, crumbled dried tarragon, salt, and white pepper to taste.
• Bring 6 ounces cream cheese to room temperature and mash with 2 or 3 drained sardine

fillets and 3 tablespoons *each* minced fresh parsley and chives. Add fresh lemon juice, salt, and white pepper to taste.
• Finely grate enough raw celeriac (celery root) to measure 1-1/2 cups. Bind with Mustard Mayonnaise and stir in 2 tablespoons *each* minced drained capers and minced fresh chives, and salt and white pepper to taste. This filling should not be prepared in advance of filling the choux.

FILLINGS FOR HOT CHOUX

• Make 1 recipe Cream Sauce, using light cream for the liquid and increasing the measure to 1-1/3 cups. When sauce is smooth and thickened, add 3/4 cup ground cooked ham; 3 hard-cooked eggs, sieved; 1 tablespoon *each* finely minced green bell pepper and pimiento or Roasted Pepper; and salt and white pepper to taste. If desired, add 1/4 cup grated Gruyère or similar cheese. Let cool before filling choux.
• Make 1 recipe Cream Sauce, using light cream for the liquid and increasing the measure to 1-1/3 cups. When sauce is smooth and thickened, add 1-1/2 cups chopped cooked shrimp, 2 tablespoons dry sherry, and freshly grated nutmeg, salt, and white pepper to taste. Let cool before filling choux.

- Combine 6 ounces cream cheese, mashed with light cream to soften; 1-1/2 cups flaked crab meat or chopped cooked shrimp; and fresh lemon juice, Worcestershire sauce, dried dill, Tabasco sauce, salt, and white pepper to taste. If desired, add 1/4 cup grated Gruyère or similar cheese.
- Drain three 7-1/2-ounce cans minced clams, reserving liquid. Beat 6 ounces cream cheese with a little of the clam liquid (reserve remainder for fish stock or chowder) until smooth, then stir in drained clams, 2 tablespoons minced fresh chives, and salt, white pepper, and Tabasco sauce to taste. Mix until well blended.
- Combine 2 cups finely minced cooked chicken or turkey, 3 tablespoons finely minced celery, 2 tablespoons minced green onion and tops, 1/4 cup mayonnaise, and fresh lemon juice, curry powder, salt, and white pepper to taste. (This mixture does not freeze well.)
- Combine 1-1/2 recipes Duxelle with 1/2 cup finely chopped walnuts.
- Combine 1-1/2 recipes Tomato and Ham Filling with 1/3 cup lightly toasted pine nuts.

PUFF PASTRIES

PUFF PASTRY ●■

There are essentially two ways to make puff pastry: the traditional complicated, labor-intensive method and the quick way in which the dough is mixed in a food processor and rolled out in three short steps. With both methods, it is important that the dough always remain chilled and that it not be worked any more than is necessary, for too much handling will toughen it and it will not puff properly in the oven.

Directions on how to make bouchées, croustades, filled squares, twists, and fingers and suggested fillings and flavorings appear after the dough recipes.

1 pound unsalted butter, chilled
3 cups unbleached flour
1 cup cake flour
1 teaspoon salt
1 tablespoon fresh lemon juice
About 1 cup ice water

TRADITIONAL METHOD Immerse butter in a bowl of cold water and work it with your fingertips until it is smooth, malleable, and has a waxy finish. Remove butter from bowl, wrap in a lightweight towel, and press out any water with the palms of your hands.

Pinch off about 1/2 cup of the butter, cut it into small bits, place the bits on a plate in a single layer, and refrigerate. Form the remaining butter into a 1/2-inch-thick round, wrap in waxed paper, and refrigerate. Sift together the flours and salt into a large mixing bowl. Remove the 1/2 cup butter from the refrigerator and with a pastry blender, 2 knives, or your fingertips, crumble the butter into the flour until the mixture is the consistency of coarse cornmeal. Sprinkle lemon juice over flour mixture and, stirring with a fork, *gradually* add ice water, using only as much as is needed for the dough to be lightly formed into a ball. The dough should be handled as little as possible at this point.

Flatten the ball into a disc on a lightly floured board and gently roll into a rectangle about 1/4 inch thick. (See Rolling the Dough in General Instructions for Pastry.) Remove butter round from refrigerator and place in center of rectangle. Bring narrow side of rectangle farthest from you over butter round to cover it, then fold narrow side closest to you over the top, forming an envelope shape. Press edges together, wrap in waxed paper, and chill 25 to 30 minutes until firm.

Remove the dough from refrigerator, unwrap, and place on a lightly floured board with one of the narrow sides facing you. Roll dough out to form a long, narrow rectangle, being careful not to split the surface of the dough and expose the butter. (Exposing the butter releases some of the air that gives the pastry its puffiness. Patching the dough is possible, but is not advisable for best results.) Fold the rectangle into an envelope shape as before, then rotate the dough a quarter turn so that a narrow side faces you. Roll as before into a long rectangle, fold again in an envelope shape, wrap in waxed paper, and chill 25 to 30 minutes.

Repeat this procedure—rolling out, folding, rotating, rolling out, and folding—two more times, chilling 25 to 30 minutes between the two procedures. After the final folding, wrap the "envelope" in waxed paper, place in a plastic bag, and chill at least 3 hours, or for up to 24 hours, then roll as described in General Instructions for Pastry.

FOOD PROCESSOR METHOD Cut butter into 16 slices, then cut each slice into quarters. Place butter pieces in one layer on a plate and refrigerate 15 to 20 minutes. Put flours and salt in the bowl of a food processor fitted with metal blade and pulse 2 or 3 times to mix. Strew pieces of butter evenly into pro-cessor bowl. With on/off pulses and stopping to check frequently, process *just* until the butter pieces are the size of large fresh peas. This should take only several seconds.

With motor running, add lemon juice and water to processor and process *just* until dough *begins* to gather on one side of bowl. Do not add all the water unless needed. Do not over-process; it is better to undermix than to overmix. Remove dough from the bowl, and with fingers, lightly form into a rough ball and then flatten into a disc about 1-1/2 inches thick. Wrap disc in waxed paper and refrigerate 20 minutes.

On a lightly floured board, roll the dough into a rectangle 3/8 to 1/2 inch thick. Fold the narrow side farthest from you over the center of the dough, then fold the side nearest you over the top, forming an envelope shape. Rotate the dough a quarter turn so that a narrow side faces you. Roll as before into a rec-tangle, fold again in an envelope shape, and rotate another quarter turn. Repeat rolling and folding again, then wrap in waxed paper, put into a plastic bag, and chill at least 3 hours or up to 24 hours before rolling out.

PETITES BOUCHEES
(Tiny Patty Shells) ■

Bouchées are flaky puff pastry shells with lids. They are often made in a size suitable for an entrée serving, but here they are tiny "cups" that are perfect hors d'oeuvre "bites."

It is best to use an assembly-line system for making bouchées. For example, while chilling the first sheet of rounds, cut out and prepare the second sheet. This way you will be able to bake a sheet at a time and always have another one ready to go into the oven. The unbaked rounds must be chilled at least 30 minutes, but can wait for baking up to 2 hours.

For 5 to 6 dozen tiny bouchées, work with one-half recipe Puff Pastry dough at a time, keeping other half refrigerated. Roll dough on a lightly floured board into a round 5/16 inch thick (see General Instructions for Pastry). The round must be no thicker than this, or the bouchées will rise and tilt during baking.

Lightly brush a large baking sheet with water. Using a round canapé or cookie cutter 1-1/2 inches in diameter, cut out rounds, dipping edge of cutter into flour with each cut. As you work, flip rounds over onto the baking sheet about 1 inch apart. Cover baking sheet with waxed paper and refrigerate 30 minutes. Repeat with remaining dough, adding rounds to the same baking sheet if there is room, or using a second sheet. Do not, however, attempt to reroll the pastry scraps and use the dough to make bouchées; the pastry is too tough at this point and can only be used to make simple cutouts (see Rolling Pastry Scraps).

Remove baking sheet from refrigerator. With a 1-inch-round cutter, cut an impression two-thirds of the way through the dough in the exact center of each 1-1/2-inch round, again dipping cutter into flour with each cut. This impression will rise during baking to form the lid of the shell. If it is even slightly off center, the bouchée may tilt when baking. Brush rounds with Egg Wash, cover sheet with waxed paper, and refrigerate 30 minutes. (The bouchées must be chilled when they go into the oven or they will not rise properly.) At this point, bouchées may be sheet frozen for up to 1 month. Defrost in the refrigerator before proceeding.

Position oven rack in center of oven. (You must not bake more than 1 sheet at a time or the bouchées will not rise evenly.) Preheat oven to 400° F. Remove baking sheet from the refrigerator, uncover, and immediately place in the preheated oven. Reduce

the heat to 375° F at once. Bake 20 minutes, or until pastry is nicely browned and puffed. Do not open the oven door until 15 minutes have elapsed. If at that point the shells are browning too quickly, cover with a sheet of parchment paper or a brown paper bag that has been buttered with Lecithin Butter.

When shells are done, remove from the oven and turn oven heat off. With a tiny two-tined fork or the point of a sharp knife, loosen and carefully lift off the "lid" of each shell and flip upside down onto the baking sheet. With a fork, lightly pull uncooked dough from the center of each shell and discard. Return the baking sheet to the turned-off oven for about 10 minutes. With a large spatula, remove shells and lids to a wire rack and let cool.

For cold fillings, the shells

must be crisp. If the air is not humid, the shells can be set out at room temperature and they will remain crisp for several hours. If they lose their crispness, reheat them in a preheated 350° F oven for 5 minutes, then cool and fill. If the bouchées are to be filled with a mixture that will be heated, the crispness is not a factor, as the pastry will crisp as the filling heats.

The baked unfilled bouchées may be sheet frozen for up to 1 month. Defrost at room temperature and crisp if necessary.

FILLINGS FOR BOUCHEES

Use about 1 teaspoon of filling for each bouchée, and remember to replace the tops after filling.
• For cold bouchées, choose from the Fillings for Cold Choux, Cold Stuffed Mushrooms, or cold stuffed artichoke bottoms (see Other Cold Filled Vegetables), or fill with a spread such as Curried Mushroom Pâté.
• For hot bouchées, select from the list of Fillings for Hot Choux, Baked Stuffed Mushrooms, or Baked Filled Artichoke Bottoms, or use Duxelle, or Tomato and Ham or Crab or Shrimp Filling.
• For a truly elegant hors d'oeuvre, sauté snails in butter with lots of minced garlic and then place 1 snail into each crisp bouchée. Serve at once.

PUFF PASTRY SQUARES ■

For approximately 4 dozen pastry squares, work with one-half recipe Puff Pastry dough at a time, keeping other half refrigerated. Roll dough on a lightly floured board into a rectangle 1/8 inch thick (see General Instructions for Pastry). Cut pastry into 1-1/2-inch squares. Place 1/2 teaspoon filling on each square, top with another square, and press edges together gently to seal. Arrange squares 1 inch apart on a lightly buttered baking sheet and brush each square with Egg Wash. Chill 30 minutes. Repeat with remaining dough.

Preheat oven to 375° F and bake pastry squares 15 to 20 minutes, or until golden. Transfer squares to a serving plate and serve at once.

Unbaked filled pastry squares may be sheet frozen for up to 1 month. Defrost in the refrigerator before baking.

FILLINGS FOR PUFF PASTRY SQUARES

GORGONZOLA FILLING Combine 1 cup (4 ounces) crumbled Gorgonzola or other blue cheese, 1 egg yolk, 1 teaspoon Worcestershire sauce, 1/4 cup finely minced green onion and tops, 2 tablespoons finely minced fresh parsley, 3 drops of Tabasco sauce, and salt and white pepper to taste.

HAM FILLING Combine 1 cup finely minced cooked ham, 2 tablespoons grated onion, 2 tablespoons minced fresh parsley, 2 tablespoons finely minced sweet pickles, and Dijon-style mustard to taste. Season to taste with salt and black pepper.

GRUYERE CHEESE FILLING Combine 1 egg, lightly beaten; 1 egg yolk; 1 tablespoon butter, melted; 2/3 cup finely shredded Gruyère cheese; and salt and cayenne pepper to taste. After filling and brushing with egg wash, sprinkle lightly with additional shredded cheese.

SEAFOOD FILLING Season 1 cup Cream Sauce with dry sherry and freshly grated Parmesan cheese to taste. Add 2/3 cup finely minced cooked shrimp, monkfish, or pollack and season to taste with salt, white pepper, and cayenne pepper.

OTHER FILLING IDEAS Fillings for Pastry Rounds; Duxelle or Crab or Shrimp Filling; Fillings for Hot Choux; fillings for Baked Stuffed Mushrooms or Filled Artichoke Bottoms; chèvre mixed to taste with Pumate Purée; or cream cheese softened with a little light cream and mixed with anchovy paste, fresh lemon juice, minced chives and/or parsley, and white pepper to taste.

PUFF PASTRY TWISTS ●■

Makes Approximately Six Dozen
1 recipe Puff Pastry dough
Egg Wash
1/2 cup finely grated or shredded Cheddar, Monterey Jack, or Gruyère cheese
Paprika
Cayenne pepper

Working with one-half recipe puff pastry dough at a time and keeping other half refrigerated, roll dough on a lightly floured board into a rectangle about 1/4 inch thick (see General Instructions for Pastry). Brush with egg wash. Sprinkle with cheese, paprika, and a light dusting of cayenne pepper. Cut into 1/2-inch-wide strips 2 inches long. Twist each strip into a spiral and place on a lightly buttered or oiled baking sheet. Chill 30 minutes.

Preheat oven to 375° F. Bake twists 10 to 15 minutes until puffed and golden. Serve immediately.

Unbaked twists may be covered and refrigerated for up to 1 day, or sheet frozen for up to 1 month. Defrost in the refrigerator before baking.

PASTRY CROUSTADES ●■

Croustades, made with Puff Pastry dough and also with bread (see Ways with Breads), are tiny shells, fully baked and cooled, that are filled just before serving with a cold mixture such as Curried Mushroom Caviar, Avocado Cream Cheese Spread, any of the Fillings for Cold Choux, or any of the fillings for Cold Stuffed Mushrooms or Other Cold Filled Vegetables.

Croustades may also be served hot. Fill fully baked croustades with Duxelle, Tomato and Ham Filling, Crab or Shrimp Filling, or with any of the Fillings for Hot Choux. Sprinkle lightly with freshly grated Parmesan cheese and bake in a preheated 375° F oven 10 minutes, or until filling is bubbly and cheese is melted.

To make pastry croustades, follow the General Instructions for Pastry to prepare and roll out the dough. Refer to Making Tartlets and Barquettes for directions on lining muffin-tin wells and to Fully Baking Pastry Shells for baking information. Each croustade, hot or cold, will hold 1 to 1-1/2 teaspoons filling.

Unbaked croustades may be covered and refrigerated for up to 1 day, or sheet frozen for up to 1 month. Defrost in the refrigerator before baking.

PHYLLO

Phyllo dough, paper-thin pastry sheets almost identical to strudel dough, is very difficult to make at home. It may be purchased in one-pound packages in Greek and Armenian specialty shops, in most delicatessens, and in many supermarkets. It is best to purchase fresh phyllo, but most markets carry the dough frozen, in which case always defrost it overnight in the refrigerator. An unopened package will keep for up to four days in the refrigerator.

The quality of the numerous brands varies widely, as do the size and thickness of the sheets. You may have to try the product of several different companies to find the one you prefer. I have found Athens brand to be the best. Also, if the grocer has been careless and the packages have defrosted and then been refrozen, you will find the sheets are impossible to work with, an aggravating discovery when you're right in the midst of making phyllo pastries.

WORKING WITH PHYLLO SHEETS

The phyllo sheets, 20 to 24 to a package, dry out easily, which makes them crumble. Before starting to work with them have everything ready. The butter (salted or unsalted) should be melting, the filling(s) should be prepared, and the baking sheets should be handy.

Carefully unwrap the sheets, saving the waxed paper, and place the stack flat on the work surface. Because phyllo is so fragile, you must work quickly and in an assembly-line fashion. Peel 3 sheets off the stack. Wrap remaining sheets in the reserved waxed paper and cover with a *very* lightly dampened tea towel. (If the dough gets wet, it will stick together and be unusable.)

Place 1 of the 3 sheets flat on the work surface. With a feather or other soft brush, lightly cover the sheet with a thin layer of melted butter. Stack the second sheet on top and brush with butter, and then cover with the third sheet, brushing it with butter as well. If the sheets tear, "mend" them by patting the tears together with melted butter. These breaks will not affect the final result.

When you have reached this point, you can use the buttered

sheets to make filled triangles or rolls (directions follow), repeating the procedure with the remaining sheets, again using 3 at a time. You will need approximately 3/4 cup butter for 1 pound of phyllo. A few suggestions for using excess sheets follow the filling recipes.

Most filled phyllo pastries freeze well. Sheet freeze, then wrap tightly and store for up to 4 months.

GENERAL INSTRUCTIONS FOR PHYLLO TRIANGLES ■

Cut the buttered stack of layered sheets widthwise into 6 to 8 even strips (depending upon the size of the sheets and the size of the triangles desired). Place 1-1/2 to 2-1/2 teaspoons of filling 1/2 inch in from the bottom of each strip. Lift up pastry on which filling is resting and fold it over to form a triangular shape. Continue in flag fashion, straight edge up, cross over, up, cross over, to make a triangle. Be careful no filling shows at tips of triangle. Tuck last fold under and seal closed with melted butter.

Place triangles seam side down 1 inch apart on ungreased baking sheet and brush lightly with melted butter. Repeat with remaining phyllo and filling.

At this point, the triangles may be covered and refrigerated for several hours, or frozen for up to 2 months. Defrost before baking.

To bake, preheat oven to 375° F. Place triangles in the preheated oven for 15 minutes, or until golden. Ovens vary; check that the triangles are baking evenly. The filling stays very hot, so cool briefly before serving.

GENERAL INSTRUCTIONS FOR PHYLLO ROLLS
(Cigars or Borek) ■

Cut the buttered stack of layered sheets widthwise into 5 even strips. Place 2-1/2 teaspoons filling on end of each strip 1/2 inch in from sides. Working from filling end, roll pastry 2 turns to encase filling. Fold in sides of strip over the filling and lengthwise along the entire strip. Continue to roll the strip, forming a cylinder. Seal seam with melted butter, place seam side down 1 inch apart on ungreased baking sheet, and brush lightly with melted butter. Repeat with remaining phyllo and filling.

At this point, the rolls may be covered and refrigerated several hours, or frozen for up to 2 months. Defrost before baking.

To bake, preheat oven to 375° F. Place rolls in the preheated oven and bake 15 minutes, or until golden.

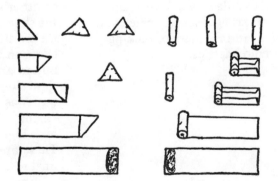

FILLINGS FOR PHYLLO TRIANGLES AND ROLLS

The following filling recipes are for approximately one pound of phyllo and will yield between forty and sixty triangles or rolls, depending on size. The fillings may be made one day in advance of encasing in pastry. Cover and store in the refrigerator.

SPINACH FILLING ●

1/2 cup finely minced onion
2 tablespoons butter
4 ounces cream cheese, at room temperature
2 eggs
1-1/2 cups *well-drained* finely chopped cooked spinach
1/2 cup minced fresh parsley
2 tablespoons minced fresh dill
2 tablespoons minced green onion tops
4 ounces feta cheese, crumbled (1 cup)
1/2 cup ricotta cheese
1/4 teaspoon salt
1/4 teaspoon freshly ground white pepper

In a covered nonstick skillet, cook onion in butter over medium heat 5 minutes until soft. Set aside to cool.
   In a large mixing bowl, mash cream cheese with a wooden spoon and gradually blend in eggs, one at a time. Mix in reserved onion mixture, spinach, parsley, dill, green onion tops, feta and ricotta cheeses, salt, and pepper. Taste and adjust seasonings.

CRAB FILLING ●

1/2 cup finely minced onion
3 medium-size dried shiitake mushrooms, soaked in warm water to soften, drained, stems discarded, and caps finely minced
3 tablespoons butter
2 tablespoons unbleached flour
3/4 cup chicken stock
1/2 cup minced fresh parsley
1/4 cup finely minced green onion tops
2 tablespoons minced drained Roasted Peppers or pimientos
1/2 to 1 teaspoon dried dill
1/2 teaspoon Worcestershire sauce
1/4 teaspoon freshly ground white pepper
4 or 5 drops Tabasco sauce
2 teaspoons fresh lemon juice, or to taste
1/2 pound crab meat or cooked pollack (see Basics), finely flaked
Salt to taste

In a covered nonstick skillet, cook onion and mushrooms in butter over medium heat 5 minutes, or until onion is soft.

Sprinkle with flour and cook, stirring, 3 minutes. Gradually add stock and cook and stir until sauce is thickened. Add parsley, green onion tops, roasted peppers, dill, Worcestershire sauce, pepper, Tabasco sauce, and lemon juice. Stir crab in with a fork. Taste and adjust seasonings, adding salt if needed. Let cool.

CHICKEN-CHEESE FILLING ●

1/4 cup finely minced onion
1/4 pound mushrooms, finely minced
2 tablespoons butter
2 cups finely minced cooked chicken
3 tablespoons minced fresh parsley
1 teaspoon minced fresh tarragon or basil
1/2 teaspoon salt
1/4 teaspoon freshly ground white pepper
1 egg, lightly beaten
3/4 cup shredded Gruyère or Emmenthaler cheese

In a covered nonstick skillet, cook onion and mushrooms in butter over medium heat 5 minutes, or until soft. Remove cover and cook until almost all the moisture has evaporated. Cool and combine with chicken, parsley, tarragon, salt, pepper, egg, and cheese. Taste and adjust seasonings.

FETA CHEESE FILLINGS
(Tiropetes) ●

Any one of these feta cheese mixtures makes excellent *tiropetes,* the classic Greek phyllo triangles, though they all depart slightly from the traditional recipe.

FILLING I
6 ounces feta cheese, crumbled (1-1/2 cups)
3 ounces cream cheese, at room temperature
1 egg, lightly beaten
1/4 cup minced green onion and tops
2 tablespoons minced fresh parsley
1 teaspoon minced fresh chives
1 teaspoon minced fresh dill
Salt and freshly ground white pepper to taste

Combine all ingredients, taste, and adjust seasonings.

FILLING II
8 ounces feta cheese, crumbled (2 cups)
1/2 cup low-fat small-curd cottage cheese
1/2 cup minced fresh parsley
1 egg, lightly beaten
1/2 teaspoon ground cumin
1/2 teaspoon ground thyme
1/2 teaspoon crumbled dried oregano

1/4 teaspoon freshly ground black pepper
1/8 teaspoon cayenne pepper

Combine all ingredients, taste, and adjust seasonings.

FILLING III
6 ounces feta cheese, crumbled (1-1/2 cups)
6 ounces Kefalotyri cheese, grated, or Monterey Jack cheese, shredded
1 egg, lightly beaten
1/2 cup minced fresh parsley
2 tablespoons minced green onion and tops
Salt and freshly ground white pepper to taste

Combine all ingredients, taste, and adjust seasonings.

PHYLLO SPINACH PIE
(Spanakopitta)

Serve this special spinach and feta cheese pie warm or at room temperature. It may be presented in the baking dish, in which case guests can remove their own small squares, or it can be cut in the kitchen and the squares arranged on a serving plate with a garnish of grape clusters or Frosted Grapes.

Approximately Forty Servings
3/4 pound phyllo
1 cup (1/2 pound) butter
1/4 cup olive oil
Sesame seeds (optional)

FILLING
2 pounds fresh spinach
1/2 cup minced onion
1/2 cup minced green onion and tops
2 tablespoons butter
6 eggs
1/2 cup finely chopped fresh parsley
1/2 tablespoon minced fresh dill
1/2 tablespoon minced fresh oregano
12 ounces feta cheese, crumbled (3 cups)
1/4 cup freshly grated Kefalotyri or Parmesan cheese
1/4 cup low-fat small-curd cottage cheese
1/4 teaspoon salt
1/4 teaspoon freshly ground white pepper

To make the filling, trim stems from spinach, rinse leaves under cold running water, and pat dry with paper toweling. Chop finely and set aside.

In a large covered nonstick skillet, cook onion and green onion and tops in butter over medium heat 5 minutes, or until soft. Add spinach, stir well, cover, and cook until spinach is wilted. Stir frequently so spinach cooks evenly. Remove cover and let all moisture cook away. Set aside to cool.

In a large mixing bowl, beat eggs lightly. With a fork, stir in parsley, dill, and oregano. Add cheeses, salt, and pepper. Stir in spinach mixture, taste, and adjust seasonings.

Butter a 9-by-13-by-2-inch shallow baking dish with Lecithin Butter. Preheat oven to 375° F. In a small saucepan, combine butter and olive oil and heat until butter is melted.

Following directions in Working with Phyllo Sheets, brush 1 sheet at a time with the oil and butter mixture and place in the prepared baking dish, pressing the sheets into the corners of the dish and letting them drape over the sides. (You will not need to make stacks of 3 sheets; add each sheet to the dish once it is brushed with the butter mixture.) Reserving 7 sheets for the top of the pie, continue to layer oiled and buttered sheets in the dish. Pour the spinach filling into the dish and level gently with a spatula or back of a wooden spoon. Bring overhanging sheet edges up over the spinach and cover with remaining 7 sheets, brushing each with the butter mixture as you layer. Lightly brush top with butter mixture and sprinkle evenly with sesame seeds.

Place dish in the preheated oven and bake 10 minutes. Lower heat to 350° F and continue baking 35 minutes, or until phyllo is golden brown.

Remove pie to a wire rack and let cool at least 10 minutes. Serve warm or at room temperature.

IDEAS FOR EXCESS PHYLLO SHEETS

BAKED BRIE Wrap 3 buttered and layered phyllo sheets around a room-temperature 8-ounce wheel of Brie. Bake in a preheated 375° F oven 10 minutes, or until phyllo is lightly browned. The cheese should be just warmed through and starting to melt.

Serve immediately with baguette slices and Roasted Garlic. The cheese will cool and start to harden if not eaten promptly.

The unbaked wrapped brie may be sheet frozen for up to 1 month. Defrost in the refrigerator, then bring to room temperature before baking.

BAKED BRIE WITH CRANBERRIES Cut 3 buttered and layered phyllo sheets into 3-inch squares. Carefully line tiny muffin tin wells with the squares, pushing

them in firmly. Refrigerate for 30 minutes, or freeze for up to 1 month.

Fill each phyllo "shell" with about 1-1/2 tablespoons finely diced room-temperature Brie. Top Brie with approximately 3/4 teaspoon cranberry sauce. Bake in a preheated 375° F oven 5 minutes, or until cheese is melted and phyllo is just golden. Let cool briefly before serving, as the cheese retains heat.

Alternative fillings for phyllo shells include any one of the Potted Blue Cheese mixtures; chèvre topped with a dab of pressed garlic and a tiny basil leaf; Stilton cheese topped with minced onion lightly sautéed in butter and olive oil; or Boursin cheese topped with finely chopped cooked spinach.

CHICKEN LIVER PATE FILLING Combine 1/2 cup Chicken Liver Pâté; 1 hard-cooked egg, finely chopped; and 2 tablespoons minced green onion. Chill and form into a log about 6 inches long. Fold 3 buttered and layered phyllo sheets in half lengthwise and place log of chicken liver mixture on the short end. Roll and bake as for Phyllo Rolls, reducing oven heat to 350° F and increasing baking time by 5 or 10 minutes, or until phyllo is golden.

BASICS

To create a first-class hors d'oeuvre, each of the ingredients that goes into it must be of the highest caliber: a perfectly thickened cream sauce, a beautifully smooth mayonnaise, a full-flavored meat stock, a fine-textured gelled aspic. This chapter includes the whole range of these basic elements—sauces, seasoned butters, stocks, fillings, and breads.

There are sections on working with aspic jellies and on fashioning garnitures, and recipes for a number of special ingredients, such as pumate, roasted peppers, roasted garlic, garlic olive oil, and so on. Basic directions on freezing, steaming, clarifying butter, and preparing lecithin oil and butter are also included, along with a number of other useful kitchen tips.

SAUCES

CREAM SAUCE ●■

This is a basic light white sauce that can be used to make creamed foods, such as creamed spinach, for fillings. The use of stock in place of some of the cream lightens the sauce, adds additional flavor, and reduces calories.

For 1 cup of sauce, melt 2 tablespoons butter and/or rendered chicken fat in a nonstick saucepan until foamy. Sprinkle with 1-1/2 to 2 tablespoons unbleached flour and cook, stirring, 2 to 3 minutes to cook away the raw taste of the flour; do not brown. (This cooked butter and flour mixture is called a *roux.*) Now gradually add 1 cup of liquid (1/2 cup *each* rich stock and milk or light cream, or any combination that appeals to your taste). Cook and stir until the mixture is smooth and thickened. This will take several minutes.

It is not necessary to heat the liquid before adding it, though heated liquid helps keep the sauce from lumping. If using cold liquid, remove the *roux* from the heat, add the liquid, stirring it in well, then return the pan to the heat and proceed. Once the sauce is made, you may find it is necessary to thin it with stock, milk, and/or cream, as it may thicken when it cools.

If making the cream sauce in advance, jar, cool, cover, and refrigerate for up to 2 days, or freeze for up to 1 month. Defrost in the refrigerator. Heat gently and stir well to bring back to sauce consistency before using in a recipe.

BASIC MAYONNAISE ●

Mayonnaise made by beating egg yolks and oil together by hand is more delicate than whole-egg mayonnaise prepared in a blender or food processor, and it does not hold up as well when combined with other ingredients to make spreads or similar preparations. Therefore, only "machine-beaten" mayonnaise appears here.

The consistency of mayonnaise made in a blender or processor is like that of commercial mayonnaise. It keeps its firmness better and can be stored longer than handmade mayonnaise, and the flavor, though less rich, remains full.

Makes Approximately One and One-fourth Cups
1 egg
2 tablespoons cider, tarragon, or other vinegar
1/2 teaspoon salt
1/4 teaspoon paprika
1/4 teaspoon freshly ground white pepper
1 to 1-1/2 cups olive or safflower oil

Place egg, vinegar, and seasonings in a blender or food processor. Blend to mix well. With motor running, pour in oil in a slow, steady stream until it is all incorporated and mayonnaise is smooth and glossy. Taste and adjust seasonings.

Transfer mayonnaise to a jar or other nonmetallic container. Cover and refrigerate for up to a week.

MAYONNAISE VARIATIONS

ANCHOVY MAYONNAISE Follow directions for Basic Mayonnaise. Add with egg 1 to 2 teaspoons anchovy paste.

CAPER MAYONNAISE Follow directions for Lemon or Lime Mayonnaise. Finely mince 3 tablespoons parsley leaves in blender or food processor before adding egg. Stir into finished mayonnaise 1 to 2 tablespoons finely chopped drained capers.

CURRY MAYONNAISE Follow directions for Lemon or Lime Mayonnaise. Add 1 teaspoon curry powder, or to taste, with the egg.

GARLIC MAYONNAISE (AIOLI) Follow directions for Lemon or Lime Mayonnaise. Finely mince 3 or 4 large garlic cloves in a blender or food processor before adding egg.

LEMON OR LIME MAYONNAISE Follow directions for Basic Mayonnaise. Substitute fresh lemon or lime juice for the vinegar.

MIXED HERB MAYONNAISE Follow directions for Basic or Lemon or Lime Mayonnaise. Finely mince 1 garlic clove and 1/4 cup chopped mixed fresh herbs of choice in a blender or food processor before adding the egg.

MUSTARD MAYONNAISE Follow directions for Basic Mayonnaise. When blending egg, add 1 teaspoon dry or Dijon-style mustard, or to taste.

ONION MAYONNAISE Follow directions for Basic Mayonnaise. Add 1 teaspoon grated onion with the egg.

SHALLOT MAYONNAISE Follow directions for Basic Mayonnaise. Finely mince 2 or 3 shallots in a blender or food processor before adding the egg.

TARRAGON MAYONNAISE Follow directions for Lemon or Lime Mayonnaise. Finely mince 3 tablespoons chopped fresh tarragon in a blender or food processor before adding the egg.

WATERCRESS MAYONNAISE Follow directions for Lemon or Lime Mayonnaise. Finely mince 1 cup watercress leaves in a blender or food processor before adding the egg and then add 1 teaspoon grated onion.

SALMON MAYONNAISE SAUCE ●

This delicate sauce may be served as a dip with crudités and/or breads and crackers, or may become the filling for cold stuffed mushrooms, cherry tomatoes, or artichoke bottoms. It is also excellent mixed with sieved hard-cooked egg yolks when preparing stuffed eggs.

Makes Approximately One Cup
1 tablespoon chopped fresh
   tarragon leaves
1 tablespoon chopped fresh dill
5 ounces smoked salmon, minced
   (approximately 3/4 cup
   firmly packed)
1 egg
1 tablespoon fresh lemon juice
1/8 teaspoon freshly ground
   white pepper
1/3 cup olive oil
Salt

In a blender or food processor, finely mince tarragon and dill. Add salmon and whirl to purée, then add egg, lemon juice, and pepper and whirl until well mixed.

With motor running, add oil in a slow, steady stream. Taste and adjust seasonings with lemon juice and pepper, adding salt if desired. Transfer to a jar, cover, and refrigerate for at least 2 hours, or for up to 3 days.

HOLLANDAISE SAUCE ●

Makes Approximately One Cup
2 eggs
2 tablespoons fresh lemon or
   lime juice
1/4 teaspoon salt
1/4 teaspoon paprika
1/8 teaspoon freshly ground
   white pepper
2 drops Tabasco sauce (optional)
3/4 cup butter, cut into small
   bits and chilled

In the top pan of a double boiler, combine eggs, lemon juice, salt, paprika, pepper, and Tabasco sauce. With a small electric beater or a wire whisk, beat until mixture is thoroughly mixed, smooth, and airy. Set pan over simmering water in bottom pan of double boiler and beat until mixture thickens to the consistency of mayonnaise. Beat in butter, one bit at a time, until sauce is slightly thickened and creamy.

Remove sauce from the heat. If not using immediately, let stand at room temperature, stirring occasionally, for up to 1 hour. If making ahead to serve with oysters or to use for a dip, cover and refrigerate for up to 3 days. Bring to room temperature and stir well before using. Do not reheat.

BEARNAISE SAUCE ●

This béarnaise sauce is a variation of the preceding hollandaise. The ingredients are combined, reduced over heat, and then used in place of the lemon juice.

Makes Approximately One Cup
1/4 cup white wine vinegar
1/4 cup dry white wine
1 tablespoon finely minced
   shallot or white of green onion
1/2 teaspoon finely minced garlic
2 teaspoons minced fresh
   tarragon
2 teaspoons minced fresh parsley
1/8 teaspoon freshly ground
   white pepper
Dash cayenne pepper

In a saucepan, combine vinegar, wine, shallot, garlic, tarragon, parsley, white pepper, and cayenne pepper. Bring to a boil and cook until liquid is reduced to 2 tablespoons. Strain and use in place of lemon or lime juice in hollandaise sauce.

CREME FRAICHE ○

Crème fraîche is a cultured cream of French origin with a rich, slightly tangy flavor and smooth consistency. It can be substituted for heavy cream in sauces (use a little less), is delicious spooned over fresh fruit or as a dressing for fruit salads, and can replace sour cream in most recipes. Most of the crème fraîche sold in the United States comes from France, though local manufacturers are now appearing. It should be stored in the same way as sour cream.

To make a mock crème fraîche at home, combine in a jar equal parts sour cream and heavy cream with a butterfat content of 40 percent. Stir to form a smooth blend and then let stand uncovered at room temperature for twelve hours. Cover and refrigerate. Crème fraîche will keep approximately one week.

YOGHURT SAUCE ●

This garlicky yoghurt sauce makes an excellent dip for Dolmades or Lamb Meatballs, barbecued lamb or pork, or crudités. Decrease or increase the garlic and lemon juice to suit your taste.

Makes Approximately One Cup
1 cup plain yoghurt
1/8 teaspoon freshly ground
    white pepper
2 tablespoons fresh lemon juice
2 large garlic cloves, very finely
    minced
2 tablespoons finely chopped
    fresh mint
Salt (optional)

In a mixing bowl, combine yoghurt, pepper, lemon juice, garlic, mint, and salt. Taste and adjust seasonings.

Transfer to a storage container, cover, and refrigerate at least 1 hour, or for up to 3 days.

HORSERADISH SAUCE ●

A good complement to roast beef and corned beef platters.

*Makes Approximately
Three-fourths Cup*
1/2 cup sour cream
2 tablespoons prepared horseradish
1/2 teaspoon granulated sugar
1/2 tart apple, pared and grated
    (optional)
1/4 teaspoon ground savory
1 to 2 teaspoons fresh lemon
    juice
1/2 teaspoon freshly grated
    lemon peel
Dash cayenne pepper

In a mixing bowl, combine sour cream, horseradish, sugar, apple, savory, lemon juice, lemon peel, and pepper. Mix well with a fork or wooden spoon. Taste and adjust seasonings.

If not using immediately, jar, cover, and refrigerate for up to 3 days.

TOMATILLO SAUCE ●

This vibrant green sauce is delightfully piquant. Tomatillos, a type of green tomato with a papery brown husk, can be found both fresh and canned in Latin American markets and many supermarkets.

Makes Approximately Three Cups
1-1/2 pounds fresh tomatillos,
    husked, or 1-1/2 cups well-
    drained canned tomatillos
1 white onion, cut up
4 large garlic cloves
3 or 4 fresh hot green chili
    peppers, seeded if desired
1/4 cup fresh coriander leaves
1/2 teaspoon salt
1/4 teaspoon granulated sugar

If using fresh tomatillos, simmer in salted water about 10 minutes, or until tender; drain well. In a blender or food processor, combine the tomatillos, onion, garlic, peppers, coriander, salt, and sugar. If a coarse sauce is preferred, whirl just until ingredients are finely minced. For a smooth sauce, purée until smooth. Taste and adjust seasonings.

If not using immediately, transfer sauce to a nonmetallic storage container, cover, and refrigerate for up to 1 week.

PESTO
(Italian Basil Sauce) ●■

Though most often thought of as a sauce for pasta (in this book dressing tortellini skewered on wooden picks), this pungent sauce complements a whole range of hors d'oeuvres, including cheese tortas and stuffed mushrooms.

Makes Approximately One and One-fourth Cups
5 large garlic cloves, coarsely chopped
2 cups firmly packed chopped fresh basil leaves
1/4 cup chopped fresh parsley (preferably Italian)
1/2 cup chopped pine nuts or walnuts
1/2 teaspoon salt
1/4 teaspoon freshly grated nutmeg
1 cup olive oil
3/4 cup freshly grated Parmesan or Romano cheese

In a blender or food processor, whirl garlic until finely minced. Add basil, parsley, nuts, salt, and nutmeg. Whirl just until finely minced. With motor running, pour in oil in a slow, steady stream until mixture is smooth and thickened. Add cheese and whirl until mixed.

If not using immediately, pack into storage containers, cover, and refrigerate for up to 1 week. If freezing, omit cheese and freeze for up to 3 months. Defrost, stir well, and blend in cheese.

CHILI SAUCE ●■

Once you have made this chili sauce, the commercial version will never again appear on your shelf.

Makes Approximately Two Cups
2-1/2 to 3 pounds ripe tomatoes
1 cup finely chopped onion
1/2 cup finely chopped green bell pepper
1/2 to 1 teaspoon finely minced garlic
1/2 to 1 teaspoon finely minced ginger root
1/2 to 3/4 teaspoon crushed dried hot red chili pepper
1/2 cup cider vinegar
1 tablespoon honey
1 teaspoon mustard seeds
1 teaspoon salt
1/4 teaspoon freshly grated nutmeg
1/4 teaspoon ground coriander
2 whole cloves

Peel and chop tomatoes to measure 5 cups. In a large saucepan, combine tomatoes with onion, bell pepper, garlic, ginger root, dried pepper, vinegar, honey, mustard seeds, salt, nutmeg, coriander, and cloves. Bring mixture to a gentle boil, lower heat, and simmer, uncovered, 2-1/2 hours, or until thickened. Stir often and keep mixture at a gentle boil. Increase heat last 10 minutes of cooking if sauce appears too thin. The sauce will thicken slightly when it has cooled.

Spoon sauce into jars, cool, and cover. If not using immediately, refrigerate for up to 5 days, or freeze for up to 2 months.

BASIC PREPARATIONS

FILLINGS

These three fillings—an elegant duxelle, an easy-to-prepare ham and tomato mixture, and a creamy crab or shrimp blend—are versatile creations. They can be used to fill a variety of hot hors d'oeuvres: Pastry Croustades, Pastry Rounds, Choux, Baked Stuffed Mushrooms, and Baked Filled Artichoke Bottoms.

Have the fillings at room temperature before spooning them into any of these pastry or vegetable bases. Sprinkle Seasoned Bread Crumbs and/or freshly grated Parmesan or Romano cheese over the top, then slip the filled hors d'oeuvres into the oven.

DUXELLE ●■

Makes One and One-half Cups
1/4 cup finely minced green
    onion and tops
4 tablespoons butter
1/2 pound mushrooms, very finely
    minced (not in a blender or
    food processor)
1/4 teaspoon salt

1/4 teaspoon ground oregano
1/4 teaspoon freshly ground
    white pepper
1/2 teaspoon fresh lemon juice
2 tablespoons unbleached flour
1 cup heavy cream
2 tablespoons minced fresh parsley
1 tablespoon minced fresh chives
3 or 4 drops Tabasco sauce

In a large skillet, sauté onion in butter 3 minutes. Add mushrooms, seasonings, and lemon juice. Cook over medium-high heat, stirring often, until moisture has almost evaporated. The amount of time this will take depends upon how fresh the mushrooms are: fresher mushrooms have more moisture and thus will take longer.

Sprinkle mushrooms with flour and continue to cook, stirring, 3 minutes. Gradually add cream and cook, stirring, until mixture thickens to a pastelike consistency. With a fork, mix in parsley, chives, and Tabasco sauce. Taste and adjust seasonings. Remove from the heat and cool to room temperature before using.

If not using immediately, transfer to a nonmetallic storage container, cover, and refrigerate for up to 3 days, or freeze for up to 1 month. Defrost in the refrigerator. To bring duxelle back to its original consistency, heat, stirring to mix well, then cool and proceed with recipe.

CRAB OR SHRIMP FILLING

If the price of crab meat or shrimp is just too high, substitute flaked steamed pollack. A recipe for its preparation appears in this chapter.

Makes Approximately One and One-half Cups
1 recipe Cream Sauce
2 to 3 tablespoons dry sherry
1 teaspoon fresh lemon juice
3 drops Tabasco sauce
2 tablespoons minced fresh
    parsley
1 tablespoon minced fresh chives
1 cup flaked crab meat or tiny
    cooked shrimp
1/4 teaspoon freshly ground
    white pepper
Salt

Prepare cream sauce and stir in sherry and lemon juice with the liquid. Cook, stirring often, 5 minutes, or until sauce is smooth and thickened. With a fork, stir in Tabasco sauce, parsley, chives, crab meat, and pepper. Taste and adjust seasonings, adding salt if needed. Remove from heat and let cool, stirring occasionally to prevent a skin from forming.

TOMATO AND HAM FILLING ●■

Makes Approximately One and One-half Cups

3 large ripe tomatoes, peeled, finely chopped, and well drained
1/4 cup finely minced green onion and tops
1 teaspoon finely minced garlic
1/4 pound mushrooms, finely minced (not in a blender or food processor)
3/4 cup finely minced ham
1/4 teaspoon salt
1/4 teaspoon ground oregano or basil
1/4 teaspoon freshly ground white pepper
3 tablespoons finely minced fresh parsley
3 or 4 drops Tabasco sauce
3 egg yolks

In a large skillet, combine tomatoes, onion, garlic, mushrooms, ham, salt, oregano, and pepper and cook over medium heat, stirring often, until almost all moisture has evaporated. Stir in parsley and Tabasco sauce, taste, and adjust seasonings.

In a mixing bowl, beat egg yolks lightly and then stir in 1 cup of the ham mixture. Return to rest of ham mixture, beating constantly. Cook and stir over medium heat 2 minutes, or until thickened. Do not allow to boil. Remove from the heat and let cool.

If not using filling immediately, transfer to a container, cover, and refrigerate for up to 3 days, or freeze for up to 2 weeks. After defrosting, heat and stir well before using.

SEASONED BUTTERS ●■

The following seasoned butters are called for primarily in the Canapés chapter, where they play an important role. Without a thin coating of butter, bread is apt to become soggy when topped with mayonnaise or spreads. Plain butter, of course, may be used, but the flavors of the canapé toppings are often enhanced by the addition of seasonings to the butter. Seasoned butters also complement cold meat platters and can be served as simple spreads for crackers and breads.

Depending upon your preference, use salted or unsalted butter to make seasoned butters. When choosing which one to use, keep in mind the saltiness of the other ingredients and plan accordingly. For instance, when the spread contains ham or sardines, unsalted butter is best.

Before adding the seasonings, have the butter at room temperature. It will be much easier to work with if it is soft. With a fork or wooden spoon, cream the butter in a bowl, on a work surface, or on a plate, then work in the seasonings. A food processor works well if the recipe is doubled or tripled.

Pack the seasoned butter into a small bowl or crock or form into a log. If not using immediately, cover or wrap and refrigerate. With the exception of those that contain seafood, all seasoned butters may be refrigerated for up to two weeks or frozen for up to two months. Those made with seafood should be refrigerated no more than two or three days or frozen more than two weeks.

Before using the butter, bring it to room temperature so that it is soft enough to spread easily. A spatula or wide-bladed knife is ideal for spreading.

The following suggestions call for one-quarter pound soft salted or unsalted butter. Cream the butter, then add:

ALMOND BUTTER 1/2 cup finely chopped almonds, lightly toasted.

ANCHOVY BUTTER 1 teaspoon anchovy paste and 1 teaspoon fresh lemon juice (best with unsalted butter).

BLUE CHEESE BUTTER 1 ounce blue cheese, crumbled (1/4 cup), and 1 teaspoon *each* fresh lemon juice and minced fresh chives (best with unsalted butter).

CHIVE OR GREEN ONION BUTTER 1/3 cup finely minced chives or green onion tops and 1 teaspoon fresh lemon juice.

CHUTNEY BUTTER 3 tablespoons finely minced drained chutney and curry powder or Dijon-style mustard to taste.

CURRY BUTTER 2 tablespoons minced shallots sautéed until soft in 2 teaspoons butter; season with curry powder to taste.

DILL BUTTER 2 tablespoons minced fresh dill, 1 teaspoon fresh lemon juice, and 1 or 2 drops Tabasco sauce.

EGG YOLK BUTTER 3 hard-cooked egg yolks, mashed, and 1/2 teaspoon paprika.

GARLIC BUTTER 1/2 to 1 teaspoon pressed garlic, 2 tablespoons *each* freshly grated Parmesan cheese and minced fresh parsley, and 1/4 to 1/2 teaspoon paprika.

GREEN BUTTER 1/2 cup parsley leaves, finely chopped; 1/4 cup watercress leaves, finely chopped; 4 medium-size spinach leaves, finely chopped; 4 chive leaves, minced; 1 teaspoon finely minced fresh sorrel, basil, tarragon, thyme, dill, and/or chervil; and 1 teaspoon fresh lemon juice.

HAZELNUT BUTTER 1/2 cup finely chopped hazelnuts, lightly toasted.

HORSERADISH BUTTER 1 to 2 teaspoons prepared horseradish.

LEMON OR LIME BUTTER 1-1/2 tablespoons *each* fresh lemon or lime juice and finely minced parsley and 1/2 teaspoon freshly grated lemon or lime peel.

MAYONNAISE BUTTER 1/4 cup Basic Mayonnaise, 1 teaspoon crumbled dried dill or oregano, and Tabasco sauce, salt, and white pepper to taste.

MIXED HERB BUTTER 1 tablespoon *each* minced fresh parsley, chervil, and chives and 1 teaspoon finely minced fresh basil or tarragon.

MUSHROOM BUTTER Sauté 1 cup minced mushrooms in 2 tablespoons butter with 1 tablespoon fresh lemon juice 5 to 10 minutes. Mash to a paste and season to taste with minced fresh chives, ground oregano or savory, paprika, white pepper, and cayenne pepper.

MUSTARD BUTTER 2 to 3 tablespoons homemade, Dijon-style, or other prepared mustard.

ONION BUTTER 2 tablespoons very finely minced onion and 1/2 teaspoon Worcestershire sauce.

PAPRIKA-ONION BUTTER Sauté 1/2 cup minced onion in 2 tablespoons butter until soft; add 1 teaspoon paprika.

PARSLEY OR CHERVIL BUTTER 1/3 cup minced fresh parsley or 1/4 cup minced fresh chervil and 1/2 teaspoon freshly grated lemon peel, or to taste.

PEPPER BUTTER 3 tablespoons very finely minced red or green bell pepper, 1/2 tablespoon *each* finely minced shallot and fresh parsley, 1/2 tablespoon fresh lemon juice, 1/2 teaspoon Worcestershire sauce, 1/8 teaspoon *each* salt and white pepper, and dash cayenne pepper.

ROSEMARY BUTTER 1 to 1-1/2 teaspoons finely minced fresh rosemary.

SHRIMP BUTTER 1/4 pound shrimp, cooked, peeled, and very finely minced or coarsely ground, 1 tablespoon fresh lime or lemon juice, and 1/2 teaspoon seafood seasoning (optional).

SMOKED SALMON BUTTER 1-1/2 ounces smoked salmon, mashed, and fresh lemon juice, minced fresh chives, and white pepper to taste (best with unsalted butter).

TARRAGON BUTTER 1 tablespoon minced fresh tarragon and 2 teaspoons fresh lemon juice.

TOMATO BUTTER 1/2 cup finely chopped ripe tomato, forced through a sieve, and 1 teaspoon fresh lemon juice.

WATERCRESS BUTTER 1/2 cup finely chopped watercress, 1 tablespoon fresh lemon juice, 1/4 teaspoon ground marjoram, 1/8 teaspoon onion powder, and anchovy paste to taste (optional).

CLARIFIED BUTTER ●

This process removes the milk solids from butter, resulting in what is called clarified, or drawn, butter. Cut butter into small pieces and melt in a saucepan over low heat. Remove the pan from the heat and let stand until the white milk solids sink to the pan bottom. Skim the clear liquid (the clarified butter) from the top and discard the white milk solids. Strain the clear liquid through a sieve lined with dampened cheesecloth.

Cool, jar, cover, and refrigerate clarified butter for up to 1 month. One pound of butter will yield approximately 3/4 cup clarified butter. Use as recipes indicate, or whenever sautéing foods that should not be browned.

GARLIC OLIVE OIL ○

Lightly mash 2 or 3 garlic cloves and place in a jar. Add olive oil and let stand 2 days, or up to 1 week. Discard garlic cloves and store in a covered jar as you would unflavored olive oil. Use whenever a subtle hint of garlic is desired with the olive oil called for in a recipe.

RENDERED FAT ●■

Cut chicken, ham, pork, or beef fat into tiny bits and cook slowly in a heavy skillet over low heat until melted. Strain and cool slightly. Pour into small containers, cover, and refrigerate up to 1 week, or freeze up to 3 months.

Alternatively, for a clearer rendered fat, cook bits of fat in water until melted, skimming off any scum that rises to the surface and adding water as needed. Pour into a jar and cool; fat will rise to the surface. Remove fat and wrap or jar. Storage times are as for preceding method.

EGG WASH ●■

In a small bowl, beat together 1 egg, or 1 egg white, and 1 tablespoon water with a wire whisk or fork until well mixed and slightly frothy. Brush on the tops of pastries or other dishes as designated in recipes. Egg wash may be refrigerated for up to 2 days, or frozen for up to 1 week.

LECITHIN OIL ●

Liquid lecithin, available in health-food stores, is a viscous liquid that resembles heavy molasses. A derivative of soybeans, it is the principal ingredient in commercial sprays designed to keep foods from sticking to pots and pans. To economize and to avoid inhalation from a spray can, mix your own coating. It is also far more effective than the spray.

Combine 3 parts safflower or corn oil and 1 part liquid lecithin in a squeeze bottle. Keep on hand at room temperature (it will keep at least 4 months) and shake well before using.

LECITHIN BUTTER ●■

Combine 4 tablespoons softened butter and 2 teaspoons liquid lecithin (see information on liquid lecithin in Lecithin Oil, preceding). Store in a covered jar in the refrigerator for up to 3 weeks, or freeze for up to 2 months.

ROASTED PEPPERS ○

Something wonderful happens to fresh bell peppers when they are roasted and peeled. Their flavor becomes robust and slightly sweet and they make marvelous additions to a wide variety of dishes. When your garden or produce market has an abundance of bell peppers, set aside a day to stock your larder, then you will always have them on hand.

Select firm, well-shaped red bell peppers (the green peppers are not as attractive to look at, as healthful, nor as flavorful). Rinse the peppers, pat them dry with paper toweling, and place them on a rack in a broiler pan. Broil the peppers about 3 inches from the source of heat, turning often, until charred on all sides. Alternatively, spear the peppers on the tines of a fork and hold them over the open flame of a gas stove, rotating to blacken evenly. As they blacken, remove the peppers to a paper bag. Close the bag, and let it stand 10 minutes so that steam forms inside of it. This steam helps loosen the skin of the peppers.

One at a time, remove the peppers from the bag. When cool enough to handle, peel off the skin with fingertips and a small knife. Cut each pepper lengthwise into quarters or eighths, cut out stem end and veins, and discard along with all of the seeds. Pack pepper pieces into sterilized 1/2-pint canning jars and pour olive or safflower oil over to cover. If desired, tuck a halved garlic clove into the jar.

Cover jar tightly and store in a cool, dry place for at least 2 weeks; if not using within 6 months, refrigerate. If you have topped them with olive oil, which congeals when chilled, bring the jar to room temperature before removing pepper pieces.

Commercially roasted peppers are available in jars at specialty food shops and some super-markets. They are, however, quite costly. As with homemade roasted peppers, once opened they should be refrigerated and will last almost indefinitely (in contrast to pimientos, which spoil within 3 or 4 days).

Use roasted peppers in place of pimientos and in those recipes that call for them. A few additional uses follow.

• Cut roasted peppers into strips and arrange spoke fashion on a serving plate alternately with anchovy fillets. Strew chopped drained capers or ripe olives over and drizzle with a little olive oil and fresh lemon juice. Sprinkle with finely minced fresh parsley or chives. Garnish with lemon wedges and serve with crusty french bread. Place a peppermill beside the plate.

• Finely mince 1 roasted pepper, 6 pitted black olives, 4 drained anchovy fillets, and 1/4 cup firmly packed fresh parsley leaves. Transfer all ingredients to a bowl and stir in fresh lemon juice, salt, and freshly ground black pepper to taste. Moisten with olive oil, if needed, and grind black pepper over the top. Serve as a spread for baguette slices or buffet rye rounds.

• Slice drained roasted peppers into strips and add to marinated mushrooms. Let marinate several hours and sprinkle with minced fresh parsley just before serving.

• In a small bowl, combine chopped drained roasted peppers with lots of slivered garlic and salt and white pepper to taste. Cover and refrigerate overnight. Just before serving, sprinkle with minced fresh parsley and chives. Serve with Fried Bread rounds.

PUMATE
(SUN-DRIED TOMATOES) ○

Commercial sun-dried tomatoes are extremely expensive and not a bit better than those you dry at home. Your range oven or home dehydrator takes the place of the sun with excellent results.

Many chefs consider Italian plum-shaped tomatoes (Roma) to be the best for drying, but I have found that my vine-ripened round tomatoes work beautifully.

Select firm, very ripe tomatoes. Wash, wipe dry with paper toweling, and trim off ends. Slice the tomatoes 1/4 inch thick, or cut them in half lengthwise three-fourths of the way through. Lay the tomato slices flat on the rack of a dehydrator or on a wire rack set over a baking pan, or open the "halved" tomatoes and lay them cut side down on the rack. If desired, lightly sprinkle tomatoes with salt.

If you are using a dehydrator, the drying time will depend on your appliance, how crowded the tomatoes are, and how many of the tiers you are using. If you rotate the tiers several times, the tomatoes will all be done at the same time. Start checking after 3 hours have elapsed.

If you are drying the tomatoes in the oven, preheat the oven to 200° F and place the racks in the oven. Again, timing will depend on how crowded the tomatoes are and how many racks you are using. Start checking after 7 hours have elapsed. In either case, check frequently so the tomatoes do not dry too long. They should look shriveled, but should still be pliable.

Pack dried tomatoes into jars, adding a few fresh basil leaves and several small cut garlic cloves, if desired. Add olive oil to cover tomatoes completely, seal with jar lid, and store in a cool, dark place at least 1 month, or for up to 6 months. (After 6 months, store in the refrigerator.) Once opened, the jars must be refrigerated.

Pumate is called for throughout this book. Use your imagination and combine these flavorful, wonderfully textured tomatoes with other foods. Here are a few suggestions to get you started.

• Wrap slivers of pumate around chunks of feta or chèvre.
• Place slivers on Fried Bread rounds with a little of their oil.
• Spread Fried Bread rounds with cream cheese softened with sour cream and place small strips of pumate on the rounds in a crisscross pattern.
• Toss pumate strips with marinated artichoke hearts or mushrooms, and small chunks of Monterey Jack cheese.

PUMATE PUREE ●■

I once gave a friend some tomatoes I had dried too long in the dehydrator. They still had marvelous flavor, but they were too hard to use in most recipes. She came up with this refreshing tomato purée, which can also be made with properly dried tomatoes.

Drain the olive oil from the pumate and cook them in a little dry vermouth and/or water until they soften. Check often and add vermouth or water as needed. Purée by pressing through a sieve, or grind in a blender or food processor. The result is a thick, lovely purée redolent of tomato.

One 1/2-pint jar of home-dried tomatoes will yield approximately 1/3 cup purée. Store in an airtight container in the refrigerator or freezer for up to 1 week, for like tomato paste, pumate purée dries out and becomes gummy when frozen too long.

Use pumate purée in place of tomato paste, or for the chili sauce called for in a recipe. (Use half as much pumate purée as chili sauce.)

CHESTNUT PUREE ●

Chestnut purée is a well-known accompaniment to venison or other game; less known are its uses in spreads and stuffed eggs. You will find the latter uses surprisingly different and tasty.

Makes Approximately One and One-half Cups

1 pound chestnuts, peeled and
    chopped (see Note)
3 celery ribs and leaves, coarsely
    chopped
1 medium-size onion, halved
2 whole cloves
1 bay leaf, broken
1/3 cup water, or as needed
1 tablespoon cider vinegar
1/4 teaspoon salt
1/8 teaspoon freshly ground
    white pepper
1/8 teaspoon freshly grated
    nutmeg
2 to 3 tablespoons butter
1/3 cup heavy cream, or as
    needed

In a saucepan, combine chestnuts, celery, onion, cloves, bay leaf, water, vinegar, salt, pepper, and nutmeg. Cover, bring to a gentle boil, and simmer 20 minutes, or until chestnuts are tender, adding water if mixture starts to dry out. Discard celery, onion, and cloves. Boil until all moisture has evaporated.

Purée mixture in a blender or food processor with butter and cream. Return purée to saucepan and reheat gently. Taste and adjust seasonings and if purée appears too thick, thin with a little additional cream.

If not using immediately, cover and refrigerate for up to 2 days. Stir well before using.

NOTE To peel raw chestnuts, cut an X on the flat side of each chestnut. Working with a dozen or so at a time, place the chestnuts in a saucepan, add water to cover, and boil until the skins can be peeled off with a sharp knife, about 10 minutes. Be sure to peel them while they are still hot or the inner brown furlike skin, which must be removed, will not come off easily.

ROASTED GARLIC

Roasted garlic is for garlic lovers and for those who shy away at the mention of raw garlic. Its sweet yet pungent flavor is like nothing you've ever tasted. The simple preparation and ease of serving make it a must for small and large parties alike.

Select well-formed garlic heads with large cloves. Trim off the very top of the head and carefully pull off the outer skin, leaving each clove covered with its tight skin. Gently loosen the cloves from the center without pulling them off.

Oil muffin-tin wells with olive oil and set a garlic head in each well. Drizzle olive oil generously over each head and then dot each head with a tiny bit of butter. Set the muffin tin on the lowest rack of a preheated 300° F oven and bake, drizzling occasionally with additional oil, 45 minutes, or until garlic cloves are nicely browned.

The garlic is now ready to eat. Here are two ways to serve it:

● Arrange garlic heads on a serving platter alongside a piece of Brie or Camembert and surround with slices of sourdough french bread. Provide each guest with a small plate and a napkin. The guests spread the bread with cheese, then squeeze the garlic out of the papery skins onto the cheese.
● Make a purée by squeezing the soft garlic out of the skins and mashing well with a fork. Toast bread cutouts on one side, flip over, and spread untoasted side of cutouts with the garlic purée. Sprinkle lightly with paprika and broil until bubbly and heated through. Serve immediately.

HOMEMADE STOCKS

A superior stock is essential to the success of aspics, soups, and sauces. Homemade stocks have better flavor and are more economical than commercial preparations, plus they use up foods, such as meat and vegetable trimmings, that might otherwise be wasted.

Acquire the habit of saving bones, scraps, and other leftovers to add to stocks you are making from fresh bones and ingredients. Or simply boil the trimmings alone in a little water to use as a base for stock. Once you begin routinely making stock, you will never be without a good stock to use in cooking.

The bones and vegetables in the following stocks may be browned in butter and/or rendered beef or chicken fat before combining with water. This step will produce what is termed a brown stock. The resulting stock will have a stronger, richer flavor than stock prepared without browned ingredients. The browning can be done in the soup kettle on top of the stove, or in a shallow baking pan in a preheated 375° F oven.

Richer flavor is also produced by boiling down the strained stock to produce a thicker, more concentrated liquid. Boil the stock, uncovered, until liquid is reduced to desired concentration. When adjusting seasonings, keep in mind that an aspic jelly will need to be slightly overseasoned because the chilling dulls the flavors.

When the finished stock is refrigerated, a layer of fat will rise to the top and harden. This fat layer acts as protection against spoilage, and the stock should keep for one week. Before you use the stock, lift off and discard the fat. If you will not be using the stock within a week's time, bring it back to a boil, rejar, and refrigerate.

If you intend to freeze the stock, leave at least an inch of head space at the top of the container to allow for expansion. Stock will keep in the freezer for as long as six months. The consistency changes, however, so defrost and bring to a boil, then rejar, cool, and refrigerate to congeal fat. Once the fat has congealed, it can be lifted off and discarded, and then the stock can be used.

BEEF STOCK ●■

Makes Approximately Three Quarts

4 pounds beef bones with meat, cut up
1 to 2 pounds marrow bones, sawed into 3-inch pieces
1 pair pigs' feet
2 quarts cold water
3 quarts plain water or water in which vegetables have been cooked
3 carrots, cut up
2 celery ribs and leaves, chopped
2 turnips, chopped
2 unpeeled whole onions, each stuck with 2 whole cloves
2 ripe tomatoes, chopped
6 parsley sprigs
2 thyme sprigs
2 oregano or marjoram sprigs
1 large bay leaf
4 garlic cloves, lightly crushed
8 black peppercorns, lightly crushed
1/2 tablespoon salt

Cover bones and pigs' feet with 2 quarts cold water, bring to a rapid boil, drain, and rinse bones and feet. Place bones and feet in a clean soup kettle, add 3 quarts plain water or vegetable cooking water, cover kettle, and bring slowly to a rapid boil. Skim off any surface scum, lower heat, cover, and simmer for 2 hours.

Add carrots, celery, turnips, onions, tomatoes, herbs, garlic, peppercorns, and salt. Bring back to a gentle boil, cover, and simmer 2 hours. Strain, jar, cool, cover, and refrigerate.

LAMB STOCK ●■

Follow directions for Beef Stock, substituting lamb blocks or leg of lamb or other bones and trimmings for the beef and adding 2 rosemary sprigs.

CHICKEN STOCK ●■

Makes Approximately Three Quarts
6 pounds chicken backs, necks, and wing tips, cut up
3 quarts water
2 onions, unpeeled and quartered
2 carrots, chopped
1 turnip, chopped
2 celery ribs and leaves, chopped
2 leeks (white and a little green), chopped
2 large garlic cloves, lightly crushed
1 large bay leaf
6 parsley sprigs
1 thyme sprig
1 savory sprig, or 2 fresh sage leaves
1/2 tablespoon salt
1 teaspoon ground turmeric
1/2 teaspoon poultry seasoning
6 white peppercorns, lightly crushed

Put bones and water in a soup kettle, cover, bring slowly to a rapid boil, and skim off any surface scum. Lower heat, cover, and simmer 2 hours.

Add onions, carrots, turnip, celery, leeks, garlic, bay leaf, herbs, salt, turmeric, poultry seasoning, and peppercorns. Bring back to a gentle boil, lower heat, and simmer 2 hours. Strain, jar, cool, and refrigerate.

PORK STOCK ●■

Follow directions for Chicken Stock, substituting pork bones for chicken bones and ground sage for turmeric; add 2 oregano sprigs.

FISH STOCK ●■

Makes Approximately One Quart
1 pound fish heads, bones, and trimmings
3 cups water
1 cup dry white wine
1/2 cup sliced celery ribs and leaves
1/2 cup sliced onion
1/2 cup sliced carrot
6 parsley sprigs
3 thyme sprigs
3 fresh tarragon leaves, or 1 bay leaf
8 black peppercorns, lightly crushed
1/2 teaspoon salt

In a large saucepan, combine fish parts, water, wine, celery ribs and leaves, onion, carrot, herbs, peppercorns, and salt. Cover, bring to a boil, lower heat, and simmer 30 minutes.

Strain, jar, cool, and refrigerate for up to 2 days, or freeze for up to 3 weeks. For a more concentrated flavor, boil strained stock to reduce to 3 cups, or add bottled clam juice to taste.

VEGETABLE STOCK ●■

Makes Approximately One Quart
1 quart water and/or water in which vegetables have been cooked, or part tomato juice
3 cups chopped fresh vegetables and vegetable trimmings of choice
5 or 6 garlic cloves, lightly crushed
4 or 5 parsley sprigs
1 cup potato skins (optional)
Herbs and seasonings of choice

In a large saucepan, combine water, vegetables, garlic, parsley, potato skins, and herbs and seasonings. Cover, bring to a boil, lower heat, and simmer 2 hours.

Strain, jar, cool, and refrigerate for up to 3 days, or freeze for up to 2 months.

TO CLARIFY STOCK

It is imperative that stock to be used in aspic jelly be clarified, for the aspic must be absolutely clear. If you are making jellies other than those in this chapter, you will need to clarify the stock before proceeding.

In a saucepan, combine 3 cups stock, 1 lightly beaten egg white, and the crumbled shell of 1 egg. Slowly bring to a boil (it should take about 10 minutes), add 2 teaspoons cold water, and bring back to a gentle boil for 2 minutes. Remove from heat and let stand without stirring 20 minutes. Rinse quadrupled cheesecloth or a piece of muslin with cold water and use it to line a large strainer. Place the strainer over a tall saucepan and pour the stock into the strainer, allowing it to drain through the cloth without disruption. The straining may take as long as 30 minutes.

STEAMED POLLACK OR MONKFISH ●

When steamed, pollack takes on the texture of crab meat and monkfish takes on that of lobster. With prices of crab and lobster so high, you may want to substitute these salt-water fish for the crab or lobster called for in recipes in this book.

For 12 ounces of pollack or monkfish fillets you will need 2 tablespoons fresh lemon juice. Arrange the fillets in a single layer in a large shallow dish or platter. Drizzle the lemon juice over and sprinkle the fillets with salt and freshly ground white pepper.

Place the dish or platter on a rack over boiling water in a large steamer or electric frypan. (If you do not have a large steamer or frypan, steam the fish in batches.) The water should be at least 1/2 inch below the top of the rack. Cover the steamer or frypan (with air vent slightly open) and steam the fish 7 to 10 minutes, depending upon the thickness of the fillets. To test for doneness, pull the flesh apart with a fork; it should be just barely opaque.

Remove the dish or platter from the steamer and lift out the fillets. Save the juices that have accumulated for making fish stock. Let the fish cool, then wrap in plastic wrap and refrigerate for no longer than 1 day.

When flaking the fish for a recipe, check carefully for any bones that may still be in the flesh.

BASIC SWEETBREADS ○ ■

The herbs and other seasonings that go into this stock for cooking sweetbreads give the delicate variety meat an extraordinarily good flavor.

Two pounds of sweetbreads will yield about five dozen hors d'oeuvre "bites" for combining with sauces and other ingredients to make a finished dish.

2 pounds veal sweetbreads
Ice water
1/4 cup fresh lemon juice
1 teaspoon salt
1 large carrot, cut up
1 large celery rib and leaves, cut up
1 medium-size onion, chopped
6 parsley sprigs
2 thyme sprigs
2 bay leaves, crumbled
8 black peppercorns, lightly crushed
2 cups dry white wine

In a saucepan, soak sweetbreads in ice water several hours. Drain and return to saucepan with lemon juice, salt, vegetables, herbs, bay leaf, peppercorns, and wine. Add water to cover the sweetbreads, cover pan, and bring to a boil. Lower heat and cook at a gentle boil 10 to 15 minutes, depending upon size. Cool in liquid, cover, and refrigerate overnight.

Remove sweetbreads from liquid and set aside. Heat liquid slightly and strain, discarding the vegetables, herbs, and seasonings. Remove any fat and membrane from the sweetbreads and break or cut into bite-size pieces.

If not using immediately, transfer sweetbreads to a jar or non-metallic storage container, pour strained liquid over and refrigerate for up to 2 days, or freeze for up to 1 month. Freeze any excess liquid separately for use in recipes or soup stocks.

WAYS WITH BREADS

Today, most of us have access to good-quality European-style breads, as new bakeries catering to ever more sophisticated palates open in communities across the country. The appearance of these breads means that you no longer need to spend hours in the kitchen baking loaves of bread with which to make canapés or to accompany pâtés, terrines, molds, and other hors d'oeuvres.

In general, the finest breads are those that are neither too heavy nor too bland and are not crumbly, rubbery, or diaphanous. This would include everything from whole wheat, french, a variety of ryes, and pumpernickel to hearty black bread. When selecting the appropriate bread, keep in mind that it should complement what it accompanies, not overpower it.

There are an additional number of breads that will add visual interest as well as distinctive flavor to the hors d'oeuvre table. These include croissants, miniature breadsticks and bagels, English muffins trimmed into small rounds and toasted, and halved tiny baking-powder biscuits.

Crackers also make good bases for spreads and dips, pâtés, cheeses, and other appetizer fare. Any mildly seasoned whole-grain, wheat, or rye crackers are good choices, as well as the Armenian cracker bread called lahvosh. Among the recommended commercial brands are Waverly, Cracotte wheat or rye rectangles, Premium (unsalted tops), Bremner, Wheat Thins, Croquille, Carr's table and whole-wheat crackers, Finn Crisp, Kavli Norwegian flatbread, CracklBred, Wesa, and the toastlike Cresca.

Some hors d'oeuvres are best suited to particular breads. Parker House rolls pair beautifully with a roast beef platter, tiny bagels are good with smoked salmon, and mini corn muffins are naturals with thinly sliced baked ham. Whimsical bread cutouts are attractive bases for a whole range of canapés (see Canapés), pita bread triangles are the perfect dippers for Eggplant Caviar, and crisp chips made from corn or flour tortillas are ideal "scoops" for chunky Guacamole.

The most important things to remember about breads are that

they be fresh, flavorful, and of a texture that won't detract from the hors d'oeuvre itself. The delicate flavor of Chèvre Cheesecake would be destroyed by the distinct flavor of rye, whereas a platter of corned beef or ham would benefit from it.

Slice the breads for the buffet table shortly before the party begins and keep covered with plastic wrap or a tea towel until the last minute.

The following recipes transform already baked breads into special breads—melba toast, fried bread, croustades, pita bread crisps, and so on—for the hors d'oeuvre table. The only made-from-scratch "bread" that appears here is a pizza dough, with a variation for making my version of the northern Italian specialty called focaccia. I have included my own recipe because of the absence of a commercial pizza crust that meets my standards.

FRIED BREAD ●■

Cut french, sourdough, Italian, or homemade-style white or light whole-wheat bread into slices approximately 3/8-inch thick. With a canapé cutter, cut 1-1/2-inch rounds or other shapes from the slices.

In a large skillet, heat 2 tablespoons Clarified Butter or unsalted butter and 1 table-spoon olive oil. Brown the bread rounds on both sides over medium heat and drain on paper toweling. Cool on a wire rack and store in an airtight container for up to 3 days, or freeze for up to 3 months. Serve with spreads and as a base for cold canapés.

MELBA TOAST ●■

With canapé cutters, cut 1-1/2- to 2-inch rounds or other shapes from thinly sliced french, Italian, homemade-style white or whole wheat, or light rye bread. Brush cutouts with melted butter or butter which has been melted with lightly crushed garlic.

Place the cutouts on an oiled baking sheet and bake in a 400° F oven until golden and crisp. Alternatively, broil to brown on one side, brush other side with melted butter, and bake buttered side up in a 300° F oven 30 minutes or until crisp. Cool on wire racks and store in an airtight container for up to 4 days, or freeze for up to 3 months. Serve with spreads, dips, pâtés, and other molded dishes.

CROUSTADES ●■

The word "croustade" refers to a pastry or bread "shell" that is to be filled with a hot or cold food. For croustades made of puff pastry, see the Pastries chapter.

To make bread croustades, slice 2-day old homemade-style white or light whole-wheat bread 1 inch thick, cut into rounds with a 1-3/4-inch cutter and then with a 1-1/8-inch cutter press down on the center of the round to cut halfway through.

Deep fry cutouts in hot (375° F) peanut oil until just golden. Drain on crumpled paper toweling. When cool enough to handle, lift out the center portion of each cutout to form a shell with sides and bottom of equal thickness.

Alternatively, butter tiny muffin-tin (tartlet) wells. Slice homemade-style white or light whole-wheat bread 1/4 inch thick and cut into rounds with a 2-5/16-inch cutter. Press rounds into wells as you would if lining for tartlets.

Lightly brush bread with melted butter and bake in a preheated 350° F oven 10 to 15 minutes, or until golden. When shells have cooled slightly, lift out of muffin tins and cool on wire racks. Store in an airtight container for up to 2 days, or freeze for up to 3 months.

Croustades may be filled with any of the Hot Fillings for Choux or with Duxelle, Tomato and Ham Filling, or Crab or Shrimp Filling. Sprinkle lightly with freshly grated Parmesan cheese or finely shredded Gruyère cheese and heat in a 375° F oven until bubbly and cheese is melted.

TORTILLA CHIPS ●■

Unless your favorite Mexican restaurant has outstandingly good chips for sale, you will want to make your own from good-quality flour or corn tortillas.

Pour corn oil into a cast-iron or other heavy skillet up to a depth of 1/2 inch. Heat the oil to 375° F, or until a piece of bread sizzles when added. With scissors, cut a tortilla into triangles, cutting just to the center so the triangles are still attached. With tongs, lower the tortilla into the oil and fry just until crisp. Remove to crumpled paper toweling to drain, sprinkle lightly with salt if desired, and when cool enough to handle, break the triangles apart. Adding additional oil as needed to keep original level, repeat with remaining tortillas.

If not using chips within 3 or 4 hours, transfer the cooled chips to an airtight container. They will stay crisp several days, or they may be frozen for up to 3 months.

PITA BREAD ●■

Pita bread, also called pocket bread or sahara bread, is available in a variety of guises—white, whole wheat, with sesame seeds, and so on. Most supermarkets carry a good selection of pita breads. Some brands have a better pocket than others, so shop until you find your favorite "flavor" and a good, roomy slit.

Crisped pita bread makes excellent "scoops" for dips. To crisp, slit the pocket with a sharp knife and pull the rounds apart. Arrange the rounds on a baking sheet and place in a preheated 375° F oven 10 minutes, or until just starting to turn golden. Remove from the oven and let cool. Break into sizes appropriate for dipping. If not using within 3 or 4 hours, transfer to an airtight container. They will stay crisp for several days, or they may be frozen for up to 3 months.

Seasoned pita bread crisps are a simple hors d'oeuvre that needs no embellishment. Make a slit in the pocket with a sharp knife and gently pull the rounds apart.

Cut each round into 6 or 8 pieces and spread the cut side of each piece with butter. Sprinkle with ground dried herbs of choice, such as oregano, basil, thyme, or marjoram. If desired, sprinkle freshly grated Parmesan or Romano cheese and paprika on top of the herb. Crisp in a preheated 350° F oven 5 minutes, or until cheese is melted. Serve immediately in an attractive basket.

LAHVOSH

Lahvosh is traditional Armenian leavened cracker bread made from wheat flour and sesame seeds. It is difficult to bake in the home, but excellent commercial brands are available. Lahvosh comes in large (15 inch), medium (5 inch), or small (3 inch) discs. The discs can be broken up and served with dips or spreads. They can also be softened, layered with various ingredients, rolled into a cylinder, and in the case of the large discs, sliced to form pinwheel hors d'oeuvres.

To soften lahvosh, hold the round under running cold water to wet both sides thoroughly. Place the round between 2 dampened terry-cloth towels and set aside for 45 minutes; if not softened in that length of time, sprinkle with a little more water, or spray with a mister. To test for proper softening, start to roll the round. If it cracks, it needs more soaking. If it tears, it is too wet; let stand 10 minutes or until it dries out enough to be rolled smoothly. You may need to test the round a few times before it is properly pliable.

The 3-inch discs can be softened in this manner and spread and layered with any of the suggestions that follow. For 36 discs, plan on about 1-1/2 cups of spread to form the base of the layers. With a flexible spatula, cover each disc with a generous layer of spread. The spread must be at room temperature so that the lahvosh will not tear. Cover the spread with cheese, meat, or other ingredients to be layered and roll each disc into a tight cylinder. Wrap tightly in plastic wrap, and refrigerate at least 1 hour, or for up to 3 hours. To serve, unwrap and arrange in spoke fashion on a round serving plate. Garnish with a garniture that complements the filling.

The 15-inch discs can be treated in the same manner, except that they must be cut into 1/2-inch-thick slices just before serving. You will need 1-1/2 to 2 cups of spread for each disc. The cylinder must be very tightly formed, or the filling will come away from the bread when sliced.

Appropriate fillings for lahvosh include: Avocado Cream Cheese Spread covered with thinly sliced smoked salmon; Mushroom Cream Cheese Spread covered with shredded Gruyère cheese; Olive Cream Cheese Spread covered with sliced ripe olives and *very thinly* sliced green bell pepper; Pecan Cream Cheese Spread covered with lightly toasted finely chopped pecans and crumbled crisply cooked bacon; and Shrimp Cream Cheese Spread covered with chopped toasted slivered blanched almonds and watercress leaves. For more ideas, see Quick-and-Easy Cream Cheese Spreads and Spread Suggestions.

BOBOLI

Named after the Boboli Gardens of Florence, Italy, this tasty bread shell, baked commercially in Marin County, California, and distributed throughout the country, is essentially a prebaked cheese crust. It has no preservatives, so despite special wrapping, it has a very short shelf life

when unrefrigerated (3 days). Look for it in the delicatessen or refrigerator section of your supermarket. It may be kept under refrigeration for up to 2 weeks, or may be frozen for up to 3 months.

Bake the Boboli in a preheated 400° F oven for 7 minutes, or until heated and slightly crisp. Cut into pieces suitable for munching and serve warm.

To make a Boboli "pizza," top the unbaked shell with your favorite pizza toppings—tomato sauce, sliced salami, grated cheese, minced parsley, whatever comes to mind—and then bake in a preheated 450° F oven 7 minutes. Cool briefly and cut into bite-size pieces to serve.

SEASONED BREAD CRUMBS ●■

Combine 1 cup fresh or dry bread crumbs with 1/2 teaspoon *each* salt and paprika and 1/4 teaspoon *each* freshly ground black or white pepper and ground oregano, basil, thyme, and/or sage. Store in an airtight container in the refrigerator for up to 1 week, or freeze for up to 4 months.

PIZZA

This recipe for basic pizza dough will make one large pizza, or approximately four dozen individual pizzas. With a few changes, the dough can become focaccia, onion bread, or onion pie (see Zwiebelkuchen in Vegetables).

To make a pizza, simply spread the prebaked pizza crust with Pesto Sauce and sprinkle with finely minced fresh herbs, then return the crust to the oven to finish baking. For a more elaborate presentation, spread the prebaked crust with tomato sauce and layer ingredients such as prosciutto or thinly sliced ham or salami, mushrooms, anchovy fillets, halved ripe olives, and thinly sliced onion and/or red or green bell pepper on the sauce. Finish with a generous sprinkling of grated mozzarella, Monterey Jack, or Parmesan cheese and bake as directed.

Approximately Twenty-four Servings
1 tablespoon active dry yeast
1/4 cup lukewarm water
1 teaspoon honey
1/2 cup nonfat milk, scalded and
    cooled to lukewarm
2 tablespoons olive oil
3/4 cup whole-wheat pastry flour
1/2 teaspoon salt
1 cup unbleached flour, or as
    needed
Olive oil

In a large mixing bowl, sprinkle yeast over water, stir in honey, and let stand 10 minutes, or until foamy. Stir in milk and oil and gradually beat in whole-wheat pastry flour. Beat vigorously for 3 minutes until bubbles form, then beat in salt and 3/4 cup of the unbleached flour.

Mound remaining 1/4 cup flour near the edge of a wood or marble work surface and sprinkle about 1 tablespoon of the flour onto the center of the board. Turn dough out onto flour and knead 8 minutes, incorporating all the remaining flour and adding more flour only if needed to prevent sticking. If dough is still sticky after 6 minutes, lightly oil board and hands with olive oil and continue kneading without adding more flour. Too much flour will toughen the dough and the resulting pizza shell will be heavy.

Form dough into a ball, place in mixing bowl oiled with olive oil, turn to coat all sides with oil, cover with a tea towel, and let rise in a warm place 1 hour, or until double in bulk. Punch dough down, place on board, and knead briefly. Cover with a tea towel and let rest 10 minutes.

Lightly oil a large pizza pan (about 14 inches in diameter), or 2 baking sheets, with olive oil. Preheat oven to 425° F.

Place dough on a lightly floured board. With a long slender rolling pin and your fingertips, roll and pat dough into a round slightly larger than the pizza pan. Dough will be approximately 1/8 inch thick. Carefully lift round onto prepared pan and with fingers build up sides to form a rim. If making small pizzas, cut rolled-out dough into rounds, using a 3-inch cookie cutter. Place rounds on prepared baking sheets at least 1 inch apart. Gather up scraps, roll out, and cut into rounds.

Brush round(s) lightly with olive oil and bake in the preheated oven 7 minutes for the large pizza, 5 minutes for the small pizzas. Top as desired and return to oven for 15 minutes for large pizza, 10 minutes for small, or until topping is bubbly.

To serve, cut large pizza into wedges with kitchen shears. Arrange wedges, or small pizzas, on a serving plate and serve immediately.

FOCACCIA

A cousin to the pizza, focaccia is a thicker, airier bread that is a favorite in northern Italy. The dough is rolled and patted into a rectangle, indentations are made in the dough, and the surface is brushed with a heavy coating of olive oil. Then a simple topping is added: a sprinkling of coarse salt; chopped green onion; or tomato sauce and a sprinkling of freshly grated Parmesan cheese.

Approximately Twenty-four Servings
1 recipe Pizza dough, preceding
Olive oil

Prepare pizza dough, omitting honey and substituting unbleached flour for the whole-wheat pastry flour. Oil a large baking sheet and set aside.

After dough has rested, roll and pat into a rectangle approximately 1/3 inch thick. Transfer to prepared pan, cover with a tea towel, and let rise in a warm place 40 minutes, or until double in size.

Preheat oven to 400° F. With fingertips, press indentations into dough, making rows of "dimples." Brush with a heavy coating of olive oil and top as directed in introduction. Bake in the preheated oven 20 to 30 minutes, or until golden.

To serve, cut into squares with kitchen shears and serve hot or at room temperature.

ONION BREAD

Approximately Twenty-four Servings
1 recipe Pizza dough, preceding
2 cups minced onion
1/2 tablespoon crumbled dried oregano
2 tablespoons olive oil
Coarse salt

Prepare pizza dough. While dough is rising, combine onion, oregano, and oil in a nonstick skillet, cover, and cook over medium heat 5 minutes or until onion is soft; do not brown. Remove from heat and let cool.

Oil a large baking sheet with olive oil.

After dough has rested, roll and pat it into a large rectangle, 1/4 inch thick, or several small rectangles. Transfer rectangle(s) to prepared sheet, cover with a tea towel, and let rise in a warm place 20 minutes.

Preheat oven to 400° F. Carefully spread onion mixture evenly over the rectangle(s) and sprinkle generously with coarse salt. Bake onion bread in the preheated oven 20 minutes, or until golden brown.

To serve, cut onion bread into squares with kitchen shears and arrange on a serving platter.

WORKING WITH ASPIC JELLIES

ASPIC JELLIES

An aspic jelly can turn any galantine or a platter of rare sliced beef, into an even more elegant presentation, one that will become the topic of conversation around the buffet table. It can be used to line a mold; to encase a pâté or terrine; to coat small items such as hard-cooked egg slices, blanched carrot slices, or cherry tomatoes to be used as garnishes; to make cutouts or mounds of chopped aspic for garnishing; or it can serve as the matrix for chopped foods such as parsley and ham.

The preparation of an aspic jelly is simple: unflavored gelatin granules are sprinkled over a small amount of water or other liquid in a dish and allowed to sit until softened without stirring. Then the gelatin mixture is added to the specified liquid, usually stock or juice, and heated until dissolved. Now the aspic jelly is chilled until it is the right consistency for the particular recipe you are making. The only tricky part of this procedure is establishing the correct gelling consistency, which takes some experimentation.

If gelatin is to be used to "set" puréed or other combined ingredients, the preparation is different. The granules are softened in water in a small dish, the dish is placed in a pan of hot water, and the water is heated until the gelatin is dissolved. Then the gelatin is cooled briefly and folded into the ingredients.

GELATIN

The purest and finest gelatin comes from boiling bones—pigs' feet, beef and veal knuckles and shinbones, chicken bones, and fish bones—in water. The resulting *naturally thickened* stock, or aspic jelly, has a more refined texture and more delicate flavor than stock to which gelatin granules have been added. It is, however, unnecessary to strive for this natural product; its superiority over a jelly made with granules or with gelatin sheets (or leaves, as they are sometimes known) is not significant.

There are two teaspoons of gelatin in the quarter-ounce packets sold in supermarkets, and usually six medium sheets (about nine by three inches each) in the one-third-ounce packages of sheet gelatin. Since sheet gelatin is only carried in German delicatessens and a limited number of food specialty shops, directions for its use are not given here. It is considerably more expensive than the granular form, but it does result in a finer-textured gelatin. Should you find it, instructions on the package explain how to use it.

TO PREPARE ASPIC JELLY

The best proportion to use to make aspic jelly is one envelope (two teaspoons) unflavored gelatin granules to approximately two cups of liquid. These amounts will vary depending upon how gelatinous your stock is, so it is best to test the aspic before attempting any of the suggested uses.

To test aspic jelly, pour an inch of the jelly into a small custard cup and place the cup in a bowl of crushed ice until the jelly sets. (Keep the remaining jelly at room temperature so it won't harden.) The jelly should reach this stage in about thirty minutes. If it is still syrupy, reheat the entire batch with a little more softened gelatin. If it is too solid, reheat the batch with more liquid. In either case, retest before proceeding.

Now chill the whole batch of jelly in the refrigerator until it is the consistency of unbeaten egg white or of syrup, at which point the jelly is called "coating" or "lining" jelly. To chill it more quickly than is possible by refrigeration, nest the container of dissolved gelatin mixture in a bowl of crushed ice and stir the mixture occasionally. Should the jelly become too stiff to work with, stir in a few drops of boiling water, or reheat it briefly. Work quickly to avoid this step.

When too much gelatin has been added to the stock or other liquid, the aspic becomes rubbery. A proper aspic is firm but not rigid and should tremble a little when shaken.

A small mold of clear aspic jelly will take from three to four hours to set properly. A larger mold may take up to five or six hours to firm up enough to unmold cleanly.

If you are adding solid ingredients (no kiwis or pineapple, which contain an enzyme that counteracts the gelling properties of gelatin) to an aspic jelly, allow approximately a cup and a half of solid ingredients for each cup of jelly. A small mold of jelly mixed with ingredients will firm up in approximately four hours; a larger mold will take at least six hours.

ASPIC JELLIES
FOR LINING AND COATING

Because good, rich consommé and madrilène are difficult and time-consuming to make in the home kitchen, canned products are used in the two recipes that follow. These two stocks do not need to be clarified.

Commercial consommés contain gelatin, so you will need to add less gelatin than you would if working with homemade stocks. The commercial consommés are usually stiff enough to use straight from the can, but refrigerate two hours and check just to be sure (see To Prepare Aspic Jelly). Gelatin will need to be added, however, if you are diluting with water and/or adding lemon juice or wine.

CONSOMME ASPIC JELLY

Makes Approximately Two Cups
1 teaspoon unflavored gelatin
3 tablespoons fresh lemon juice, dry vermouth, or other wine
One 10-ounce can consommé
1/3 cup water

In a small dish, sprinkle gelatin over lemon juice and let stand until softened. In a saucepan, heat consommé and water and stir in softened gelatin until dissolved. Use as directed in To Prepare Aspic Jelly.

MADRILENE ASPIC JELLY

There are two types of commercial madrilène available. One is clear and contains beef extract. The other, termed red madrilène, is milder tasting and has a rich ruby color, which is, unfortunately, artificial. Therefore, I recommend the clear madrilène.

Makes Approximately
One and Three-fourths Cups
1/2 teaspoon unflavored gelatin
3 tablespoons fresh lemon juice or dry vermouth
One 13-ounce can madrilène

In a small dish, sprinkle gelatin over lemon juice and let stand until softened. In a saucepan, heat madrilène and stir in softened gelatin until dissolved. Use as directed in To Prepare Aspic Jelly.

SOUR CREAM ASPIC JELLY

Makes Approximately One Cup
1 envelope (2 teaspoons) unflavored gelatin
3 tablespoons cold water
1/3 cup clarified stock, heated
1 cup sour cream

In a small dish, sprinkle gelatin over water and let stand until softened. In a saucepan, heat stock and stir in softened gelatin until dissolved. Cool briefly and stir in sour cream. Use as directed in To Prepare Aspic Jelly.

TOMATO ASPIC JELLY

Makes Approximately
Two and One-half Cups
1-1/2 cups tomato juice
1 cup chicken stock
4 slices onion
1 bay leaf
2 whole cloves
1 teaspoon granulated sugar
1/4 teaspoon crumbled dried oregano
1-1/2 envelopes (3 teaspoons) unflavored gelatin

In a saucepan, combine 1 cup of the tomato juice, chicken stock, onion, bay leaf, cloves, sugar, and oregano. Bring to a boil and simmer 10 to 15 minutes. Strain, return to saucepan, and keep warm. (Because of the tomato juice, the stock does not need to be clarified.)

In a small dish, sprinkle gelatin over remaining 1/2 cup tomato juice and let stand until softened. Stir softened gelatin into tomato stock until dissolved. Use as directed in To Prepare Aspic Jelly.

MADEIRA ASPIC JELLY

The quality of the stock is especially important when making this jelly. Fortify the stock, if needed, with chicken or beef stock base. Dry vermouth, port, dry white wine, or brandy may be substituted for the Madeira. Fresh lemon juice or distilled white vinegar may also be used in place of the Madeira, in which case halve the measurement.

In this recipe, the stock is simmered and clarified in the same step. Once the stock is strained, it can be boiled down longer than specified here to produce an even more concentrated flavor.

Makes Approximately Three Cups
4 cups rich chicken or beef stock
2 medium-size ripe tomatoes, chopped
3 green onions and tops, chopped
6 fresh tarragon leaves
2 egg whites, lightly beaten
Crumbled shells of 2 eggs
1 cup Madeira
2 envelopes (4 teaspoons) unflavored gelatin

In a large saucepan, combine stock, tomatoes, green onions, tarragon, egg whites, egg shells, and 1/2 cup of the Madeira. Bring slowly to a boil (it should take 10 to 15 minutes), add 2 teaspoons water, bring back to a boil, and boil 2 minutes. Remove from heat and let stand 20 minutes.

Strain stock according to directions in To Clarify Stock. Return clarified stock to medium-high heat, bring to a boil, lower heat slightly, and boil until reduced to approximately 3 cups.

In a small dish, sprinkle gelatin over remaining 1/2 cup Madeira. Stir softened gelatin into hot stock until dissolved. Use as directed in To Prepare Aspic Jelly.

LINING CONTAINERS WITH WITH ASPIC

Prepare one of the preceding aspic jellies and chill it to the coating stage. At the same time, select a mold and place it in the freezer for thirty minutes or so, then nest it in a large bowl of crushed ice.

Pour the coating jelly into the mold and quickly tip the mold to coat the entire inner surface with an even layer of jelly approximately one-eighth to one-fourth inch thick. If excess jelly settles to the bottom of the mold,

scoop it out with a spoon that has been heated in boiling water. Alternatively, pour jelly into the mold to make a layer on the bottom only; the layer should be between one-fourth and one-half inch deep, or more if a thicker aspic "topping" is desired.

Chill the jelly-lined mold fifteen minutes and then check it. Keep checking regularly until the jelly is stiff but still a little sticky on the surface. When the jelly has reached this stage, gently pack in the pâté or other mold mixture to be coated, cover, and refrigerate at least six hours.

To unmold the aspic-coated molded dish, see General Instructions for Molds in Charcuterie and Molds.

GARNISHING ASPIC-LINED MOLDS

Molds lined with aspic jelly can be adorned with additional garnitures. The items must be readied and thoroughly chilled before the container is lined. The design of the decorations depends upon the shape and content of the molded food. Keep color and the appropriateness of the garniture in mind when selecting from the list below or creating your own. For instance, a dish that contains ripe olives can be garnished with olive halves, a lemon-flavored dish with lemon slices.

Line the mold as described above, but do not fill. When the lining has set properly, i.e., is "stiff but still a little sticky on the surface," secure the garnitures with tweezers, dip them into the bowl of syrupy coating jelly, and arrange them artistically on the aspic lining. Carefully pour in enough of the coating jelly to cover the garnitures with a layer of jelly about an eighth of an inch thick. Refrigerate mold until aspic jelly is firm but still a little sticky on the surface. If you are creating a number of different garniture layers to achieve a lining with visual depth, coat and chill each layer separately.

Pack in the pâté or other mold mixture, cover, and refrigerate at least six hours. Unmold as you would any aspic-lined mold.

GARNITURES FOR LINED MOLDS

- Lightly blanched sliced or julienned vegetables
- Hard-cooked egg whites, cut into strips, dice, or tiny cutouts
- Hard-cooked egg yolk forced through a sieve, then mixed with softened butter and shaped into small balls or fingers

- Ripe olives, cut in half or into small slivers
- Pimiento-stuffed olives, sliced crosswise
- Raw or blanched red or green bell pepper, cut into strips or dice
- Green onion or leek tops or tarragon, sage, nasturtium, violet, geranium, or spinach leaves, lightly blanched, rinsed in cold water, drained, and patted dry with paper toweling
- Well-drained pimientos or Roasted Peppers, cut into thin strips or small pieces

COATING FOODS WITH ASPIC JELLY

The following method can be used to coat canapés, meats, poultry, fish, terrines, pâtés, or simple garnitures, such as hard-cooked egg slices, vegetable cutouts, Roasted Pepper or Pumate strips, or olives.

Thoroughly chill the foods to be coated. Prepare one of the aspic jellies and set aside at room temperature. Ladle out a little of the jelly into a small bowl nested in crushed ice and let the jelly become syrupy. (It is best to work with only a small amount of jelly at a time so that the entire batch does not become cloudy from bits of food.) To test for the proper consistency, see the instructions in To Prepare Aspic Jelly.

On a wire rack, arrange the foods you are coating. With a feather brush, spread a thin layer of the coating jelly over the tops and sides of the foods. Chill them in the refrigerator, then repeat the procedure as many times as is necessary to achieve a coating one-eighth to one-fourth inch thick.

If you are preparing aspic-coated garnitures for a pâté, terrine, or other molded dish, unmold the dish to be decorated directly onto a serving plate. Brush the surface of the food with several thin layers of aspic jelly, chilling between each layer. When the aspic jelly is about one-eighth inch thick, the garnitures can be arranged on the food and will adhere to the "sticky" aspic.

If the garnitures are to decorate a serving plate, once their aspic coating is of the proper thickness and is fully gelled, set them on the plate in an attractive pattern. Coated canapés, meats, or other foods should be arranged on platters and decorated with appropriate garnishes.

GARNITURES

Garnitures are not only the decorations that rest on top of a prepared food. They are also handcrafted "containers" for holding foods and such elaborate creations as a turnip chyrsanthemum or a tomato rose that will "bloom" at the edge of the serving platter. The appearance of food, how it looks on a dish and the attractiveness of the table arrangement, adds greatly to the overall appeal and enjoyment of the presentation. Imaginative garnishing makes the difference between a good dish and a spectacular one.

There are presently several books on the market that explore the world of garnitures, including one that discusses the special gadgets for forming them and comes with a few of the tools. These works describe dozens of lovely handmade garnitures: red

onion cups, orange baskets, accordian radishes, apple birds, pineapple crisscross wedges, mushrooms fashioned out of radishes, and so on.

Choose garnishes that complement the food being served and include a variety of tastes, textures, and colors. Technically garnitures should be edible, but do take liberties. Use an ivy leaf as a base for a tomato rose, or form a mound of pâté on a large saxifraga or maple leaf. Tuck fresh chrysanthemums or daisies into the center of a ring mold or along the rim of a fluted avocado mold.

Garnishing takes thought, time, and effort. As you improve your techniques, you will want to invest in a book that describes more intricate creations than those given here. But whether your creations are simple or elaborate, there are a few things to remember when forming garnishes and displaying them:

- A very sharp knife is a must.
- Make enough garnitures so that you can replace those that wilt or are eaten while the party is in progress.
- Choose attractive crystal, silver, or ceramic bowls, plates, and platters that will show off the garnitures as well as the food.

- Garnitures should be a part of the planning schedule for entertaining whether the party is large or small. Decide which dishes need elaborate garnishes and which need only simple parsley or watercress sprigs, and then have the necessary ingredients on hand.

GARNITURE SUGGESTIONS

ASPIC CUTOUTS Prepare one cup aspic jelly. Rinse a large shallow dish in cold water, pour in jelly to a depth of approximately one-fourth inch, and refrigerate until firm. With tiny hors d'oeuvre cutters, cut into shapes.

CARROT CURLS, RIBBONS, AND BOWS Use large, fat, new carrots (old carrots tend to crack when a toothpick is put through them) for these creations and be sure to use flat toothpicks to secure them, as round cocktail picks are too thick. Use your imagination; if the curls, ribbons, or bows don't form as you'd hoped, twist them and play with them to form other shapes.

With a vegetable peeler, lightly peel the carrot. Still using the peeler, slice paper-thin lengthwise strips from the carrot. Trim the strips to three-inch lengths and roll around your finger. Secure with a toothpick and place in ice water for at least two hours. Remove pick and let the "curl" open slightly. To make a whimsical flower, secure three curls with a toothpick and spear a small ripe olive to make a center. Tuck the back end of the toothpick under a parsley sprig to hide it.

To fashion a "ribbon," weave the thin strip of carrot onto the toothpick. Crisp in ice water as above, remove the picks, and arrange the ribbons on a bed of greens.

To form a bow, cut a one-inch slit in the center of the carrot strip. Soak in salted water thirty minutes to soften and then pull one end of the carrot strip through the slit. Be inventive: if the carrot breaks, arrange several "bows" together on a bed of greens.

CARROT FLOWERS Cut lengthwise grooves in carrots one-fourth inch deep, making five or six notches on each carrot, then cut crosswise into thin slices. Arrange in groupings directly on the food to be garnished, or alongside, tucking watercress leaves in and around the "flowers."

CHOPPED ASPIC Follow directions for Aspic Cutouts, preceding. When aspic jelly is firm, chop it into tiny cubes with a sharp knife and arrange the cubes in shimmering mounds around foods to be garnished.

CHRISTMAS CHERRY CLUSTERS Cut green maraschino cherries in eighths almost through to the stem end. Carefully pull apart the wedges and spread open just wide enough to place a red maraschino cherry half in center. Nestle the cherries into tiny juniper or holly sprigs to form clusters.

CITRUS CUPS Cut a lemon or small orange into thin slices. Make a slit almost to the center of the slice and then twist the slice so that the cut ends are brought together and overlapped to form a cup.

CITRUS FLOWERS Cut a lemon, lime, or small orange in half crosswise and place cut side down on a cutting board. With an ice pick, punch holes all over the surface of the fruit. Push the stems of flowers, such as small daisies, geraniums, or chrysanthemums, into the holes until the citrus base is completely covered with the flowers and no stems are showing.

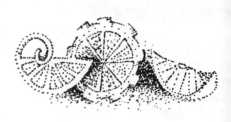

CITRUS TWISTS Cut a lemon or small orange into thin slices. Cut each slice in half. Through the center of each half slice, cut a slit from the cut edge almost to the peel edge. Twist the inside cut corners to form a bow-tie shape.

CRANBERRY SPEARS Skewer three or four cranberries on a toothpick and tuck the picks into a bed of parsley, with the cranberries showing at different angles.

CUCUMBER-RADISH CATERPILLARS Cut a lengthwise strip about one-half inch deep from one side of a cucumber. With cut surface facing up, cut crosswise slices almost all the way through the cucumber, spacing the cuts about one-fourth inch apart. Into each cut tuck a slice of radish.

DAISY OUTLINES On a leaf or paper doily, fashion daisy petals of hard-cooked egg white. Place a ripe olive half (cut crosswise) in the center of the petals, and fashion a stem from green bell pepper. Alternatively, cut petals from pineapple slices, make leaves and stems of green pepper, and make a center with sieved hard-cooked egg yolk or a green maraschino cherry.

EGG-ASPIC CUTOUTS Prepare one and one-half cups aspic jelly. Rinse an eight-inch pie plate with cold water, pour in three-fourths cup of the jelly, and re-frigerate until firm. Purée yolks of three hard-cooked eggs and remaining three-fourths cup jelly in a blender or food processor and pour over aspic. Chill until firm. With tiny hors d'oeuvre cutters, cut into desired shapes.

FROSTED GARNITURES Frost mint leaves, grapes, violets, small nasturtiums, or other leaves and flowers to place artistically on a plate or platter. Beat egg whites until frothy. Dip leaves into whites, and then into superfine sugar, repeating process until the items are well coated. Dry on a wire rack.

GREEN ONION BRUSHES Trim ends of green onions, cut off all but three inches of tops, and shred tops down to white to make a "brush." Crisp in ice water.

ONION CUPS Peel and halve round onions and scoop out centers, leaving a shell about one-fourth inch thick. Stand green onion brushes or cranberry spears upright in shells.

PICKLE FANS Slice small pickles into five or six strips almost to stem end. Spread strips apart to fashion a fan.

RADISH ROSES Cut a slice off both ends of a red radish. Make slashes about halfway to the center from tip to stem on a slight diagonal, completely covering the surface of the radish. Spread "petals" and crisp the radish in ice water.

RICKRACK CITRUS HALVES Place a halved lemon or small orange cut side down on cutting board. With a sharp knife, cut a zigzag pattern along the edge, as you would for a jack-o'-lantern. Turn right side up, tuck a parsley leaf in the center, and place on an ivy leaf.

RIPE OLIVE STARS Halve or quarter large pitted ripe olives. Arrange the pieces on a small paper doily in a spoke pattern, using two or three olive pieces to form each spoke. Place a tiny sliver of celery between the spokes of the decorative "star." Fashion a center from tiny celery leaves.

TOMATO ROSES Partially cut a slice off the stem end of a tomato; place knife point under skin at that spot and start to peel tomato in spiral fashion, leaving peel attached to stem slice. Be careful the skin does not break; the band should be about one-half inch wide. When you have finished peeling the tomato, the peel will be fully detached from it. Place stem slice with peel attached on board and wind peel up and around to make a rose. Alternatively, cut tomato into eighths within one inch of bottom. Peel back skin of each eighth about halfway down and curl to resemble a rose.

TURNIP CHRYSANTHEMUMS Trim root end of a turnip. Cut a slice from the stem (top) of the turnip about one-third of the way down. Being careful not to cut too deeply (in which case the turnip will fall apart), make cuts one-eighth inch apart across the cut surface of the turnip, then across the opposite direction to make a tiny crosshatch pattern. Plunge into ice water and refrigerate several hours until the "flower" opens up. If desired, put food coloring into ice water to color the flower, or when the flower has been removed from the ice water, dab a bit of undiluted coloring onto the tips of the "petals."

VEGETABLE CUTOUTS Thinly slice vegetables such as lightly steamed turnips, beets, carrots, or zucchini. Cut into shapes with canapé cutters and arrange artistically in clusters, daisy patterns, or in form desired.

VEGETABLE FANS Cut zucchini, carrots, green onions, or celery ribs into two-inch lengths. Cut each piece lengthwise into thin shreds to within one-half inch of end. Crisp in ice water. Alternatively, make the cuts from both ends, leaving one-fourth to one-half inch uncut in the center.

VEGETABLE OR FRUIT BOWLS Hollow out a green pepper, an eggplant, a head cabbage, a dumpling squash, a large pattypan (scallop) squash, a small pumpkin, or a grapefruit or large orange half. Use as a "bowl" to hold cold sauces, dips, or spreads.

SIMPLE GARNISHES

This list of garnishes is meant to give you ideas to build on when designing the garnishes that will complement your hors d'oeuvre presentations. All of these items can be easily purchased at a market or found in your backyard garden.

When selecting the appropriate garnish for the hors d'oeuvre to be decorated, consider the color and the ingredients of the dish. For example, deep green herb sprigs dramatically set off a liver pâté, pieces of chutney are perfect with a curry-scented dip, or julienned carrot can show off a mixed-vegetable terrine.

- Pickled fruits and vegetables of all kinds
- Parsley, coriander, watercress, or chervil sprigs; dill or fennel feathers
- Julienned carrots, string beans, or other vegetables; grated carrots or daikon; whole or halved cherry tomatoes; broccoli or cauliflower buds
- Citrus slices, kumquats
- Drained capers, anchovy curls
- Firm-cheese cutouts
- Chutneys (tamarind, gooseberry, mango, peach, cranberry, or pineapple), marmalades
- Sieved hard-cooked egg yolk and/or white
- Seasoned Butter pipings, anchovy-paste piping or stars
- Chicory (curly endive), escarole, kale, turnip greens, romaine or red leaf lettuce, arugula, radicchio, mâche
- Mint, nasturtium, violet, ivy, saxifraga, or chrysanthemum leaves
- Blossoms such as nasturtiums, daisies or marguerites, chrysanthemums, columbine, azalea, lantana, roses, pot marigolds, pansies, geraniums, violets, lavender, or day lilies; or herb flowers such as borage, chives, or sage
- Roasted Pepper, Pumate, or pimiento strips
- Pomegranate or papaya seeds

KITCHEN HINTS

BONING FOWL

Lay the fowl breast down on a cutting board. With a small, sharp, thin, pointed knife, cut skin down along backbone from the neck to the tail. With the point of the knife always tight against the backbone, separate the meat from one side of the carcass. You will be cutting almost to the breastbone, so use short shallow strokes to avoid piercing the skin on the breast. As you work, lift the skin and meat away from the frame so the tissue to be cut is visible.

On one side of the carcass, remove the wing at the shoulder and the drumstick at the knee, leaving minimum-size holes in the skin. Sever the hip joint internally. Remove the thigh bone by making a single lengthwise slit on the inside of the thigh and then gradually cutting the meat away from the bone.

Repeat this procedure on the other side of the carcass. Cutting between the ribs and breastbone on both sides, lift the ribcage out. Now, cut out the collarbone and shoulder blade on both sides and then remove the wishbone. With almost-detached meat flat

on either side and taking extra care to avoid slitting the skin, delicately cut the meat away from the breastbone leaving meat and skin intact and in one piece.

GENERAL INSTRUCTIONS FOR PIPING

Using a pastry bag to pipe on the topping of a canapé or the border on a stuffed egg gives the hors d'oeuvre a particularly professional look. If you are new to using a pastry bag and tube, the procedure will take some practice to perfect.

If possible, purchase a pastry bag with a plastic lining, as it is much easier to clean than the old-fashioned all-cloth type. Average-size bags are twelve to sixteen inches long and have a narrow opening at one end. Plain and fluted tubes are sometimes boxed with the bag or can be purchased separately. Plain tubes are used for making circles or mounds or for filling a pastry shell, while fluted tubes make decorative borders or other garnishes, such as those for canapés.

Drop the plain or fluted tube through the top of the pastry bag so that it lodges securely, with tip protruding, in the narrow opening at the opposite end. (On some bags, the tips screw onto the narrow ends rather

than being "dropped" into place.) Fold back the top half of the bag so that the substance to be piped can be easily spooned in, and then fill the bag no more than half full.

Unfold the bag so that the sides again stand upright. With your right hand (if you are right-handed) grasp the top neatly so that it comes together in even pleats. Twist the pleats and gently grasp the top of the bag with the thumb and fingers of your right hand. The bag must be tightly closed.

Press the piping mixture through the tip by applying even pressure with the palm and fingers of your right hand. Your left hand should guide the tip so that the piping hits the desired mark. As the piping mixture is used, continue to twist the top of the bag so that steady pressure is exerted on what remains in the bag.

As has been said, attractive piping takes considerable practice. You may want to experiment with mashed potatoes or some other "pipable" mixture until you master the art. Then you can turn the pastry bag on your hors d'oeuvres with confidence.

FREEZING

Foods that freeze well are marked with ■ and the recipes designate the approximate length of time they will remain "fresh" in the freezer. Note that the flavor of spices such as pepper, cumin, and chili powder grows stronger when foods are frozen. Mayonnaise, unless it is a small quantity incorporated in a mixture, should not be frozen. Hard-cooked egg white takes on a rubbery quality when frozen for any length of time, even when incorporated in a mixture.

Airtight wrapping is essential to keep foods from drying out. Use freezer paper or aluminum foil, press out as much air from the package as possible as you wrap, and seal tightly. Mark the package with the item and the date. Most foods may also be frozen in airtight containers, such as cookie tins or self-sealing plasticware.

SHEET FREEZING

When freezing such food items as pastry rounds, phyllo triangles, dolmades, chicken wings, and the like, arrange them on a baking sheet or tray, not touching, and place the sheet in the freezer until the items are frozen solid. Remove them from the baking sheet and wrap well in freezer paper or in plastic wrap and then aluminum foil, or place in an airtight freezer container. Return to the freezer for the time indicated in recipes.

STEAMING

Chinese dumplings and a few of the pâté and meatball recipes call for the steam method of cooking. You can use bamboo steamers, which are particularly suitable for Chinese dumplings, two- or three-tiered metal steamers, or a steamer improvised with standard kitchen equipment.

To use bamboo steamer baskets, set one filled basket (the foods, especially dumplings, may be set directly on the rungs, or they can be arranged in a shallow bowl) in a wok filled with water to come within one inch of the base of the basket. Top with up to three more filled baskets, and then cover the final basket with its lid. Bring the water to a boil, and start timing the cooking when steam is first visible. Lower heat to maintain a steady, moderate boil. Check from time to time to make sure the water has not boiled away. If the water level drops substantially, add boiling water.

A two- or three-tiered metal steamer works essentially the same way as a bamboo steamer, except that the vessel that holds the water is part of the steaming unit and the water can be brought to the boil before the tiers are stacked on top. (Bringing the water to a boil first is not advisable with bamboo baskets, as they are too difficult to balance on a wok filled with already boiling water.) Tiered steamers are available in several sizes. A good-sized steamer, perhaps eleven or twelve inches in diameter, is the best kind to have, as it can accommodate a large shallow dish for holding the foods. Bring the water to a boil in the pan of the steamer (the water should be low enough so that it will not touch the base of the tier), set the filled dish on the tier, place the tier over the boiling water, cover the steamer, and steam the designated time.

As the water boils in a metal steamer, droplets collect on the lid. If you are steaming dumplings or a custard, for example, you will want to prevent the droplets from falling onto the foods. To do so, wrap the lid of the steamer in a tea towel, being careful that the ends of the towel don't hang down and touch the range burner.

To improvise a steamer, place a cake rack on the bottom of a large, deep saucepan with a tight-fitting lid. Set three soup cans, opened at both ends, on the rack and add water to come halfway up the sides of the cans. Place a second rack on top of the cans and set the shallow dish on the rack. (If you do not have a second rack, place a pair of square-sided chopsticks, with a narrow end facing a broad end, parallel on the cans.) Set the dish on the rack and cover the steamer. To improvise a second tier, place another pair of chopsticks on top of the dish and set a second dish on top of the chopsticks.

To steam foods directly on a rack, oil a fine-mesh rack with Lecithin Oil. Place a high-sided can, with ends removed, or similar platform in a deep saucepan with a tight-fitting lid and top with the oiled rack. Add water to the saucepan to come about halfway up the sides of the can. Place foods on rack, cover saucepan, bring water to a boil, and steam time specified.

TO CUT A ROUND QUICHE OR CHEESECAKE INTO SQUARES

With a sharp knife, carefully cut a complete circle one inch in from the outer rim of the quiche or cheesecake. Be sure to cut all the way through the crust. Now cut the area between the rim and the circle into one-inch pieces. Continue cutting the quiche into one-inch-wide circles and the circles into one-inch pieces until you reach the center.

Leave the cut quiche or cheesecake in the pan and let guests lift out their own pieces. Remove a few pieces to get them started. Alternatively, remove all of the pieces and arrange them on a serving plate. In either case, a small flexible metal spatula is the best tool for lifting out the pieces.

SERVING TEMPERATURES

When a recipe states "serve at room temperature," set the dish out on a table or counter in the kitchen or pantry until serving time. In contrast, a dish that is to be put "in a cool place" should be kept in a laundry room, dry basement, or other spot in the house where it is away from a heat vent or the stove.

BLANCHING FOODS

Bring a saucepan of water to a rolling boil, add the food to be blanched, and boil one to two minutes to cook partially. Drain immediately, plunge the food into ice water, and drain again.

HERB EQUIVALENTS

One-half teaspoon dried herbs or one-fourth teaspoon ground herbs is equivalent to one tablespoon minced fresh herbs.

GENERAL COOKING HINTS

• Pat parsley or other fresh herbs dry before mincing in a food processor or blender. Also, be sure the blender or processor container is dry.
• When mixing foods in a food processor or blender, stop the motor frequently and scrape down the sides of the container.
• Ovens vary greatly, so watch timing carefully. Never crowd the oven or baking sheets.
• Unless otherwise specified, use grade A large eggs in all recipes calling for eggs.
• When baking in glass dishes, lower specified oven temperature by 25° F.
• When draining fried foods on paper toweling, crumple the toweling. More oil will be absorbed and you will use less toweling.
• Always freshly grind white and black peppers, and freshly grate nutmeg.
• Foods that are served chilled need more intense seasoning than those served at room temperature or hot.

BUFFETS

The buffets described in this chapter are designed as full meals. Only those guests who are just dropping by on the way to another function will need to make dining plans.

First, make a guest list and then set the date of the buffet, checking on the availability of helpers and possible entertainers before finalizing it. Next, invite guests by mail or phone. Once that is done, immediately begin to plan your menu.

The majority of buffet menus give a choice of dishes. Choose dishes that will complement one another: consider color, texture, and especially variety. You would not want to serve two dishes that are coated with aspic, or a blue cheese mold and a potted blue cheese. There must also be a good balance of meat and fowl, seafood, vegetables, and so on. Don't let the menus limit you, however. Look through the book to see if other recipes better fit your tastes or the theme of the party. Plan on approximately fourteen bites per person; some guests leave early, some stay on. Remember to include helpers and any entertainers in your count.

For a large group, select a number of items that can be made several weeks ahead and frozen, and other dishes that can be made several days in advance. Keep in mind which foods must be kept chilled and how much refrigerator space is available. Don't plan more broiled or baked dishes than your oven or ovens can handle. Complete everything possible before the day of the party, leaving you and your helper(s) with only last-minute details.

How many helpers you need will depend upon how well you have planned the buffet, how many guests are coming, how formal the party will be, and the types of foods that will be served. If there are several dishes that must be passed rather than set on the table, or if there are many preparations that require attention in the kitchen, you will need at least one helper for even a small buffet and up to four or five for a very large one.

Make a comprehensive list of what you are serving. Include the ingredients necessary for each dish, what kinds of breads or crackers are to accompany the dishes, and what equipment—chafing dish, spirit stove, and/or warming trays—and serving plates, platters, bowls, and utensils will be needed. Plan for other supplies as well, such as cocktail picks and/or forks, napkins, coasters. and small (six- to seven-inch) plates or hors d'oeuvre trays on which guests can place their foods. The latter can be high-quality paper or your best china. Always have more of these items on hand than the number of people expected. Extra people may come, or guests sometimes misplace their plates and need second ones. Decide on your beverage needs, both cold and hot.

Make a detailed sheet that shows at what time during the party hot dishes must be heated and how to heat them, oven temperatures for items such as pastry rounds or phyllo triangles, and any other specific directions. You and your helpers will need these reminders. Then draw a rough diagram of the main buffet table that shows where each dish will be placed and what utensils it will need.

The area around the main table must be unobstructed so guests can circulate freely, and the dishes must not be crowded onto the table. Consider other "food areas": tables or counters in other rooms or outdoors. A barbecue set up on a patio or in a recreation room helps disperse the crowd and takes pressure off the kitchen, especially if guests can cook their own skewered foods.

The morning of the party, set out all the utensils, such as serving spoons, trivets, and mats. Place an attractive sign with the name of the dish in the appropriate spot on the table—guests like to know what they are eating. Just before the guests arrive, set out the foods, using the signs to double-check their positions.

Once the buffet has begun, check frequently for "dead" plates left on the tables and serving platters that need replenishing and/or garnishing. Never leave an empty platter or one with wilted garnishes in view of guests.

This chapter has menus for eight ethnic buffets. Two of the them, the Chinese and Japanese buffets, include all of the recipes necessary to prepare the menu. The remaining buffets—American, Greek or Middle East, French, Italian, Spanish, and Latin American—for the most part draw upon recipes that appear in earlier chapters. Each menu specifies the size of the party, but these numbers can be increased or decreased. For example, if you find that fewer people will be attending than you originally planned, cut down on the number of dishes or halve one or more of the larger recipes.

Remember, most people are flattered when they arrive at a party and find the beautiful food before them is homemade. Don't be apologetic if the pâté isn't perfectly shaped, or the walnut cake crumbles when it is picked up. Appearance is important, but taste is more important (and no one else is as aware of little failures as you are). Relax, let guests help if they offer, and be proud your efforts are so successful.

AMERICAN BUFFET FOR ONE HUNDRED

Advance planning and preparation will make a party of this size possible without the help of a professional caterer. Carefully read the chapter introduction so that you understand what entertaining on this scale entails.

Once the date is set, find at least three helpers, one to oversee the kitchen, one to pass the hot appetizers, remove the empty platters and plates, and empty ashtrays, and one to help the bartender. You may want at least one of the helpers to arrive the morning of the party to assist with unmolding the molded dishes, stuffing eggs, readying the garnishes, and the million other tasks that seem to appear out of nowhere.

Use your organizational abilities to make this large buffet run more smoothly. For example, prepare a pâté in two small vessels rather than one large one. Place each pâté on a garnished serving plate and set one on the buffet table and keep one in the refrigerator until the first has been eaten. Any mold or spread may be treated in the same way.

There are a great number of dishes to choose from on the American buffet menu, and many more throughout the book that would be suitable. Look at the recipes carefully, paying close attention to whether they can be prepared in advance and their yields, garnishes, and serving instructions, before making your final selections. Yields for the cold meat and poultry platters can be adjusted to your needs. For some dishes, doubling or tripling the recipe may be required. If you have more helpers than the number suggested here, consider serving cold canapés and/or lahvosh pinwheels, too. They are always popular inclusions. Keep in mind that you should plan on about fourteen individual servings per person.

Soup is always welcome at a large party, especially with guests who linger after the crowd has left. I have included two hot soups for cool-weather entertaining, and two cold ones for balmy evenings.

Dessert possibilities range from crispy oatmeal cookies studded with white chocolate to lemony tartlets. Make as many of the following desserts as you like, or look to the other buffets for additional suggestions.

COLD DISHES

Three or Four of the Dips or
   Spreads ●

CHOICE OF TWO
Smoked Turkey Platter
Roast Beef Platter
Corned Beef Platter ○
Ham Platter
Tongue or Smoked Tongue
   Platter ○
Steak Tartare
Raw Beef Platter

CHOICE OF ONE
Poached Whole Salmon ○
Gravlax ○
Pickled Herring ○
Cooked Seafood Platter
Terrine of Salmon ○
Terrine of Pollack, Shrimp, and
   Smoked Salmon ○
Smoked Salmon and Broccoli
   Custard
Shrimp on Ice ●

CHOICE OF TWO
Blue Cheese Mold ○
Red Caviar Mold ○
Braunschweiger Mold with
   Caviar ○
Braunschweiger Cream Cheese
   Mold ○
Caviar Surprise ●
Watercress Cream Mold ○
Avocado Mold ○
Parslied Ham Mold ○

CHOICE OF ONE
Cream Cheese-Caviar Pie
Chèvre Cheesecake

CHOICE OF ONE
Zwiebelkuchen
Pissaladière
One of the Quiches

CHOICE OF ONE
Assorted Stuffed Eggs
Red Eggs ○
Tea Eggs ○

CHOICE OF ONE
Chicken Pâté with Spinach ○
Chicken Liver Pâté ○
One of the Terrines ○
One of the Galantines ○
Three-Vegetable Terrine ○

One of the Tortas ●

HOT DISHES

One or Two of the Pastry
   Rounds and/or Piroshki ■
Puff Pastry Twists ●■
Assorted Phyllo Triangles or
   Rolls, or Phyllo Spirals ■
Chicken Wings ●■
Bacon Roll-ups ●■

CHOICE OF TWO
Mushroom Canapés ●■
Crab and Clam Canapés ●■
Green Olive Canapés with
    Pecans ●■
Ripe Olive Canapés with
    Cheddar ●■
Gorgonzola Canapés ●■
Artichoke-Parmesan Canapés ●
Hot Stuffed Mushrooms
Baked Filled Artichoke Bottoms

CHOICE OF TWO
Clam and Pork Sausage Meatballs
    with Clam-Dill Sauce ●■
Pork Sausage and Beef
    Meatballs ●■
Veal and Beef Meatballs with
    Sorrel Sauce ●■
Turkey Tofu Meatballs ●■
Sweet-and-Sour Meatballs ●■

CHOICE OF ONE
Crab Melba
Sweetbreads and Mushrooms
Chicken Livers and Gizzards
Hot Artichoke with Parmesan
    Spread ●

CHOICE OF ONE
Turkey Sausages
Pork Link Sausages with Rum or
    Cranberry Sauce ●■
Skewered Meat or Poultry*

One of the Soups

CHOICE OF ONE, TWO, OR THREE
One of the Cheese Trays
Fruit Desserts
Assorted cookies and tartlets

*See Barbecue Cookery. Consider also larger cuts, such as flank or skirt steak or butterflied leg of lamb.

SOUPS

The soup served at a buffet should be regarded by guests as a subtle reminder that it's time to think about going home—sip on a little soup, try a few cookies, and bid farewell. If your party is a long one, such as an open house, you will need to present the soup at several intervals during the affair, as guests come and go. At a shorter event, bring out the soup only once, about two-thirds of the way through the party.

Any soup you serve at a buffet must be smooth, so that it requires no spoons and can be sipped from a mug or punch cup. Hot soups must be served piping hot. A crockpot set on the sideboard in the dining room, or on a table or counter in another room, is ideal for keeping the soup at serving temperature and can easily be refilled from a soup kettle kept hot on the stove. (Have two or three cups of extra stock handy in the kitchen to thin the soup, for it tends to thicken when kept on the heat for any length of time.) Place the crockpot, or other warming vessel, on a large tray so there is a spot for guests to set the lid while they ladle out a serving. Have plenty of mugs on hand in which to serve the soup, and don't let the pot run low.

Cold soups are only good if they remain icy cold. Pour the soup into an attractive chilled tureen or other vessel, then nest the tureen in a bowl of ice placed in the coolest part of the house or patio. Cold soups are often rich because of the addition of cream, so punch cups are perfect for serving.

The four soups that follow have been chosen for their ease of preparation and use of readily available ingredients. Each recipe yields approximately eight quarts, or sixty-four half-cup portions, usually sufficient for a party for one hundred. The recipes, however, can be easily increased or decreased. Unless you have a *giant* soup kettle, you will need to make the soups in several batches.

The recipes can be used as guidelines to help you determine ingredient proportions and combinations for creating your own soups. Use what you have on hand, what appeals to your tastes, and what complements the other dishes on your menu.

A well-seasoned clear broth also makes an excellent buffet soup. It is light and refreshing, and may fit into your menu better than the thicker soups presented here.

SWEET POTATO SOUP ●■

Makes Approximately Eight Quarts
1/4 cup bacon drippings
4 large onions, chopped
1 small head celery and leaves, chopped
5 pounds sweet potatoes or yams, peeled and sliced
6 quarts rich chicken stock
6 large parsley sprigs
2 teaspoons salt
1 teaspoon freshly ground black pepper
1/2 teaspoon freshly grated nutmeg
Minced fresh parsley
Sour cream or Crème Fraîche

In a large kettle, heat the bacon drippings and add onions, celery, and sweet potatoes. Cover and cook, stirring several times, 5 minutes, or until lightly browned. Add 2 quarts of the stock and the parsley sprigs, cover pot, bring to a boil, lower heat, and simmer until vegetables are very soft.

In batches, purée mixture in a blender or food processor. Pour the purée into 1 or more storage containers, cool, cover, and refrigerate for up to 3 days, or freeze for up to 2 months.

To serve, heat the vegetable base with the remaining stock and season with salt, pepper, and nutmeg. Taste and adjust seasonings. As each batch of soup is transferred to the crockpot, sprinkle it with minced parsley. Place a bowl of sour cream on the side. Guests should top their servings with a small dollop of the cream.

LETTUCE SOUP ●■

Makes Approximately Eight Quarts
4 large heads iceberg or romaine lettuce, shredded
1 small bunch watercress (leaves and tender stems only)
1 tablespoon granulated sugar
6 quarts rich chicken stock
5 large garlic cloves, minced
1 teaspoon freshly ground white pepper
1/2 teaspoon freshly grated nutmeg
2 cups light cream
1/4 pound butter, cut into small bits
Very finely chopped watercress leaves

In a large kettle, combine lettuce, watercress leaves and stems, sugar, 2 quarts of the stock, garlic, pepper, and nutmeg. Cover and bring to a gentle boil. Boil 5 minutes, or until lettuce is soft.

In batches, purée mixture in a blender or food processor. Pour the purée into 1 or more storage containers, cool, cover, and refrigerate for up to 3 days, or freeze for up to 2 months.

To serve, reheat lettuce purée with remaining stock and cream. Adjust seasonings and transfer in batches to a crockpot. Swirl a few bits of butter into each batch and then sprinkle each with chopped watercress.

TOMATO-ORANGE SOUP ●

A most refreshing soup for a hot day. Easy to assemble and serve. Combine the ingredients a day ahead so flavors blend.

Makes Approximately Nine Quarts
4 quarts tomato juice
4 quarts fresh orange juice
1/2 cup fresh lemon juice
1 quart dry white wine
1 tablespoon very finely minced fresh basil
1/2 teaspoon salt, or to taste
1/4 teaspoon freshly ground black pepper, or to taste
1/8 teaspoon ground red pepper, or to taste
1 cup heavy cream, whipped

In a large container, combine tomato juice, orange juice, lemon juice, wine, basil, salt, and black and red peppers. Chill thoroughly and transfer to a chilled bowl. Place a bowl of whipped cream alongside so each guest can put a tiny dollop on his or her serving.

VICHYSSOISE O ■

Makes Approximately Eight Quarts
2 or 3 bunches leeks
6 tablespoons butter, or
     as needed
6 tablespoons rendered chicken
     fat
1 cup minced onion
6 large garlic cloves, minced
1-1/2 tablespoons mushroom
     powder (see Note)
1 teaspoon freshly ground
     white pepper
8 thick-skinned potatoes
     (approximately 6 ounces each)
2 quarts rich chicken stock
2 quarts rich beef stock
2 quarts milk
1/4 cup fresh lemon juice,
     or to taste
Salt to taste
1 quart heavy cream
Finely minced fresh chives or
     green onion tops

Wash leeks thoroughly and chop the white and 1/2 inch of the green to measure approximately 6 cups. In a large kettle, melt butter and rendered chicken fat. Add leeks, onion, garlic, mushroom powder, and pepper. Cover and cook, stirring occasionally, 10 minutes, or until leeks and onions are soft.

Peel and dice enough potatoes to measure 8 cups. Add to kettle, stir, cover, and cook 5 minutes. Add chicken stock, cover, bring to a boil, lower heat, and boil gently until potatoes are very soft, adding a little of the beef stock if too much of the liquid cooks away.

In batches, purée mixture in a blender or food processor. Pour purée into 1 or more storage containers, cool, cover, and refrigerate for up to 3 days, or freeze for up to 2 months.

To serve, reheat purée with beef stock and milk. Add lemon juice. Taste and adjust seasonings with more white pepper, if needed, and a little salt (heavy cream is salty, so be careful). Cool and chill at least 1 day. Stir in heavy cream and again adjust seasonings. Transfer in batches to a chilled serving bowl and sprinkle each batch with chives.

NOTE To make mushroom powder, whirl 1 ounce dried mushrooms (cèpes) in a blender or food processor until ground to a powder. Store in an airtight container in the refrigerator for up to 3 months.

FRUIT DESSERTS

• Soak melon, papaya, or mango balls, small chunks of pineapple, seedless grapes, or strawberries (halved if large) in kirsch, sweet sherry, port, Madeira, rum, bourbon, brandy, or a fruit-flavored liqueur several hours. Skewer a selection of 2 or 3 of the fruits on small wooden skewers and arrange in spoke fashion on a round serving plate. Garnish with mint sprigs.
• Mound large strawberries with stems attached in the center of a round serving platter. Surround with small bowls of Crème Fraîche, sour cream, low-fat cottage cheese, and/or plain yoghurt and confectioner's sugar and/or brown sugar. Tuck mint sprigs around the bowls. Guests pick up the strawberries and dip into the accompaniments as desired. For an extra treat, offer small bowls of Curaçao, Triple Sec, Cointreau, or other liqueur for dipping.
• Arrange apple and/or pear wedges and halved or quartered apricots and/or plums around a wheel of Brie, Camembert, or Gorgonzola cheese. Tuck several small bowls filled with walnuts in between the fruits.
• Stuff large pitted prunes with halved pecans, walnuts, or almonds; cubes of cream cheese; or a piece of candied ginger. Marinate the prunes in sweet

sherry, Madeira, port, or brandy for at least 8 hours, or overnight. Arrange on a serving plate and garnish with Lemon Twists.

• Present a large serving platter of fruits that can be speared with cocktail picks or picked up with fingers: halved or quartered apricots or plums; fresh pineapple chunks; kiwi slices; melon, papaya, or mango balls; seedless grapes. Arrange the fruits attractively and tuck cubes of provolone, Monterey Jack, or Cheddar cheese in among the fruits. Alternate the cheese cubes with marinated stuffed prunes (preceding), if desired.

COOKIES

An assortment of cookies is always a hit with a buffet crowd; bring them out about halfway through the party. Here are a few hints for the baker, followed by four foolproof recipes.

• For baking cookies in a conventional oven, baking sheets should have a rim no higher than one-half inch.

• Do not crowd the oven; bake one sheet at a time.

• If your oven bakes unevenly, turn the sheet once during baking, or remove any cookies that have baked faster than others.

• While the first batch is baking, ready a second baking sheet and pop it into the oven at the same time you take the first one out.

• Have wire racks ready on the counter, and an airtight container handy so you can put the cookies in it as soon as they are cool. This way the racks are empty for the next batch.

ALMOND MACAROONS ●■

Makes Four to Five Dozen
1 cup almonds
3 egg whites
1/8 teaspoon cream of tartar
1/8 teaspoon salt
1-1/3 cups firmly packed brown sugar, sieved
1/2 teaspoon ground cinnamon
1/4 teaspoon ground allspice
1 teaspoon pure vanilla extract, or 1/2 teaspoon almond extract

Oil 2 baking sheets with Lecithin Oil.

Finely grind almonds in a nut grinder (a blender or processor will release too much oil) to measure 2-1/3 cups very loosely packed. Set aside.

Preheat oven to 325° F. Beat together egg whites, cream of tartar, and salt until stiff peaks form. Combine sugar, cinnamon, and allspice. Two tablespoons at a time, beat sugar mixture into egg whites until stiff and glossy; the mixture should hold firm peaks. Beat in vanilla. Sprinkle about 2 tablespoons ground almonds over egg-white mixture

and gently fold in, being careful not to overmix. Repeat with remaining almonds until all are incorporated.

Drop macaroon mixture by heaping half tablespoonfuls onto a prepared baking sheet about 1 inch apart, swirling top to form a cookie about 3/4 inch thick. Bake in the preheated oven 12 minutes, or until a pale gold. Remove immediately to wire rack. Repeat with remaining dough, reoiling sheets between batches if cookies seem to be sticking.

When the macaroons are cool, store in an airtight container up to 2 days, or freeze up to 3 weeks.

CHOCOLATE ALMOND MACA- ROONS Mix 1/2 cup finely grated semisweet baking chocolate with almonds before folding nuts into egg-white mixture.

COOKIE RINGS ●■

Butter is usually a must in baking, but here is a cookie that tastes best made with good-quality margarine. During the holiday season, sprinkle these irresistible crisp rings with colored sugar for a festive touch.

You will need a cookie press to form the rings. Once baked, the cookies freeze well and are even better when eaten while still frozen.

Makes Approximately Fourteen Dozen
1 pound margarine, at room
  temperature
1 cup granulated sugar
2 teaspoons pure vanilla extract
1 teaspoon freshly grated lemon
  peel
3-1/2 to 4 cups unbleached flour
1 teaspoon salt
Coarse granulated sugar

In a large mixing bowl, beat
margarine with a wooden spoon
until softened and smooth. Gradually beat in sugar, mixing until
smooth. Stir in vanilla and lemon
peel. Sift 1 cup of the flour with
the salt and mix into the batter.
Gradually add remaining flour as
is needed to form a stiff dough;
do not add too much flour. The
dough should be just past the
sticky stage and as firm as pastry
dough. It will stiffen further
when it is chilled. If the dough is
too firm, it will be difficult to
work it through the cookie press.
If it is too soft, the cookies will
not hold their shape.

Form the dough into 2 logs,
each about 3 inches in diameter.
Wrap the logs individually in
waxed paper, place the logs in a
plastic bag, and refrigerate at
least 1-1/2 hours, or overnight.

When ready to bake the
cookies, preheat the oven to
350° F. Remove dough from
refrigerator and let stand at room
temperature 10 minutes (a little
longer if refrigerated overnight).
Fit the cookie press with the
star disc and fill the press with
the dough as directed in the
cookie-press kit. Now force the
dough through the press, forming
long, thin strips (they will be the
diameter of the disc opening;
make them as long as you can)
onto a work surface. Pinch strips
off into 3-1/2-inch lengths. Curl
each length to form a ring, or
wreath, and pinch ends together.

Sprinkle cookies with sugar
and arrange 1 inch apart on
ungreased baking sheets. Bake
in the preheated oven 8 to 10
minutes, or until just golden.
Remove from baking sheets onto
paper toweling and let cool.

Store cookies in an airtight
container for up to 1 week, or
freeze for up to 3 months.

OATMEAL COOKIES WITH WHITE CHOCOLATE ●■

Makes Approximately Eight Dozen
3/4 cup (12 tablespoons) butter,
  at room temperature
1-1/3 cups firmly packed dark
  brown sugar
2 eggs
1 teaspoon almond extract
1 cup sifted unbleached flour
3/4 teaspoon baking soda
1/4 teaspoon salt
1/4 teaspoon freshly grated
  nutmeg
1/4 teaspoon ground coriander
1/4 teaspoon ground allspice
2 cups unprocessed rolled oats
3/4 cup dark raisins, chopped
4 ounces white chocolate, finely
  chopped (3/4 cup)

Preheat oven to 350° F. Oil 2 or
3 baking sheets with Lecithin Oil.

In a mixing bowl, beat butter
with a wooden spoon until
softened and smooth. Gradually
beat in sugar, mixing until smooth.
One at a time, beat in eggs,
mixing well after each addition.
Stir in almond extract. Sift together flour, baking soda, salt,
and spices and gradually stir into
butter mixture. Stir in oats until
well mixed and fold in raisins
and chocolate.

Drop batter by heaping tea-
spoonfuls 2 inches apart on prepared baking sheet. Bake in the
preheated oven 7 to 8 minutes,
or until just starting to brown.
Remove baking sheet from oven
and let cookies cool 1 minute,
or until they can be removed
from sheet without breaking.
Cool on wire racks and store in
an airtight container for up to 3
days, or freeze for up to 2
months. Defrost at room temperature.

DESSERT TARTLETS

Always popular with the host or hostess because the shells and filling can be made ahead, these melt-in-the-mouth tartlets are certain to disappear in record time.

BASIC SWEET TARTLET SHELLS ●■

Especially easy to work with, this dough recipe can be easily doubled or tripled, as can the filling recipe that follows.

Makes Two Dozen
4 tablespoons butter, cut into
    8 pieces and at room
    temperature
1/4 cup confectioner's sugar,
    sifted
1 egg yolk
1 teaspoon pure vanilla extract
1 cup unbleached flour

In a mixing bowl, mix together butter and sugar with a wooden spoon until mixture is creamy and smooth. Beat in egg yolk and vanilla and blend well. Gradually beat in flour until well mixed. Divide dough in half and, with fingers, gently form the dough into 2 rough balls. Flatten each ball into a disc about 1-1/2 inches thick, wrap the discs in waxed paper, place in a plastic bag, and refrigerate at least 1 hour, or overnight.

Working with one disc at a time and keeping second disc chilled, let disc stand at room temperature for 4 or 5 minutes (a little longer if the dough has been refrigerated overnight). Then roll out and cut as directed in section on tartlets in General Instructions for Pastry. The dough will be delicate but very workable. Because of the amount of butter, scraps will have to be thoroughly chilled before they can be rolled a second or third time.

Line the muffin-tin wells as directed and chill at least 20 minutes. Preheat oven to 375° F. Bake tartlets 10 minutes, or until lightly golden. Remove to wire rack, cool, and store in an airtight container for up to 1 day, or freeze for up to 2 months. Defrost at room temperature before filling.

LEMON CREAM TARTLET FILLING ●■

This tangy, creamy filling will fill two dozen tartlets. Lighten it with one cup heavy cream, whipped until stiff, to produce a larger yield and a richer flavor. Any excess filling can be spooned into small dishes and refrigerated for the next evening's dessert.

Makes Approximately
One and Three-fourths Cup
3 eggs
2 egg yolks
1/2 cup granulated sugar
1/2 cup fresh lemon juice
1 tablespoon freshly grated
    lemon peel
4 tablespoons butter, cut into
    bits and at room temperature

PRESENTATION
Tiny fresh mint sprigs, or small
    strawberries, halved lengthwise
Mint sprigs
Whole strawberries

In the top pan of a double boiler, beat together eggs, egg yolks, and sugar with an electric beater 5 minutes, or until thickened, creamy, and lemon colored. Place top pan over lower pan of simmering water and stir in lemon juice and lemon peel with a wooden spoon. Stirring almost constantly, cook until mixture heavily coats the spoon. (When the spoon is lifted from the cream, the mixture should fall from it in heavy "sheets.") Remove pan from heat and, bit by bit, stir in butter, whisking after each addition until well blended.

Let lemon cream cool, stirring occasionally to prevent a skin from forming. Cover and refrigerate 2 hours, or for up to 5 days, or freeze for up to 1 month. Let come to room temperature and stir well before using.

To serve, fill each tartlet with approximately 1 tablespoon filling and top with a tiny mint sprig or tiny strawberry half. Nest the tartlets in small paper cupcake liners. Arrange the tartlets on a serving tray and garnish the tray with mint sprigs and a cluster of whole strawberries.

PECAN TARTLETS ●■

These rich, sweet tartlets are best eaten the day they are baked. They may, however, be stored one day in an airtight container or frozen for several weeks. The crust will not be as light and the texture of the filling will be a bit chewy, but the excellent flavor will remain. The pastry-lined muffin tins may be frozen, however, for up to one month. Defrost in the refrigerator before filling.

Makes Three Dozen
1 recipe Cottage Cheese or Sour
   Cream Pastry
Egg Wash

FILLING
3/4 cup firmly packed dark
   brown sugar
3/4 cup light corn syrup
1 cup coarsely chopped pecans
1 teaspoon pure vanilla extract
1/4 teaspoon salt
3 tablespoons butter, melted
   and cooled briefly
3 eggs, lightly beaten
3 dozen pecan halves

PRESENTATION
1 orange
Unshelled pecans
2 small mint sprigs

To prepare the tartlet shells, make pastry dough and line 3 dozen tiny muffin-tin wells as directed in section on tartlets in General Instructions for Pastry. Brush lightly with egg wash, let dry, and refrigerate.

To prepare the filling, combine brown sugar and corn syrup in a heavy saucepan. Bring to a boil and stir with a wooden spoon until sugar is dissolved. Remove from heat and stir in chopped pecans, vanilla, salt, and melted butter. Add eggs and mix well.

Preheat the oven to 350° F. Carefully fill each tartlet shell with the pecan mixture, dividing it evenly among the shells and making sure each shell has a well-combined portion of the mixture.

Top each filled tartlet with a pecan half and place in the preheated oven. Bake 35 minutes, or until a cake tester inserted in center of a tartlet comes out clean and egg is set. Tartlets should be just golden brown. Do not overbake.

While the tartlets are baking, cut the orange in half and scoop out the center pulp, leaving a shell about 1/2 inch thick. Mound the unshelled pecans in the orange and tuck mint sprigs in among the nuts.

Remove tartlets from oven and let cool 5 minutes, then carefully remove them to a wire rack and cool completely. Arrange tartlets on a serving tray and garnish the tray with the orange and pecan garniture.

BERRY TARTLETS

Prepare Basic Sweet Tartlet Shells, or fully baked tartlet shells as described in General Instructions for Pastry, using Cream Cheese, Cottage Cheese, Lemon Egg White, Sour Cream, or Short Crust Pastry. Just before serving, mound lightly sweetened (optional) fresh strawberries, raspberries, blueberries, or other berries in the shells and top with a dollop of Crème Fraîche or sour cream. Alternatively, marinate the berries in a complementary liqueur and refrigerate for several hours, fill the shells with the berries, using a slotted spoon to transport them. Garnish each tartlet with a tiny fresh mint leaf and arrange on a serving plate garnished with mint sprigs.

GREEK BUFFET FOR FIFTY

The philosophers of Sophocles's day frequently discussed *the art* of cookery. Then, kitchens were the province of men and the gourmet dining club was a thriving institution. Ancient Greeks regarded eating as an important social occasion, a time to be in the company of others.

Today in Greece, philosophers talk of food less formally and women are found in the kitchen, but enjoying a meal with friends is still a way of life. To make this elaborate buffet for fifty an even more festive affair, hire a bouzouki player (or purchase some records for your stereo) and stock up on retsina, the most famous wine of the country.

The culinary traditions of Greece share much with the nearby countries of the Middle East. I have included a second buffet that incorporates dishes of this neighboring region for those who wish to serve foods from a range of nations.

COLD DISHES

Taramosalata (Caviar Dip) ●
Eggplant-Tomato Spread ○
Minted or Spinach Yoghurt Dip ●
Dolmades with Rice Filling (Stuffed Grape Leaves) ●■

Stuffed Shrimp with Feta Cheese Filling ●
Skordalia (Garlic-Potato Spread) ●
Spanakopitta (Spinach Pie)
Pickled Squid ○
Marinated Mushrooms ○*
Marinated Olives (Kalamata) ○

CHOICE OF ONE
Marinated Feta Cheese ●**
Herbed Feta Cheese Mold ○

HOT DISHES

Stuffed Clams or Mussels (Filling I)
Skewered Lamb with Oregano Marinade ***
One of the Lamb Meatballs ●■
Saganaki (Fried Cheese)
Sikotaka Tighanita (Fried Liver Bits)
Phyllo Triangles with Spinach Filling or Feta Cheese Filling ■

Greek bread or baguettes

Baklava ●■
Walnut Cake ●■
Grape clusters

*See Marinated Vegetables.
**See Suggestions for Cheese.
***See Barbecue Cookery.

MIDDLE EAST BUFFET FOR FIFTY

For a Middle East buffet, make the following adjustments in the Greek Buffet menu:
- Add Tahini Dip ●
- Substitute Baba Ghannouj ○ for Eggplant-Tomato Spread.
- Substitute Middle East Beef Balls ●■ for Lamb Meatballs.
- Substitute Kibbeh ● for Skewered Lamb with Oregano Marinade.
- Substitute Hummus ● for Skordalia.
- Prepare Phyllo Triangles with Spinach Filling, but form into rolls as directed in General Instructions for Phyllo Rolls.
- Substitute Phyllo Rolls with Walnuts and Almonds ●■ for Baklava.

BAKLAVA ●■

One piece of this honeyed dessert is usually enough to satisfy any guest with a sweet tooth. It can be prepared one day in advance and refrigerated, or frozen for up to two weeks. Purchase tiny paper cupcake liners in which to nestle the baklava diamonds. Refer to the section on Phyllo in the Pastries chapter for instructions on working with phyllo dough.

The syrup is best made the day before, so plan ahead.

Four to Five Dozen Servings

3/4 to 1 pound phyllo
3/4 to 1 pound unsalted butter, melted
Fresh mint sprigs

SYRUP

2-1/2 cups granulated sugar
1-1/2 cups honey
2 cups water
Peel of 1 large lemon
3 tablespoons fresh lemon juice
Two 3-inch cinnamon sticks
8 whole cloves

FILLING

4 cups chopped walnuts
2 cups chopped blanched almonds
1/4 cup granulated sugar
1 tablespoon ground cinnamon
1/2 teaspoon ground cloves
1/2 teaspoon ground allspice

To prepare the syrup, combine sugar, honey, and water in a heavy saucepan. Bring to a boil and cook, stirring, until sugar is dissolved and honey is incorporated. Add lemon peel, lemon juice, cinnamon sticks, and cloves. Bring to a boil, reduce heat to medium low, and boil gently 40 minutes, stirring occasionally. Syrup should thicken slightly. Cool, cover, and refrigerate overnight.

To prepare the filling, combine walnuts, almonds, sugar, cinnamon, cloves, and allspice in a mixing bowl and toss well.

To assemble the baklava, heavily butter a baking pan 17 by 11 by 2-1/2 inches with Lecithin Butter. Preheat the oven to 325° F.

Buttering 1 phyllo sheet at a time as directed in Phyllo, layer 8 sheets in the prepared baking pan. Sprinkle one-third of the walnut mixture over and layer 2 more buttered sheets on top. Sprinkle one-half of the remaining walnut mixture over and again cover with 2 buttered sheets. Sprinkle remaining walnut mixture over and cover with 8 more buttered sheets. Brush the top sheet lightly with melted butter. Score the pastry in a diamond pattern by cutting two-thirds of the way through to bottom of pan.

Bake the baklava in the preheated oven 50 to 55 minutes, or until lightly golden. Remove from the oven and immediately pour the chilled syrup over, letting it soak in evenly. Cool baklava completely.

To serve, finish cutting portions through to form diamonds and place each diamond in a cupcake liner. Arrange on a serving platter garnished with mint sprigs.

WALNUT CAKE ●■

Make the syrup several hours ahead so it cools before you pour it over the hot cake. The cake will be easier to cut if it is made one day in advance of serving.

Three to Four Dozen Servings

SYRUP
2 cups water
1-1/2 cups granulated sugar
Peel of 2 lemons
6 whole cloves
One 2-inch stick cinnamon
2 teaspoons fresh lemon juice

CAKE
4 tablespoons lard or solid
    vegetable shortening
1 cup granulated sugar
4 eggs
1 cup safflower oil
1 cup milk
1 tablespoon freshly grated
    orange peel
1 teaspoon baking soda, dissolved
    in 2 tablespoons dark rum
2 cups cake flour
3 tablespoons cultured buttermilk
    powder
2-1/2 tablespoons baking powder
1 teaspoon ground cinnamon
1/2 teaspoon ground cloves
1/2 teaspoon ground allspice
1/8 teaspoon salt
2 cups chopped walnuts

To prepare the syrup, combine water, sugar, lemon peel, cloves, stick cinnamon, and lemon juice in a saucepan. Bring to a boil, stirring to dissolve sugar, lower heat, and simmer uncovered 45 minutes. Remove from heat and let cool.

Oil a 13-by-9-inch baking pan with Lecithin Oil and set aside. Preheat oven to 350° F.

To prepare the cake, combine lard and sugar in a large mixing bowl and cream with a wooden spoon until smooth. Beat in eggs, one at a time, and then beat in oil, milk, orange peel, and baking soda and rum mixture. Sift together flour, buttermilk powder, baking powder, spices, and salt. Stir dry ingredients into wet ingredients just until mixed. Fold in walnuts and pour into prepared baking pan. Batter will be quite thin.

Bake the cake in the preheated oven 30 minutes, or until a cake tester inserted in center comes out clean and cake has pulled slightly away from sides of pan. Remove from oven and *immediately* pour cooled syrup over, distributing it evenly as it soaks into the cake. Let cool on wire rack.

To serve, cut cake into diamonds and nestle each diamond in a tiny paper cupcake liner.

Walnut cake may be frozen for up to 2 months. Defrost at room temperature.

PHYLLO ROLLS WITH WALNUTS AND ALMONDS ●■

Makes Four to Five Dozen
1 pound phyllo
Approximately 3/4 pound butter,
    melted
Fresh grape leaves

SYRUP
1/2 cup water
3/4 cup granulated sugar
2 tablespoons honey
1 tablespoon fresh lemon or
    lime juice
1/2 teaspoon ground cinnamon

FILLING
1 cup walnut meats
1 cup blanched almonds
6 tablespoons granulated sugar
2 egg yolks
3 tablespoons brandy
1/2 teaspoon pure vanilla extract
1/2 teaspoon ground allspice
1/2 teaspoon ground cinnamon
1 teaspoon freshly grated lemon
    peel

To prepare the syrup, combine water, sugar, honey, lemon juice, and cinnamon in a saucepan. Bring to a boil and stir to dissolve sugar. Simmer uncovered 10 minutes and set aside.

To prepare the filling, grind nuts in a nut grinder (if using a blender or a food processor, add a little of the sugar and be sure not to grind the nuts to the point they become a paste). Transfer ground nuts to a mixing bowl and toss with sugar. With a fork, stir in egg yolks, brandy, vanilla, allspice, cinnamon, and lemon peel.

To assemble the rolls, fill and roll as directed in Basic Instructions for Phyllo Rolls.

Unbaked sweet phyllo rolls may be refrigerated and frozen in the same manner as savory phyllo rolls. If freezing, however, do not make the syrup until the rolls are defrosting.

To bake, preheat oven to 375° F. Bake the rolls 15 minutes, or until golden. Cool 2 minutes, prick all over with tines of a fork, and pour syrup over. Serve hot or at room temperature.

Baked rolls may be sheet frozen for up to 2 months, but they will lose their distinctive texture. Defrost at room temperature.

FRENCH BUFFET FOR FORTY

A chapter on buffets would be incomplete without a French menu. After all, *buffet*—literally "sideboard"—is a French word. In addition, many of the dishes that people commonly associate with an "hors d'oeuvre meal" are classic Gallic preparations—galantines, terrines, canapés, quiches, and so on.

Your sideboard won't be large enough to display all of the delicious dishes that make up this elegant buffet. There is a savory rich cheesecake of lemon-scented chèvre, an aspic-coated galantine of chicken, a creamy chicken liver mousse flavored with brandy, eggs stuffed with a delicate chestnut purée, piping hot meatballs in a tangy sorrel sauce, classic madeleines in honor of Proust, and more. This feast is a celebration of gastronomy.

COLD DISHES

Potted Shrimp •
Oysters on the half shell
Stuffed Eggs with Sorrel and/or
    Chestnut Purée Filling
One of the Quiches
One of the Galantines or
    Terrines o
Petites Bouchées*
Crêpes**

CHOICE OF ONE
One of the Brie Tortas •
One of the Potted Cheeses o■
Potted Blue Cheese II o■
Herbed Chèvre o
Chèvre Cheesecake

CHOICE OF ONE
Duck Rillettes o■
Pork Rillettes o■

CHOICE OF ONE
Chicken Mousse with Almonds o
Chicken Liver Mousse
    with Brandy o
Chopped Chicken Liver with
    Mushrooms
Chicken Liver Pâté o
Baked Chicken Liver Pâté o
Spicy Baked Chicken Liver
    Pâté o
Pork Pâté with Savory o

CHOICE OF ONE
Parslied Ham in Aspic o
Black Caviar Mold o
Blue Cheese Mold o

CHOICE OF ONE
Crème Fraîche with Red Pepper
    Dip •
Lemony Spinach Sorrel Dip •
Tapenade with Cauliflower and
    Eggs •

CHOICE OF ONE
Caviar Surprise •
Chopped Eggs with Chestnut
    Purée •

HOT DISHES

Mushrooms Stuffed with Snails
Beef Marrow Rounds

CHOICE OF ONE
Fried Brie with Herbs and Pecans
Cheese Fondue

CHOICE OF ONE
Sweetbreads and Mushrooms
Veal and Beef Meatballs with
   Sorrel Sauce ●■

Cheese Tray I

CHOICE OF ONE OR TWO
Madeleines ●■
Allumettes
Cream Puffs
Dessert Crêpes

*Fill with crème fraîche filling
included in Fillings for Cold
Choux.
**Wrap crêpes around asparagus
tips, as described in Fillings for
Crêpes.

MADELEINES ●■

These rich, lemony miniature
"cakes" are baked in a special
pan with a dozen wells, each
shaped like an elongated scallop
shell. Since the pans are quite
expensive, you will probably have
only one of them, and thus be
able to bake only twelve cookies
at a time. Be sure to wash and
heavily oil the pan before filling
it for each baking. The recipe is
easily doubled, and the batter
will hold while the "first recipe"
is being baked.

Makes Three Dozen
1 cup superfine sugar
3/4 cup (12 tablespoons) butter
2 eggs, at room temperature,
   separated
Freshly grated peel of 1 large
   lemon
1 cup sifted cake flour
1 tablespoon fresh lemon juice

Oil the wells of a madeleine pan
generously with Lecithin Oil and
set aside. Preheat oven to 375° F.
   Measure sugar into a mixing
bowl. Melt butter, cool briefly
to lukewarm, and beat into sugar
with a wooden spoon. Stir in egg
yolks and lemon peel, beat until
smooth, and sift flour over the
mixture. Beat flour in until
smooth, then add unbeaten egg
whites and lemon juice, and
again beat until smooth.
   Transfer a heaping teaspoon
of dough to each prepared pan
well. Place the pan in the preheated oven and bake 12 minutes
or until madeleines are golden.
Cool briefly, then remove the
cakes from the wells with the
help of a small spatula. Cool on
wire racks. Repeat with remaining dough.
   Store the madeleines in an
airtight container for up to 1
day, or freeze for up to 2
months. Defrost at room temperature.

ALLUMETTES

For the best flavor, serve these
flaky pastry fingers the day they
are baked. The puff pastry dough
may be made a day ahead and
rolled just before baking; the
icing may be made several hours
ahead. See the American Buffet
for tips on cookie baking.

Makes Approximately Five Dozen
1/2 recipe Puff Pastry
1 egg white
1 cup confectioner's sugar, sifted,
   or as needed

Prepare puff pastry dough and chill. Working with half the pastry at a time, roll the dough as directed into a rectangle approximately 1/4 inch thick.

Preheat oven to 375° F. Heavily oil 2 or 3 baking sheets with Lecithin Oil. In a mixing bowl, beat egg white lightly with a wooden spoon. Gradually beat in sugar, adding enough to form an icing with the consistency of lightly whipped cream. Spread the puff pastry rectangle evenly with half the icing and cut the pastry into "fingers" that measure 1 inch by 2 inches. Carefully transfer the fingers to a baking sheet, placing them at least 1-1/2 inches apart. Place the sheet in the preheated oven and bake 8 minutes, or until lightly golden. Immediately remove to wire racks to cool. Bake remaining cut cookies, and then roll out remaining pastry dough, cut into cookies, and bake.

When cool, place allumettes in an airtight container until ready to serve.

DESSERT CREPES

Following directions for Crêpes, cook crêpes and trim into rounds as directed. Spread crêpe rounds with apricot or strawberry jam and sprinkle with chopped walnuts or pecans. Roll one turn, fold in sides, and continue to roll to form a tight cylinder. In a large skillet, melt enough butter to cover the bottom of the skillet with a thin film. Place the rolls in the skillet seam side down, cover, and cook over medium-low heat 5 minutes, or until just heated through.

Serve from a chafing or equivalent dish with cocktail picks for spearing.

Alternatively, strew finely chopped apples and shredded Gruyère cheese over the crêpes. Roll and warm as directed above.

CREAM PUFFS

Prepare Choux, adding 2 teaspoons granulated sugar and 1 teaspoon rose water or orange water to the batter after beating in eggs. Bake as directed and cool completely. Just before serving, fill puffs with lightly sweetened whipped cream laced with liqueur; Lemon Cream Tartlet Filling lightened with whipped cream; or the filling for Cannoli. Arrange the cream puffs on a round serving plate in a circular pattern and tuck thin chocolate mints in between the puffs.

ITALIAN BUFFET FOR THIRTY

Today, Italian food is definitely "in" in the United States and everything from the equipment featured in kitchenware shops to the growing number of trattorias reflects that popularity. This buffet imaginatively combines the classic preparations of the "boot" with dishes that depart from tradition.

At the center of this sophisticated meal is a large array of cold meats, seafood, and vegetables, what many Italian restaurants call an *antipasto* platter. The term, which literally means "before the meal," is roughly equivalent to the French *hors d'oeuvre*. A sumptuous display of colorful, delicious foods, from a vegetable-flecked frittata to herb-scented meatballs to tortellini in cream sauce, accompanies the platter. Cannoli, their ricotta filling pierced with candied orange peel, are the perfect finish.

COLD DISHES

Antipasto
Marinated Calimari o·
Marinated Artichokes o*
Marinated Mushrooms o*
Potted Blue Cheese IV o■
Prosciutto-wrapped asparagus
   tips**
One of the Frittatas

CHOICE OF TWO
Bagna Cauda
Black Peppercorn–Anchovy Dip •
White Beans with Pumate
    dip ○***
Caponata ○

HOT DISHES

Skewered Tortellini
Polpotte •■
Stuffed Clams or Mussels
    (Filling I)
Spinach Balls •■
Fried Mozzarella Cheese ****

CHOICE OF ONE
Focaccia
Small Pizzas
Chicken Liver or Pumate
    Crostini

Mushroom Broth •
Cheese Tray IV
Almond Biscuit Cookies •■
Cannoli

*See Marinated Vegetables.
**Wrap lightly blanched asparagus in paper-thin slices of proscuitto. Form a cluster of squash blossoms or nasturtium flowers on end of an oval serving platter. Arrange the wrapped asparagus tips in a spoke design radiating from the flower cluster.
***See Black-eyed Peas with Pumate dip. Use white beans and substitute a dash of cayenne pepper for the chili powder.

****See Fried Monterey Jack with Garlic and Chilies. Substitute mozzarella cheese for the Monterey Jack.

ANTIPASTO

Here is a score of possibilities for your antipasto platter. Six items should be considered the minimum; choose as many more than that as desired, but plan on at least one cold-meat roll for each guest.

Roll the meats, which should be sliced paper thin, into tight cylinders and arrange them seam side down in neat, well-spaced rows on a square or rectangular tray. Make small mounds of the other items between the meat rows (use a slotted spoon to transport foods that are in liquid). Garnish with young kale or curly endive leaves. Place a mug filled with breadsticks and a basket of sliced Italian bread alongside. Provide plenty of cocktail picks.

Dry salami
Mortadella
Coppa
Prosciutto or Westphalian ham
Shrimp *
Pickled pigs' feet
Sardines in oil
Anchovy fillets rolled with capers
Smoked oysters
Cubed provolone and/or
    mozzarella cheese

Quartered hard-cooked eggs
Large black and green olives
Radish Roses
Green Onion Brushes
Celery and/or carrot sticks
Green bell pepper, cut in rings
Hearts of fennel
Cherry tomatoes
Pepperoncini
Roasted Pepper or pimiento
    strips

*See Shrimp on Ice for cooking instructions. For 1 pound medium-large shrimp, immediately toss drained cooked shrimp with 1/3 cup fresh lemon juice, 1 teaspoon chopped fresh oregano, 2 garlic cloves, finely minced, and 1 tablespoon chopped fresh Italian parsley. Let stand at least 1 hour, or for up to 3 hours before serving.

SKEWERED TORTELLINI

Several recent cookbooks have included the idea of serving tortellini, stuffed "little hats," on small skewers, making pasta a popular finger food.

The quality of the tortellini is of prime importance, so purchase only the best. There are approximately sixty tortellini in one pound, which is sufficient for a buffet for thirty. The filling may be chicken, veal, cheese, or a combination, and the dough may be plain egg or spinach. For color contrast, serve both egg and spinach tortellini.

Boil the tortellini in plenty of water just until al dente; do not overcook. Drain the pasta and immediately toss it with enough olive oil to coat evenly. If you omit this step, the tortellini will stick together. When cool enough to handle, carefully thread 2 tortellini on each skewer.

To serve hot, prepare a double recipe Cream Sauce with 6 tablespoons freshly grated Parmesan cheese stirred in at the last minute. Arrange skewered tortellini on a warmed platter, with tortellini pointing toward the center of the platter, and pour the hot sauce over the pasta. Garnish the platter with a cluster of arugula leaves or parsley sprigs and nestle 1 or 2 Tomato Roses in the center. Place the platter on a warming tray. Accompany with a bowl of Roasted Garlic, if desired.

To serve at room temperature, prepare Pesto, Green Sauce, or Crème Fraîche seasoned to taste with fresh lemon juice, Garlic Purée, minced Pumate with a little of its oil, and freshly grated Parmesan cheese. Arrange the skewers on a platter as described for hot tortellini and pour sauce over the pasta. Sprinkle with Parmesan cheese. Garnish as for hot tortellini.

CHICKEN LIVER CROSTINI

Crostini are lightly toasted slices of Italian bread spread with the savory paste or other topping of your choice, such as chicken livers, flavored olive oil, bone marrow, cheese and anchovies, broccoli purée, or zesty anchovy-flavored tomato sauce. I have developed a chicken liver and an olive oil version, which are included here.

Makes Approximately Twenty-four
1 pound chicken livers
Dry sherry or Madeira to cover
12 large slices Italian bread (about 1/4 inch thick)
4 large garlic cloves, very finely minced
2/3 cup very finely minced onion
2 tablespoons rendered chicken or ham fat
3 tablespoons olive oil, or as needed
1/2 teaspoon salt
1/4 teaspoon freshly ground black pepper
1 large sage sprig
1 teaspoon fresh lemon juice
1 teaspoon anchovy paste
1/2 cup freshly grated Parmesan cheese (optional)
Parsley sprigs
Lemon Cups

Soak chicken livers in sherry 4 hours, or overnight. Drain, pat dry with paper toweling, chop finely, and set aside.

Toast the bread lightly on one side and transfer to wire racks to cool.

In a large covered nonstick skillet, cook garlic and onion in rendered fat and 1 tablespoon of the olive oil over medium heat 5 minutes. Add reserved chicken livers, sprinkle with salt and pepper, and stir well with a fork. Place the sage sprig on top, cover, lower heat slightly, and cook 10 minutes.

Preheat oven to 450° F. Discard sage sprig and stir lemon juice and anchovy paste into the chicken livers, mixing well. Taste and adjust seasonings. If not using immediately, transfer to a bowl, cover, and refrigerate for up to 4 hours. Bring to room temperature before proceeding.

To serve, spread chicken liver mixture evenly on the untoasted side of the bread slices and drizzle with remaining 2 tablespoons olive oil, or as needed to moisten evenly. If desired, sprinkle lightly with Parmesan cheese. Bake in the preheated oven 3 minutes, or until heated and crispy.

Place parsley sprigs on one corner of a serving plate and nestle 2 or 3 lemon cups on the parsley. Cut each bread slice in half and arrange on the garnished plate. Serve at once.

PUMATE CROSTINI

Following directions in Chicken Liver Crostini, ready toast slices. Drizzle about 1 teaspoon of the oil from a jar of Pumate on the untoasted side of each slice of bread. Bake as directed, remove from the oven, and place a strip of pumate on each slice. Garnish the serving plate with cherry tomatoes nestled in a bed of parsley or kale.

MUSHROOM BROTH ●

This broth, flavored with the dried mushrooms called porcini by the Italians and cèpes by the French, nicely complements the menu. The soup may be prepared a day in advance, stored in the refrigerator, and then reheated just before serving. See the American Buffet for tips on making and serving soup.

Soak 1 ounce dried Italian mushrooms in warm water to cover 30 minutes. In a large saucepan, combine 2-1/2 quarts defatted Beef Stock, 3 quarts defatted Chicken Stock, and one 10-1/2-ounce can consommé. Add soaked mushrooms and their soaking water to saucepan and bring to a boil. Boil uncovered 10 minutes, remove from the heat, and strain.

ALMOND BISCUIT COOKIES ●■

These biscuitlike cookies are complemented by freshly brewed coffee, preferably a full-bodied Italian roast. For tips on baking cookies, see the American Buffet.

Makes Two and One-half to Three Dozen
1/2 cup lard, at room
    temperature
1/3 cup granulated sugar
2 egg yolks
1/4 teaspoon anise extract
1 teaspoon freshly grated lemon
    peel
1 cup ground almonds,
    or as needed
1/2 cup sifted unbleached flour
1/8 teaspoon salt
1/4 cup dry sherry

Oil 2 or 3 baking sheets with Lecithin Oil.

In a mixing bowl, cream together lard and sugar with a wooden spoon until well blended and smooth. One at a time, beat in egg yolks. Blend in anise extract, lemon peel, and 1/2 cup of the ground almonds. Sift flour with salt and stir into almond mixture alternately with sherry, mixing well after each addition.

Preheat oven to 400° F. Spread remaining ground almonds on a sheet of waxed paper. Drop dough onto almonds in rough balls the size of a large marble. With your fingertips, gently roll dough into smooth balls, coating on all sides with the ground almonds and adding more almonds as needed.

Place balls 1 inch apart on prepared baking sheets. With 2 fingers, gently flatten balls to a thickness of 1/2 inch. Bake in the preheated oven 10 minutes, or until golden. Remove immediately to a wire rack, cool, and store cookies in an airtight container up to 3 days, or freeze for up to 2 months.

CANNOLI

You are probably surprised to find wonton skins in a recipe for an Italian dessert, but I have found that they make excellent cannoli shells, saving you considerable time and effort in the kitchen. (See the Chinese Buffet for information on wonton skins.)

You will need six cannoli tubes, which can be purchased in cookware shops. If you cannot find them, make your own tubes by cutting one-inch aluminum tubing or wooden dowels into six-inch lengths.

Once the cannoli shells are made and completely cooled, they can be stored in an airtight container for up to two days, or frozen for up to one month. Defrost at room temperature and fill just before serving.

Makes Twenty-four
24 square wonton skins
Peanut oil for deep frying
Coarsely ground unsalted pistachio nuts
Additional confectioner's sugar
Mint sprigs

FILLING
1 pound low-fat ricotta cheese, beaten until smooth or sieved
1/2 cup confectioner's sugar, sifted
1 teaspoon pure vanilla extract
1/3 cup shaved semisweet chocolate
2 to 3 tablespoons finely minced candied orange peel

In a deep fryer, heat 4 inches of peanut oil to 375° F.

Work with 6 wonton skins at a time and keep remainder well wrapped in waxed paper and draped with a lightly dampened tea towel. Place a wonton skin on work surface and set a cannoli tube diagonally across the center of it. Bring sides of skin up over tube and seal overlapping tips with a dab of water. Form wonton skins around the remaining 5 tubes.

Lower 2 wrapped tubes, seam side down, into the hot oil and fry 30 seconds, or until just golden. Remove with tongs and drain on crumpled paper toweling; while cannoli shells are still hot, gently push them off the tubes with a small metal spatula and your fingertips. Repeat with remaining 18 skins, working in batches of 6. Be sure the tubes cool completely before forming the wonton skins around them.

For the filling, combine cheese, confectioner's sugar, vanilla, chocolate, and orange peel. Cover and chill at least 2 hours or overnight.

To serve, spoon the filling into the cannoli shells. Dip each end of the filled shell in pistachio nuts and arrange on a serving plate. Sift additional sugar over each cannoli and garnish the plate with mint sprigs.

VARIATION Omit vanilla and add to cheese mixture rum or any high-quality liqueur to taste. Mix the confectioner's sugar for sifting over the cannoli with instant espresso or dark cocoa powder.

LATIN AMERICAN BUFFET FOR TWENTY

The cuisine of Latin America has been influenced by that of Spain, Portugal, black Africa, and, most importantly, the indigenous Indian population. These varied lands south of the Rio Grande and Florida offer a diverse table, one that includes native plants—potatoes, tomatoes, peppers, squash, beans—in a variety of distinctive dishes.

The recipes that make up this buffet are, for the most part, not classic preparations of the region. They are instead dishes that respect the culinary spirit of Latin America and reflect the tastes of North American cooks.

To set the mood, decorate the buffet with vases of colorful fresh flowers, wreaths of dried red chili peppers, and a tray of tropical fruits. Be sure the tortilla chips are of the highest quality.

COLD DISHES

Guacamole
Layered Bean Dip
Seviche ○
Filled Cherry Tomatoes*
Sliced jicama sprinkled with herb
    salt, surrounded by marinated
    green bell peppers**

HOT DISHES

Skewered Pork and/or Chorizo
    with Tortillas
Meatballs with Chili Peppers
    and Cheese ●■
Chili-Cheese or Beef
    Empanaditas ●■

CHOICE OF ONE
Cheese Crisps
Fried Monterey Jack with Garlic
    and Chilies

Macerated fruit on skewers***

*The shrimp and olive filling
would be appropriate with this
menu, but select any filling you
prefer.
**See Marinated Vegetables.
***See Fruit Desserts in American
Buffet; macerate the fruit in
Tequila.

SKEWERED PORK OR CHORIZO WITH TORTILLAS

Cut 1 pound lean pork into 1-inch
cubes and marinate 4 hours or
overnight in Olive Oil Marinade.
Spear 1 or 2 cubes of meat onto
each bamboo skewer (see Barbecue Cookery) and cook, basting
frequently, over hot coals 10
minutes, or until cooked through.
Place a basket of warmed corn
tortillas and a bowl of Tomatillo
Sauce alongside the grill. Guests
tuck the barbecued pork cubes
into a tortilla, spoon on a little
sauce, and fold into a packet for
eating.

    To barbecue chorizo (spicy
pork sausage), cut 1 pound sausages into 1-inch pieces and
spear 1 piece on each skewer.
Grill, basting with Olive Oil
Marinade, 10 minutes, or until
cooked through. Alternatively,
spear a sausage piece and a pork
cube on each skewer.

SPANISH BUFFET FOR TWENTY

Most first-time travelers to Spain
are surprised to discover that
when the natives dine out, they
seldom begin eating until ten
o'clock. If hunger pangs strike
before that hour, you can do as
the Spanish do and visit a tavern
where *tapas,* literally "covers"
(and in this context, "snacks"),
are served.

    Dozens of small plates holding
a variety of preparations—marinated artichokes or olives, steamed
clams, lamb kidneys in a sauce
laced with Madeira, squares of
potato omelet—are placed on
the bar top. As patrons have a
before-dinner drink, they snack
on whatever appeals to them.

    This buffet is based on the
tapas tradition, but with one
notable exception: your guests
won't need to go on to a restaurant for dinner.

COLD DISHES

Tortilla de Patata (Potato
    Omelet)
Squid Rings in Green Sauce
Tongue Platter ○ garnished with
    Potato Balls and served with
    Garlic Mayonnaise on the
    side

White Beans with Almonds
   dip • served with green
   bean crudités
Marinated Mushrooms ○*
Marinated Olives (ripe) ○
Roasted Peppers with Garlic**
Roasted Nuts
Crusty bread

HOT DISHES

Shrimp in the Shell,
   Spanish Style
Stuffed Clams or Mussels
   (Filling II)
Skewered Pork with Chili-Lemon
   or Coriander Marinade***
Lamb Kidneys in Madeira
   Sauce****

Chocolate Almond Macaroons
Orange sections

*See Marinated Vegetables; use
lots of garlic.
**See Roasted Peppers suggestions.
***See Barbecue Cookery.
****Prepare half a recipe and
add 1 cup cubed cooked ham
(3/4-inch cubes) to the kidneys
when heating.

CHINESE BUFFET FOR TWELVE

The Cantonese, native to south China, are the masters of dim sum, literally "dot heart," the savory pastries and buns and small dishes of spareribs, meatballs, paper-wrapped chicken, duck feet, and the like they traditionally eat with tea for lunch. It is common for this special meal to be taken at restaurants or teahouses, where kitchens are lined with stacks of bamboo steamers that reveal delicate dumplings at every level.

This buffet cannot include all of the wonderful dishes found at a teahouse, for no home chef has sufficient bamboo steamers and range-top burners to manage the cooking. Because of this, I have included only half a dozen preparations, among them some of the most popular dim sum.

Provide guests with chopsticks, shallow dishes for mixing dipping sauces, and small Chinese teacups. For a satisfying tea to accompany the meal, combine po nay cha, a reddish black tea from Yunnan, with dried chrysanthemum buds.

Steamed Beef or Pork
   Dumplings ■
Rice Noodle Rolls with
   Barbecued Pork
Egg Rolls
Pot Stickers
Parchment Chicken •
Steamed Pork Spareribs
Tea Eggs ○ (see Eggs)

Almond Cookies •■
Mandarin oranges

STEAMED BEEF OR PORK DUMPLINGS ▪

The round wonton skins used for making these delicate steamed dumplings, called shui mai, can be found in one-pound packages in Oriental groceries and most supermarkets. (If only square skins are available, make an impression on the stack of skins with a three-inch cookie cutter, then use kitchen scissors to cut out the rounds.) Each package contains between forty and sixty skins, or wrappers, depending upon how thinly the skins have been rolled. Well wrapped, the skins may be frozen after purchase. Noodle doughs dry out quickly, however, and should not be frozen longer than two or three weeks. Defrost the skins in the refrigerator.

Chinese bamboo basket steamers are ideal for cooking the dumplings, and are attractive enough to double as serving vessels. You will need at least three ten-inch baskets for forty-eight dumplings. See Steaming for specific directions and for alternatives to the bamboo baskets.

Choose one of the following fillings, or halve each filling recipe and present guests with a choice of dumplings

Makes Forty-eight

BEEF FILLING
1 pound ground lean beef
1 egg, lightly beaten
1/4 cup minced green onion and tops
1 teaspoon finely minced ginger root
One 1-inch piece dried tangerine peel, softened in warm water, drained, and finely minced
2 tablespoons soy sauce
1 tablespoon Chinese white wine or dry sherry
1 tablespoon cornstarch
1/2 teaspoon salt

PORK FILLING
1/2 pound ground lean pork butt
1/2 pound shrimp, shelled and finely minced
4 dried shiitake mushrooms, soaked in warm water to soften, drained, and finely minced
3 tablespoons finely minced green onion and tops
1 tablespoon minced fresh coriander
1/2 cup finely minced water chestnuts
1 tablespoon soy sauce
1 tablespoon cornstarch
1 teaspoon salt
1/2 teaspoon Oriental sesame oil
1 egg, lightly beaten

48 round wonton skins
48 tiny coriander leaves
Soy sauce
Prepared Chinese mustard

To make the beef filling, combine beef, egg, onion, ginger root, tangerine peel, soy sauce, wine, cornstarch, and salt in a mixing bowl and mix well. Pinch off a small portion and sauté until cooked through. Taste and adjust seasonings.

To form the dumplings, work with only 6 to 8 wonton skins at a time. Keep the rest well wrapped in waxed paper and draped with a lightly dampened towel. Lay 1 wonton skin across the palm of your left hand (if you are right-handed). With the fingers of your other hand, grasp about 1 tablespoon of the filling, form it into a rough ball, and place it in the center of the wonton skin. Bring the skin up and around to cover the sides and outer edge of the top of the filling. With your fingers, form tiny pleats along the top of the skin; the filling should be visible. Place a tiny coriander leaf on the center of the formed dumpling.

With your fingertips, gently press the bottom of the dumpling to flatten slightly so that it will stand upright. Place the dumpling on a platter or wooden board, cover with a tea towel, and repeat with the remaining wonton skins and filling. Do not allow the dumplings to touch. Once all of the dumplings are made, they may be steamed immediately, or covered tightly with plastic wrap and refrigerated for up to 4 hours.

To steam the dumplings, place each on a 2-inch square of aluminum foil and arrange the dumplings directly on the rungs of bamboo baskets or on the tiers of a metal steamer. The dumplings should be no closer than 1 inch, though the aluminum foil may overlap. When the tiers are filled and stacked, cover the steamer (if you are using a metal steamer, wrap the lid in a towel), bring the water to a boil, and steam 20 minutes. The skins will have a shiny look when the dumplings are done.

Serve the dumplings at once from the bamboo steamers or arrange on a warmed serving platter. Set out a cruet of soy sauce and a small bowl of mustard with a spoon. Guests may dip the dumplings in soy or mustard, or mix them to taste.

Uncooked dumplings may be sheet frozen for up to 3 days. Defrost in the refrigerator before steaming.

RICE NOODLE ROLLS WITH BARBECUED PORK

The rice noodle rounds called for in this recipe can be purchased by the piece in Chinese bakeries. They are white, opaque, usually about fourteen inches in diameter, and come loosely folded. Do not refrigerate them, or they will stiffen. The rounds can be covered with plastic wrap and kept at room temperature overnight.

Barbecued pork can be purchased in Chinese delicatessens. Select a lean piece with a moist appearance.

Makes Approximately Sixty Pieces
1 pound bean sprouts
1/2 teaspoon Oriental sesame oil
1 tablespoon soy sauce
1 teaspoon salt
1/4 teaspoon freshly ground black pepper
1/4 pound barbecued pork, slivered
1/2 cup slivered green onion with some tops
1 recipe Egg Rounds, cut into slivers
1 tablespoon lightly toasted sesame seeds
1 tablespoon slivered pickled red ginger (optional)
6 rice noodle rounds
Coriander sprigs
Soy and/or oyster sauce

In a mixing bowl, pour boiling water to cover over bean sprouts and let stand 1 minute. Drain, rinse in cold water, and drain well. Combine bean sprouts with sesame oil, soy sauce, salt, and pepper, toss well, and set aside.

Have the pork, onion, egg round slivers, sesame seeds, and pickled red ginger ready. Shortly before serving, unfold 1 rice noodle round, being careful not to break it and keeping the rest of the sheets covered. Place the sheet flat on a work surface and strew one-sixth of the bean sprouts over the sheet. In order given, layer one-sixth of the pork, onion, egg round slivers, sesame seeds, and pickled red ginger over the sprouts. Roll as tightly as possible to make a cylinder about 1-1/4 inches in diameter. Repeat with remaining rounds and filling ingredients.

Cut cylinders into 1-1/2-inch lengths and arrange cut side up on a serving plate. Garnish the plate with coriander sprigs. Serve at room temperature with soy and/or oyster sauce for dipping.

EGG ROLLS

Egg roll skins, or wrappers, are similar in appearance to wonton skins, but measure about five by six inches. A one-pound package contains about twenty wrappers. They are carried in Oriental markets and most supermarkets.

Makes Approximately Seventy Pieces

FILLING
1 tablespoon corn oil
2 celery ribs, very thinly
    sliced on diagonal
1 pound bean sprouts
3/4 cup slivered bamboo shoots
One 4-ounce can water chestnuts,
    drained and sliced into tiny
    slivers
1 tablespoon soy sauce
1 teaspoon granulated sugar
1/2 teaspoon Oriental sesame oil
1/2 cup slivered green onion
    with some tops
1 tablespoon cornstarch
1 recipe Egg Rounds, cut into
    slivers

1 pound egg roll skins
Peanut oil for deep frying
Coriander sprigs

To make the filling, heat corn oil in a wok or heavy skillet and stir-fry celery, bean sprouts, bamboo shoots, water chestnuts, soy sauce, and sugar over medium-high heat 3 minutes. Pour off any juices that accumulate and mix in sesame oil, onion, cornstarch, and egg round slivers. Set aside to cool.

Work with 3 or 4 egg roll skins at a time and keep rest wrapped with waxed paper and draped with a lightly dampened tea towel. Place 1 skin flat on work surface, with a long side facing you. Spoon 1/3 cup of the filling in a line 1/2 inch in from the edge of the egg roll skin closest to you. Bring the 1/2-inch border over the filling to encase it, fold in side edges, and roll like a jelly roll. Seal seam with a little water, place roll seam side down on another work surface or a baking sheet, and cover with a tea towel. Repeat with remaining egg roll skins and filling.

In a large skillet, electric fry-pan, or deep fryer, heat at least 3 inches of peanut oil to 375° F. Deep-fry the egg rolls seam side down, without crowding, until crisp and golden, turning once. Drain on crumpled paper toweling and cut each roll into 5 slices. Arrange on a serving plate and garnish with coriander sprigs.

POT STICKERS

These pan-fried dumplings are favorites of the northern Chinese, though their southern neighbors, the Cantonese, prepare a similar dumpling. I have simplified the forming of the pot stickers to save the cook time. Traditionally the pleating is more elaborate than what is described here.

If you cannot find pastry rounds labeled "pot sticker wrappers" (or "gyoza wrappers," the Japanese equivalent), use round wonton skins.

Makes Forty-eight

FILLING
1 pound lean pork butt, very
    finely minced
1/4 cup minced green onion
    and tops
1 cup very finely shredded
    Chinese (Napa) cabbage
1/2 tablespoon finely minced
    garlic
1 teaspoon finely minced ginger
    root
1/2 teaspoon salt
1/2 teaspoon Chinese rice wine
    or dry sherry
1/4 teaspoon freshly ground
    black pepper
1/2 teaspoon Oriental sesame oil
6 drops chili oil

48 pot sticker skins or
   round wonton skins
Peanut oil
2/3 cup chicken stock or water
Coriander sprigs
White rice vinegar or distilled
   white vinegar
Soy sauce
Chili oil

To make the filling, combine pork, onion, cabbage, garlic, ginger root, salt, wine, pepper, sesame oil, and 6 drops chili oil in a bowl and mix well. Pinch off a small portion and sauté until cooked through. Taste and adjust seasonings.

To form the pot stickers, work with only 6 to 8 skins at a time. Keep the rest well wrapped in waxed paper and draped with a lightly dampened towel. Lay 1 skin across the palm of your left hand (if you are right-handed). With the fingers of your other hand, grasp about 1 tablespoon of the filling, form into a rough ball, and place it in the center of the skin. Make 3 or 4 pleats along one half of the skin and bring that half up and over the filling to meet the other half and form a half-moon shape. Press

edges together securely. Place on work surface or baking sheet and cover with a tea towel. Repeat with remaining filling and skins.

Heat 2 heavy 12-inch skillets until very hot (a few drops of water flicked onto the skillet should sizzle). Add 2 tablespoons of the peanut oil to each skillet and heat to 375° F; a tiny piece of bread should brown within seconds when added. Quickly place half of the pot stickers on their sides in a single layer in each skillet; do not allow them to touch. Checking frequently, brown the pot stickers on that side; this should take about 3 minutes. Pour 1/3 cup of the chicken stock into each skillet, lower heat slightly, cover skillets, and cook 5 to 7 minutes until stock has almost cooked away. Remove lids and check one of the pot stickers in each skillet. The side that was browned should be crisp. Continue to cook a few more minutes if necessary, adding a little more oil if needed.

To serve, remove skillets from heat and loosen the pot stickers with a flexible spatula. Arrange browned side up on a warmed serving platter and garnish with coriander sprigs. Serve with cruets of vinegar and soy sauce and a bottle of chili oil. Guests mix the condiments on their plate to use as a dipping sauce.

STEAMED PORK SPARERIBS

Approximately Twenty Servings
One 1-pound-rack meaty pork
   spareribs, separated and each
   rib cut into 1-1/2-inch lengths
1 recipe Hoisin Marinade
Coriander sprigs

Place spareribs in 2 large shallow bowls. Prepare hoisin marinade and rub well into spareribs. Marinate at room temperature 4 hours, turning often. Place the bowls on 2 steamer racks (see Steaming) and steam 50 minutes, or until tender. Turn the ribs several times to ensure even cooking.

To serve, remove bowls from steamer and set on a warming tray. Garnish with coriander sprigs. Guests help themselves with chopsticks or fingers. Provide plenty of paper napkins and a receptacle for the bones.

PARCHMENT CHICKEN ●

Makes Twenty Four
1 pound chicken meat, cut into
  small pieces
Peanut oil for deep frying
Shredded Chinese cabbage or
  lettuce
Coriander sprigs

MARINADE
2 tablespoons dry sherry or
  whiskey
2 tablespoons corn oil
2 tablespoons soy sauce
2 tablespoons finely minced
  green onion
2 teaspoons finely minced
  ginger root
1 teaspoon finely minced garlic
1/2 teaspoon Oriental sesame oil
1/4 teaspoon five-spice powder
1 tablespoon cornstarch

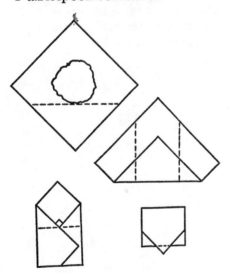

To prepare the marinade, combine sherry, corn oil, soy sauce, green onion, ginger root, garlic, sesame oil, five-spice powder, and cornstarch in a nonmetallic container. Add chicken and toss to coat thoroughly; let stand at room temperature 2 hours.

Cut parchment paper, doubled waxed paper, or butcher paper into 24 squares, each 6 inches square. Divide chicken mixture evenly among squares, encasing as illustrated in diagram.

In a large skillet, electric frypan or deep fryer, heat at least 2 inches peanut oil to 375° F. Without crowding, deep fry the packets in hot oil 2 minutes per side. Drain on crumpled paper toweling and keep warm in a moderate oven. Repeat with remaining packets.

Make a bed of shredded lettuce on a serving platter. Arrange the packets on the lettuce and garnish with coriander sprigs. Guests open the packets with their fingers and eat the chicken with chopsticks.

Parchment chicken may be made 1 day ahead and refrigerated. Reheat on a rack in a preheated 375° F oven 10 to 15 minutes.

ALMOND COOKIES ●■

For hints on baking cookies, see the American Buffet.

Makes Approximately Five Dozen
1 cup lard, at room temperature
1/2 cup granulated sugar
1/2 cup firmly packed brown
  sugar
1 egg, lightly beaten
2 teaspoons almond extract
1/4 cup finely ground almonds
2-1/2 cups unbleached flour
2 teaspoons baking powder
1/2 teaspoon salt
2-1/2 dozen blanched almonds,
  halved lengthwise
1 egg yolk, lightly beaten with
  1 tablespoon cold water

Preheat oven to 350° F. Oil 2 or 3 baking sheets with Lecithin Oil and set aside.

In a mixing bowl, beat lard with a wooden spoon until smooth. Gradually add sugars, beating until well mixed. Stir in egg, mix well, and add almond extract and ground almonds.

Sift together flour, baking powder, and salt. Gradually blend flour mixture into lard mixture to make a firm dough.

With hands, form dough into small balls about 3/4 inch in diameter. Press an almond half onto the top of each ball, flattening the ball to form a cookie about 5/16 inch thick. Arrange cookies at least 1-1/2 inches apart on prepared baking sheet. Place in the preheated oven and bake 15 minutes, or until just golden. Immediately remove cookies to wire racks to cool. Bake remaining cookies.

When completely cool, transfer cookies to an airtight container for up to 2 days, or freeze for up to 2 months. Defrost at room temperature.

CHINESE GLOSSARY

All of the following items can be found in Oriental markets and most supermarkets.

CHILI OIL Vegetable or sesame oil flavored with hot chili peppers. Available in bottles.

CHINESE MUSTARD A hot yellow mustard. Available prepared in jars, or in cellophane in powdered form, to be mixed with water.

CHINESE RICE WINE A drinking and cooking wine made from rice. Substitute dry sherry.

FIVE SPICE POWDER A finely ground spice mixture of star anise, fennel, cinnamon, cloves, and Szechwan peppercorns. Available in cellophane packages and bottles.

ORIENTAL SESAME OIL A reddish oil made from toasted sesame seeds, with a strong, distinct flavor. Do not confuse with the lighter-bodied sesame cooking oil found in health-food stores.

OYSTER SAUCE A thick brined sauce made of oysters and soy sauce. Use for flavoring foods as they cook and as a condiment. Available in bottles and cans.

PICKLED RED GINGER Ginger pickled in vinegar brine. Available in jars.

SHIITAKE MUSHROOMS, DRIED See Japanese Glossary.

TANGERINE PEEL, DRIED Tangerine peel that has been dried in the sun. Sold in small pieces packaged in cellophane or lightweight boxes.

WHITE RICE VINEGAR A mild vinegar made from rice. Do not substitute black or red Chinese vinegar, both of which are strongly flavored.

JAPANESE BUFFET FOR TWELVE

Fresh fish, colorful vegetables, lightly vinegared rice, lacquered trays, artistic garnishes—these are all present at a buffet featuring sushi and sashimi. The foremost consideration when preparing this very special Asian feast is exceptionally fresh, high-quality seafoods.

For serving, provide chopsticks, preferably the "pull-apart" bamboo type, though many sushi enthusiasts find their fingers are equally practical for grasping the morsels, and small dishes for the dipping sauces. Arrange soy sauce in easy-to-pour bottles and bowls of gari, prepared wasabi, and the suggested dipping sauces near the sushi and sashimi. Serve bowls of suimono for those who want soup.

Purchasing the ingredients for and preparing sushi and sashimi cannot be done in advance; all the pressure comes on party day. Put together a smaller sushi affair, perhaps a family meal, before attempting the buffet. The deft movements necessary for making the various forms of sushi can only be mastered with practice.

Since some guests may find a whole meal of raw fish not to their liking, I have included yakitori and a tofu dish to give the menu variety. A glossary of Japanese food items appears after the recipes.

Assorted Sushi
Sashimi
Chicken Yakitori
Cold Tofu Cubes with Dipping
    Sauce
Suimono
Melons and/or persimmons

SUSHI

Two types of sushi will be discussed here: nigiri, or hand-shaped sushi, and maki, or rolled sushi. In the first, rice is formed into a "finger," swabbed with a dab of the pungent mustard called wasabi, and then topped with a strip of prime seafood. Maki-zushi includes a variety of forms, but only nori-maki, a seaweed-encased cylinder of rice with fish or vegetables in the center, and temaki, a seaweed "cone" holding rice and fish and/or vegetables, are described.

You need only a few special tools to become a sushi chef: a flat wooden spoon or a proper wooden rice paddle; a hangiri, a shallow wooden tub, or similar vessel; a hand fan or folded newspaper; and a sudare, a bamboo mat for making the nori-maki. And finally, you must have a very sharp knife with a blade (not serrated) about eight inches long to cut the fish.

SUSHI RICE

In Japanese, this delicately seasoned rice is called sushi-meshi or shari. The kernels should be tender but firm; handle them gently to avoid bruising them.

Makes Approximately Thirteen Cups
5 cups short-grain white rice
5 cups water
1-1/2 tablespoons sake
1 3-inch piece kombu, broken
    into several pieces (optional)
4 tablespoons granulated sugar
2 teaspoons salt
7 tablespoons rice vinegar

Wash rice in at least 8 changes of cold water, or until washing water runs clear. Place rice in a bowl and add cold water to cover; let stand 30 minutes. Drain.

In a saucepan with a tight-fitting lid, bring 5 cups water to a boil and add sake. Gradually stir in rice. Top with kombu, cover saucepan, and cook on high heat until rice starts to steam over. Reduce heat to low and continue to cook 6 minutes. Turn off heat and let rice stand 20 minutes.

In a small saucepan, dissolve the sugar and salt in the vinegar over low heat. Remove from the heat, transfer to a bowl, and immerse base of bowl in cold water to cool mixture completely.

Discard kombu and turn rice out into a large shallow wooden or ceramic vessel. (Wood is best, as it absorbs moisture.) With a rice paddle, turn the rice with horizontal strokes so as not to bruise the kernels. Once large clouds of steam have stopped rising from the rice, sprinkle the cooled vinegar mixture over the rice as you continue to turn it. When all of the vinegar mixture has been added, continue to turn the rice at the same time you fan it with a hand fan. The fanning will cool it quickly and prevent it from becoming soggy. When the rice is at room temperature (the entire cooling process should take about 10 minutes), proceed to make the sushi, or cover the container with a lightly dampened cloth and let the rice stand for no more than 2 hours. Do not refrigerate the rice or the kernels will harden.

NIGIRI-ZUSHI

Select only the best-quality seafood to make nigiri-zushi. Possible toppings for the rice "fingers" include tuna, red snapper, young yellowtail, halibut, sea bass, mackerel, albacore, abalone, or boiled shrimp or octopus. For the buffet, plan on an assortment of no more than three or four different toppings: tuna, red snapper, and abalone or octopus would make a good combination, for example.

Nigiri-zushi is particularly lovely presented on a black or red lacquer serving dish or on an attractive wooden board.

Makes Approximately Sixty Pieces
6 cups sushi rice (preceding)
2 to 2-1/2 pounds fillets of
    assorted fish (see
    introduction)
2 teaspoons powdered wasabi,
    mixed with water to form
    a thick paste

HAND VINEGAR
1 cup water
1 tablespoon rice vinegar

PRESENTATION
Parsley sprigs
Carrot curls
Soy sauce, mixed with mirin
    to taste (about 4 parts soy
    to 1 part mirin)
Soy sauce
Additional prepared wasabi
Gari

Place the container of sushi rice on the work surface. In a bowl, combine the water and vinegar for the hand vinegar and place it next to the rice. (You will dampen your hands with this water-vinegar mixture as you work with the rice. It prevents the rice from sticking to your hands.) Mix up the wasabi in a small dish and set alongside the rice.

You must keep the fish as cold as possible when slicing it. Rinse your hands in ice water often to prevent their warmth from damaging the fish. With a sharp knife, cut the fillets crosswise slightly on the diagonal into slices about 1/4 inch thick and 2 inches long. If serving boiled shrimp, they should be shelled, deveined (make as shallow a cut as possible), and then butterflied along the inner curve. Boiled octopus should be cut into 1/8-inch-thick slices.

Immerse your fingers in the hand vinegar and rub the solution onto your palms. Grasp about 1-1/2 tablespoons of sushi rice in your left hand (if you are right-handed) and *gently* press it to form a rough mass. With fingers of your other hand, form the rice into an oval about 1-1/2 inches long and 3/4 inch thick. Do not mash the rice or you will bruise the kernels.

When the oval is properly formed, pick up a slice of fish in your free hand. Balance it on your fingertips and, with the index finger of the hand holding the oval of rice, smear a light streak of the prepared wasabi along the length of the fish. (A little wasabi goes a long way, so add it lightly.) Now place the rice oval evenly on the fish slice and press firmly but gently in place. Set the formed sushi rice side down on a serving platter. The fish slice should completely obscure the rice.

Repeat with remaining fish and rice. When all of the sushi have been made, garnish the serving plates with parsley sprigs and carrot curls. Serve with soy-mirin sauce and plain soy sauce for dipping. Set out additional wasabi to mix with the soy for those who like a "zestier" mouthful. Place gari in a small dish alongside.

VARIATIONS Sea urchin and salmon roe are very special nigiri-zushi toppings. They are both quite expensive, especially the latter, and have extraordinary flavor and texture. To serve them, toast nori as described in directions for Nori-Maki (below) and cut the nori into strips about 1 inch wide by 1-3/4 inches long. Form 1-1/2 tablespoons of rice into an oval about 3/4 inch high. Wrap the nori strip around the perimeter of the rice oval so that the nori stands about 1/4 inch above the surface of the rice. With a tiny spoon, carefully place a mound of urchin or roe (about 3/4 to 1 teaspoon) on the surface of the rice. If desired, arrange a "fan" of tiny cucumber slices in the corner of the salmon roe sushi.

NORI-MAKI

A sudare, or bamboo mat, is best for forming the rolls, though a heavy cloth napkin can be substituted. The mushrooms, egg strips, kampyo, and mitsuba can be readied a few hours in advance.

Makes Five Rolls
10 mitsuba or watercress sprigs, or approximately 3 ounces spinach leaves
5 thin carrot strips, each about 7 inches long and 1/8 inch thick
6-1/4 cups sushi rice
5 standard nori sheets
1 recipe Egg Rounds, cut into long strips about 1/4 inch wide

MUSHROOMS
10 dried shiitake mushrooms, soaked in warm water to soften, drained, tough stems removed, and caps cut into 1/8-inch-thick strips
2/3 cup Dashi
2 teaspoons sugar
1 tablespoon soy sauce

KAMPYO
10 strips kampyo (each about 6 inches long)
1/2 teaspoon salt
2/3 cup Dashi
2 teaspoons sugar
3 tablespoons soy sauce

HAND VINEGAR
1 cup water
2 teaspoons rice vinegar

PRESENTATION
Mitsuba sprigs
Carrot curls
Gari

To prepare the mushrooms, soften and cut as dirrected and set aside. In a small saucepan, combine dashi, sugar, and soy sauce and heat, stirring to dissolve sugar. Add mushroom slices and simmer uncovered over low heat about 15 minutes, or until almost all of the liquid has evaporated and mushrooms are well flavored. Drain well and set aside.

To prepare the kampyo, rinse the strips under running cold water. Rub the strips with the salt to break down the fibers and again rinse under water. In a small saucepan, combine the dashi, sugar, and soy sauce and heat, stirring to dissolve sugar. Add kampyo strips and simmer uncovered over low heat about 20 minutes. Drain well and set aside.

Blanch the 10 mitsuba sprigs 1 minute, drain well, and set aside. Blanch the carrot strips 2 minutes, drain well, and set aside.

Arrange the container of sushi rice and all the filling ingredients on the work surface. In a small bowl, mix the water and rice vinegar for the hand vinegar. Place the sudare (or a heavy cloth napkin) flat on the surface, with the mat's slats running crosswise as you face them. Take 1 nori seaweed sheet and hold it shiny side down about 2 inches above a low flame on a gas range or a burner turned to medium-high heat on an electric range. When the seaweed sheet turns dark green, remove it immediately to the sudare, shiny side down. Position the nori sheet in the middle of the mat so that bamboo is exposed on all sides.

Lightly dampen your fingertips with the hand vinegar and transfer about 1-1/4 cups of the sushi rice to the center of the nori sheet. With your fingertips, spread the rice over the surface of the nori all the way to the edges, leaving a 1-inch strip uncovered along the edge farthest from you. The rice should be about 3/8 inch thick.

Arrange one-fifth of the mushroom slices on the rice in a row running crosswise about one-third of the way in from the sheet edge nearest you. Place 2 kampyo strips right next to the mushrooms so the ingredients touch, then one-fifth of the egg strips, and finally 2 mitsuba sprigs and 1 carrot strip.

While securing the filling ingredients in place with the fingers of both hands, lift the mat up with thumbs and forefingers so that the sheet edge nearest you meets the uncovered portion of the sheet beyond the filling. At this point, the uncovered portion of the mat that was nearest you will be extended over the edge of the mat portion farthest from you. Viewed from the side, the filling should be centered in the rice roll. Firmly but gently press the bamboo mat around the roll for 20 seconds.

Remove the mat and place the roll on a cutting surface. Make the other 4 rolls in the same manner as you made the first roll. With a very sharp

knife, cut each roll in half with a smooth, even stroke. Wiping the knife blade clean between each cut, cut each half into 4 equal-size slices. (If the roll's ends are ragged, trim them off before slicing the roll.) Attractively arrange the slices on a serving platter, cut side up to reveal their beautiful centers, grouping the slices in threes to form flower shapes. (The sushi chef may eat the extra slice.)

When all the rolls are cut and arranged on the platter, tuck sprigs of fresh mitsuba around slices and set carrot curls along the edge of the plate. Place a mound of gari in the center of the plate, or put it in a small bowl alongside. No dipping sauce is necessary with this sushi.

VARIATIONS Do not limit yourself to the filling ingredients specified here. Shelled shrimp or fillet of any firm white fish that has been boiled in dashi seasoned with soy and sugar and then coarsely cut can be used in place of or added to these ingredients. Or fill with thin strips of raw tuna fillet (tekka-maki) or of peeled and seeded cucumber (kappa-maki). With the latter two suggestions, smear a light streak of prepared wasabi on the rice where the filling will be placed and then serve these rolls with soy sauce for dipping.

TEMAKI-ZUSHI

To make your guests active participants in the preparation of the food for the buffet (and to save yourself time in the kitchen), serve temaki-zushi instead of nori-maki zushi. With temaki, guests form their own servings of nori-wrapped rice and you need only ready the ingredients.

On the buffet table, place a wooden container with 3 cups of Sushi Rice. Toast 6 to 8 standard nori sheets as described in the directions for Nori-Maki, cut each into 4 equal-size squares, and arrange on a plate alongside the rice. Prepare any of the filling ingredients for nori-maki and/or those suggested in the variations (you will need to cut the ingredients into smaller pieces) and arrange them attractively in a number of small dishes or on a single large platter.

Each guest takes a square of nori, places it on a flat surface (put a wooden board on the buffet table for this purpose), spreads about 2 tablespoons of rice over one of the corners, and arranges the filling ingredient(s) of choice on top. (A streak of prepared wasabi can precede the filling, if desired.) Now, the guest folds the corner opposite the rice-covered one over the rice and then folds in the sides to form a cone shape. The roll can then be dipped in soy sauce and easily eaten in 1 or 2 bites.

SASHIMI

Nothing can match the light, delicate flavor of absolutely fresh raw fish, or sashimi. The same rules apply for sashimi as for sushi: only the *freshest* fish or shellfish should be served, making the choices dependent upon what is in season. The seafoods suggested in nigiri-zushi are equally suitable for sashimi. Also consider regional specialties, such as cherrystone or geoduck clams, as possible candidates for the sashimi platter.

The fish is most easily cut when it is very cold. For the most flavorful results, delay the preparation of the sashimi platter(s) until just before your guests arrive.

Approximately Thirty-six Servings
2 pounds fish or shellfish
    of choice

PRESENTATION
Daikon, very finely shredded
    into long strands
Finely shredded carrot
Chrysanthemum leaves and
    flowers, ivy or maple leaves,
    or Turnip Chrysanthemums
Shredded cabbage, cucumber, or
    turnip
Parsley sprigs
Thin lemon wedges
Prepared wasabi
Grated or finely minced
    ginger root
Dipping sauces (following)
Soy sauce

See the method for Nigiri-Zushi for general information on working with fish. For sashimi, most fish should be cut across the grain into slices about 3/8 inch thick. Particularly firm-fleshed fish (red snapper and sea bass) can be cut as thin as 1/8 inch, while soft-fleshed fish (tuna) may need to be cut as thick as 1/2 inch for the slice to hold together properly. Cut squid, white meat fish, or abalone into 1/4-inch-wide threadlike slices and form into an attractive mound.

Cover a chilled serving platter with shredded daikon and surround the daikon with a border of finely shredded carrot. Arrange fish in overlapping slices on top of the daikon and garnish as desired with suggested garnishes. In separate dishes place the lemon wedges; wasabi, formed into a cone shape; and ginger root. Place one or both of the dipping sauces in small bowls. Set out a cruet of soy sauce.

In their own sauce dishes, guests mix wasabi and/or grated ginger with one of the dipping sauces or plain soy sauce. They help themselves to the fish with chopsticks and swirl the fish in the mixed sauce. Provide each guest with a small plate to catch the drips.

DIPPING SAUCES FOR SASHIMI

• For white-meat fish, use soy sauce diluted with sake or dry sherry and a little rice vinegar.
• For other fish or shellfish, combine equal parts soy sauce and fresh lime juice. Or combine cup soy sauce, 2 tablespoons sake or dry sherry, 1 teaspoon granulated sugar, and a pinch of katsuobushi and simmer 10 minutes. Strain and cool.

CHICKEN YAKITORI

You will need to refer to Barbecue Cookery to prepare this tasty skewered chicken. Slice 2 large chicken breasts, skinned and boned, into pieces approximately 1 by 2 inches. Place the pieces in a nonmetallic container and pour 1 double recipe Yakitori Marinade over the chicken. Cover and let stand 2 hours, turning chicken occasionally.

Thread 1 piece of chicken on each bamboo skewer and place over hot coals. Barbecue 4 to 5 minutes on each side, basting frequently with marinade. Arrange skewers on a bed of shredded daikon that has been sprinkled lightly with ground ginger and white pepper.

ADDITIONAL BUFFET SUGGESTIONS

• Arrange thin slices of cucumber in a square pan, fill with sushi rice, and pat down. Let stand for 20 minutes, then invert on a cutting board. Cut into small squares or diamonds and arrange on a platter. Garnish each piece with a tiny cooked shrimp.
• Mix minced softened shiitake mushrooms, raw fish or cooked shrimp, or blanched carrot or other vegetable of choice into 1-1/2 cups Sushi Rice. Trim edges of Egg Rounds (prepare a triple recipe) to make twelve 5-inch squares. Form about 2 tablespoons of the rice mixture into a square and place on the center of the egg square. Fold in sides to form a square packet, envelope style. Place flap side down on a serving plate. Garnish each package with a tiny strip of toasted nori.

COLD TOFU
WITH DIPPING SAUCE

Drain a 1-pound package of firm tofu (bean curd) and place the tofu in a strainer for 20 minutes. Remove the tofu to a cutting board and cut it into 1-inch cubes.

Make a bed of chrysanthemum leaves on a large platter and artistically arrange the tofu cubes on top of the leaves. Sprinkle lightly toasted sesame seeds and minced green onions over the tofu.

For the dipping sauce, combine 3 tablespoons *each* soy sauce and Dashi and 1/2 tablespoon freshly grated ginger root in a small bowl. Stir well and place next to the platter of tofu.

SUIMONO

The base of this simple, refreshing soup is dashi, the classic fish-based stock used in Japanese cooking. If you are pressed for time, look for instant dashi in Japanese markets.

The dashi portion of the recipe makes enough for twelve soup-course servings of suimono and for the dashi called for in the preceding recipes.

Serves Twelve

DASHI
2 pieces kombu (each 6 inches square)
3 quarts water
3 cups katsuobushi

6 cooked shrimp, shelled, deveined, and halved lengthwise
2 medium-size spinach leaves, each cut into 6 thin strips
12 tiny lemon peel strips

To make the dashi make several slashes in the kombu pieces, place them in a large saucepan, and add the water. Let stand 30 minutes, turn heat to medium, and bring water slowly to a boil. Remove kombu (reserve) and add katsuobushi. Bring water back to a boil for 30 seconds, remove from heat, and let stand *just* until all the katsuobushi has settled on the bottom of the saucepan.

Line a colander or large sieve with dampened cheesecloth and set over a saucepan. Pour dashi through the colander and set aside. (The kombu and katsuobushi can be reused to make a lighter-flavored dashi.)

To prepare the suimono, reheat the dashi. Place 1 shrimp, 1 strip of spinach, and 1 strip of lemon peel in each of 12 small (6-ounce) cups or mugs. Pour piping hot dashi into cups and serve at once.

EGG ROUNDS

Makes Four
2 eggs
1-1/2 tablespoons Dashi or water (see Note)
1/2 teaspoon soy sauce
Dash salt
Peanut oil

In a mixing bowl, beat eggs lightly with a whisk, chopsticks, or fork. Beat in dashi, soy sauce, and salt. Heat a 7-inch skillet over medium heat. Brush skillet with peanut oil and pour in 2 tablespoons of the egg mixture. Immediately tilt pan so that the entire bottom is covered with egg mixture. Cook until egg is set and bottom of round is just turning golden. Turn out onto a plate or work surface and repeat with remaining egg mixture, making 4 rounds in all.

To make slivers, cool rounds completely. Roll each round into a tight cylinder and slice cylinder at 1/4-inch intervals. Shake slices loose to form slivers.

NOTE If making egg rounds for a Chinese dish, use water in place of the dashi.

JAPANESE GLOSSARY

All of the following items can be found in Japanese markets, some Asian-food shops, and many supermarkets.

DAIKON A very large white radish (usually about 14 inches long) with a tart flavor.

GARI Sushi-shop jargon for pink vinegared ginger; also called amazu shoga. Available in plastic tubes and packets.

KATSUOBUSHI Flaked dried bonito sold in cellophane packages.

KOMBU Deep olive-brown kelp leaves sold dried in cellophane packets.

MIRIN Heavily sweetened rice wine used for cooking. Available in bottles.

MITSUBA Called trefoil in English, this member of the parsley family has a pale green stalk topped by three flat green leaves. The overall length of a sprig is about 6 inches. Wrapped in plastic, mitsuba sprigs will keep in the refrigerator crisper for up to 1 week.

NORI Often called laver in English. Dried seaweed sold in thin 8-by-7-inch sheets, usually packaged in cellophane. Can be purchased toasted or untoasted, seasoned or unseasoned. Use the unseasoned type for sushi; buy the untoasted variety to save money, as it is easy to toast the nori yourself. Nori may be frozen several months; it defrosts almost instantly. Most commonly available in cellophane packets; very high-quality nori can be quite expensive.

RICE VINEGAR A mild-flavored vinegar with just a hint of sweetness. Do not confuse with other Asian vinegars; purchase only the white Japanese variety. Available in bottles.

SAKE Rice wine that is used both as a beverage and for cooking. Available in bottles in most liquor stores as well as the outlets listed above.

SHIITAKE MUSHROOMS, DRIED Brown-black mushrooms, also known as forest or dried black mushrooms. They have a wrinkled-looking cap and light-colored gills. Available in cellophane packages.

SHORT-GRAIN WHITE RICE Short-grain rice, which produces a plump, firm kernel when cooked, is essential for successful sushi. Excellent short-grain rice is grown in California.

WASABI A root vegetable whose pungent flavor is often compared to the horseradish of the West, though the two are not related. It can be purchased in powder form in small cans. To prepare, add tepid water to the powder and mix to a smooth paste, then cover and let stand for about 15 minutes to mellow the flavor. Also available premixed in tubes, though the powder is preferred.

INDEX

ABOUT THE AUTHOR

Since the publication in 1971 of her first book, *Soup,* Coralie Castle has written or coauthored nine other popular cookbooks, which have over 350,000 copies in print. Editions of her books have also been issued in Holland, England, and Australia, and by all of the major book clubs in America.

Among her best-selling or recent titles are *Soup* (which was completely revised in 1980), *The Art of Cooking for Two, Country Inns Cookery, Leftovers,* and *Real Bread,* all published by 101 Productions, and *The Complete Book of Steam Cookery,* published in 1985 by Jeremy P. Tarcher, Inc.

Ms. Castle was born and raised on Chicago's North Shore, but has lived in San Rafael, California, since 1958. When she is not creating recipes for new books, she tends her half-acre vegetable garden and is active in local food and wine societies.